DICTATORIAL GRIMOIRE
VOLUME 1

story & art by Ayumi Kanou

STAFF

translation	
adaptation	
lettering	
logo design	Courtney Williams
cover design	Nicky Lim
proofreader	Janet Houck
editor	Adam Arnold
publisher	Jason DeAngelis
	Seven Seas Entertainment

DICTATORIAL GRIMOIRE VOL. 1
Copyright ©2011 Ayumi Kanou
First published in Japan in 2011 by MEDIA FACTORY, Inc.
English translation rights reserved by Seven Seas Entertainment, LLC.
under the license from MEDIA FACTORY, Inc., Tokyo.

ISBN: 978-1-937867-93-5

Printed in Canada

First Printing: September 2013

10 9 8 7 6 5 4 3 2 1

Seven Seas

FOLLOW US ONLINE: www.gomanga.com

READING DIRECTIONS

This book reads from *right to left*, Japanese style. If this is your first time reading manga, you start reading from the top right panel on each page and take it from there. If you get lost, just follow the numbered diagram here. It may seem backwards at first, but you'll get the hang of it! Have fun!!

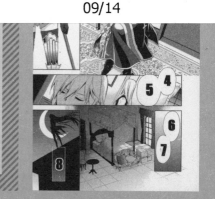

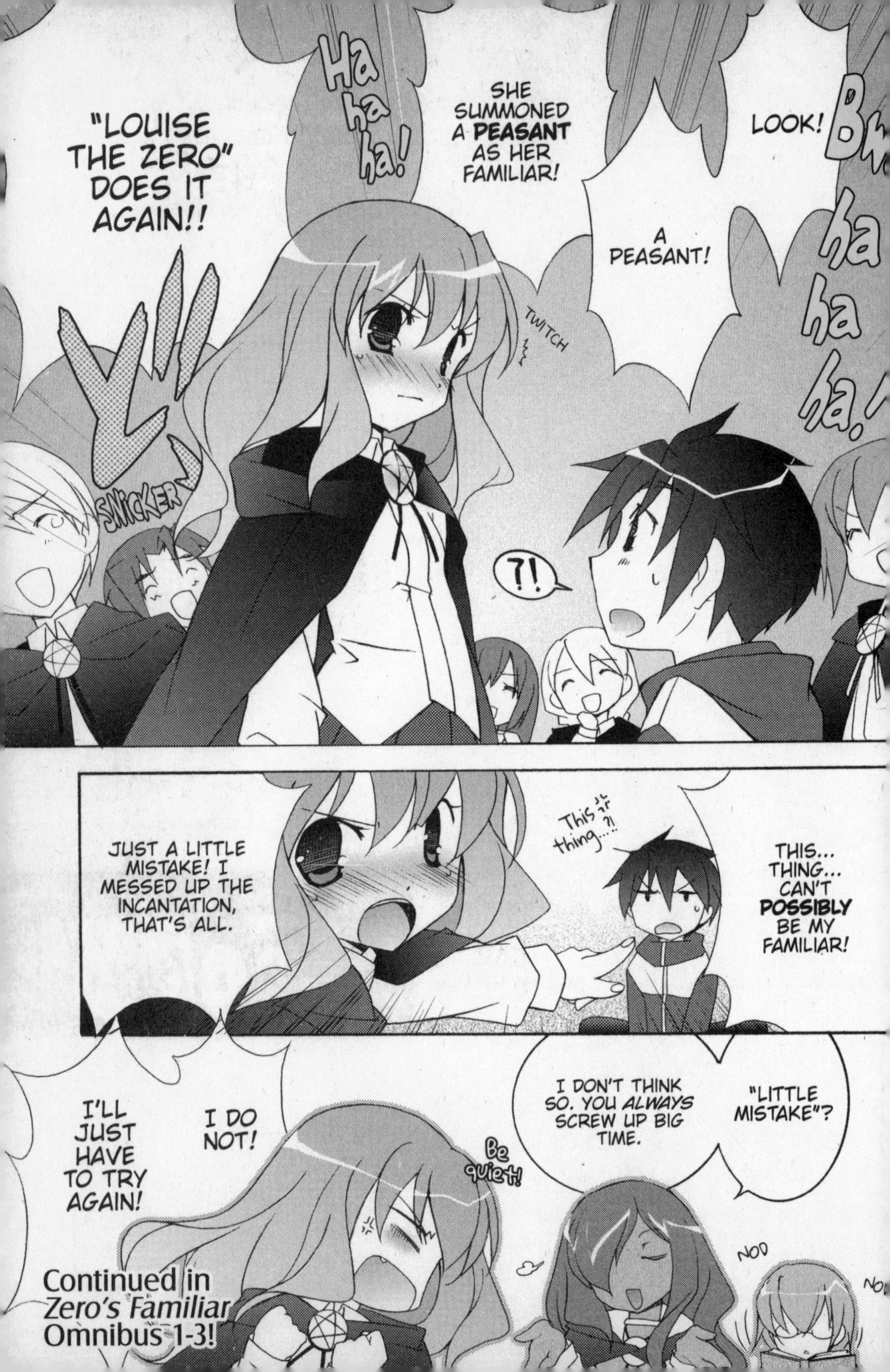
Bw ha ha ha ha!
LOOK!
A PEASANT!
SHE SUMMONED A **PEASANT** AS HER FAMILIAR!
Ha ha ha!
"LOUISE THE ZERO" DOES IT AGAIN!!
TWITCH
?!
SNICKER
THIS... THING... CAN'T **POSSIBLY** BE MY FAMILIAR!
This thing...?!
JUST A LITTLE MISTAKE! I MESSED UP THE INCANTATION, THAT'S ALL.
"LITTLE MISTAKE"?
I DON'T THINK SO. YOU *ALWAYS* SCREW UP BIG TIME.
Be quiet!
I DO NOT!
I'LL JUST HAVE TO TRY AGAIN!
NOD
NO

Continued in *Zero's Familiar Omnibus 1-3!*

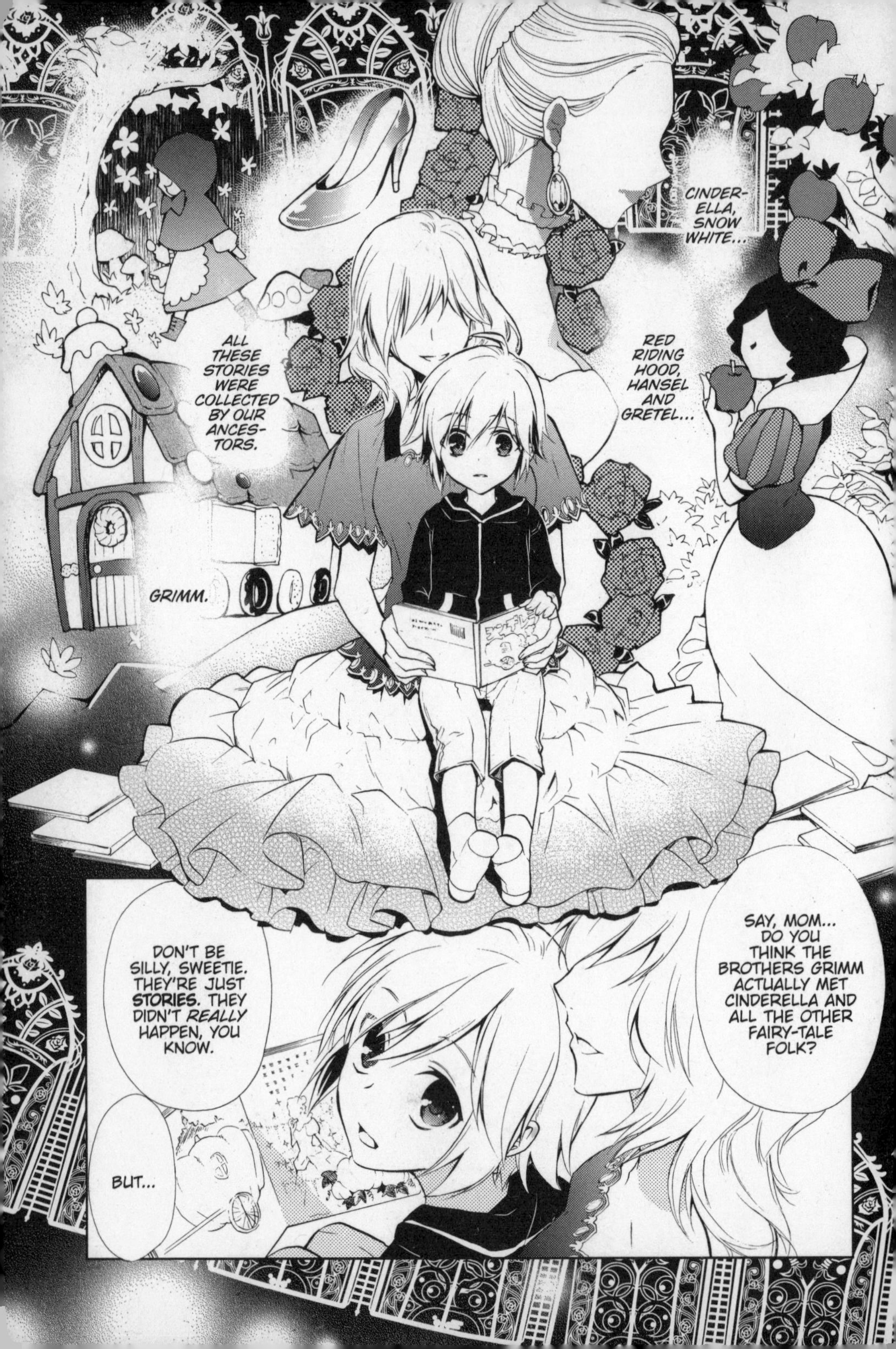
CINDER-ELLA, SNOW WHITE...
RED RIDING HOOD, HANSEL AND GRETEL...
ALL THESE STORIES WERE COLLECTED BY OUR ANCES-TORS.
GRIMM.
SAY, MOM... DO YOU THINK THE BROTHERS GRIMM ACTUALLY MET CINDERELLA AND ALL THE OTHER FAIRY-TALE FOLK?
DON'T BE SILLY, SWEETIE. THEY'RE JUST STORIES. THEY DIDN'T REALLY HAPPEN, YOU KNOW.
BUT...

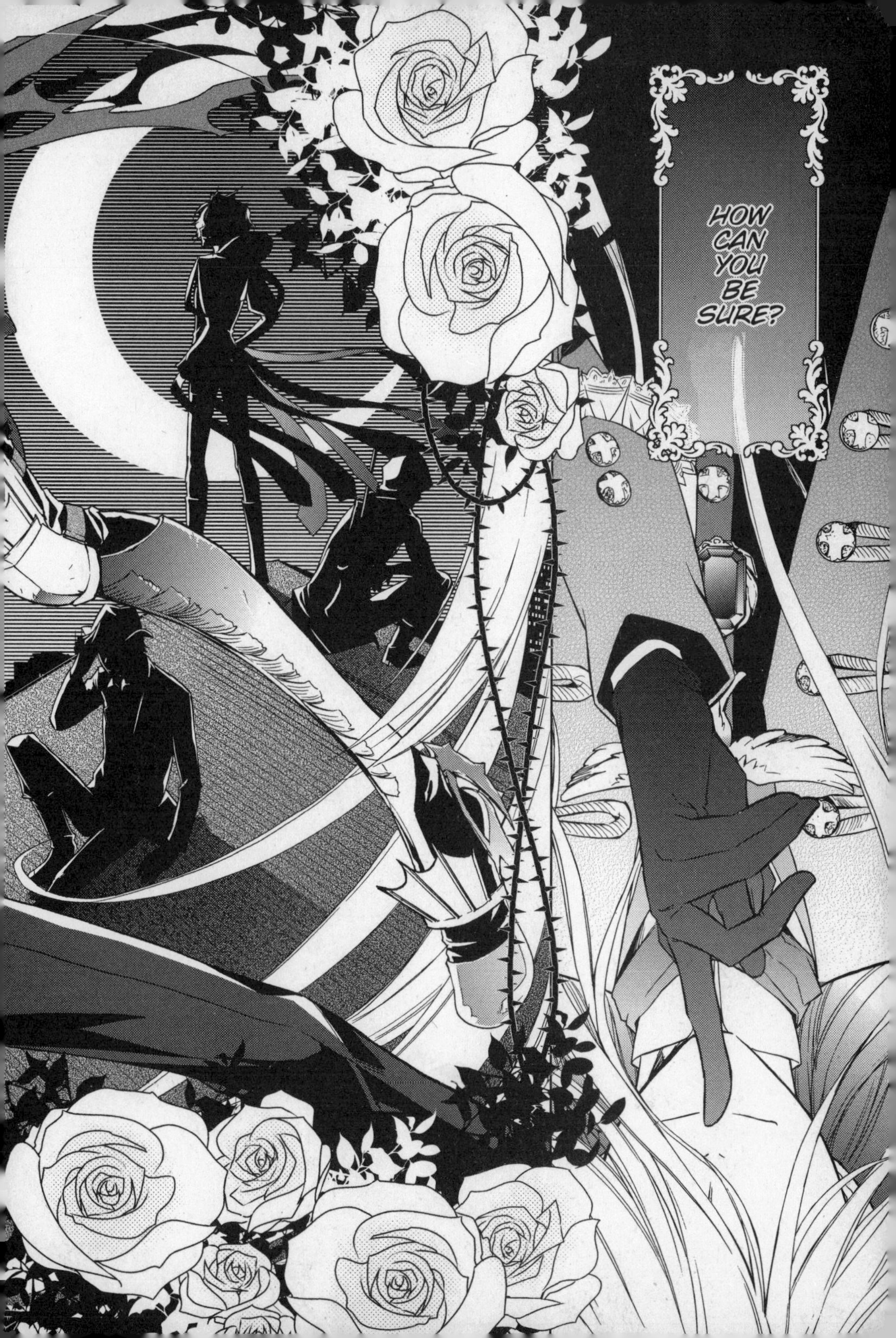
HOW CAN YOU BE SURE?

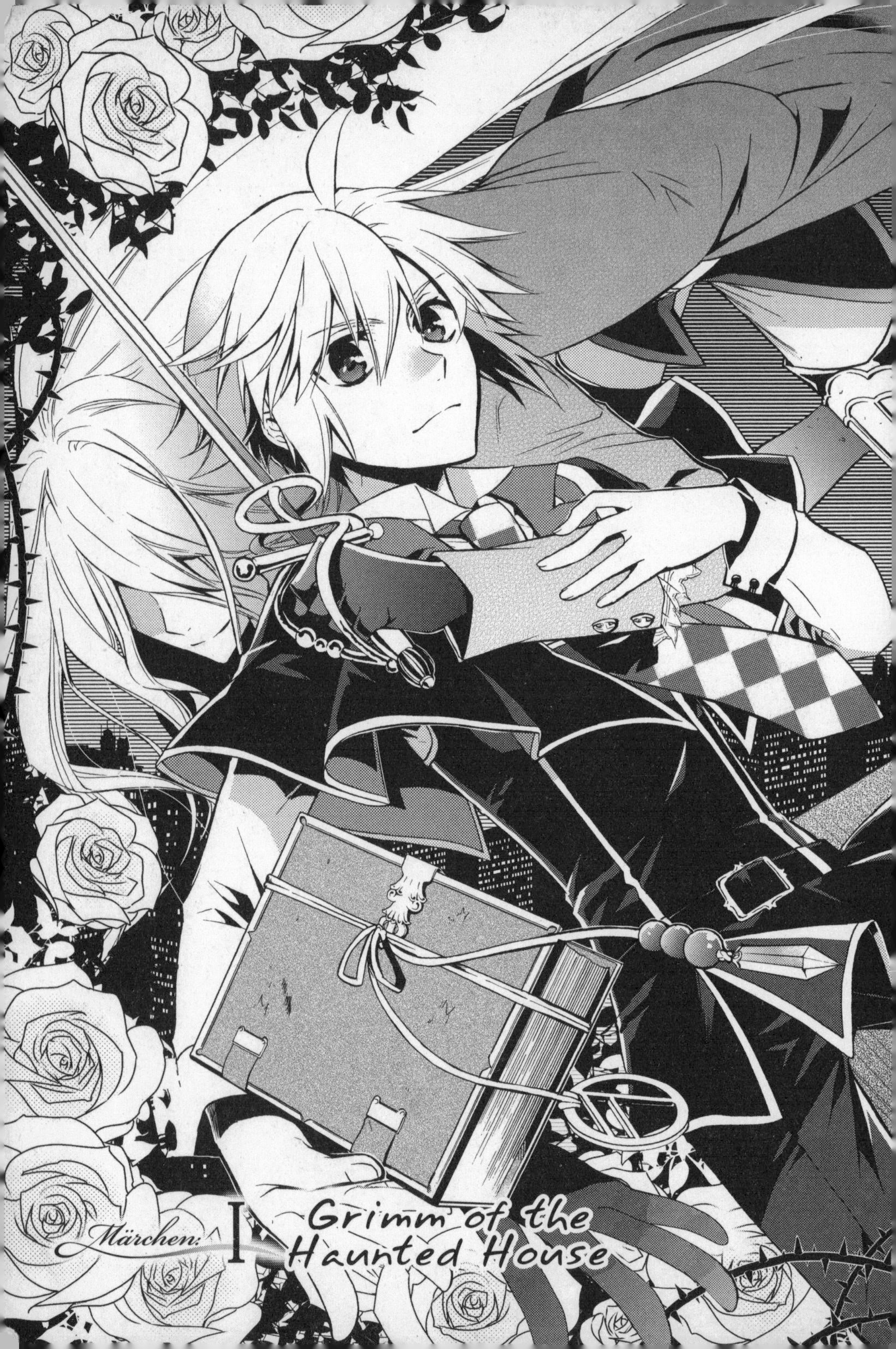
Märchen: I
Grimm of the Haunted House

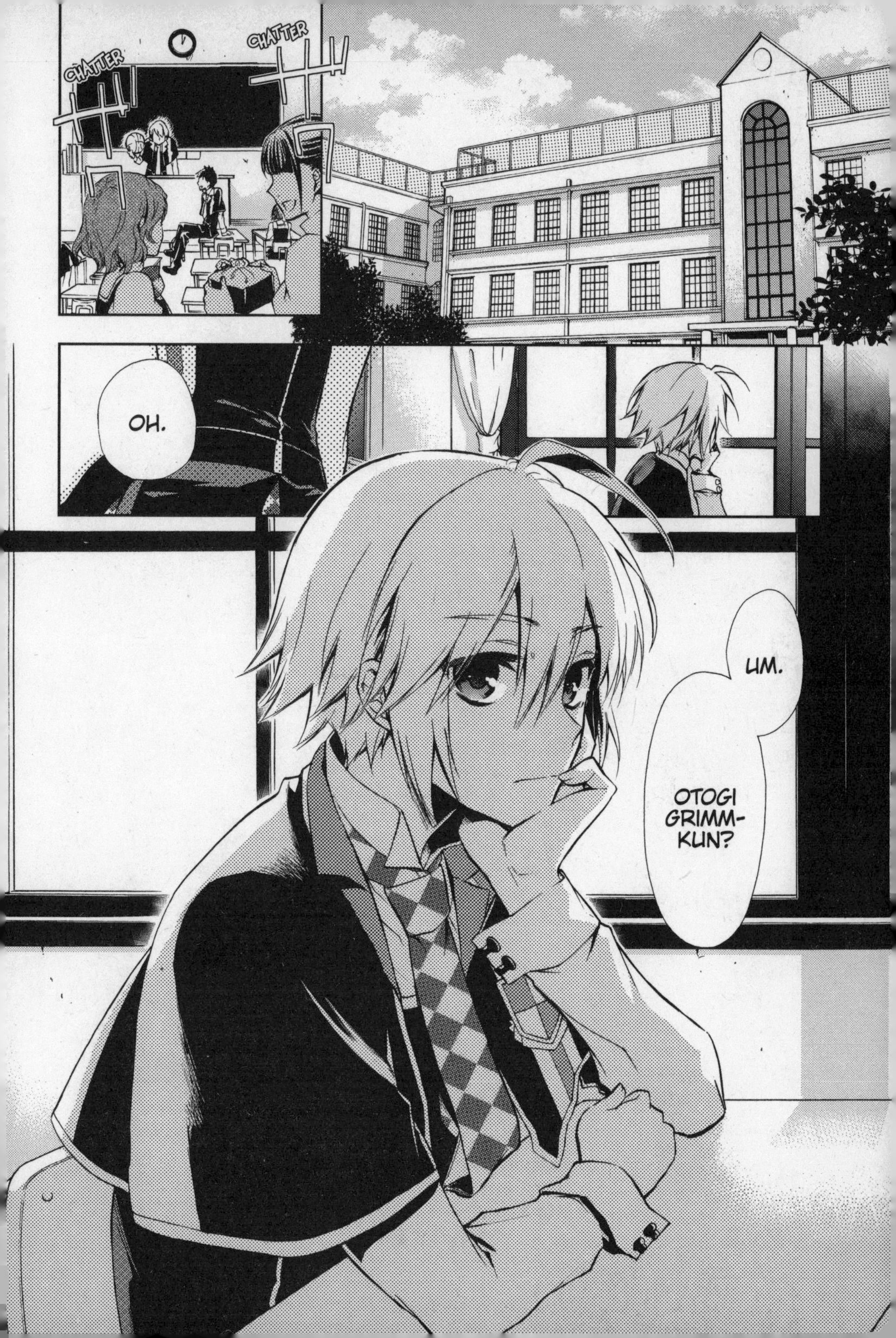
CHATTER
CHATTER
OH.
UM.
OTOGI GRIMM-KUN?

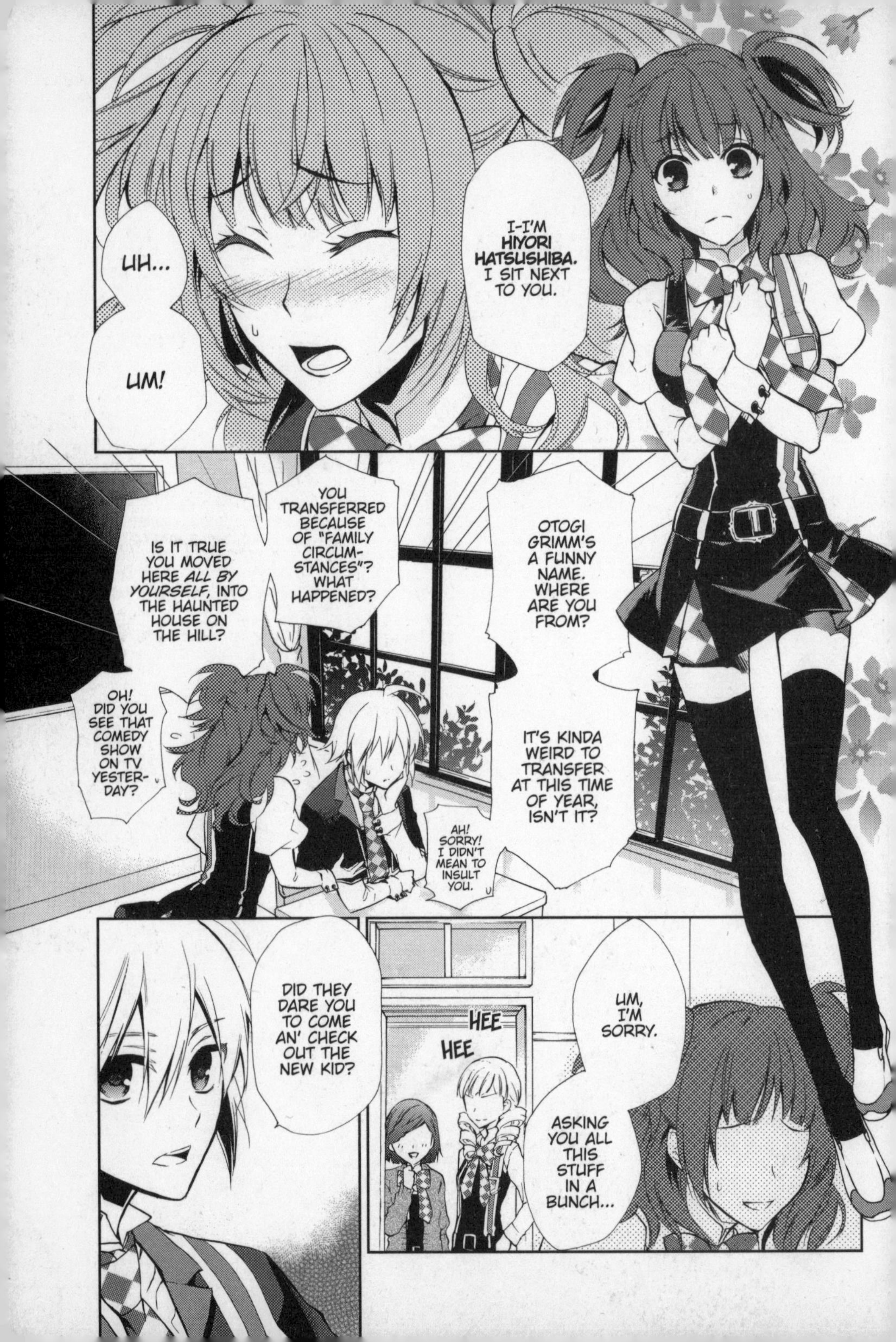
I-I'M HIYORI HATSUSHIBA. I SIT NEXT TO YOU.
UH...
UM!
OTOGI GRIMM'S A FUNNY NAME. WHERE ARE YOU FROM?
YOU TRANSFERRED BECAUSE OF "FAMILY CIRCUM-STANCES"? WHAT HAPPENED?
IS IT TRUE YOU MOVED HERE *ALL BY YOURSELF*, INTO THE HAUNTED HOUSE ON THE HILL?
IT'S KINDA WEIRD TO TRANSFER AT THIS TIME OF YEAR, ISN'T IT?
AH! SORRY! I DIDN'T MEAN TO INSULT YOU.
OH! DID YOU SEE THAT COMEDY SHOW ON TV YESTER-DAY?
UM, I'M SORRY.
ASKING YOU ALL THIS STUFF IN A BUNCH...
HEE
HEE
DID THEY DARE YOU TO COME AN' CHECK OUT THE NEW KID?

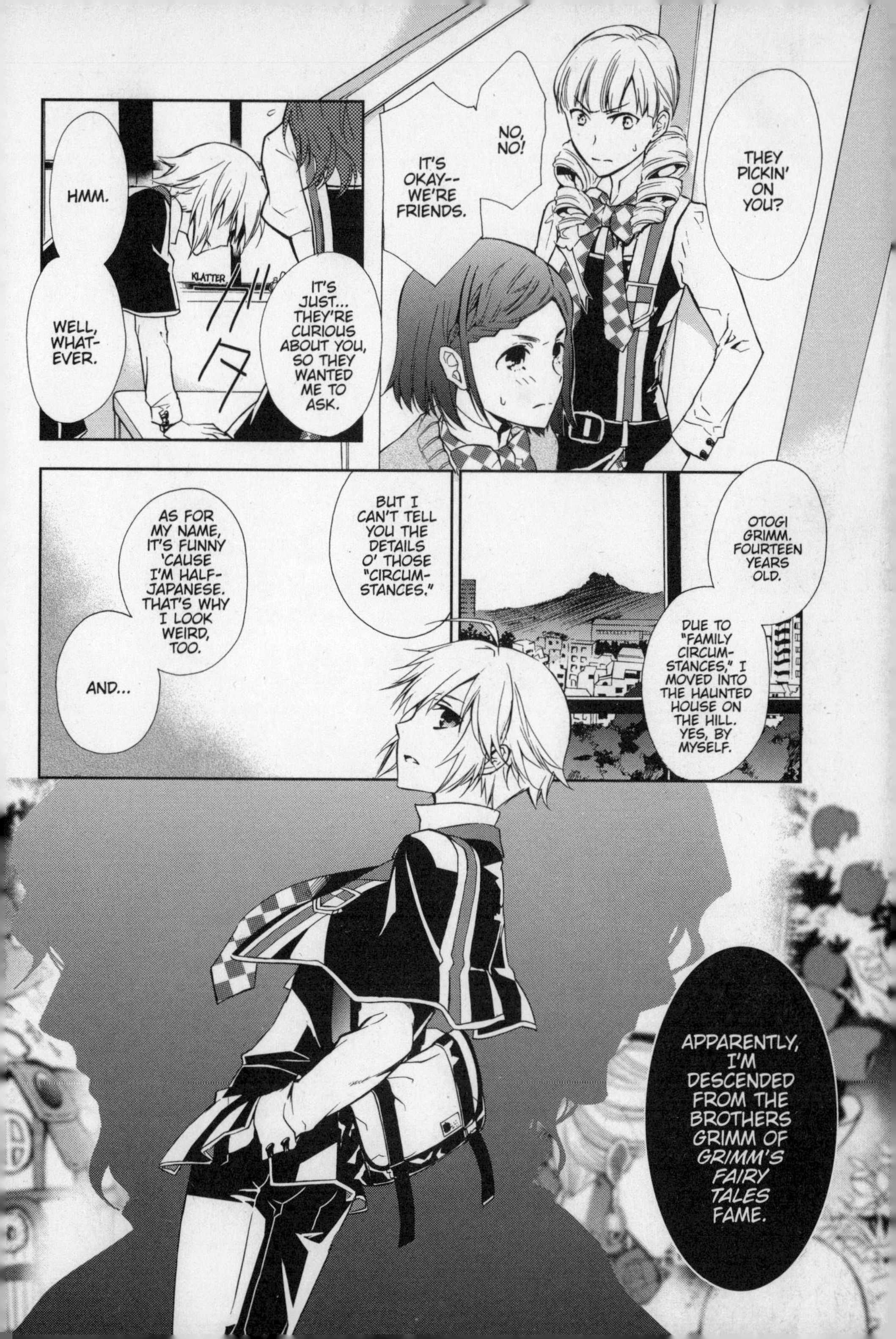
THEY PICKIN' ON YOU?
NO, NO!
IT'S OKAY-- WE'RE FRIENDS.
IT'S JUST... THEY'RE CURIOUS ABOUT YOU, SO THEY WANTED ME TO ASK.
HMM.
KLATTER
WELL, WHAT-EVER.
OTOGI GRIMM. FOURTEEN YEARS OLD.
DUE TO "FAMILY CIRCUM-STANCES," I MOVED INTO THE HAUNTED HOUSE ON THE HILL. YES, BY MYSELF.
BUT I CAN'T TELL YOU THE DETAILS O' THOSE "CIRCUM-STANCES."
AS FOR MY NAME, IT'S FUNNY 'CAUSE I'M HALF-JAPANESE. THAT'S WHY I LOOK WEIRD, TOO.
AND...
APPARENTLY, I'M DESCENDED FROM THE BROTHERS GRIMM OF *GRIMM'S FAIRY TALES* FAME.

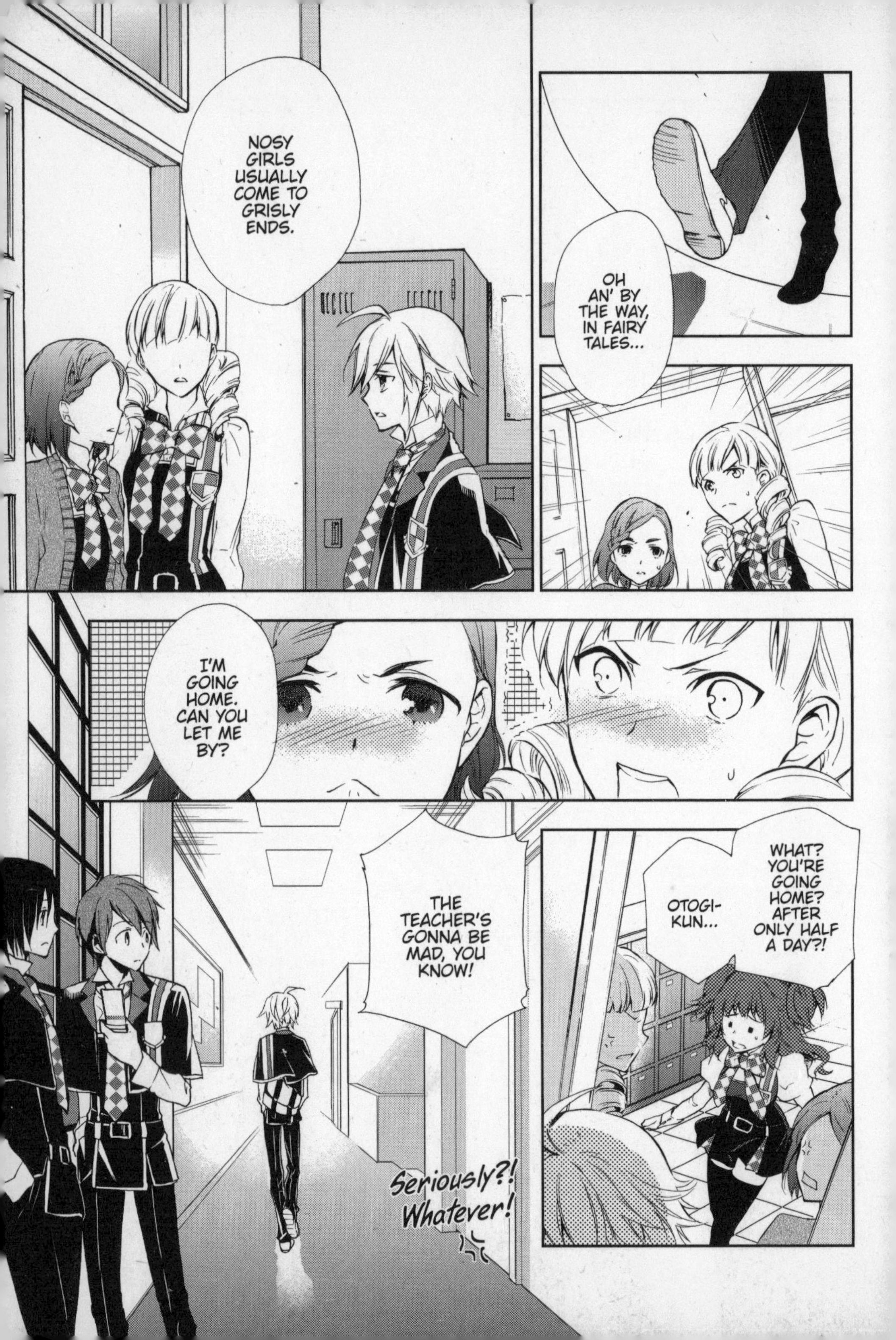
OH AN' BY THE WAY, IN FAIRY TALES...
NOSY GIRLS USUALLY COME TO GRISLY ENDS.
I'M GOING HOME. CAN YOU LET ME BY?
WHAT? YOU'RE GOING HOME? AFTER ONLY HALF A DAY?!
OTOGI-KUN...
THE TEACHER'S GONNA BE MAD, YOU KNOW!
Seriously?! Whatever!

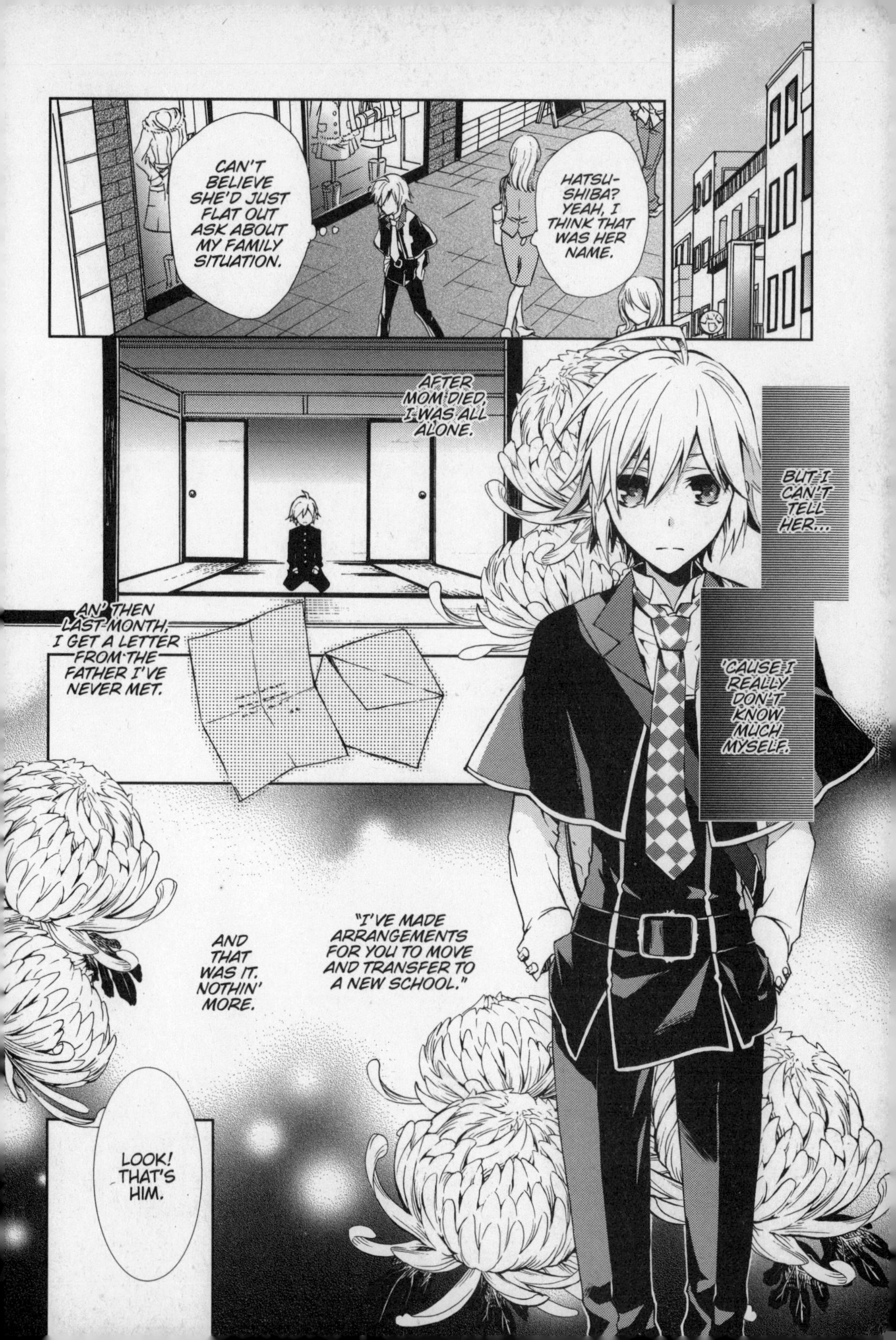
HATSU-SHIBA? YEAH, I THINK THAT WAS HER NAME.
CAN'T BELIEVE SHE'D JUST FLAT OUT ASK ABOUT MY FAMILY SITUATION.
AFTER MOM DIED, I WAS ALL ALONE.
AN' THEN LAST MONTH, I GET A LETTER FROM THE FATHER I'VE NEVER MET.
"I'VE MADE ARRANGEMENTS FOR YOU TO MOVE AND TRANSFER TO A NEW SCHOOL."
AND THAT WAS IT. NOTHIN' MORE.
BUT I CAN'T TELL HER...
'CAUSE I REALLY DON'T KNOW MUCH MYSELF.
LOOK! THAT'S HIM.

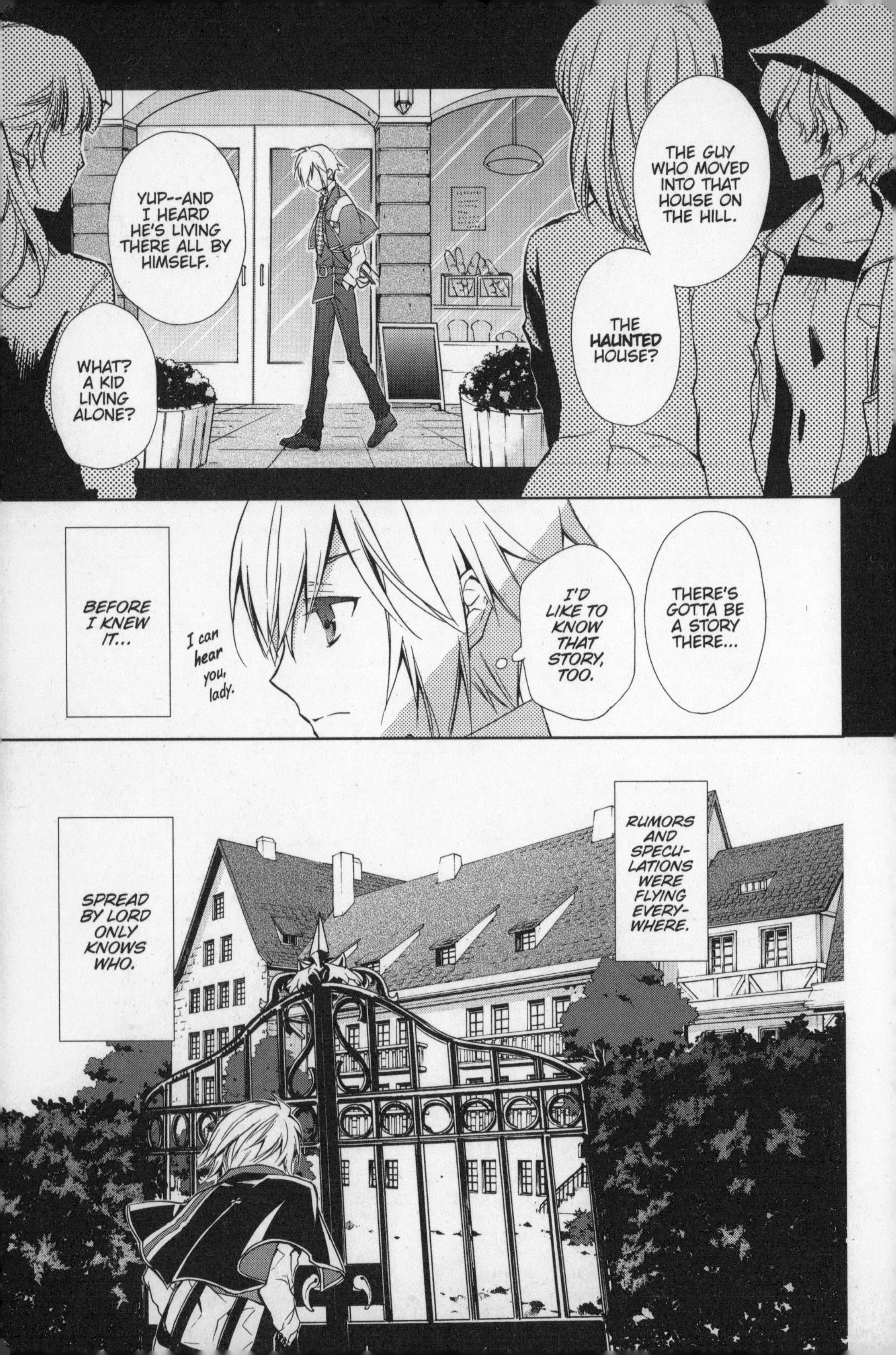
THE GUY WHO MOVED INTO THAT HOUSE ON THE HILL.
THE HAUNTED HOUSE?
YUP--AND I HEARD HE'S LIVING THERE ALL BY HIMSELF.
WHAT? A KID LIVING ALONE?
THERE'S GOTTA BE A STORY THERE...
I'D LIKE TO KNOW THAT STORY, TOO.
I can hear you, lady.
BEFORE I KNEW IT...
RUMORS AND SPECULATIONS WERE FLYING EVERYWHERE.
SPREAD BY LORD ONLY KNOWS WHO.

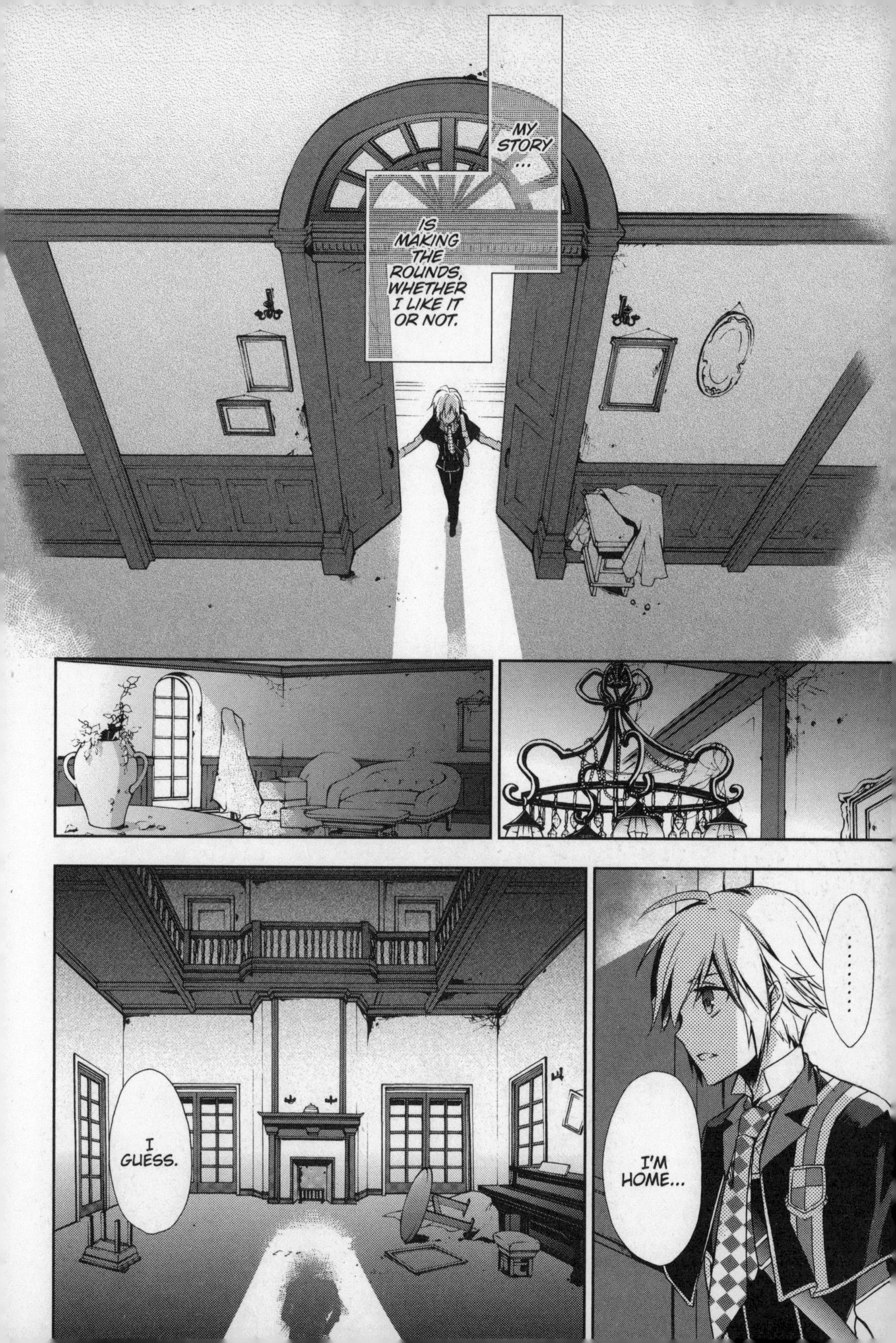
—MY STORY ...
IS MAKING THE ROUNDS, WHETHER I LIKE IT OR NOT.
......
I'M HOME...
I GUESS.

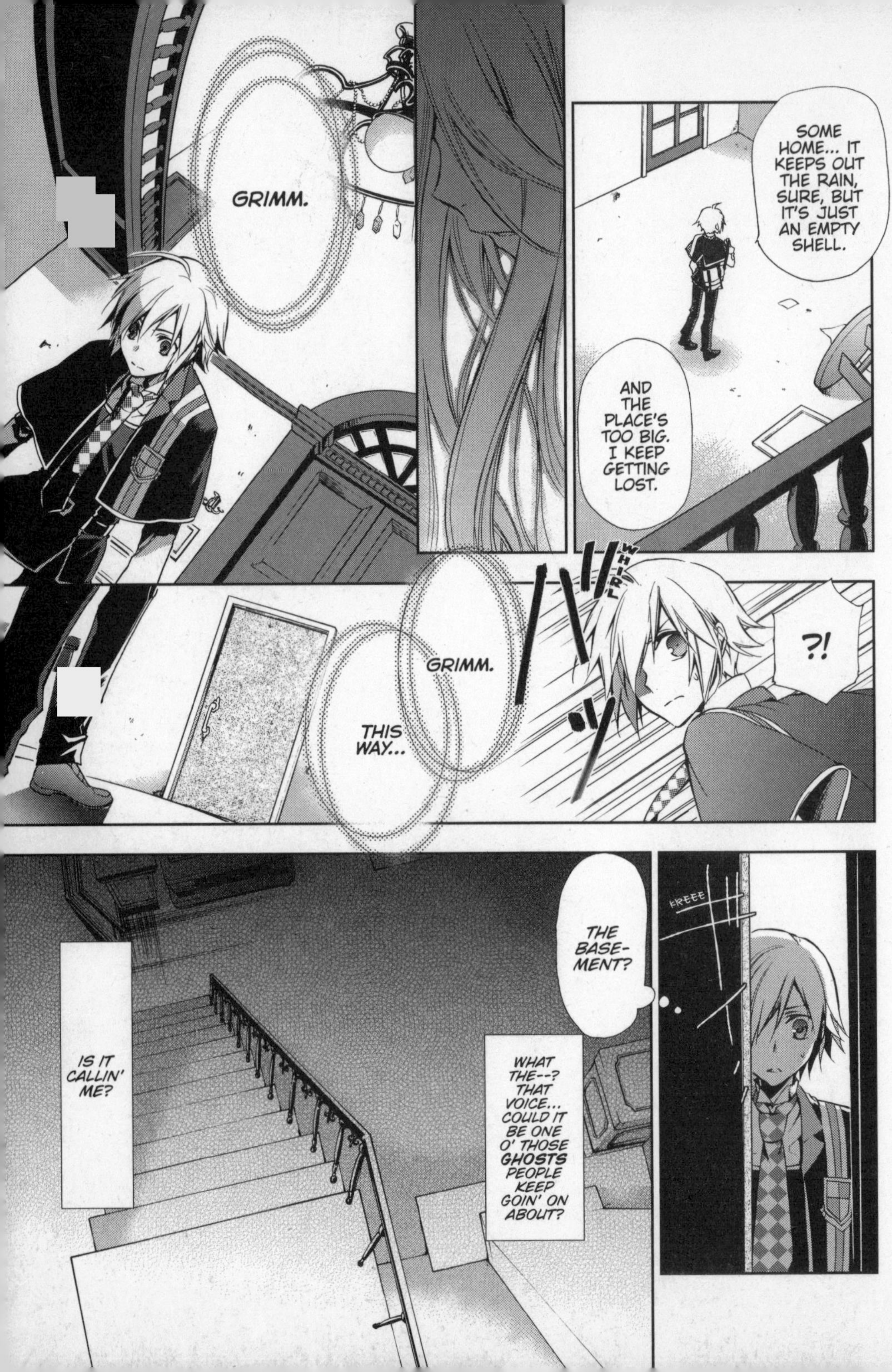
SOME HOME... IT KEEPS OUT THE RAIN, SURE, BUT IT'S JUST AN EMPTY SHELL.
AND THE PLACE'S TOO BIG. I KEEP GETTING LOST.
GRIMM.
WHIRL
?!
GRIMM.
THIS WAY...
FREEE
THE BASE-MENT?
WHAT THE--? THAT VOICE... COULD IT BE ONE O' THOSE **GHOSTS** PEOPLE KEEP GOIN' ON ABOUT?
IS IT CALLIN' ME?

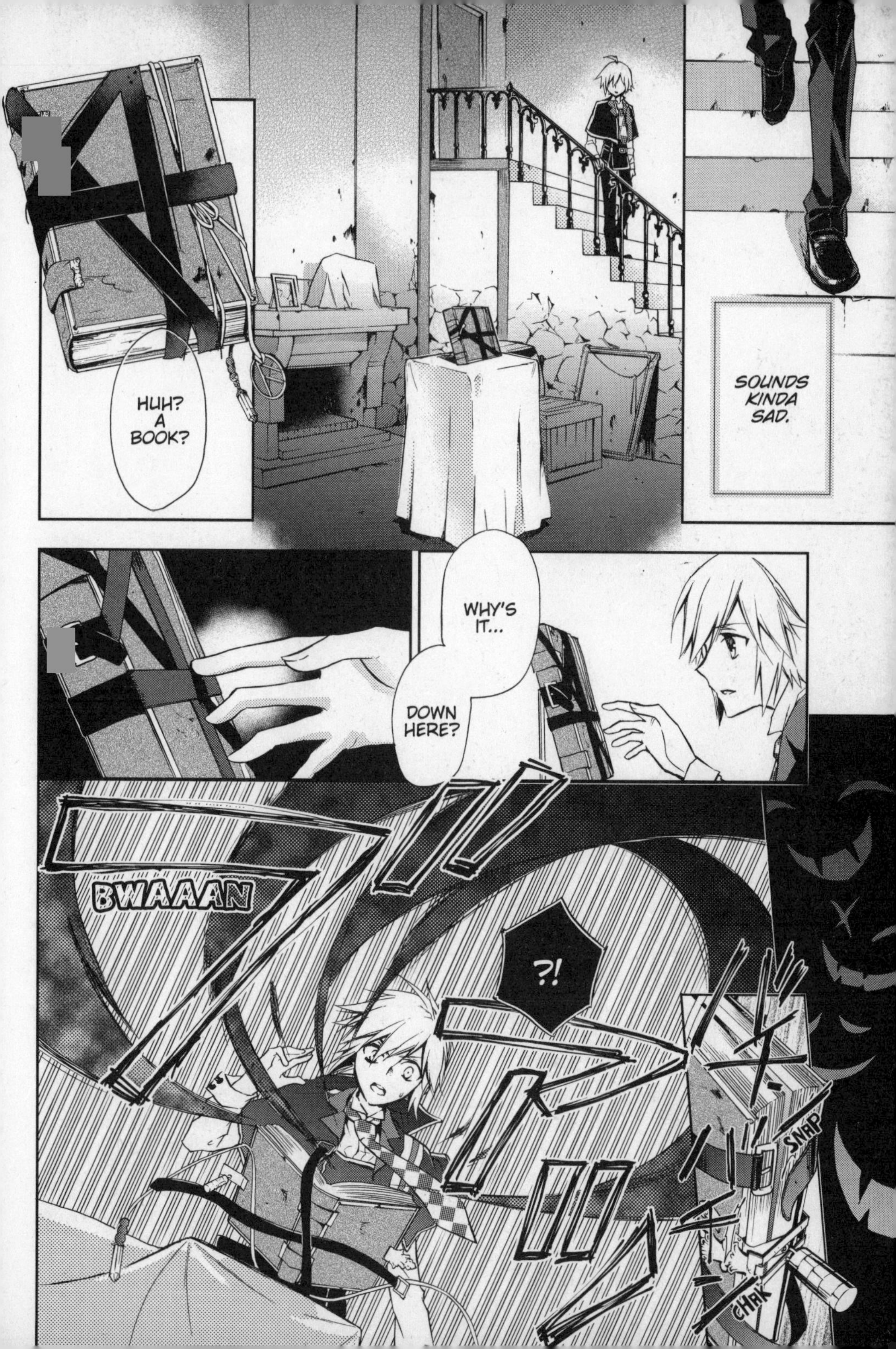
SOUNDS KINDA SAD.
HUH? A BOOK?
WHY'S IT...
DOWN HERE?
SNAP
?!
BWAAAAN
CHAK

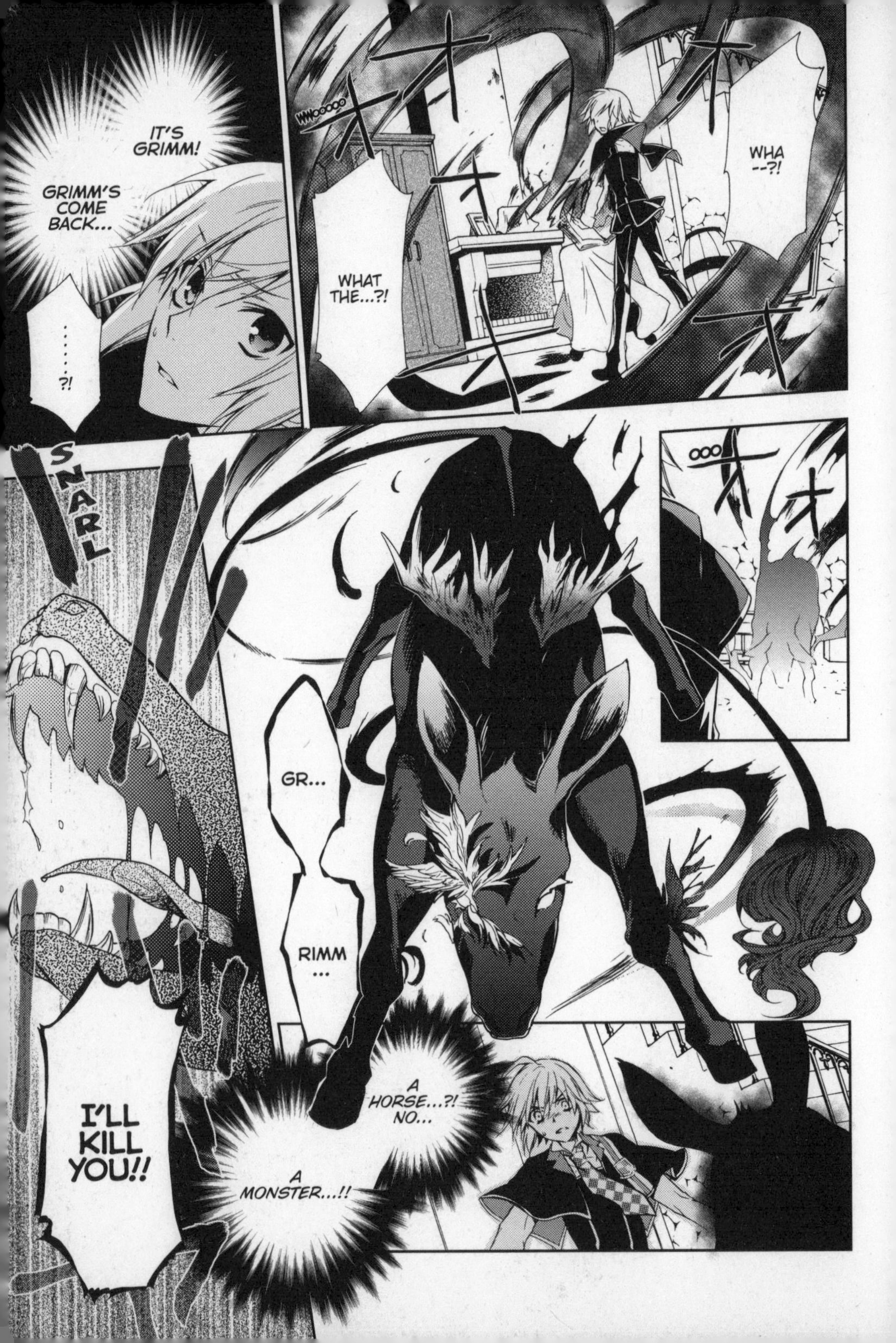
WHOOOOO
WHA --?!
WHAT THE...?!
IT'S GRIMM!
GRIMM'S COME BACK...
......?!
OOO
GR...
RIMM ...
A HORSE...?! NO...
A MONSTER...!!
SNARL
I'LL KILL YOU!!

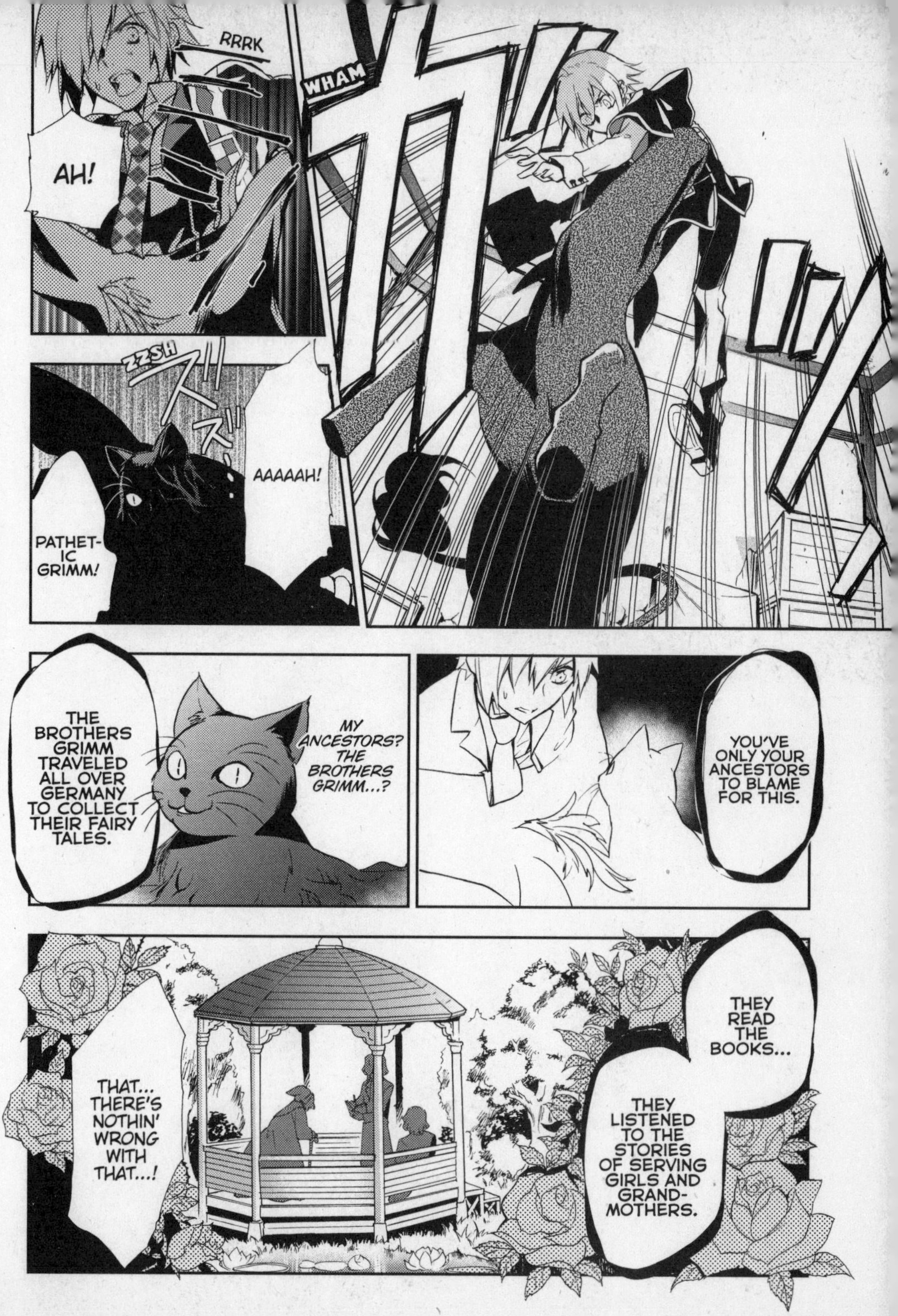
WHAM
RRRK
AH!
ZZSH
AAAAAH!
PATHET-IC GRIMM!
YOU'VE ONLY YOUR ANCESTORS TO BLAME FOR THIS.
MY ANCESTORS? THE BROTHERS GRIMM...?
THE BROTHERS GRIMM TRAVELED ALL OVER GERMANY TO COLLECT THEIR FAIRY TALES.
THEY READ THE BOOKS...
THEY LISTENED TO THE STORIES OF SERVING GIRLS AND GRAND-MOTHERS.
THAT... THERE'S NOTHIN' WRONG WITH THAT...!

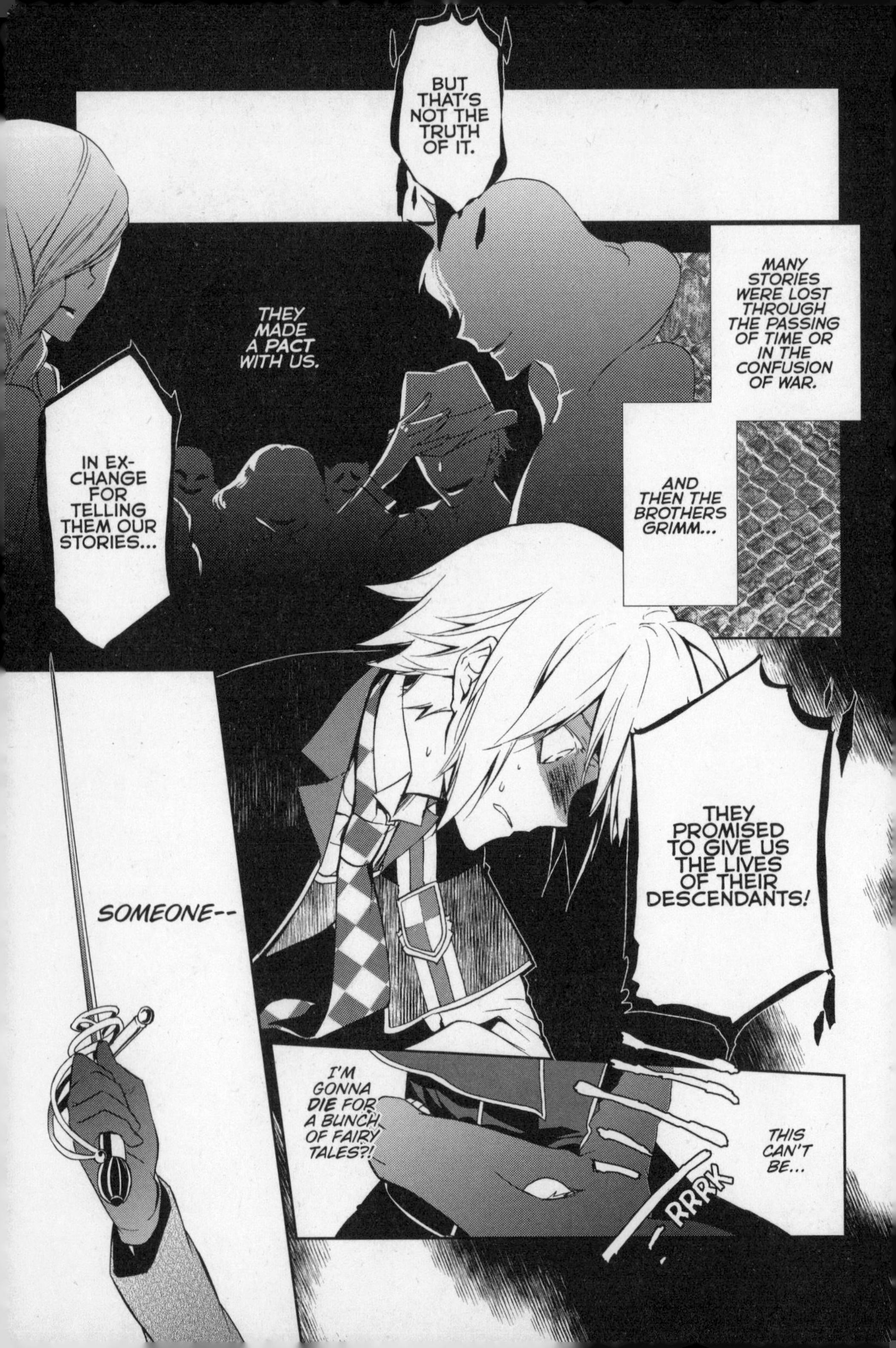
BUT THAT'S NOT THE TRUTH OF IT.
MANY STORIES WERE LOST THROUGH THE PASSING OF TIME OR IN THE CONFUSION OF WAR.
AND THEN THE BROTHERS GRIMM...
THEY MADE A PACT WITH US.
IN EX-CHANGE FOR TELLING THEM OUR STORIES...
THEY PROMISED TO GIVE US THE LIVES OF THEIR DESCENDANTS!
THIS CAN'T BE...
I'M GONNA DIE FOR A BUNCH OF FAIRY TALES?!
RRRK
SOMEONE--

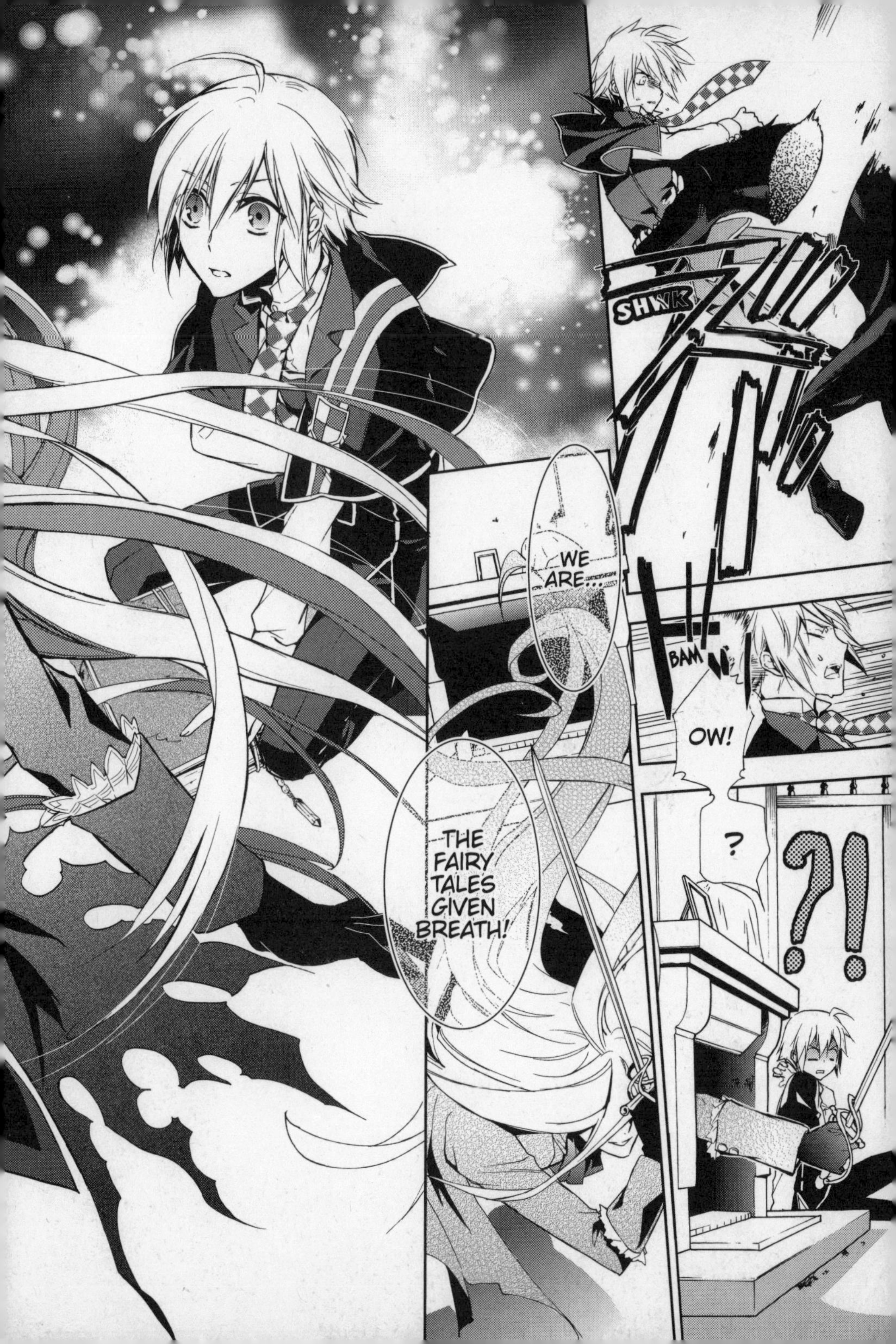
SHWK
BAM
OW!
?
?!
WE ARE...
THE FAIRY TALES GIVEN BREATH!

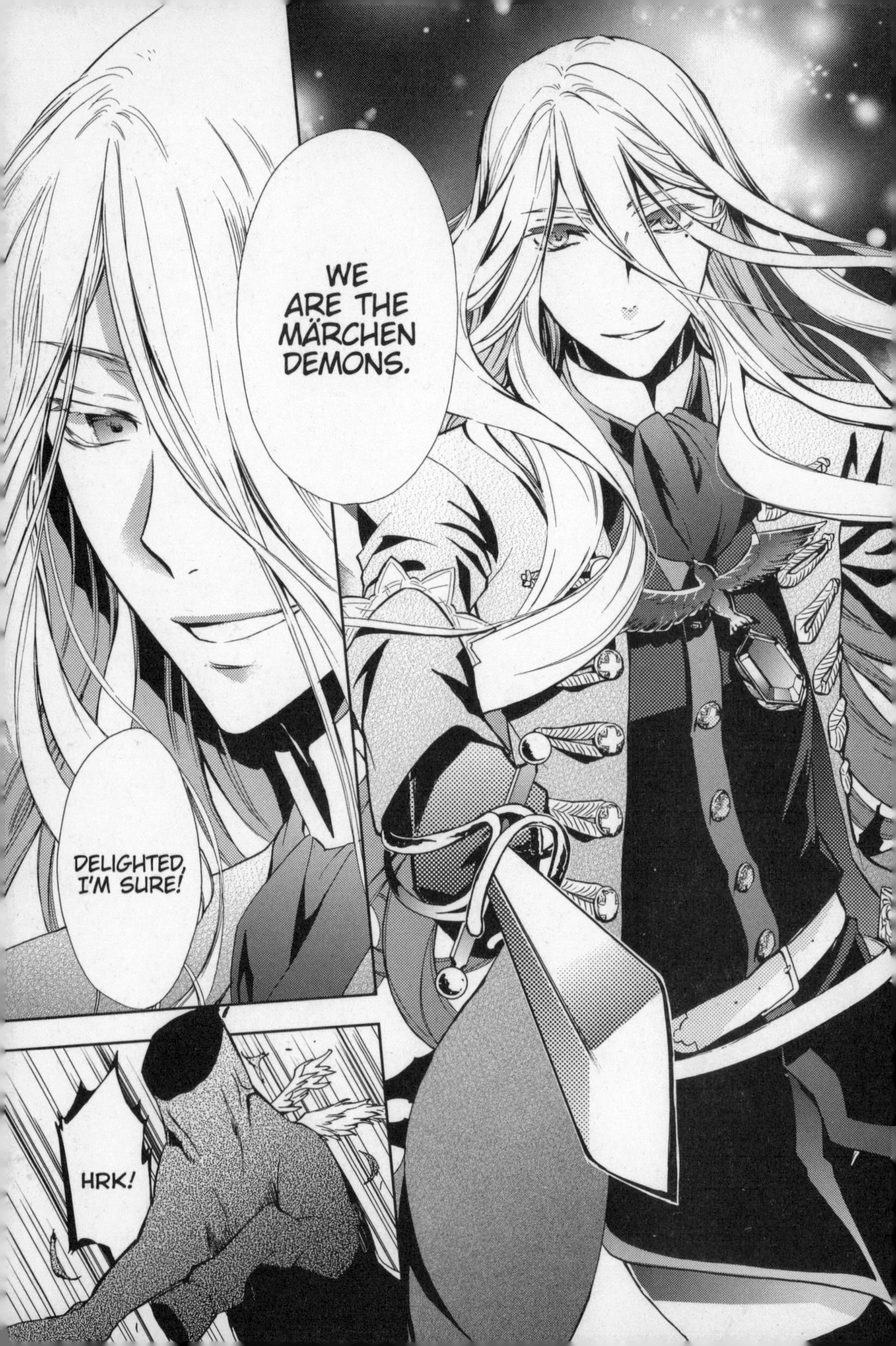
WE ARE THE MÄRCHEN DEMONS.
DELIGHTED, I'M SURE!
HRK!

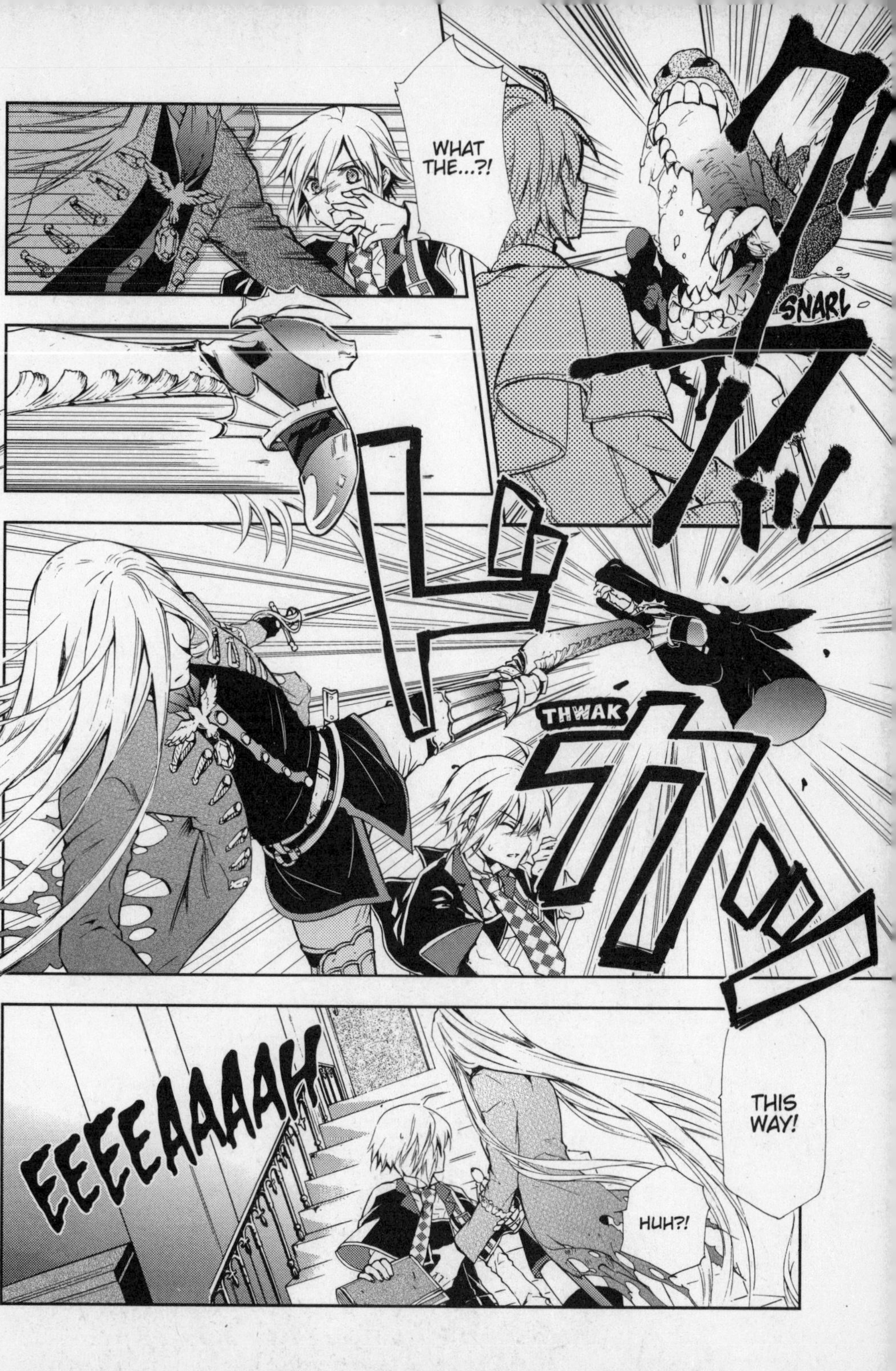
SNARL
WHAT THE...?!
THWAK
THIS WAY!
HUH?!
EEEEAAAAH

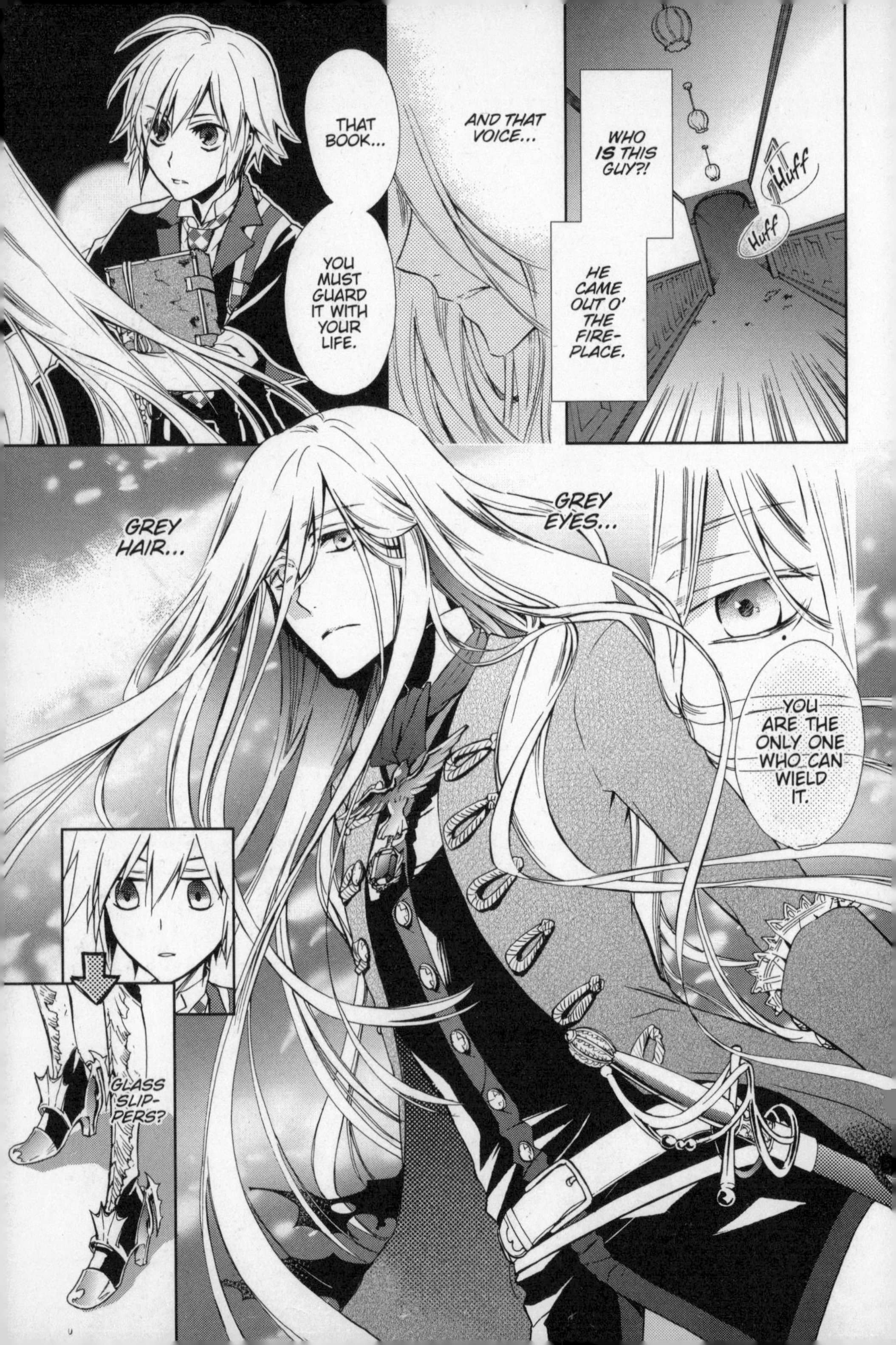

WHO IS THIS GUY?!
Huff
Huff
HE CAME OUT O' THE FIRE-PLACE.
AND THAT VOICE...
THAT BOOK...
YOU MUST GUARD IT WITH YOUR LIFE.
YOU ARE THE ONLY ONE WHO CAN WIELD IT.
GREY EYES...
GREY HAIR...
GLASS SLIPPERS?

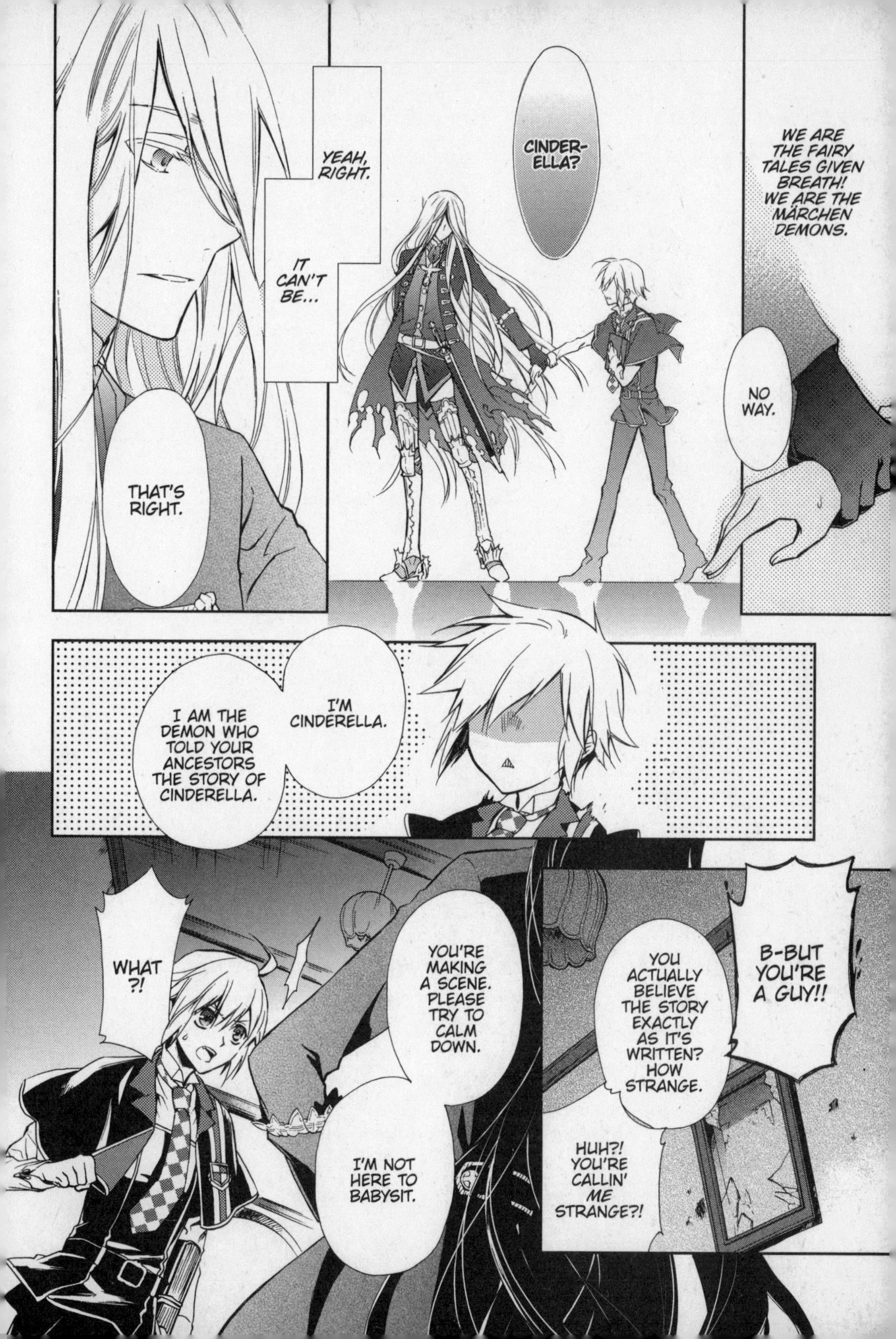
WE ARE THE FAIRY TALES GIVEN BREATH! WE ARE THE MÄRCHEN DEMONS.
NO WAY.
CINDER-ELLA?
YEAH, RIGHT.
IT CAN'T BE...
THAT'S RIGHT.
I'M CINDERELLA.
I AM THE DEMON WHO TOLD YOUR ANCESTORS THE STORY OF CINDERELLA.
B-BUT YOU'RE A GUY!!
YOU ACTUALLY BELIEVE THE STORY EXACTLY AS IT'S WRITTEN? HOW STRANGE.
HUH?! YOU'RE CALLIN' ME STRANGE?!
YOU'RE MAKING A SCENE. PLEASE TRY TO CALM DOWN.
WHAT?!
I'M NOT HERE TO BABYSIT.

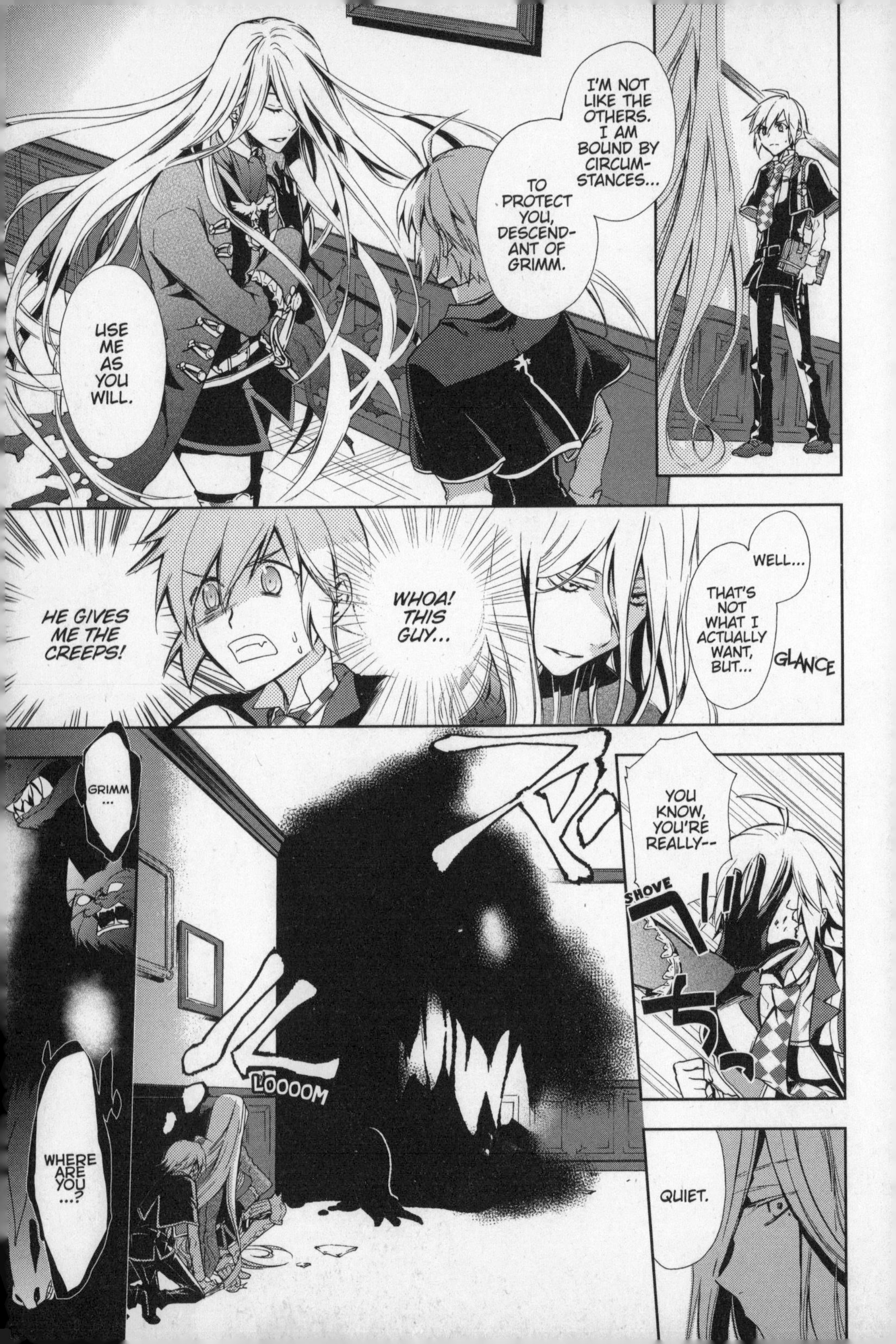
I'M NOT LIKE THE OTHERS. I AM BOUND BY CIRCUMSTANCES...
TO PROTECT YOU, DESCENDANT OF GRIMM.
USE ME AS YOU WILL.
WELL...
THAT'S NOT WHAT I ACTUALLY WANT, BUT...
GLANCE
WHOA! THIS GUY...
HE GIVES ME THE CREEPS!
YOU KNOW, YOU'RE REALLY--
SHOVE
QUIET.
GRIMM...
LOOOOM
WHERE ARE YOU...?

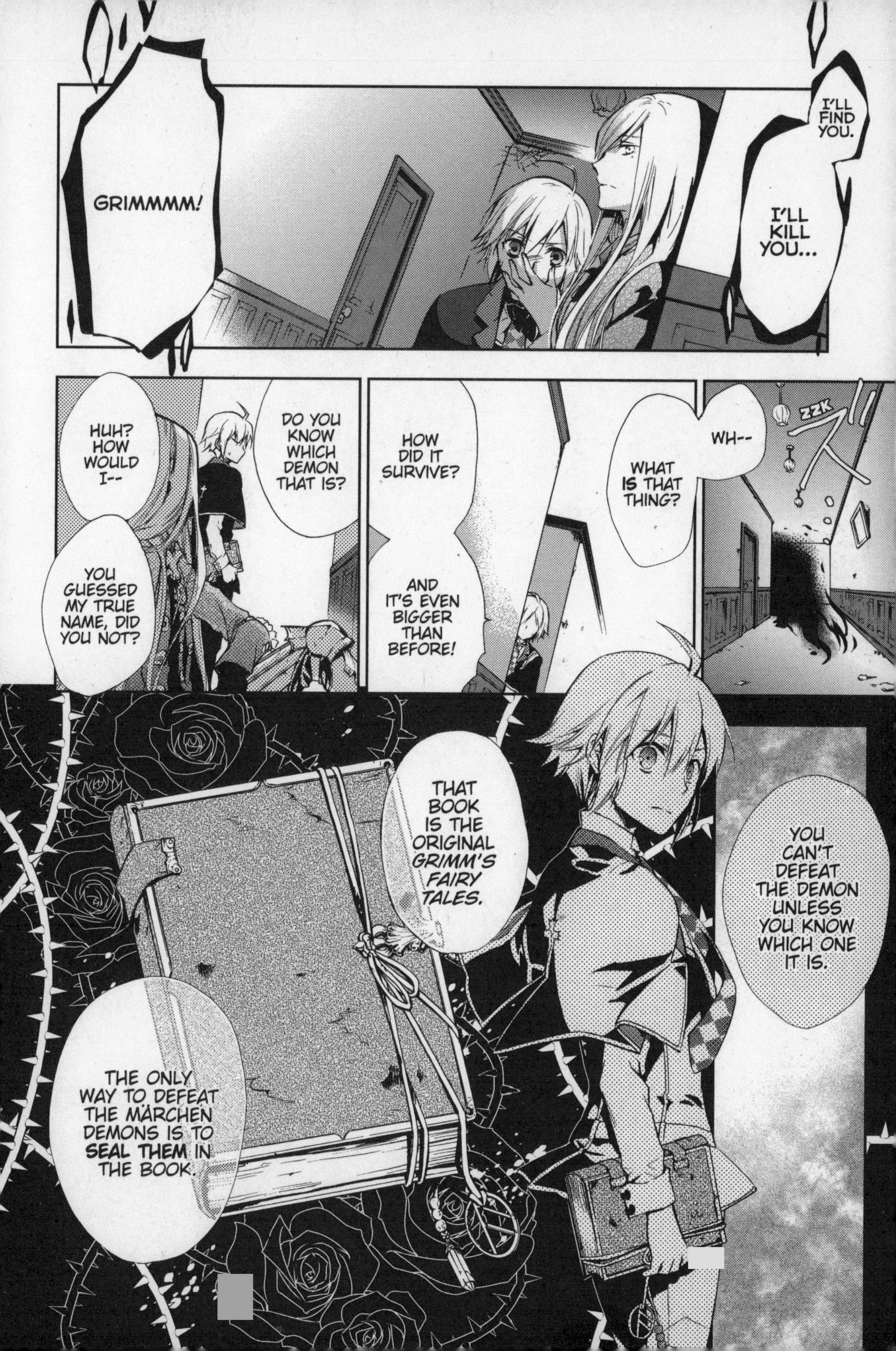
I'LL FIND YOU.
I'LL KILL YOU...
GRIMMMM!
ZZK
WH--
WHAT IS THAT THING?
HOW DID IT SURVIVE?
AND IT'S EVEN BIGGER THAN BEFORE!
DO YOU KNOW WHICH DEMON THAT IS?
HUH? HOW WOULD I--
YOU GUESSED MY TRUE NAME, DID YOU NOT?
YOU CAN'T DEFEAT THE DEMON UNLESS YOU KNOW WHICH ONE IT IS.
THAT BOOK IS THE ORIGINAL *GRIMM'S FAIRY TALES.*
THE ONLY WAY TO DEFEAT THE MÄRCHEN DEMONS IS TO **SEAL THEM** IN THE BOOK.

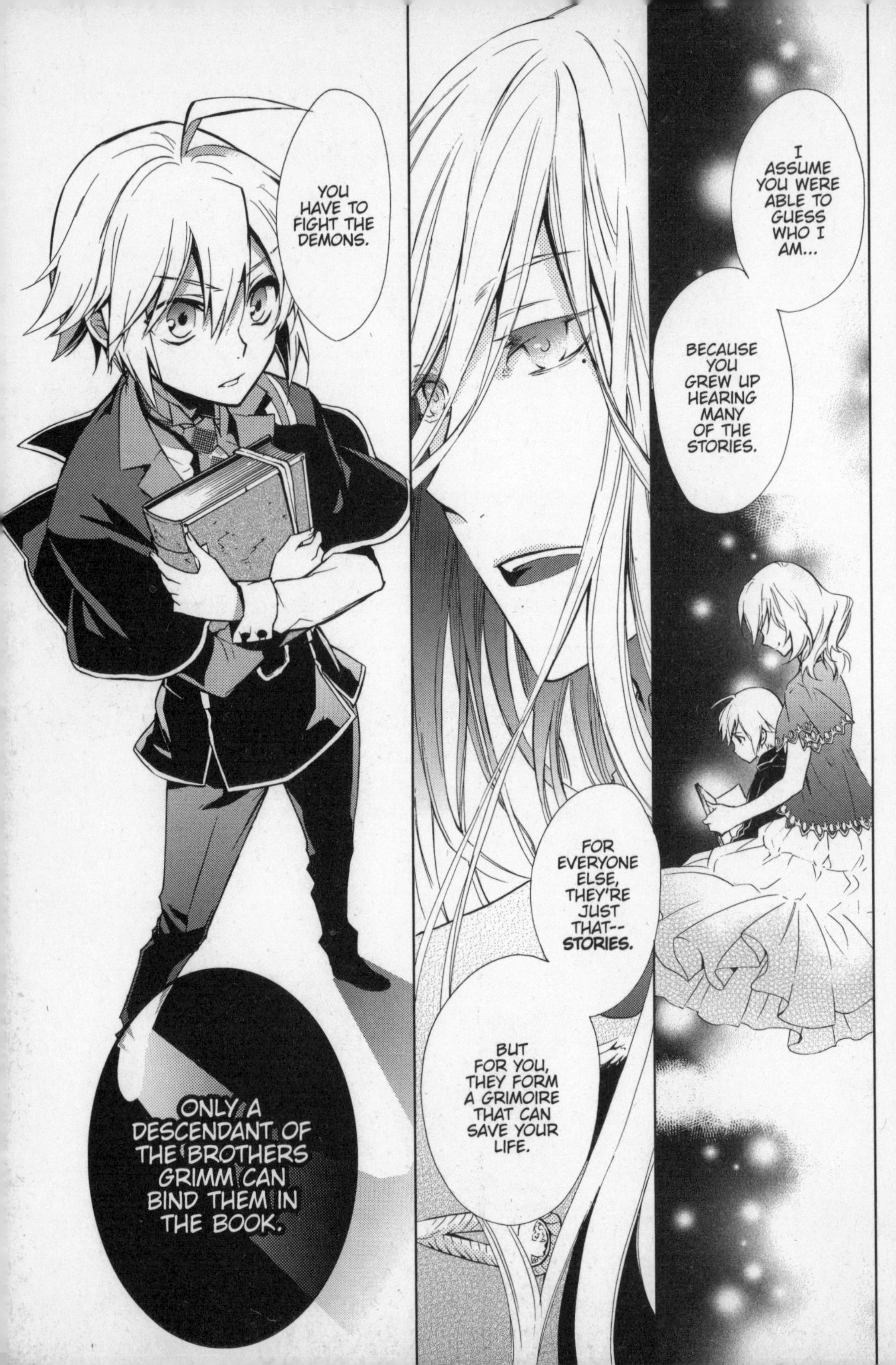
I ASSUME YOU WERE ABLE TO GUESS WHO I AM...
BECAUSE YOU GREW UP HEARING MANY OF THE STORIES.
FOR EVERYONE ELSE, THEY'RE JUST THAT--**STORIES.**
BUT FOR YOU, THEY FORM A GRIMOIRE THAT CAN SAVE YOUR LIFE.
YOU HAVE TO FIGHT THE DEMONS.
ONLY A DESCENDANT OF THE BROTHERS GRIMM CAN BIND THEM IN THE BOOK.

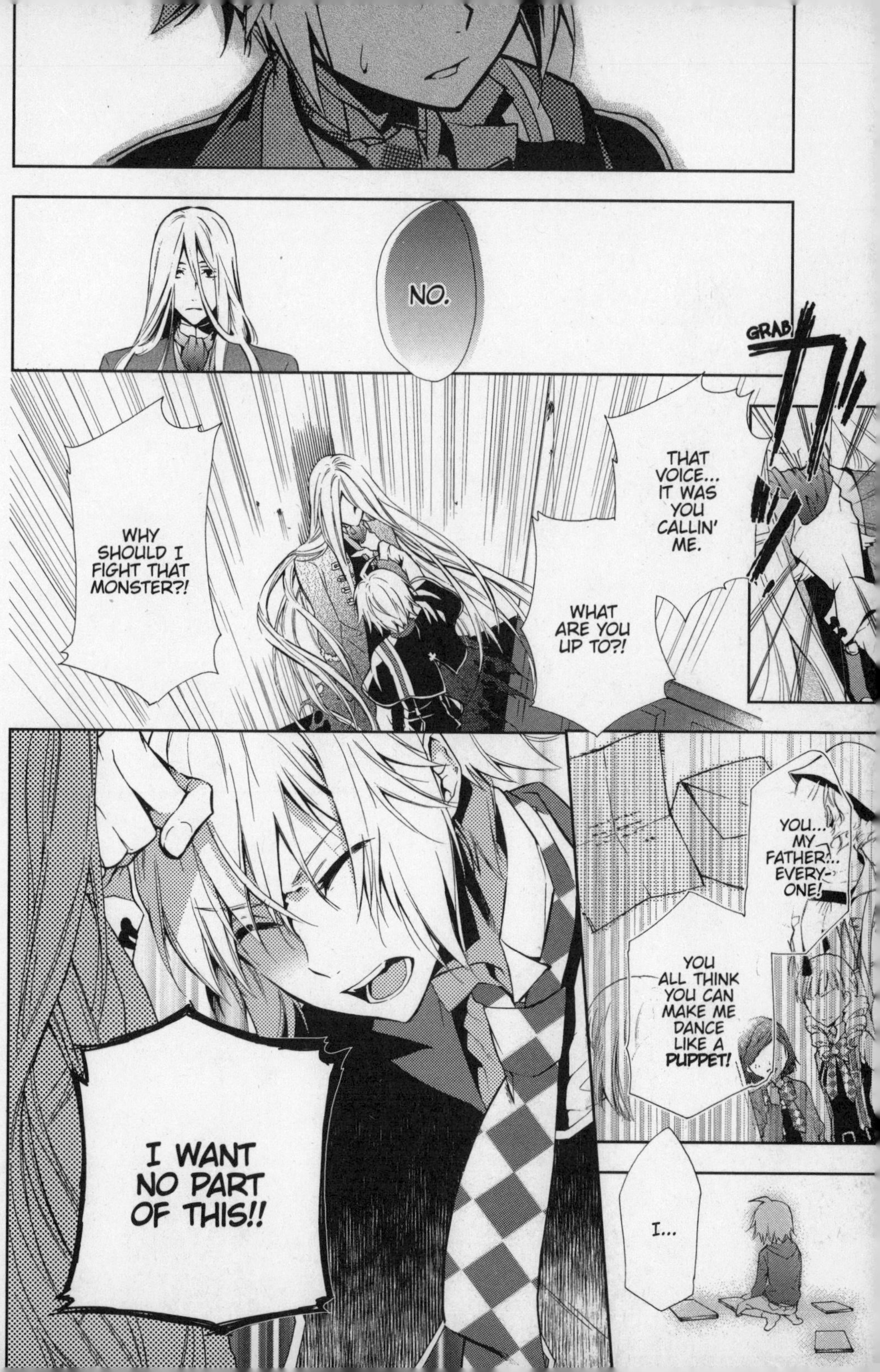
NO.
GRAB
THAT VOICE... IT WAS YOU CALLIN' ME.
WHAT ARE YOU UP TO?!
WHY SHOULD I FIGHT THAT MONSTER?!
YOU... MY FATHER... EVERY-ONE!
YOU ALL THINK YOU CAN MAKE ME DANCE LIKE A PUPPET!
I...
I WANT NO PART OF THIS!!

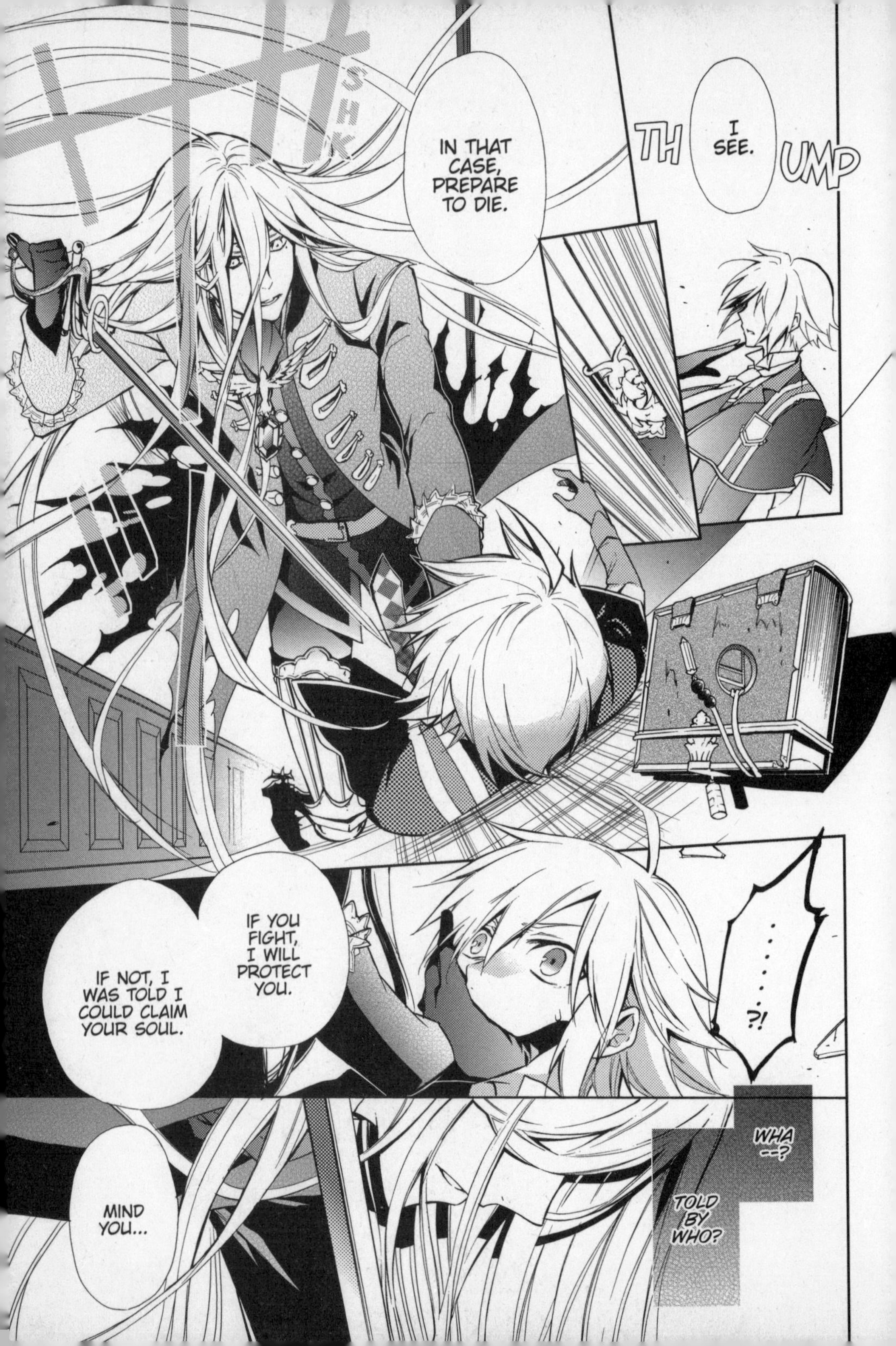
THUMP
I SEE.
SHK
IN THAT CASE, PREPARE TO DIE.
......?!
IF YOU FIGHT, I WILL PROTECT YOU.
IF NOT, I WAS TOLD I COULD CLAIM YOUR SOUL.
WHA--?
TOLD BY WHO?
MIND YOU...

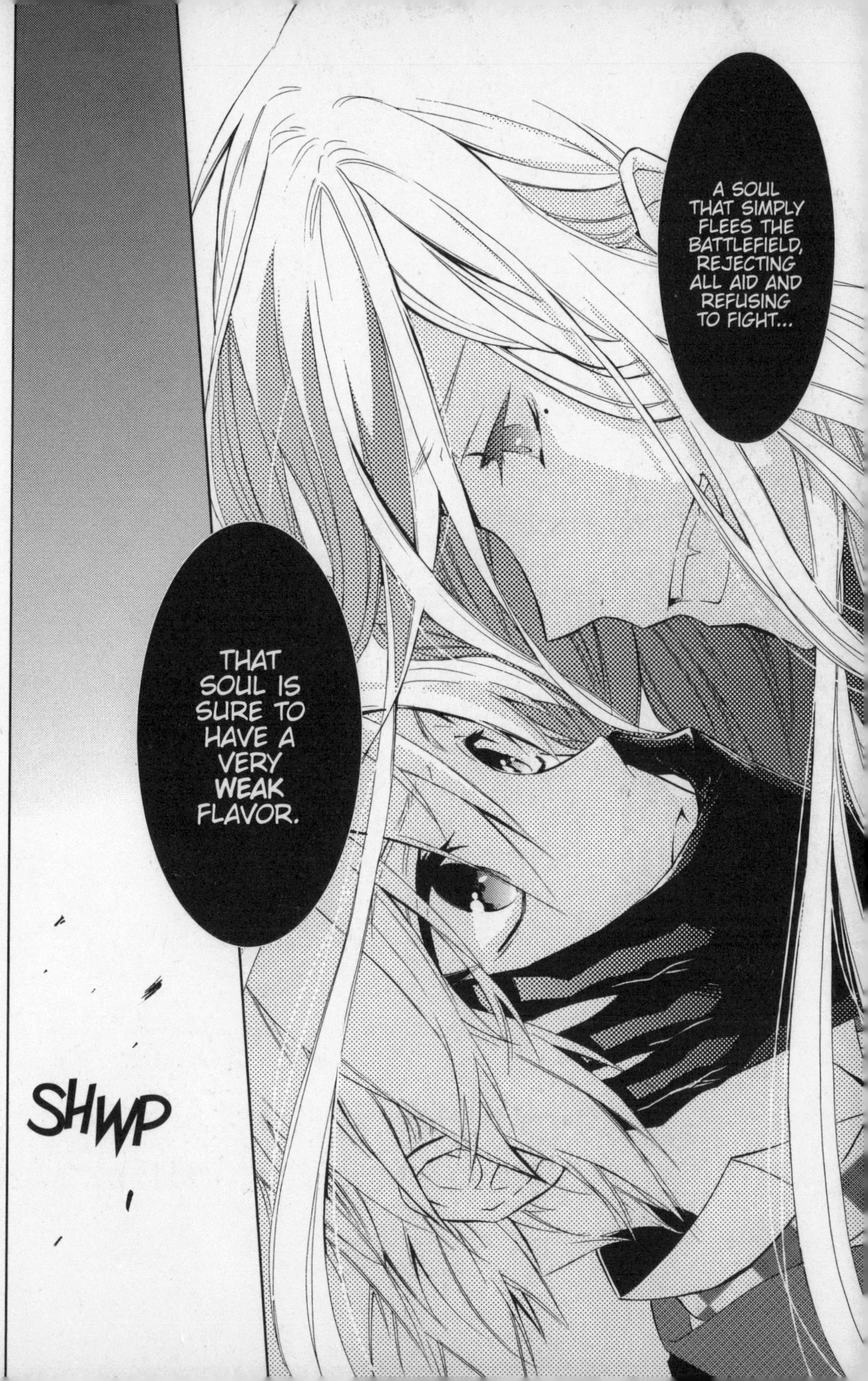
A SOUL THAT SIMPLY FLEES THE BATTLEFIELD, REJECTING ALL AID AND REFUSING TO FIGHT...
THAT SOUL IS SURE TO HAVE A VERY WEAK FLAVOR.
SHWP

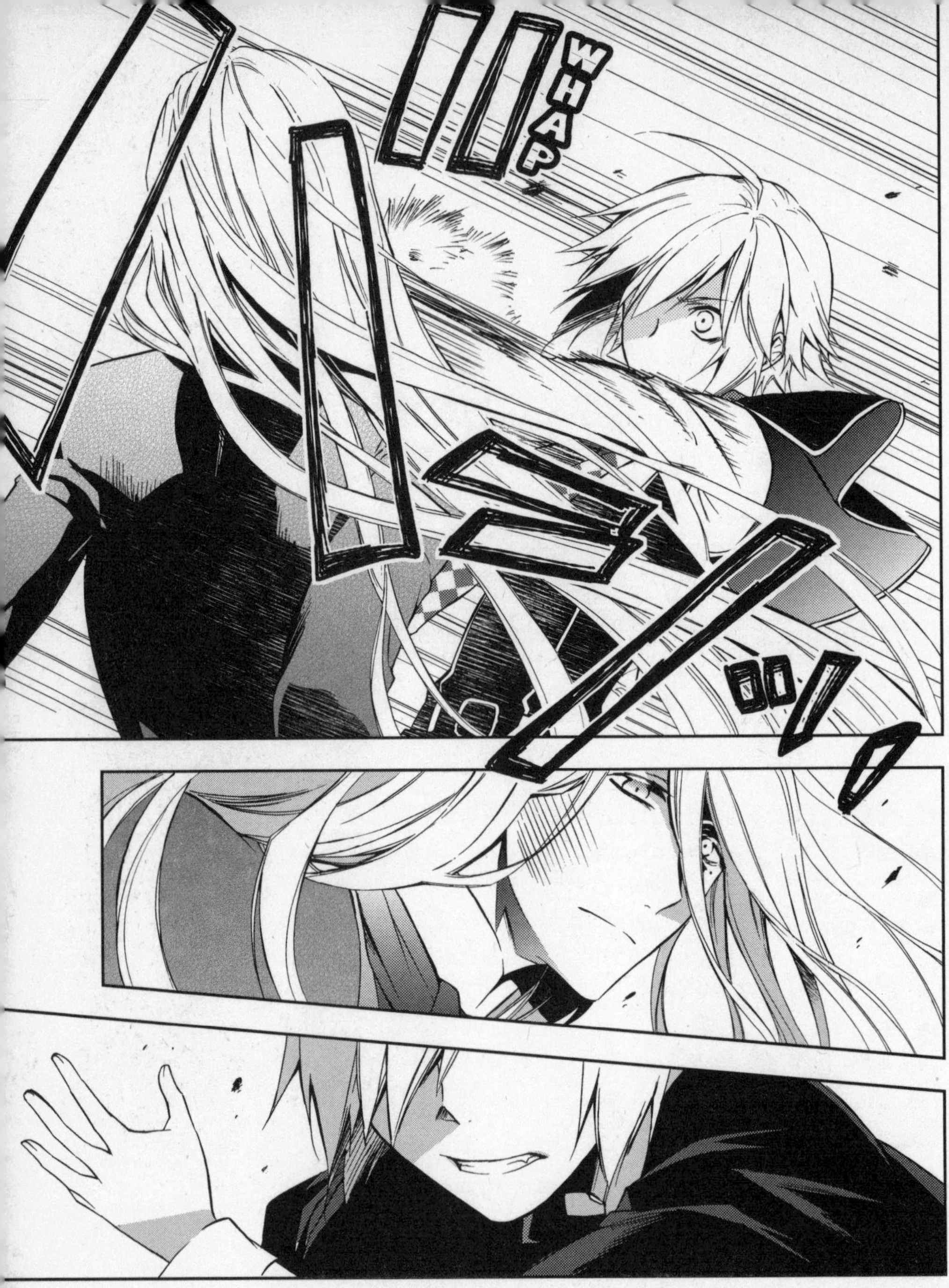
WHAP

NO FRICKIN' WAY!

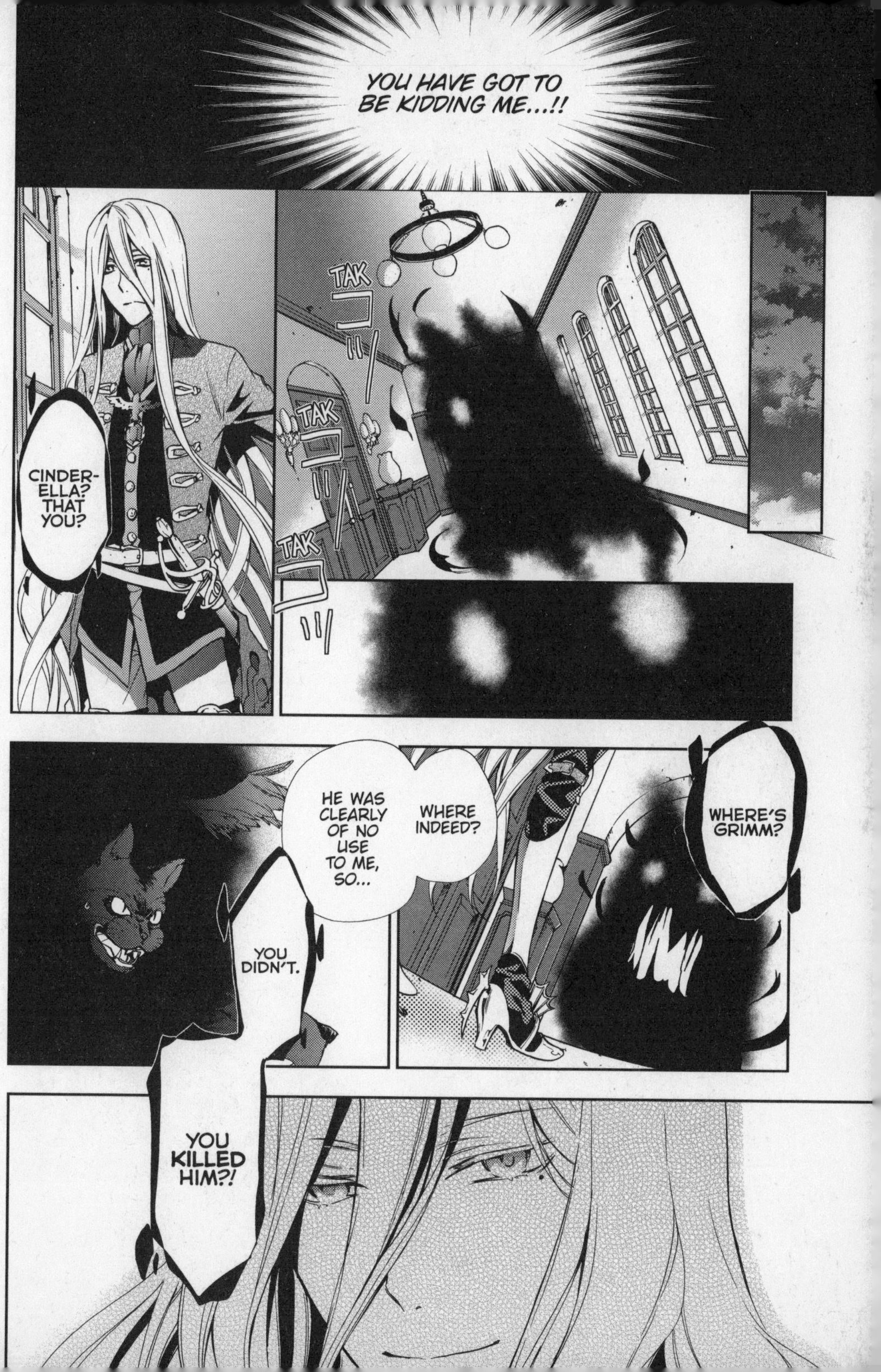
YOU HAVE GOT TO BE KIDDING ME...!!
TAK
TAK
TAK
CINDERELLA? THAT YOU?
WHERE'S GRIMM?
WHERE INDEED?
HE WAS CLEARLY OF NO USE TO ME, SO...
YOU DIDN'T.
YOU KILLED HIM?!

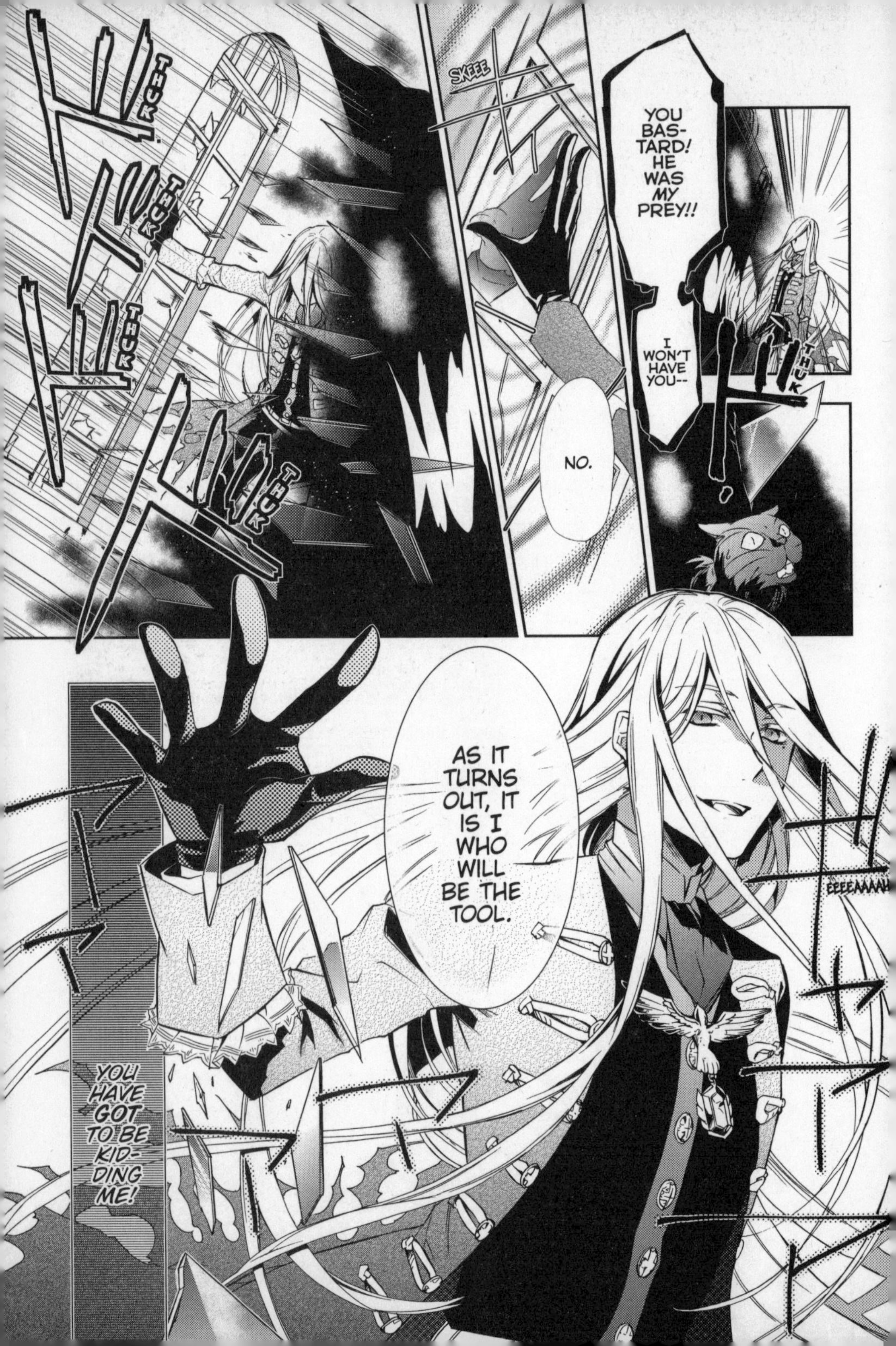
YOU BASTARD! HE WAS MY PREY!!
I WON'T HAVE YOU--
THUK
SKEEE
NO.
THUK
THUK
THUK
THUK
AS IT TURNS OUT, IT IS I WHO WILL BE THE TOOL.
EEEEAAAAH
YOU HAVE GOT TO BE KID-DING ME!

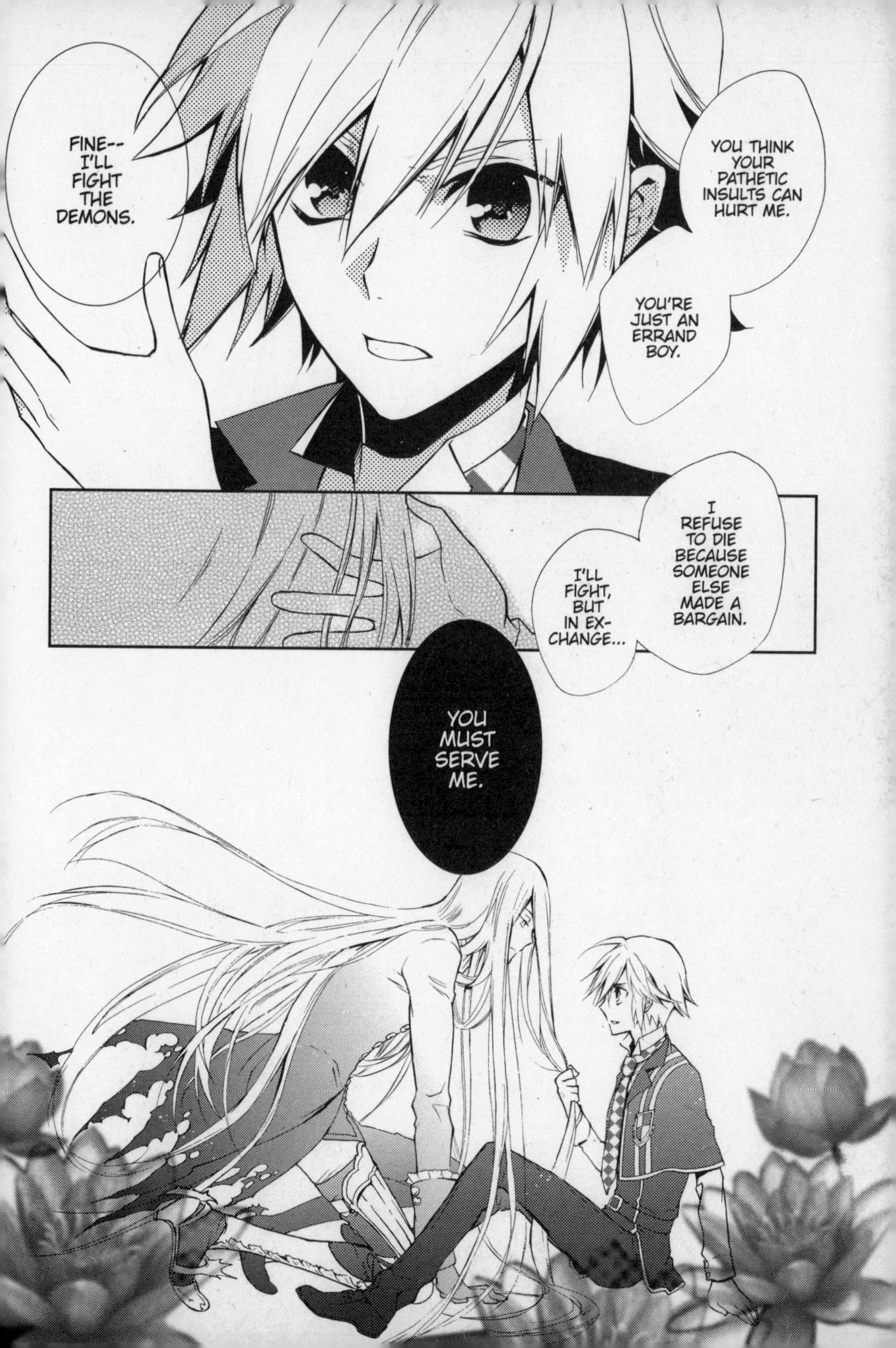
YOU THINK YOUR PATHETIC INSULTS CAN HURT ME.
YOU'RE JUST AN ERRAND BOY.
FINE-- I'LL FIGHT THE DEMONS.
I REFUSE TO DIE BECAUSE SOMEONE ELSE MADE A BARGAIN.
I'LL FIGHT, BUT IN EX-CHANGE...
YOU MUST SERVE ME.

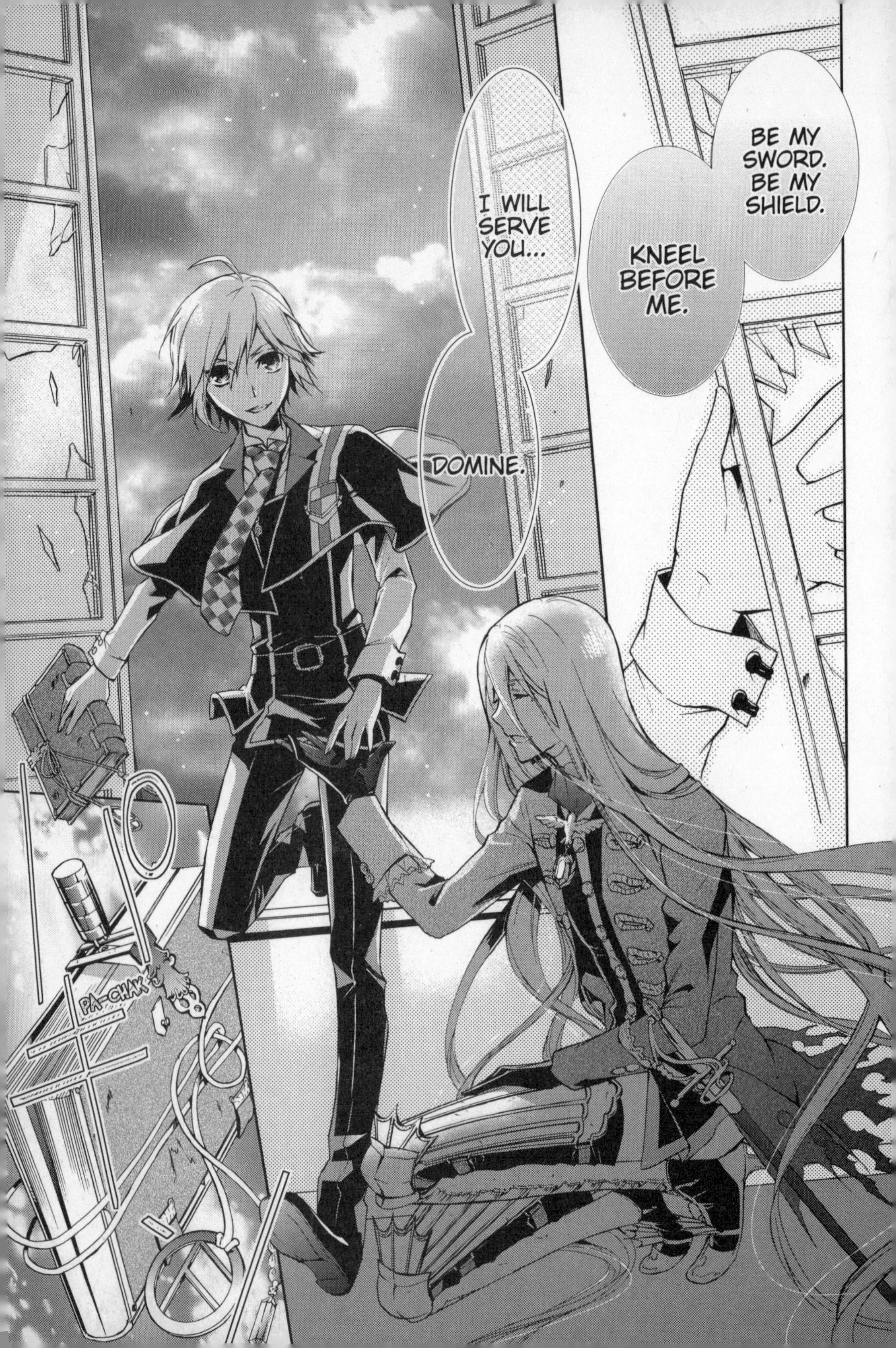
BE MY SWORD. BE MY SHIELD.
KNEEL BEFORE ME.
I WILL SERVE YOU...
DOMINE.
PA-CHAK

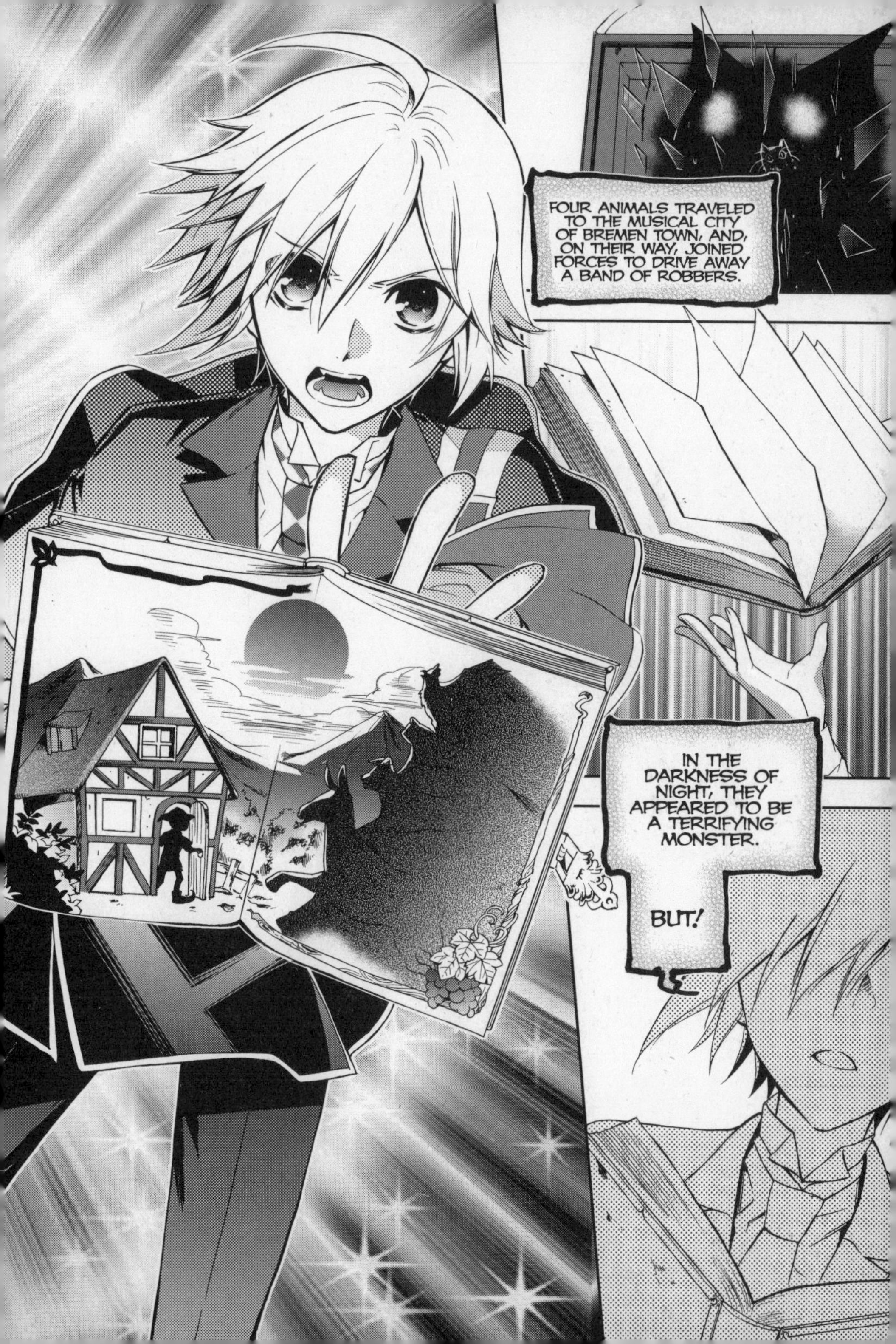
FOUR ANIMALS TRAVELED TO THE MUSICAL CITY OF BREMEN TOWN, AND, ON THEIR WAY, JOINED FORCES TO DRIVE AWAY A BAND OF ROBBERS.
IN THE DARKNESS OF NIGHT, THEY APPEARED TO BE A TERRIFYING MONSTER.
BUT!

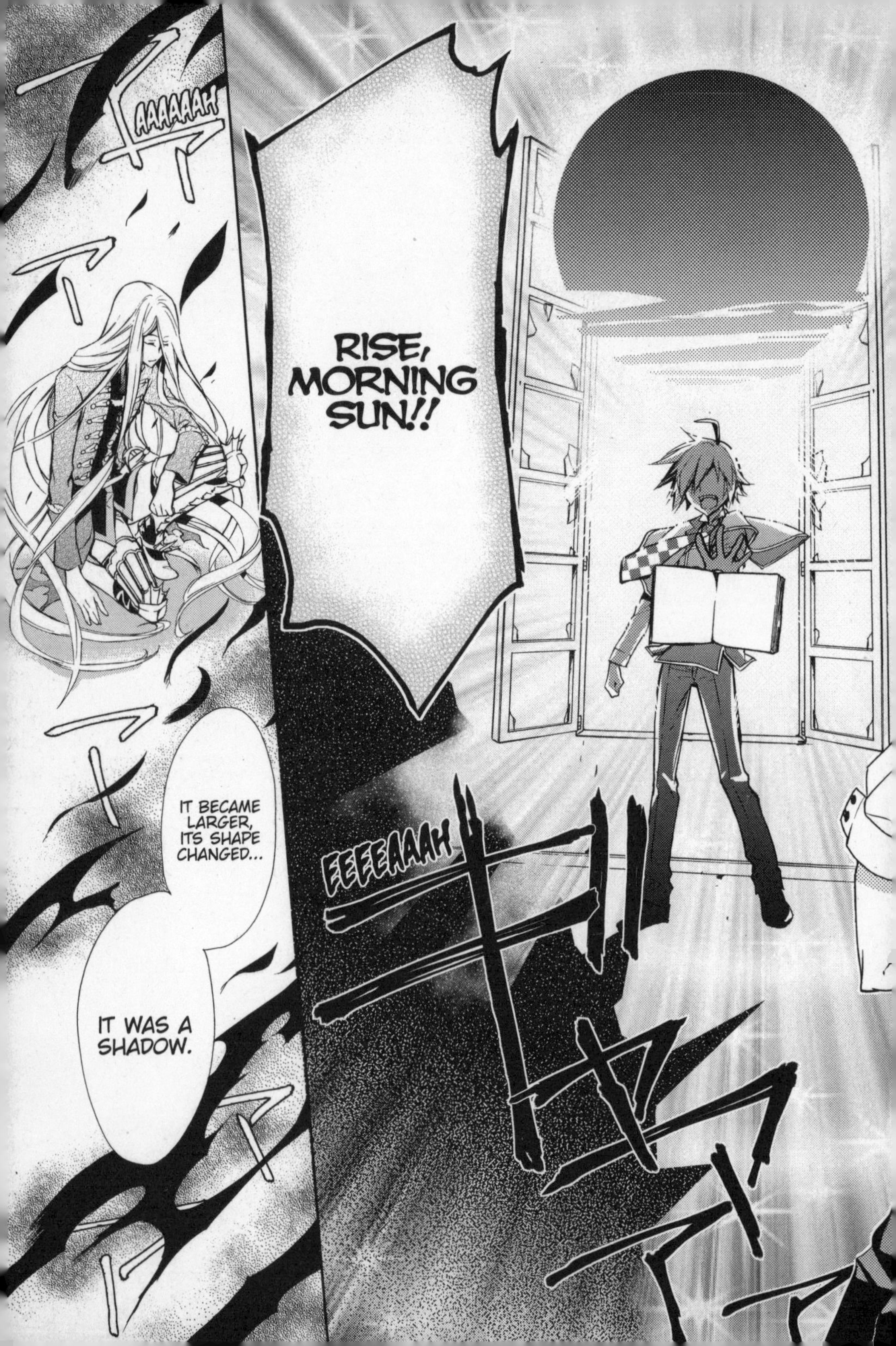
RISE, MORNING SUN!!
EEEEAAAH
AAAAAAH
IT BECAME LARGER, ITS SHAPE CHANGED...
IT WAS A SHADOW.

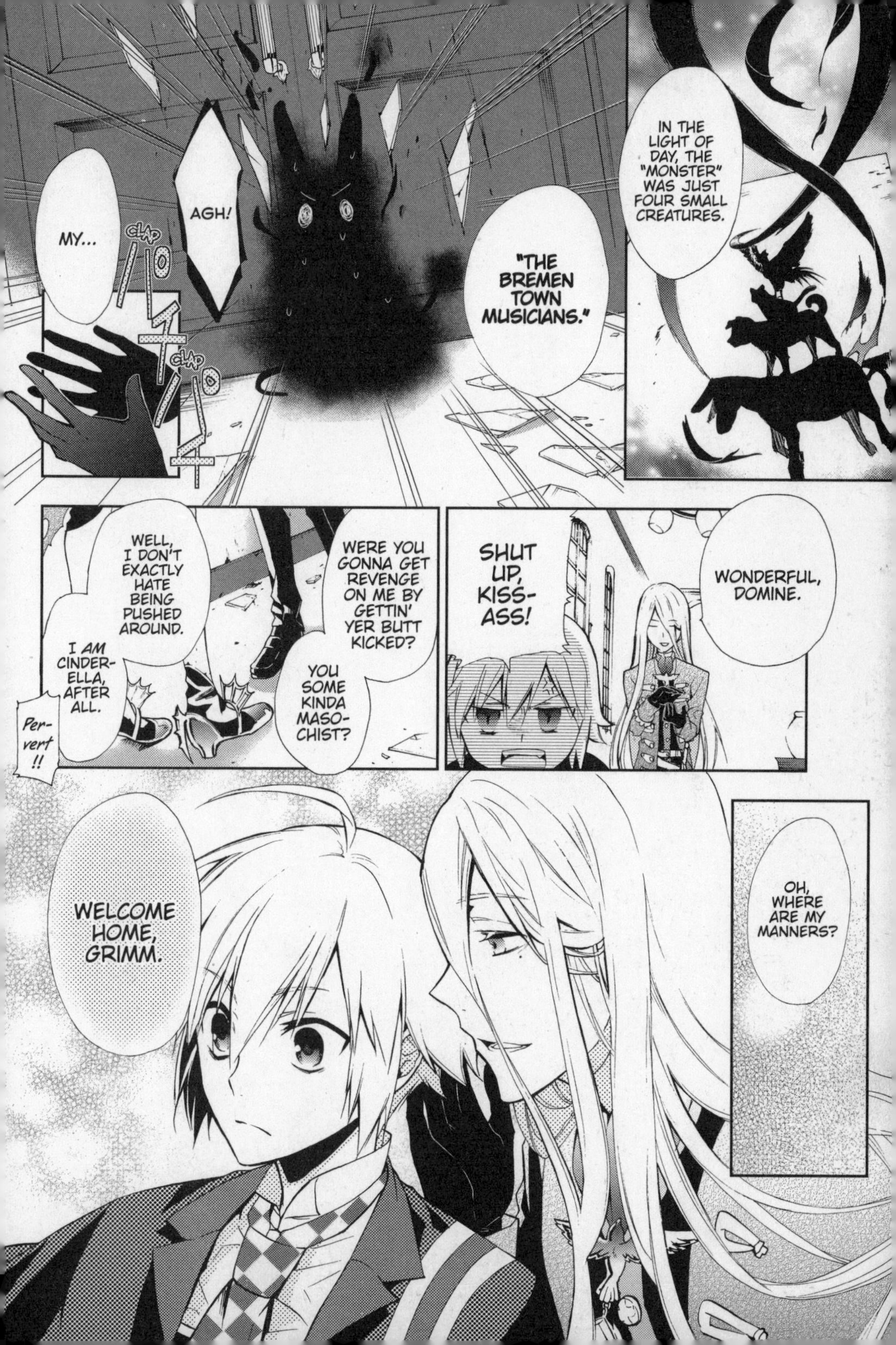
IN THE LIGHT OF DAY, THE "MONSTER" WAS JUST FOUR SMALL CREATURES.
"THE BREMEN TOWN MUSICIANS."
AGH!
MY...
CLAP
CLAP
WONDERFUL, DOMINE.
SHUT UP, KISS-ASS!
WERE YOU GONNA GET REVENGE ON ME BY GETTIN' YER BUTT KICKED?
YOU SOME KINDA MASO-CHIST?
WELL, I DON'T EXACTLY HATE BEING PUSHED AROUND.
I AM CINDER-ELLA, AFTER ALL.
Per-vert!!
OH, WHERE ARE MY MANNERS?
WELCOME HOME, GRIMM.

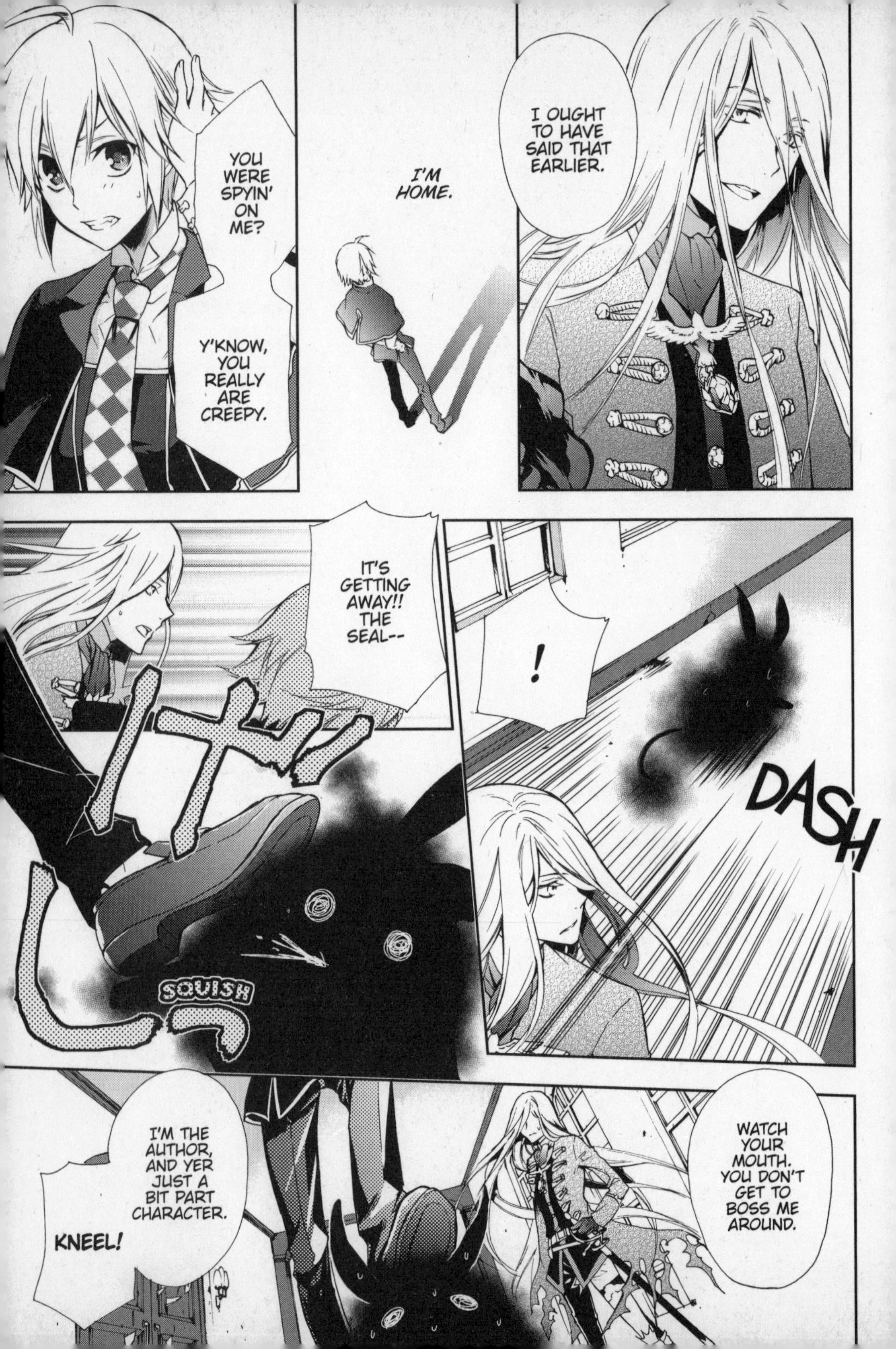
I OUGHT TO HAVE SAID THAT EARLIER.
I'M HOME.
YOU WERE SPYIN' ON ME?
Y'KNOW, YOU REALLY ARE CREEPY.
!
DASH
IT'S GETTING AWAY!! THE SEAL--
SQUISH
WATCH YOUR MOUTH. YOU DON'T GET TO BOSS ME AROUND.
I'M THE AUTHOR, AND YER JUST A BIT PART CHARACTER.
KNEEL!

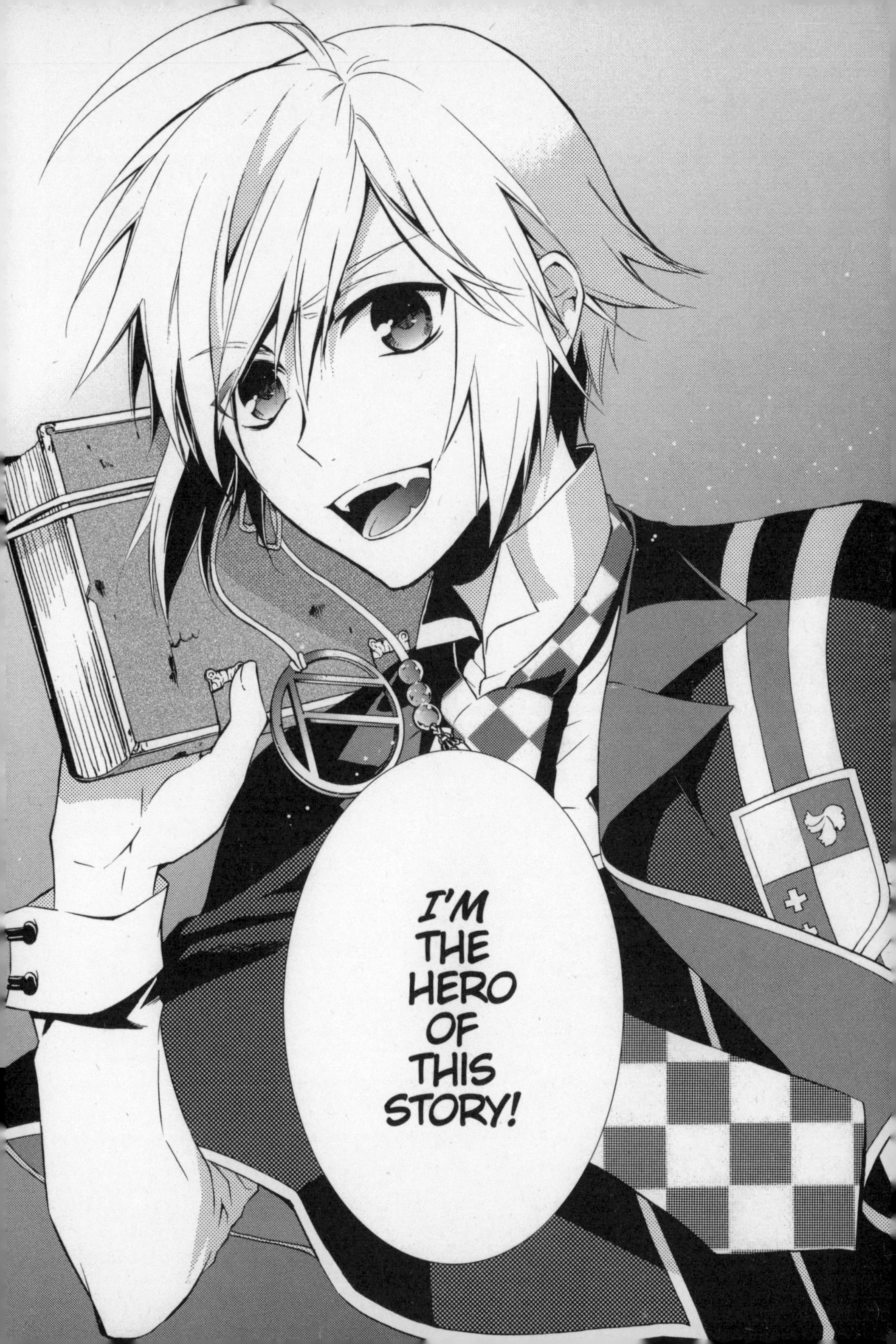
I'M THE HERO OF THIS STORY!

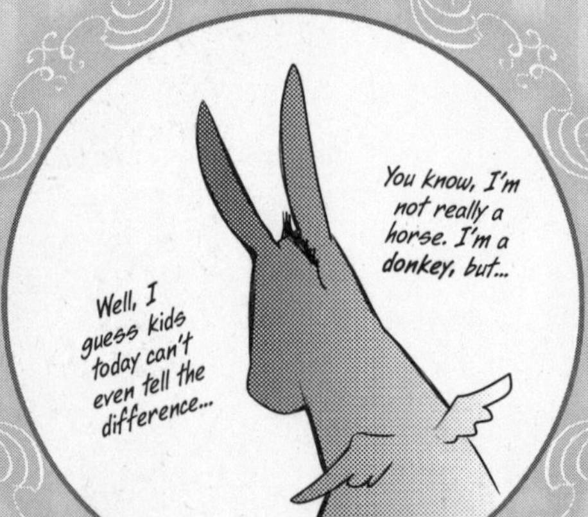
You know, I'm not really a horse. I'm a donkey, but...
Well, I guess kids today can't even tell the difference...

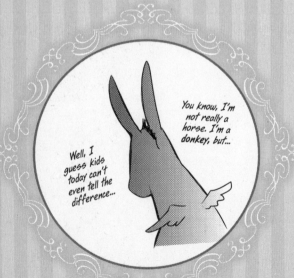

Dictatorial Grimoire

独裁グリムワール

Dictatorial Grimoire

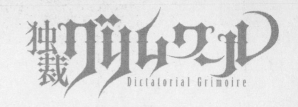

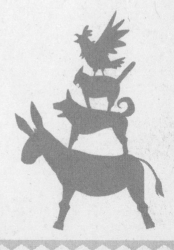

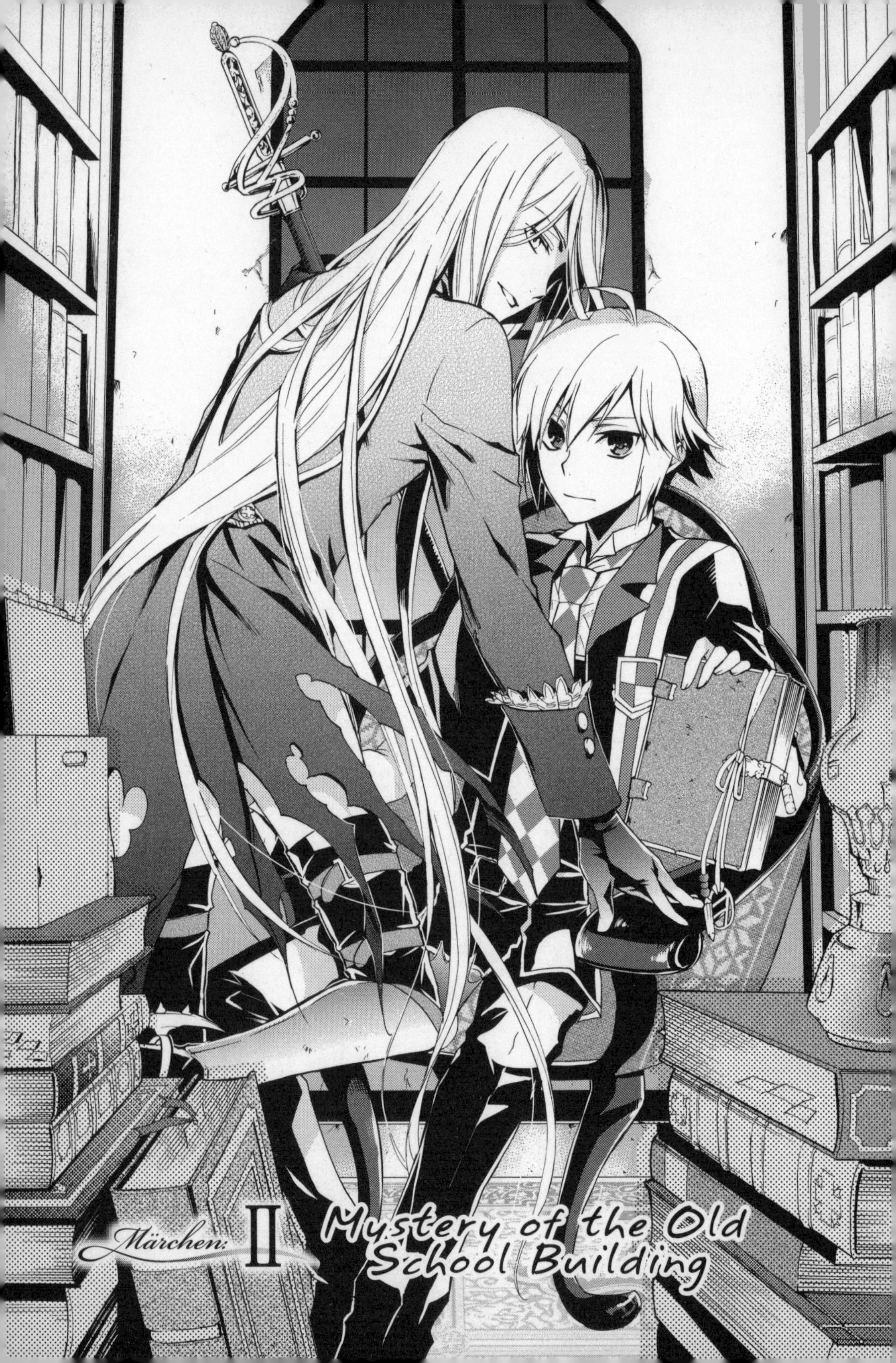
Märchen: II
Mystery of the Old School Building

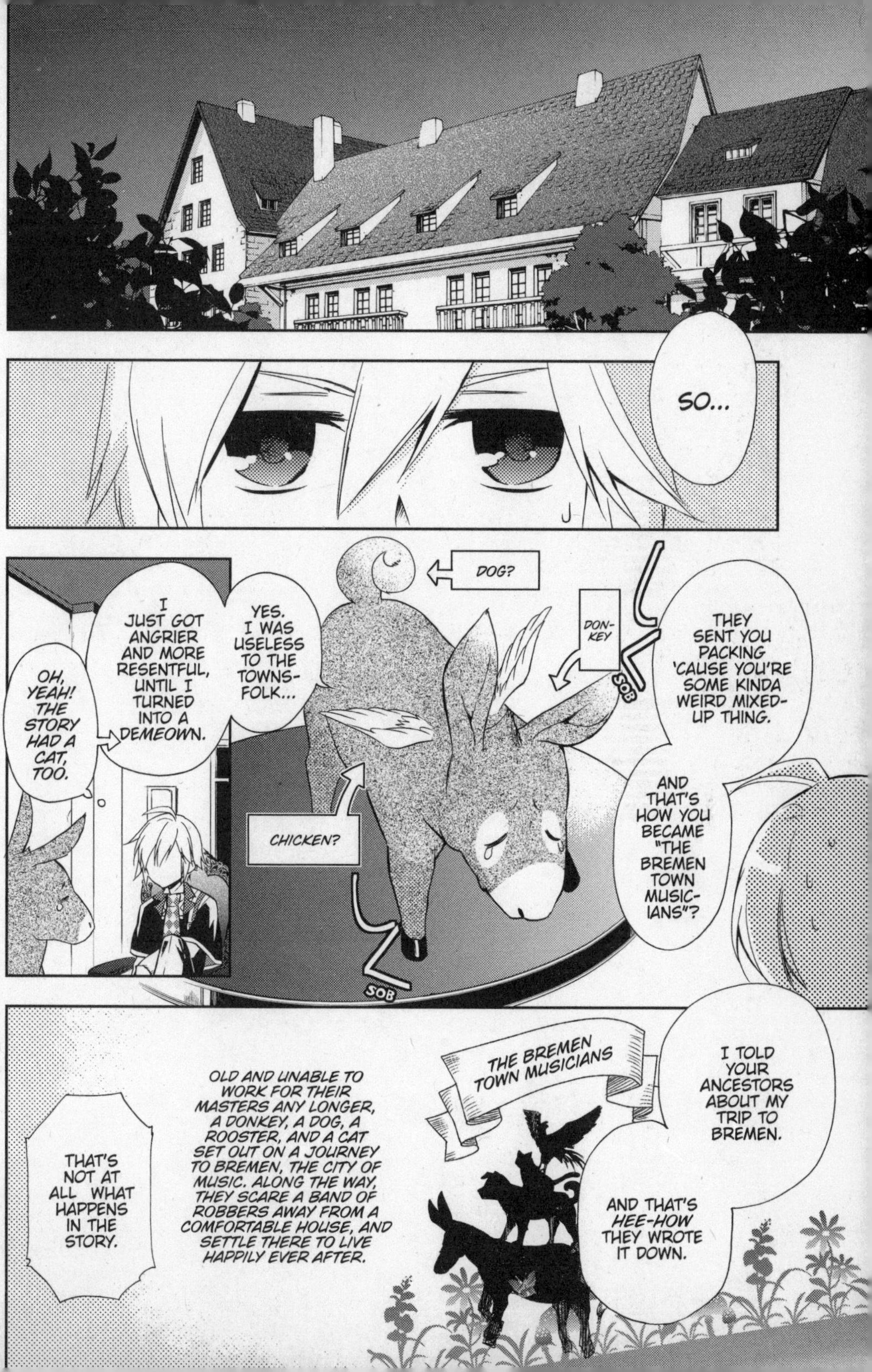
SO...
THEY SENT YOU PACKING 'CAUSE YOU'RE SOME KINDA WEIRD MIXED-UP THING.
DON-KEY
SOB
DOG?
AND THAT'S HOW YOU BECAME "THE BREMEN TOWN MUSICIANS"?
CHICKEN?
SOB
YES. I WAS USELESS TO THE TOWNSFOLK...
I JUST GOT ANGRIER AND MORE RESENTFUL, UNTIL I TURNED INTO A DEMEOWN.
OH, YEAH! THE STORY HAD A CAT, TOO.
I TOLD YOUR ANCESTORS ABOUT MY TRIP TO BREMEN.
AND THAT'S HEE-HOW THEY WROTE IT DOWN.
THE BREMEN TOWN MUSICIANS
OLD AND UNABLE TO WORK FOR THEIR MASTERS ANY LONGER, A DONKEY, A DOG, A ROOSTER, AND A CAT SET OUT ON A JOURNEY TO BREMEN, THE CITY OF MUSIC. ALONG THE WAY, THEY SCARE A BAND OF ROBBERS AWAY FROM A COMFORTABLE HOUSE, AND SETTLE THERE TO LIVE HAPPILY EVER AFTER.
THAT'S NOT AT ALL WHAT HAPPENS IN THE STORY.

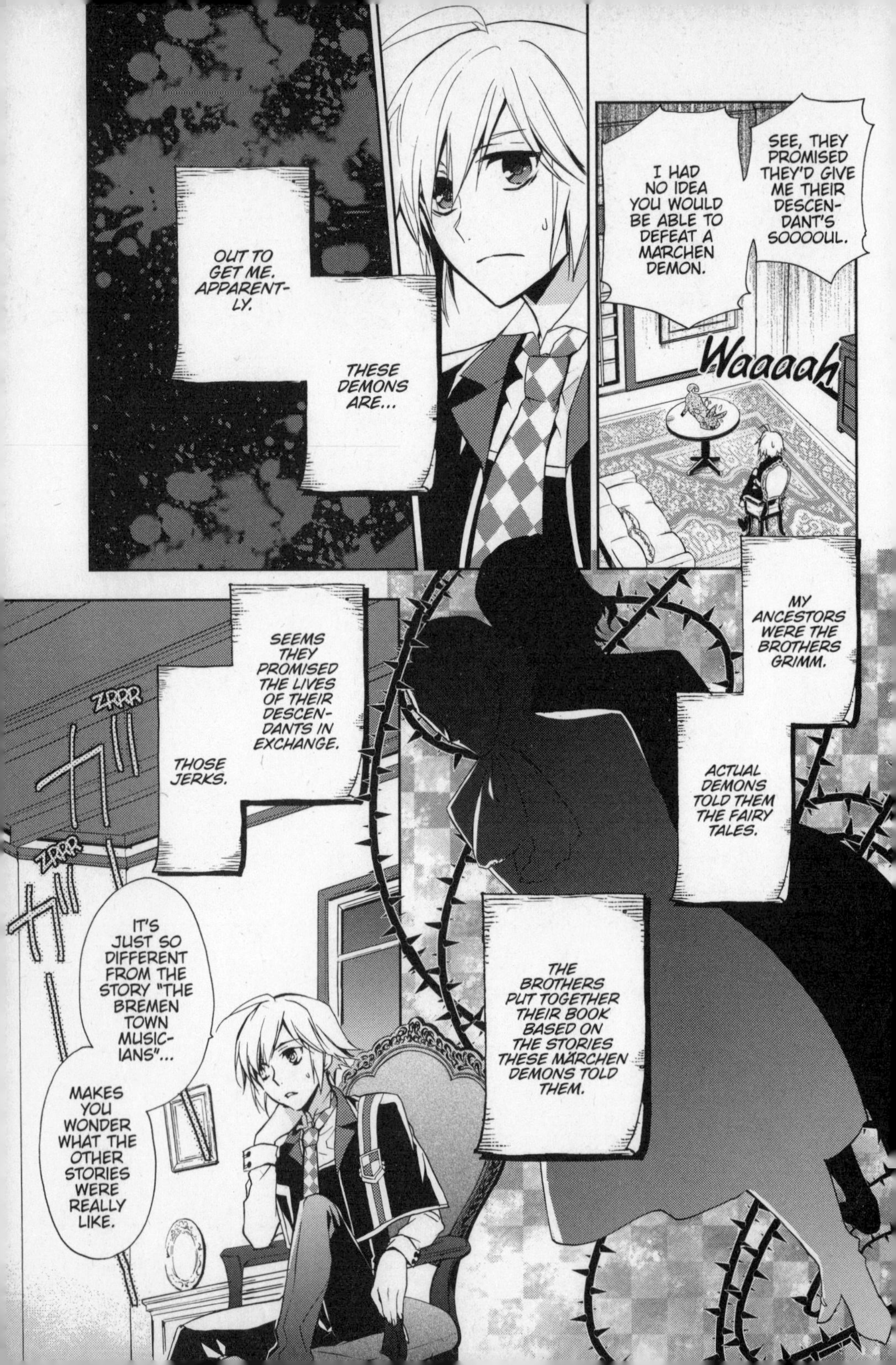
SEE, THEY PROMISED THEY'D GIVE ME THEIR DESCENDANT'S SOOOOOUL.
I HAD NO IDEA YOU WOULD BE ABLE TO DEFEAT A MARCHEN DEMON.
Waaaah
THESE DEMONS ARE...
OUT TO GET ME. APPARENTLY.
MY ANCESTORS WERE THE BROTHERS GRIMM.
ACTUAL DEMONS TOLD THEM THE FAIRY TALES.
THE BROTHERS PUT TOGETHER THEIR BOOK BASED ON THE STORIES THESE MÄRCHEN DEMONS TOLD THEM.
SEEMS THEY PROMISED THE LIVES OF THEIR DESCENDANTS IN EXCHANGE.
THOSE JERKS.
ZRRR
ZRRR
IT'S JUST SO DIFFERENT FROM THE STORY "THE BREMEN TOWN MUSICIANS"...
MAKES YOU WONDER WHAT THE OTHER STORIES WERE REALLY LIKE.

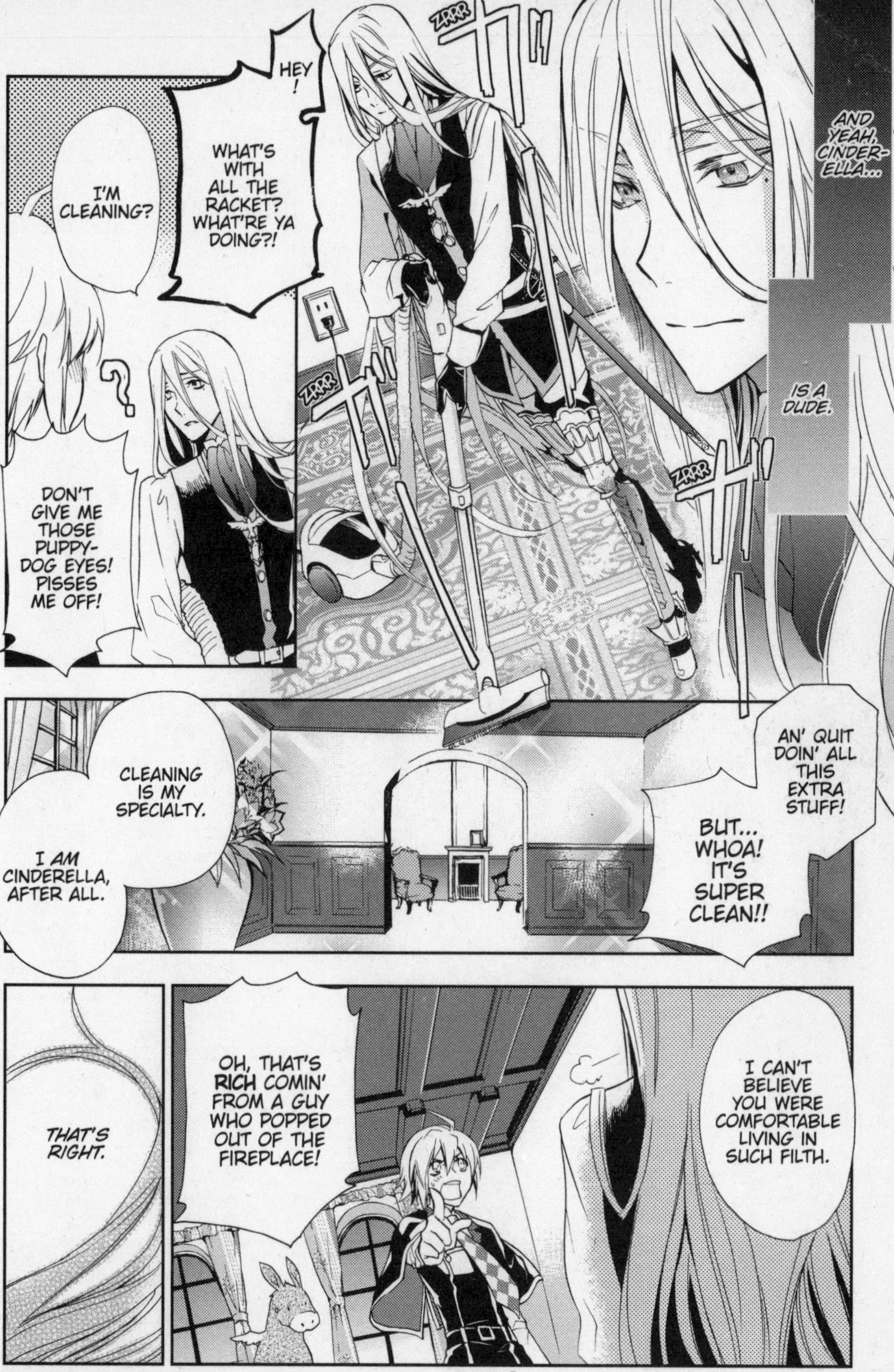

ZRRR
AND YEAH, CINDER-ELLA...
IS A DUDE.
ZRRR
ZRRR
HEY!
WHAT'S WITH ALL THE RACKET? WHAT'RE YA DOING?!
I'M CLEANING?
?
DON'T GIVE ME THOSE PUPPY-DOG EYES! PISSES ME OFF!
AN' QUIT DOIN' ALL THIS EXTRA STUFF!
BUT... WHOA! IT'S SUPER CLEAN!!
CLEANING IS MY SPECIALTY.
I AM CINDERELLA, AFTER ALL.
I CAN'T BELIEVE YOU WERE COMFORTABLE LIVING IN SUCH FILTH.
OH, THAT'S RICH COMIN' FROM A GUY WHO POPPED OUT OF THE FIREPLACE!
THAT'S RIGHT.

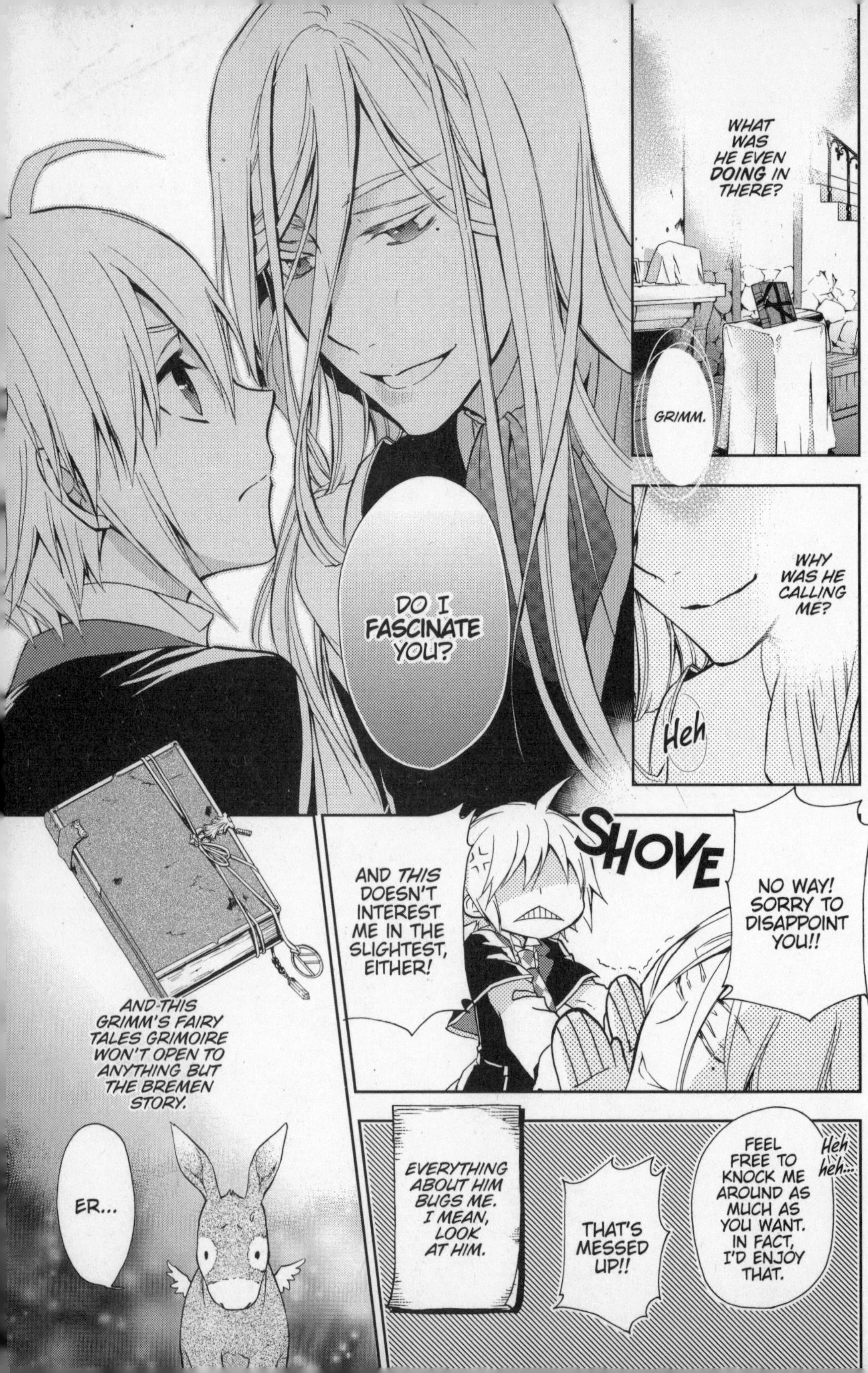
WHAT WAS HE EVEN DOING IN THERE?
GRIMM.
WHY WAS HE CALLING ME?
Heh
DO I FASCINATE YOU?
NO WAY! SORRY TO DISAPPOINT YOU!!
SHOVE
AND THIS DOESN'T INTEREST ME IN THE SLIGHTEST, EITHER!
AND THIS GRIMM'S FAIRY TALES GRIMOIRE WON'T OPEN TO ANYTHING BUT THE BREMEN STORY.
Heh heh...
FEEL FREE TO KNOCK ME AROUND AS MUCH AS YOU WANT. IN FACT, I'D ENJOY THAT.
THAT'S MESSED UP!!
EVERYTHING ABOUT HIM BUGS ME. I MEAN, LOOK AT HIM.
ER...

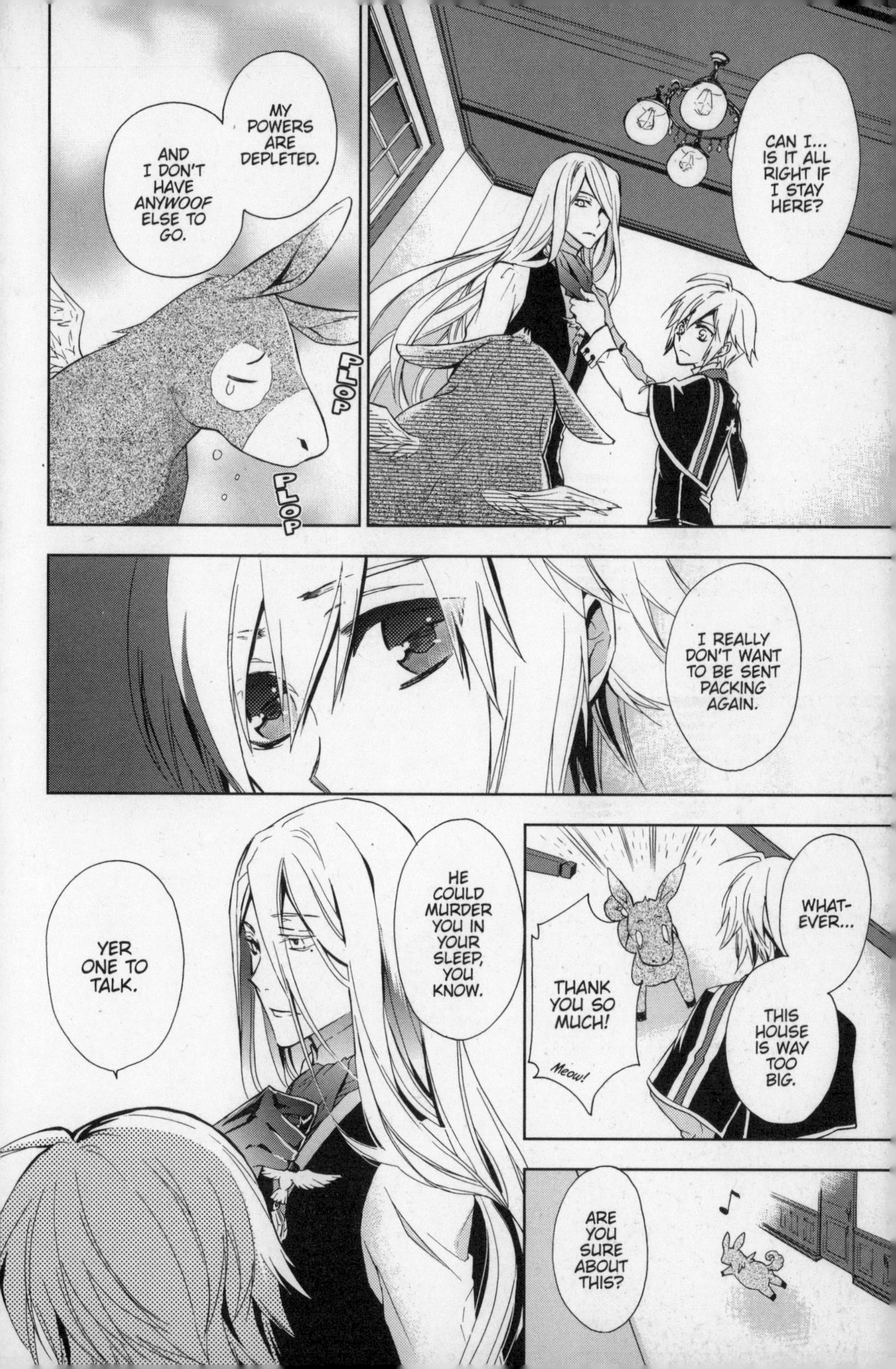
CAN I... IS IT ALL RIGHT IF I STAY HERE?
MY POWERS ARE DEPLETED.
AND I DON'T HAVE ANYWOOF ELSE TO GO.
PLOP
PLOP
I REALLY DON'T WANT TO BE SENT PACKING AGAIN.
WHAT-EVER...
THIS HOUSE IS WAY TOO BIG.
THANK YOU SO MUCH!
Meow!
ARE YOU SURE ABOUT THIS?
HE COULD MURDER YOU IN YOUR SLEEP, YOU KNOW.
YER ONE TO TALK.

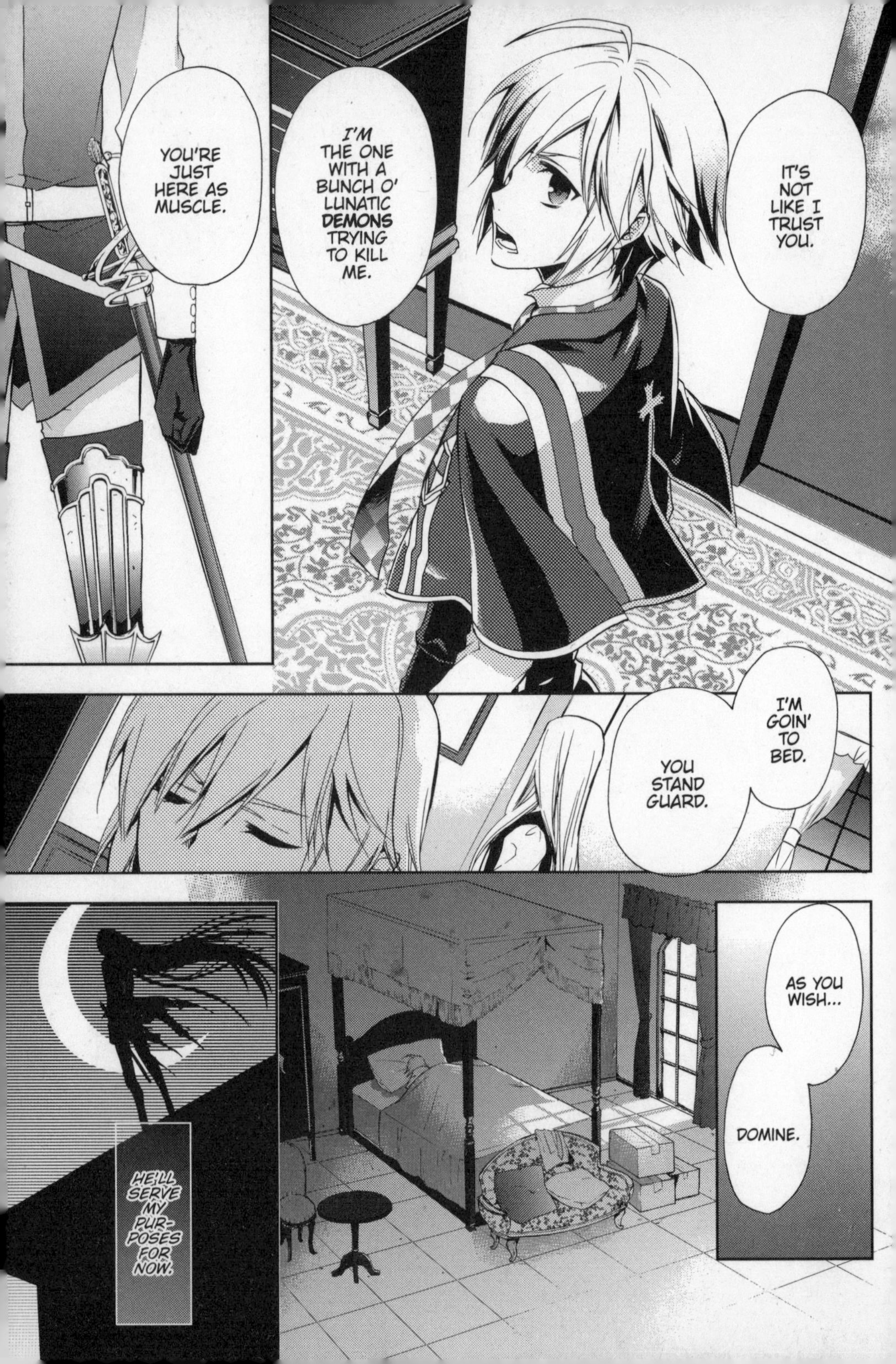
IT'S NOT LIKE I TRUST YOU.
I'M THE ONE WITH A BUNCH O' LUNATIC **DEMONS** TRYING TO KILL ME.
YOU'RE JUST HERE AS MUSCLE.
I'M GOIN' TO BED.
YOU STAND GUARD.
AS YOU WISH...
DOMINE.
HE'LL SERVE MY PURPOSES FOR NOW.

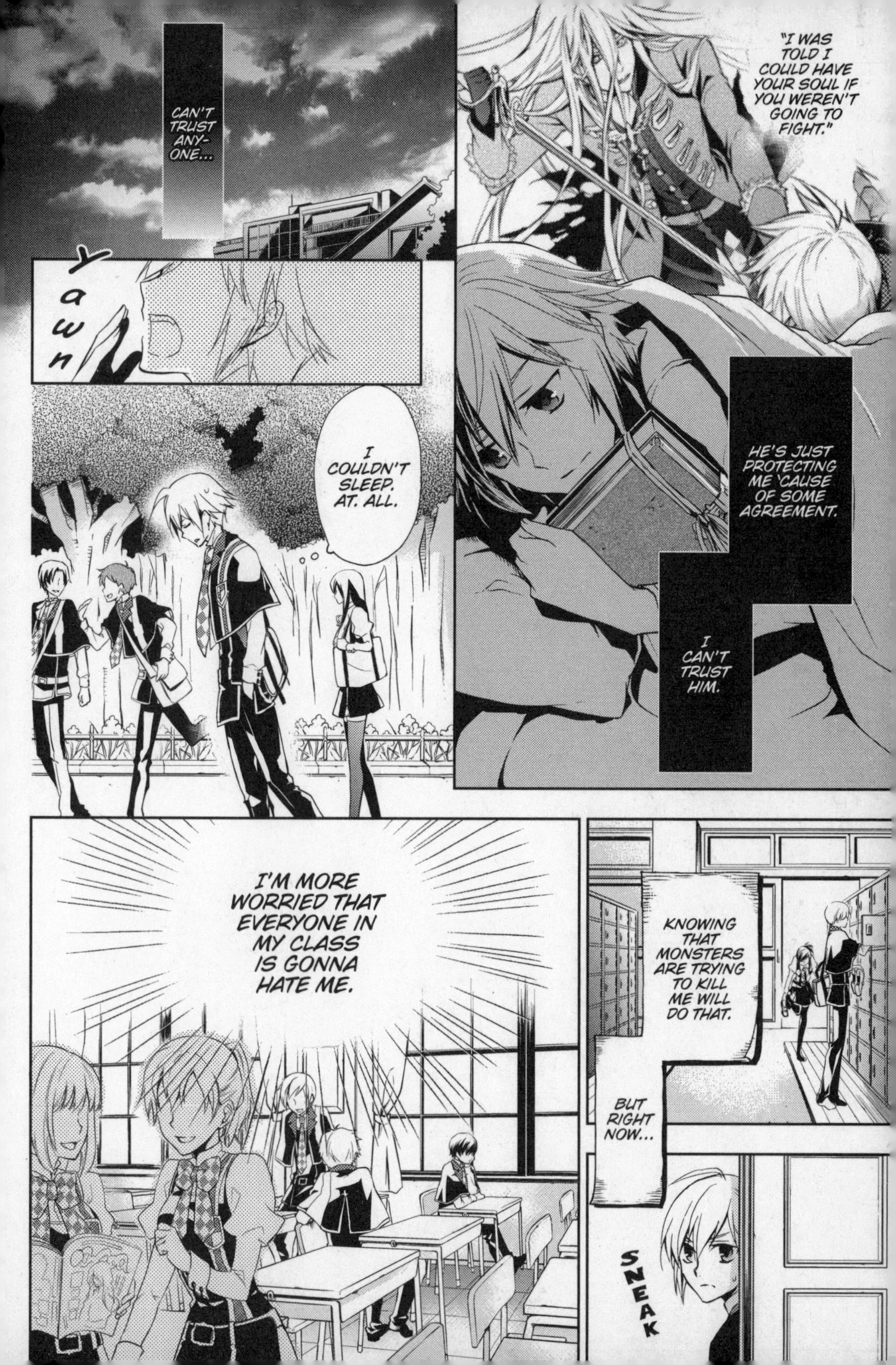
"I WAS TOLD I COULD HAVE YOUR SOUL IF YOU WEREN'T GOING TO FIGHT."
HE'S JUST PROTECTING ME 'CAUSE OF SOME AGREEMENT.
I CAN'T TRUST HIM.
CAN'T TRUST ANY-ONE...
Yawn
I COULDN'T SLEEP. AT. ALL.
KNOWING THAT MONSTERS ARE TRYING TO KILL ME WILL DO THAT.
BUT RIGHT NOW...
SNEAK
I'M MORE WORRIED THAT EVERYONE IN MY CLASS IS GONNA HATE ME.

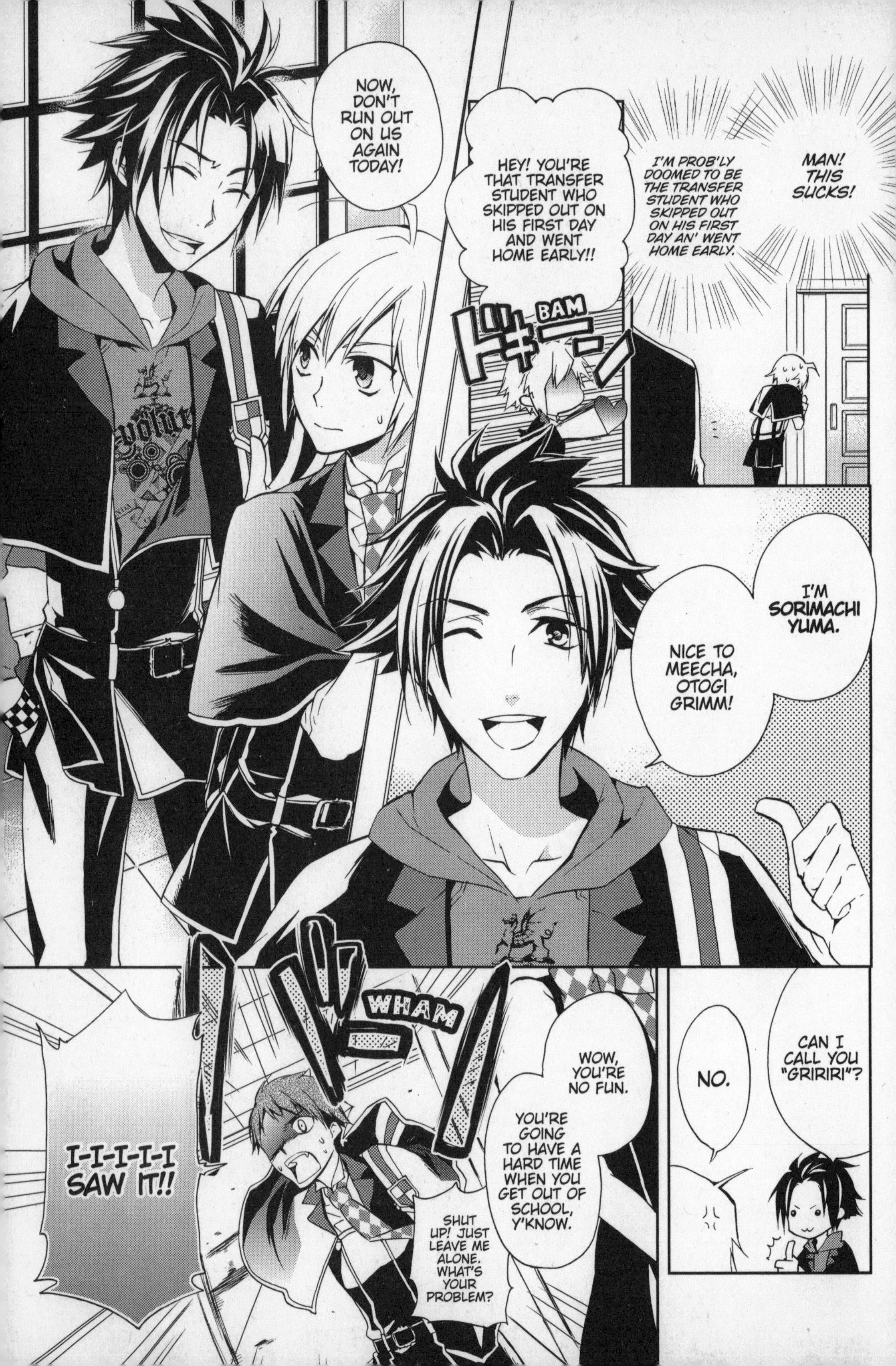
MAN! THIS SUCKS!
I'M PROB'LY DOOMED TO BE THE TRANSFER STUDENT WHO SKIPPED OUT ON HIS FIRST DAY AN' WENT HOME EARLY.
BAM
HEY! YOU'RE THAT TRANSFER STUDENT WHO SKIPPED OUT ON HIS FIRST DAY AND WENT HOME EARLY!!
I'M SORIMACHI YUMA.
NICE TO MEECHA, OTOGI GRIMM!
NOW, DON'T RUN OUT ON US AGAIN TODAY!
CAN I CALL YOU "GRIRIRI"?
NO.
WHAM
WOW, YOU'RE NO FUN.
YOU'RE GOING TO HAVE A HARD TIME WHEN YOU GET OUT OF SCHOOL, Y'KNOW.
SHUT UP! JUST LEAVE ME ALONE. WHAT'S YOUR PROBLEM?
I-I-I-I-I SAW IT!!

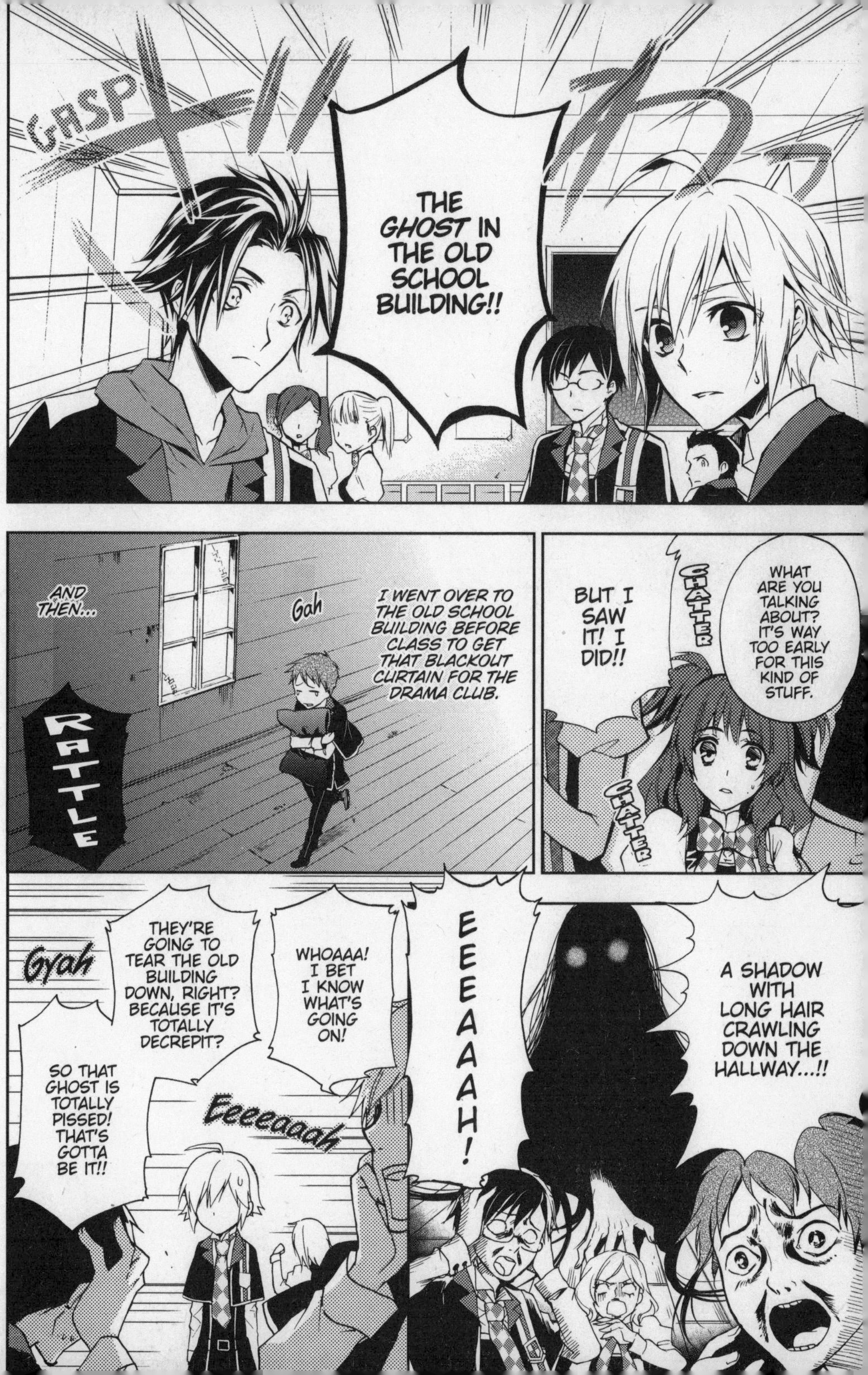
GASP
THE GHOST IN THE OLD SCHOOL BUILDING!!
WHAT ARE YOU TALKING ABOUT? IT'S WAY TOO EARLY FOR THIS KIND OF STUFF.
CHATTER
BUT I SAW IT! I DID!!
CHATTER
I WENT OVER TO THE OLD SCHOOL BUILDING BEFORE CLASS TO GET THAT BLACKOUT CURTAIN FOR THE DRAMA CLUB.
Gah
AND THEN...
RATTLE
Gah
A SHADOW WITH LONG HAIR CRAWLING DOWN THE HALLWAY...!!
EEEEAAAAH!
WHOAAA! I BET I KNOW WHAT'S GOING ON!
THEY'RE GOING TO TEAR THE OLD BUILDING DOWN, RIGHT? BECAUSE IT'S TOTALLY DECREPIT?
Gyah
Eeeeaaah
SO THAT GHOST IS TOTALLY PISSED! THAT'S GOTTA BE IT!!

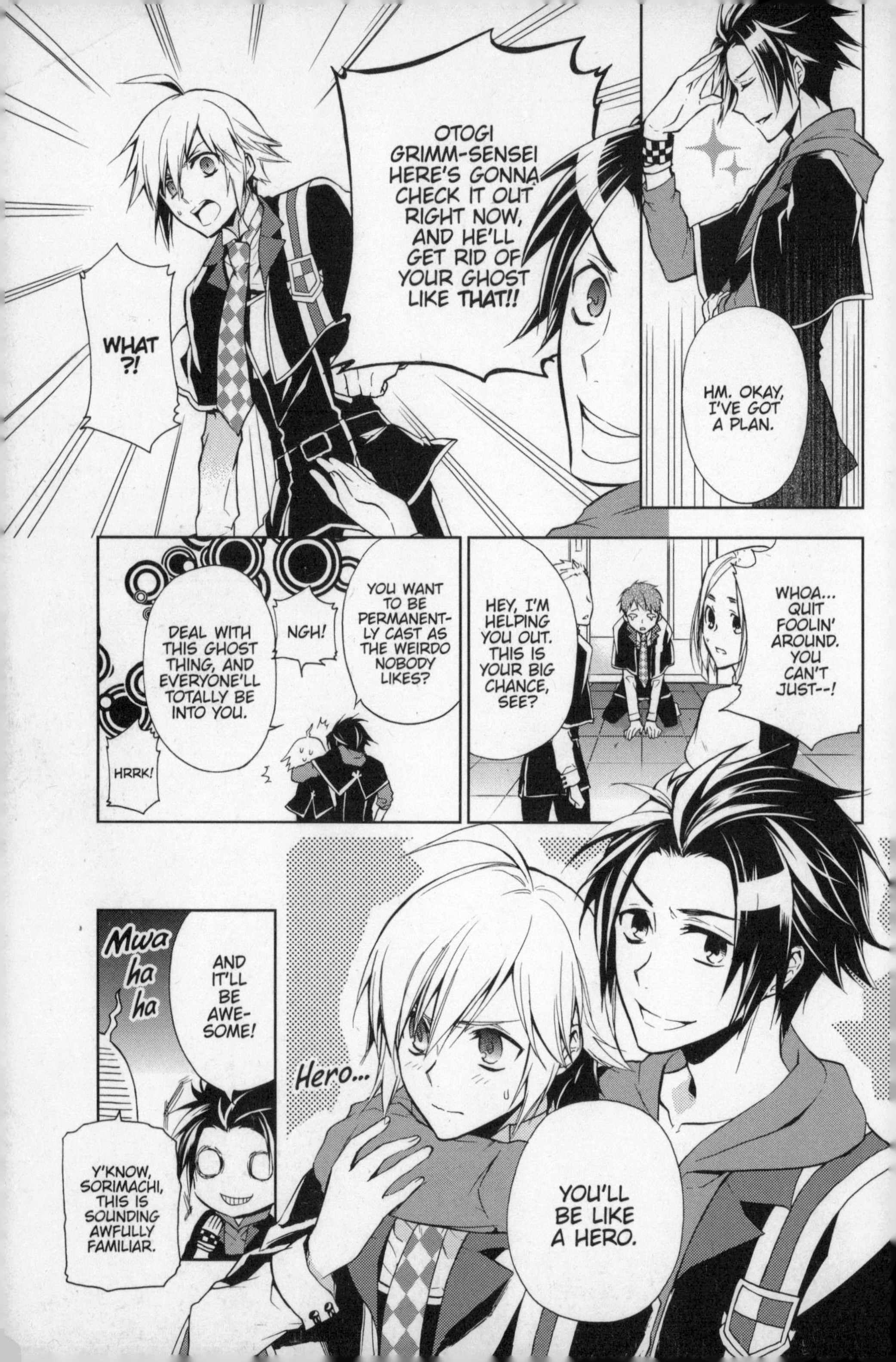
HM. OKAY, I'VE GOT A PLAN.
OTOGI GRIMM-SENSEI HERE'S GONNA CHECK IT OUT RIGHT NOW, AND HE'LL GET RID OF YOUR GHOST LIKE THAT!!
WHAT ?!
WHOA... QUIT FOOLIN' AROUND. YOU CAN'T JUST--!
HEY, I'M HELPING YOU OUT. THIS IS YOUR BIG CHANCE, SEE?
YOU WANT TO BE PERMANENT-LY CAST AS THE WEIRDO NOBODY LIKES?
NGH!
DEAL WITH THIS GHOST THING, AND EVERYONE'LL TOTALLY BE INTO YOU.
HRRK!
YOU'LL BE LIKE A HERO.
Hero...
AND IT'LL BE AWE-SOME!
Mwa ha ha
Y'KNOW, SORIMACHI, THIS IS SOUNDING AWFULLY FAMILIAR.

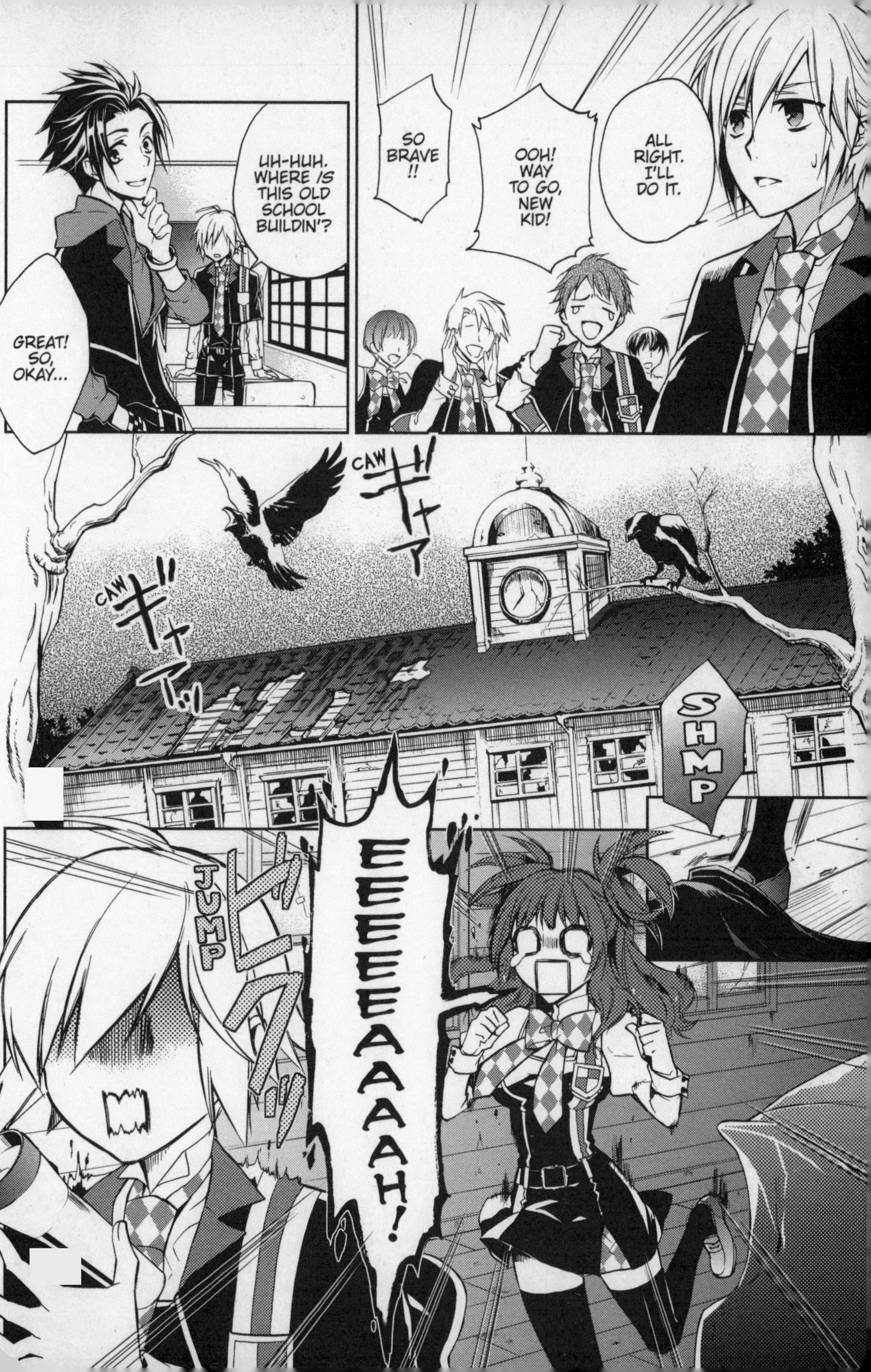
ALL RIGHT. I'LL DO IT.
OOH! WAY TO GO, NEW KID!
SO BRAVE!!
UH-HUH. WHERE IS THIS OLD SCHOOL BUILDIN'?
GREAT! SO, OKAY...
CAW
CAW
SHMP
EEEEEEAAAAAH!
JUMP

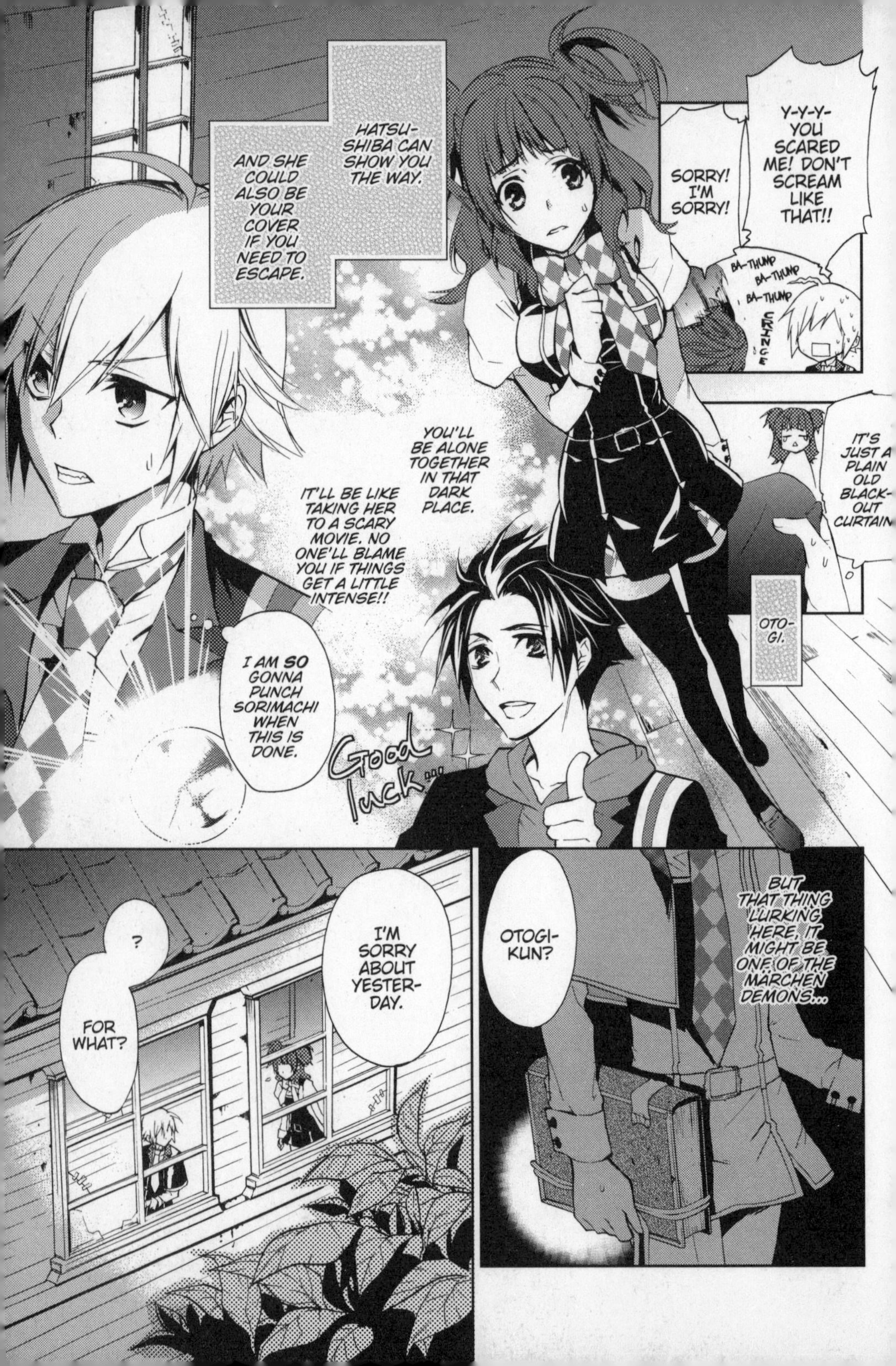
Y-Y-Y-YOU SCARED ME! DON'T SCREAM LIKE THAT!!
SORRY! I'M SORRY!
BA-THUMP BA-THUMP BA-THUMP
CRINGE
IT'S JUST A PLAIN OLD BLACK-OUT CURTAIN
OTOGI.
HATSU-SHIBA CAN SHOW YOU THE WAY.
AND SHE COULD ALSO BE YOUR COVER IF YOU NEED TO ESCAPE.
YOU'LL BE ALONE TOGETHER IN THAT DARK PLACE.
IT'LL BE LIKE TAKING HER TO A SCARY MOVIE. NO ONE'LL BLAME YOU IF THINGS GET A LITTLE INTENSE!!
I AM SO GONNA PUNCH SORIMACHI WHEN THIS IS DONE.
Good luck...
BUT THAT THING LURKING HERE, IT MIGHT BE ONE OF THE MARCHEN DEMONS...
OTOGI-KUN?
I'M SORRY ABOUT YESTER-DAY.
?
FOR WHAT?

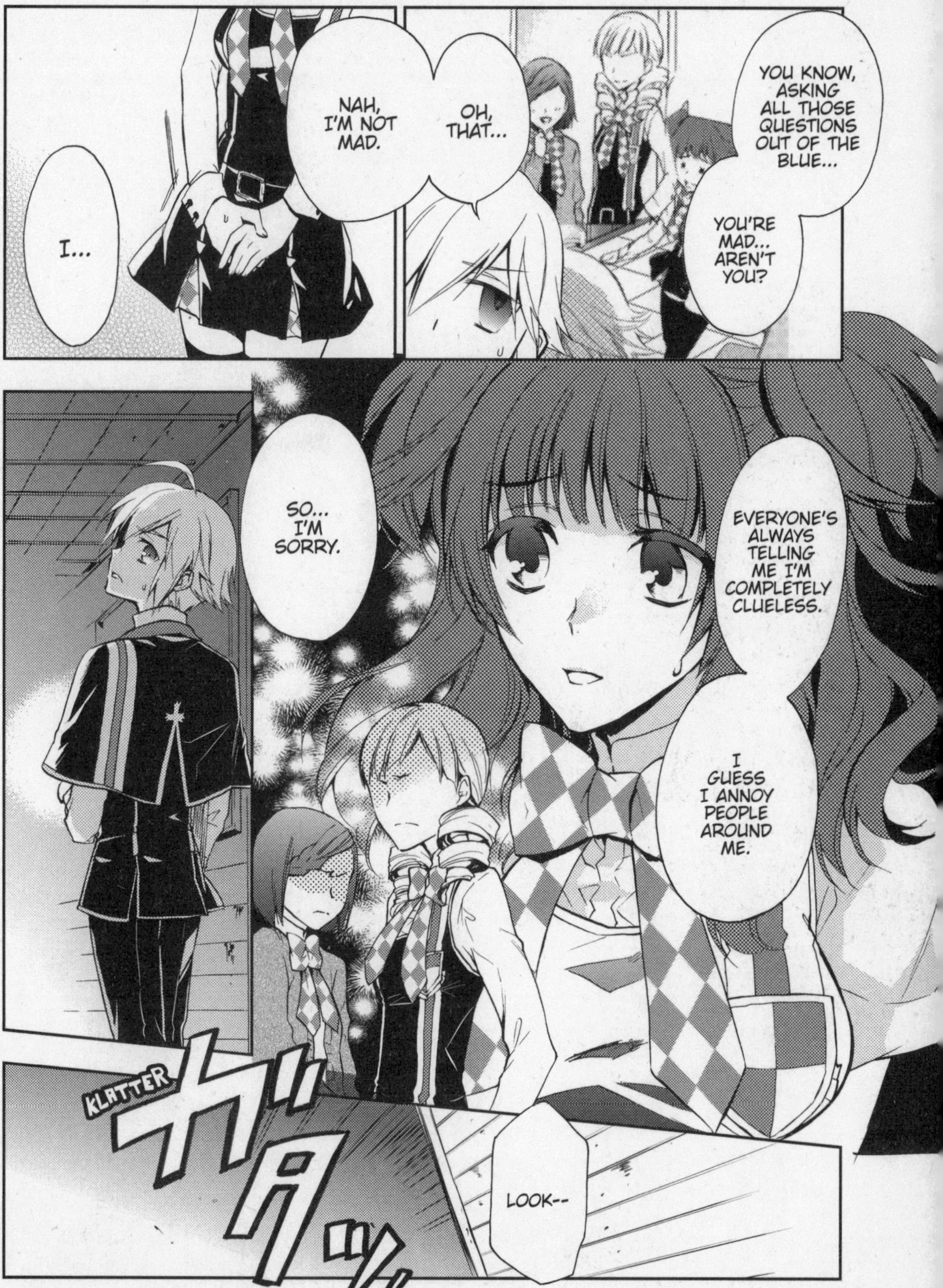
YOU KNOW, ASKING ALL THOSE QUESTIONS OUT OF THE BLUE...
YOU'RE MAD... AREN'T YOU?
OH, THAT...
NAH, I'M NOT MAD.
I...
EVERYONE'S ALWAYS TELLING ME I'M COMPLETELY CLUELESS.
I GUESS I ANNOY PEOPLE AROUND ME.
SO... I'M SORRY.
LOOK--
KLATTER

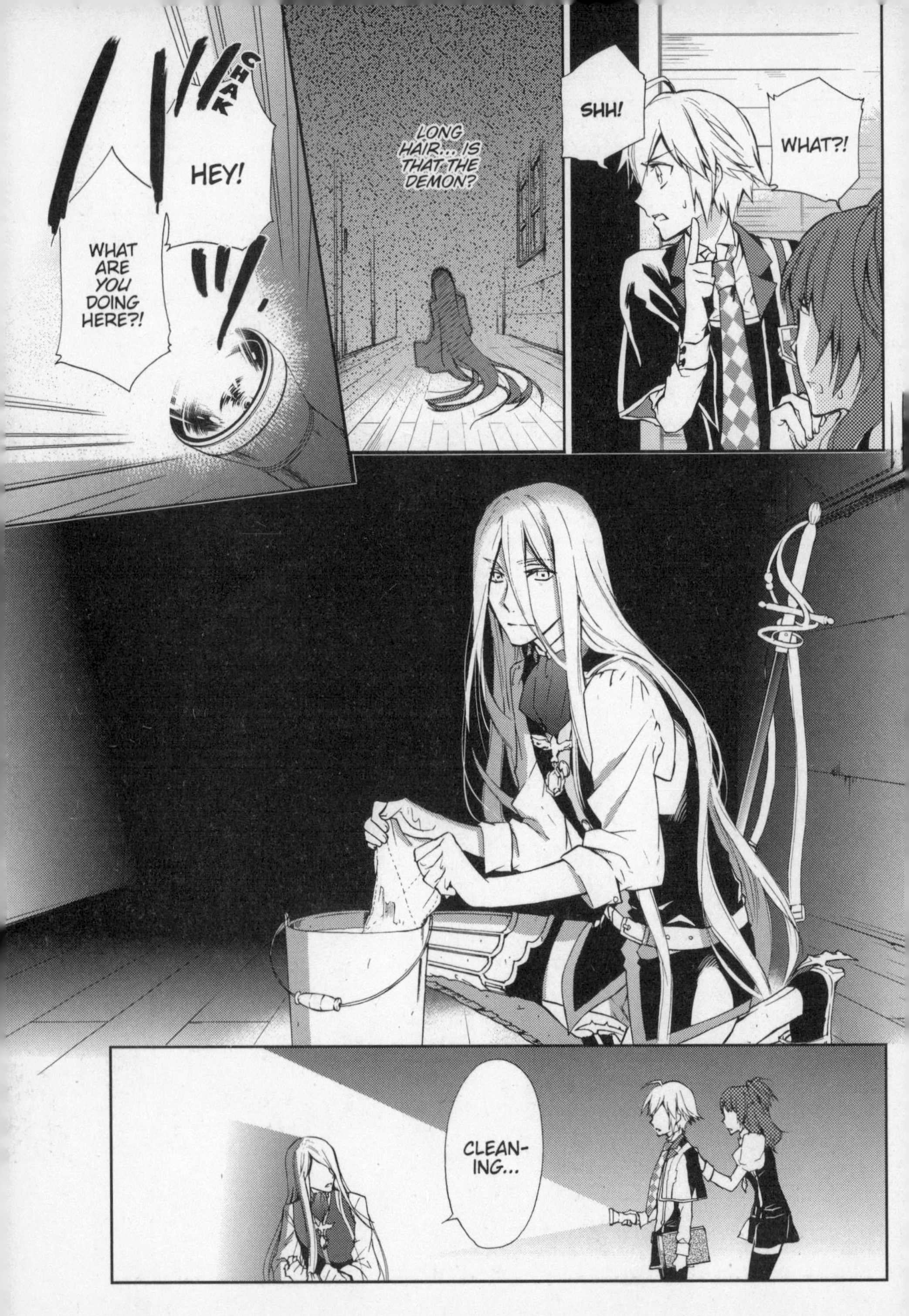
WHAT?!
SHH!
LONG HAIR... IS THAT THE DEMON?
CHAK
HEY!
WHAT ARE YOU DOING HERE?!
CLEANING...

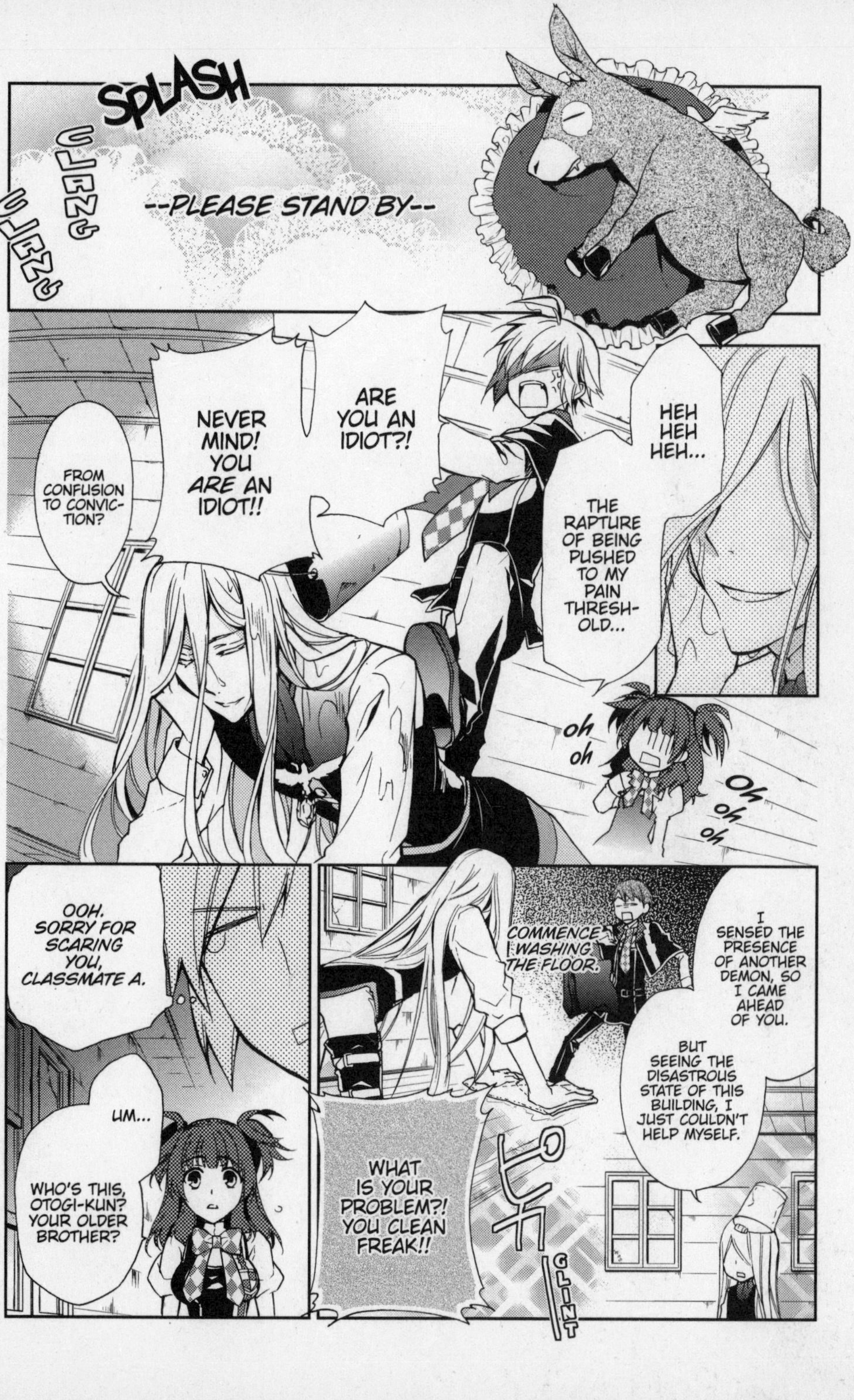
SPLASH
--PLEASE STAND BY--
CLANG
CLANG
HEH HEH HEH...
THE RAPTURE OF BEING PUSHED TO MY PAIN THRESH-OLD...
ARE YOU AN IDIOT?!
NEVER MIND! YOU ARE AN IDIOT!!
FROM CONFUSION TO CONVIC-TION?
Oh oh oh
oh oh
I SENSED THE PRESENCE OF ANOTHER DEMON, SO I CAME AHEAD OF YOU.
COMMENCE WASHING THE FLOOR.
BUT SEEING THE DISASTROUS STATE OF THIS BUILDING, I JUST COULDN'T HELP MYSELF.
GLINT
WHAT IS YOUR PROBLEM?! YOU CLEAN FREAK!!
OOH. SORRY FOR SCARING YOU, CLASSMATE A.
UM...
WHO'S THIS, OTOGI-KUN? YOUR OLDER BROTHER?

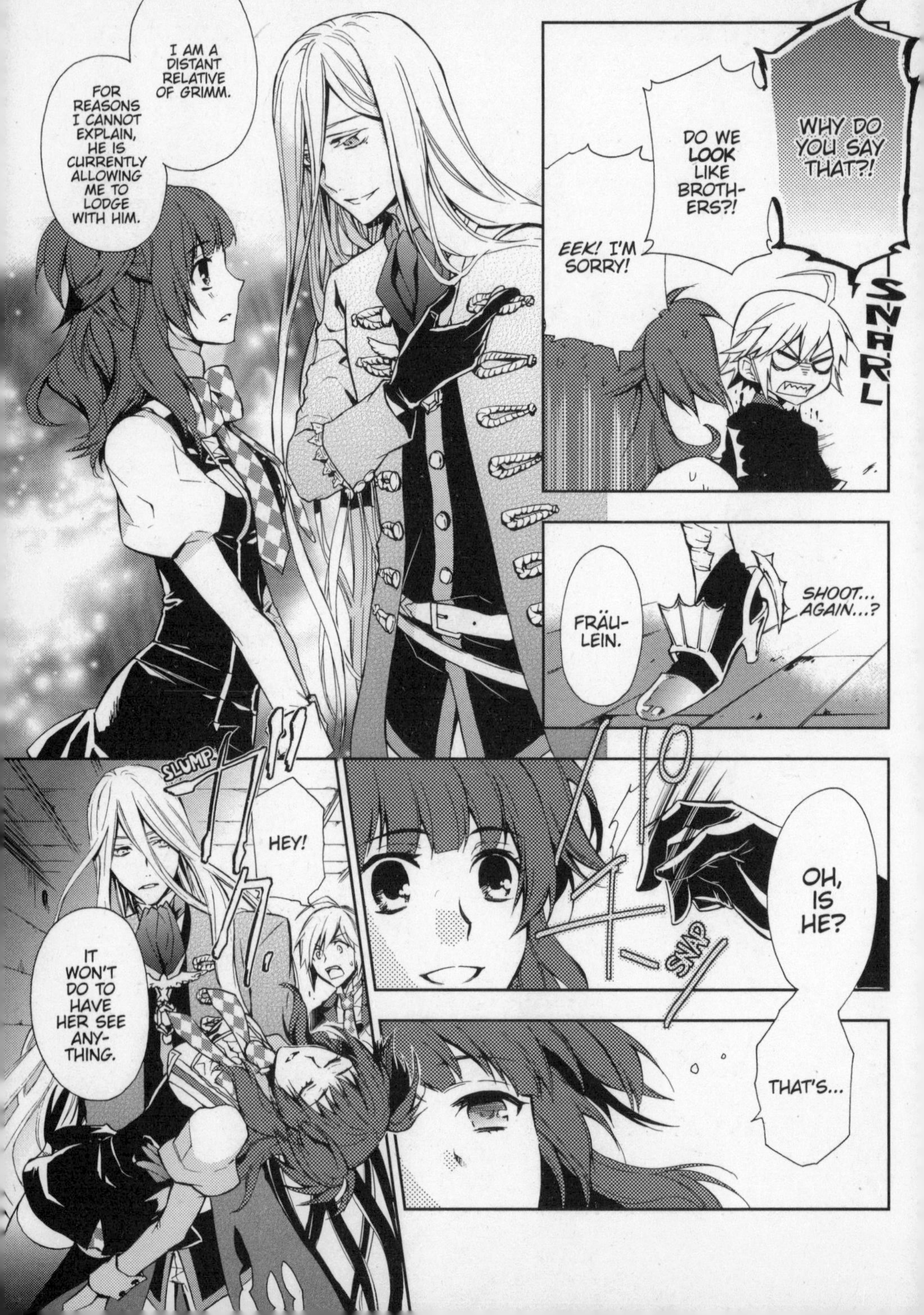
WHY DO YOU SAY THAT?!
DO WE LOOK LIKE BROTHERS?!
SNARL
EEK! I'M SORRY!
SHOOT... AGAIN...?
FRÄULEIN.
I AM A DISTANT RELATIVE OF GRIMM.
FOR REASONS I CANNOT EXPLAIN, HE IS CURRENTLY ALLOWING ME TO LODGE WITH HIM.
OH, IS HE?
SNAP
THAT'S...
SLUMP
HEY!
IT WON'T DO TO HAVE HER SEE ANYTHING.

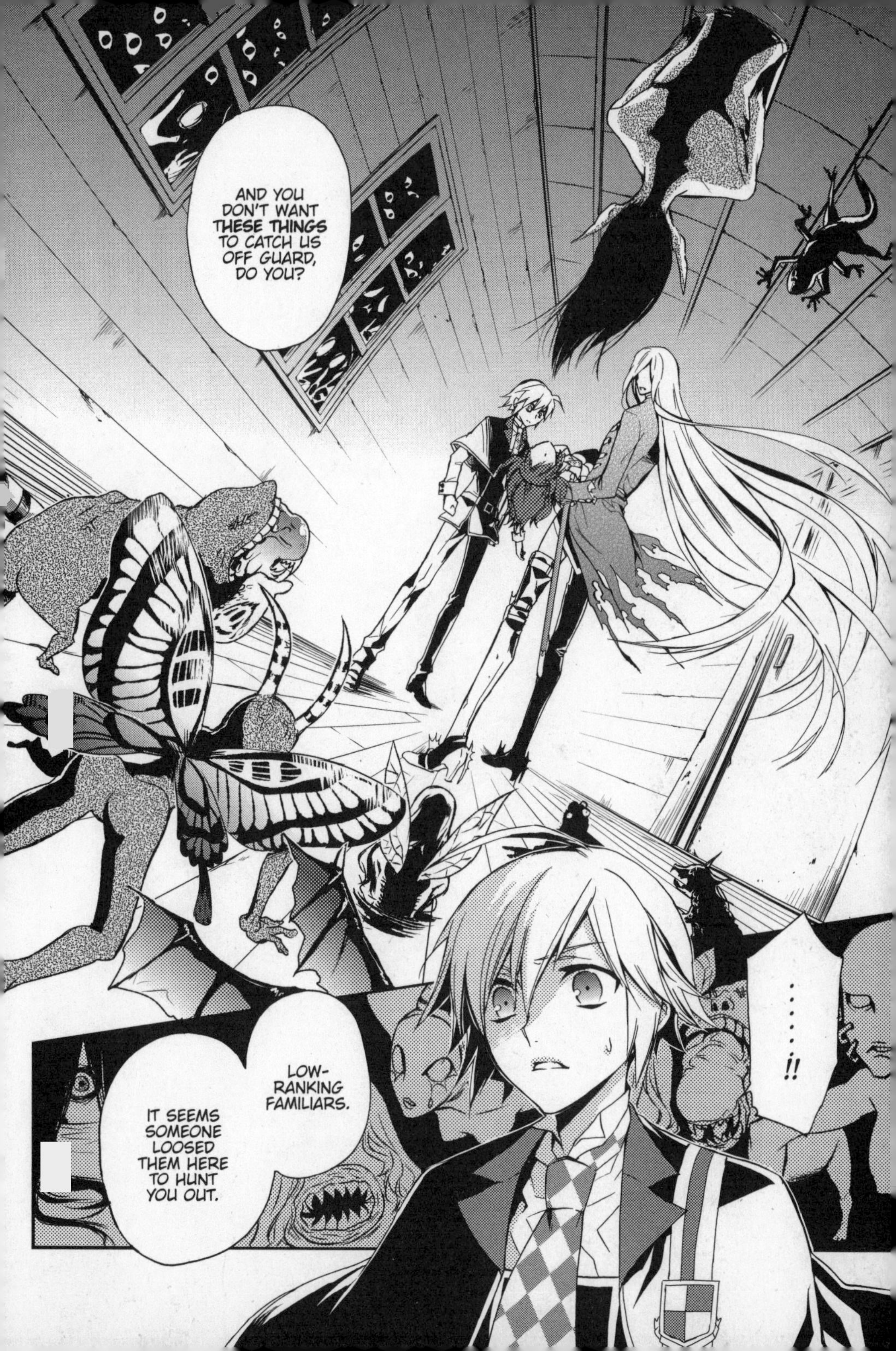
AND YOU DON'T WANT THESE THINGS TO CATCH US OFF GUARD, DO YOU?
......!!
LOW-RANKING FAMILIARS.
IT SEEMS SOMEONE LOOSED THEM HERE TO HUNT YOU OUT.

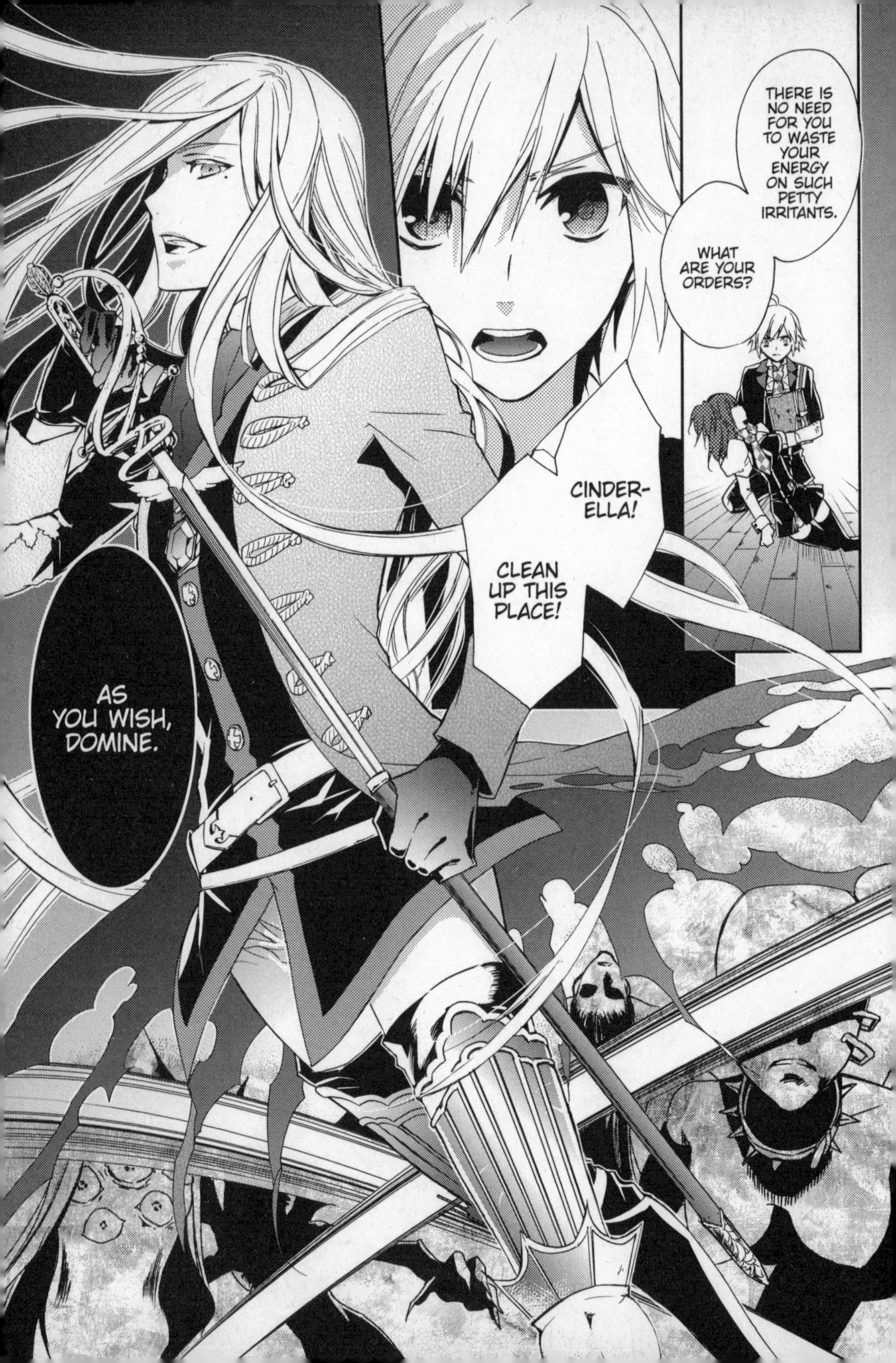
THERE IS NO NEED FOR YOU TO WASTE YOUR ENERGY ON SUCH PETTY IRRITANTS.
WHAT ARE YOUR ORDERS?
CINDER-ELLA!
CLEAN UP THIS PLACE!
AS YOU WISH, DOMINE.

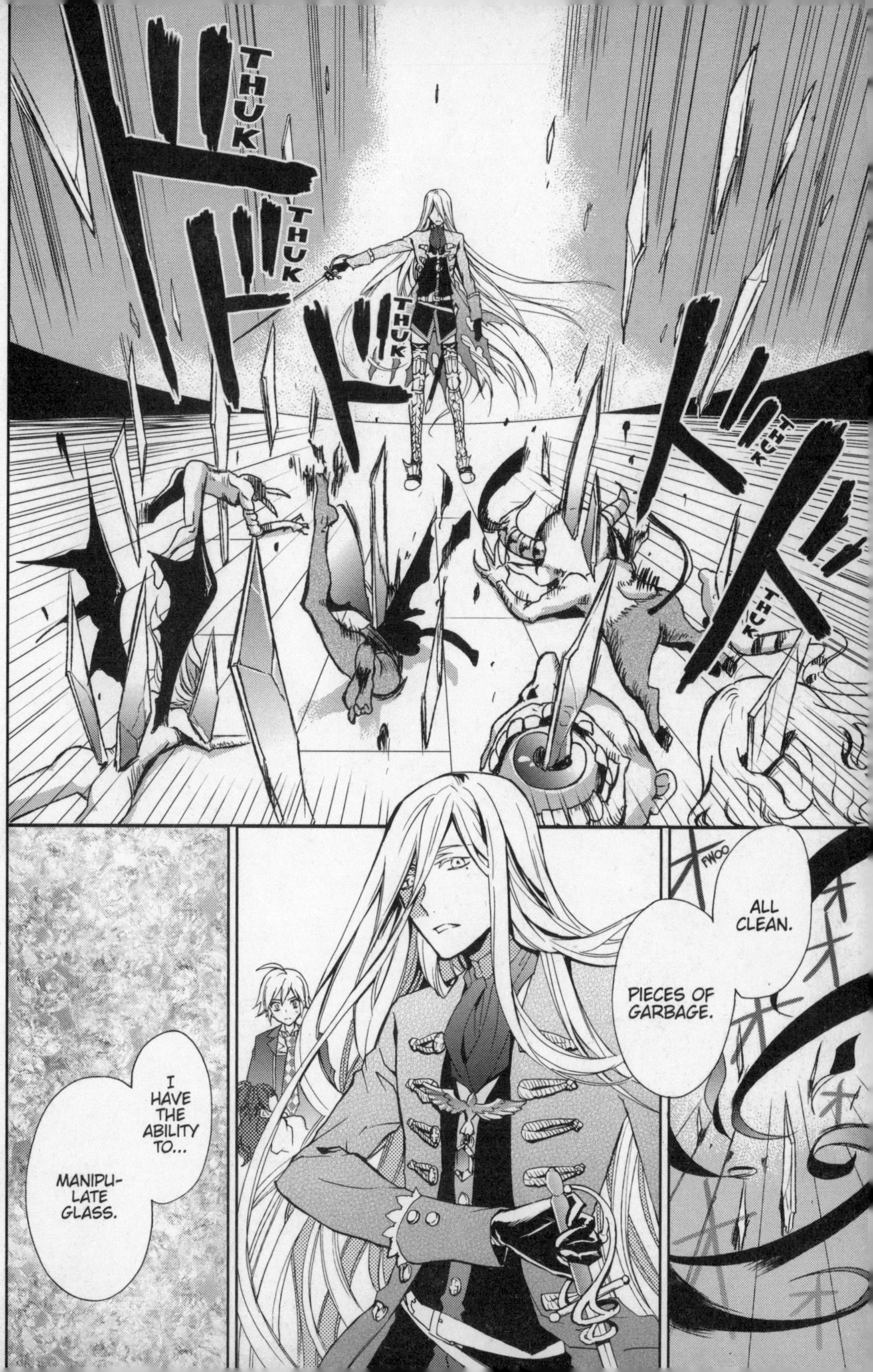
THUK
THUK
THUK
THUK
THUK
FWOO
ALL CLEAN.
PIECES OF GARBAGE.
I HAVE THE ABILITY TO...
MANIPU-LATE GLASS.

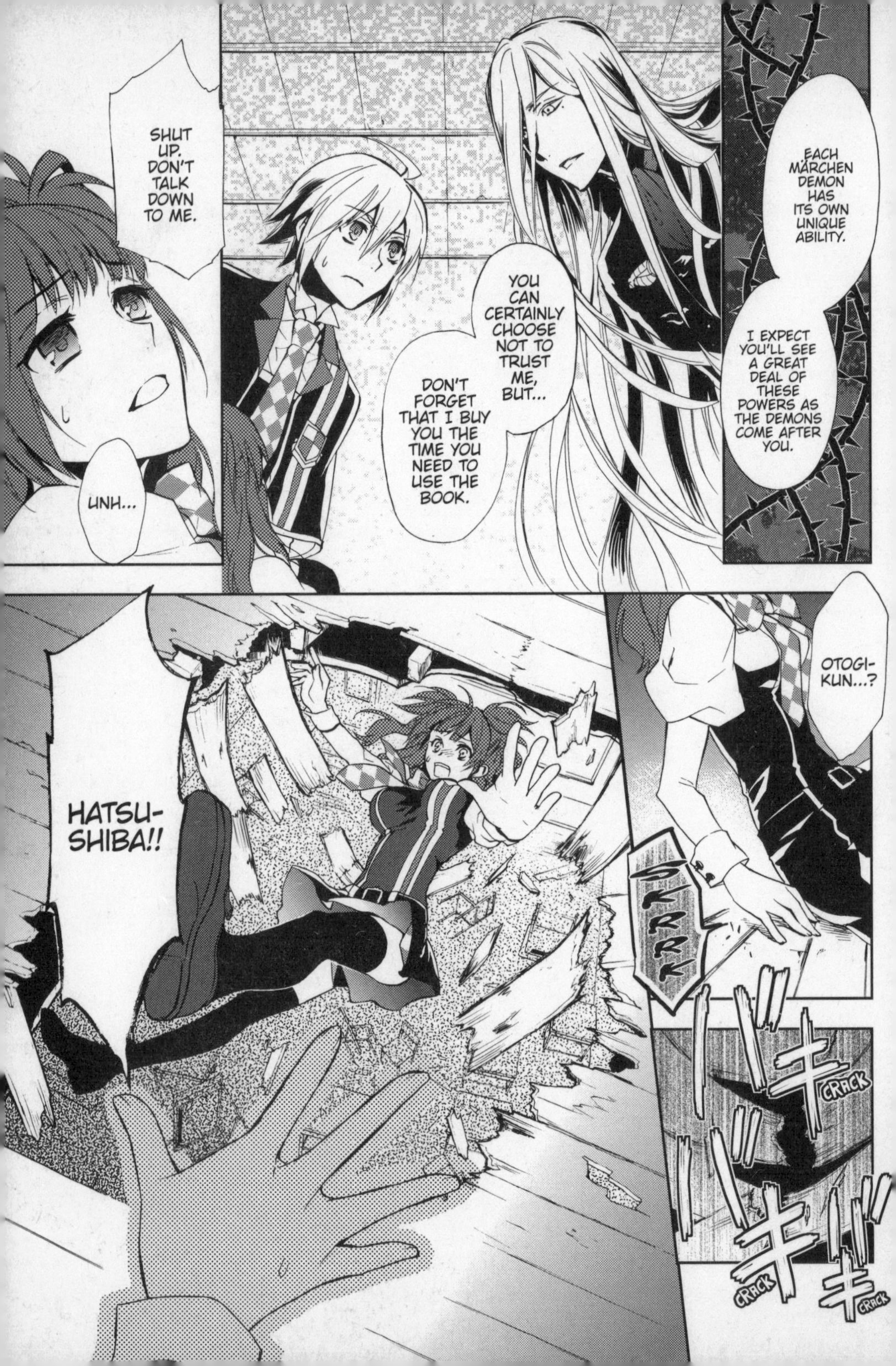
EACH MÄRCHEN DEMON HAS ITS OWN UNIQUE ABILITY.
I EXPECT YOU'LL SEE A GREAT DEAL OF THESE POWERS AS THE DEMONS COME AFTER YOU.
YOU CAN CERTAINLY CHOOSE NOT TO TRUST ME, BUT...
DON'T FORGET THAT I BUY YOU THE TIME YOU NEED TO USE THE BOOK.
SHUT UP. DON'T TALK DOWN TO ME.
UNH...
OTOGI-KUN...?
SRRRK
CRACK
CRACK
CRACK
HATSU-SHIBA!!

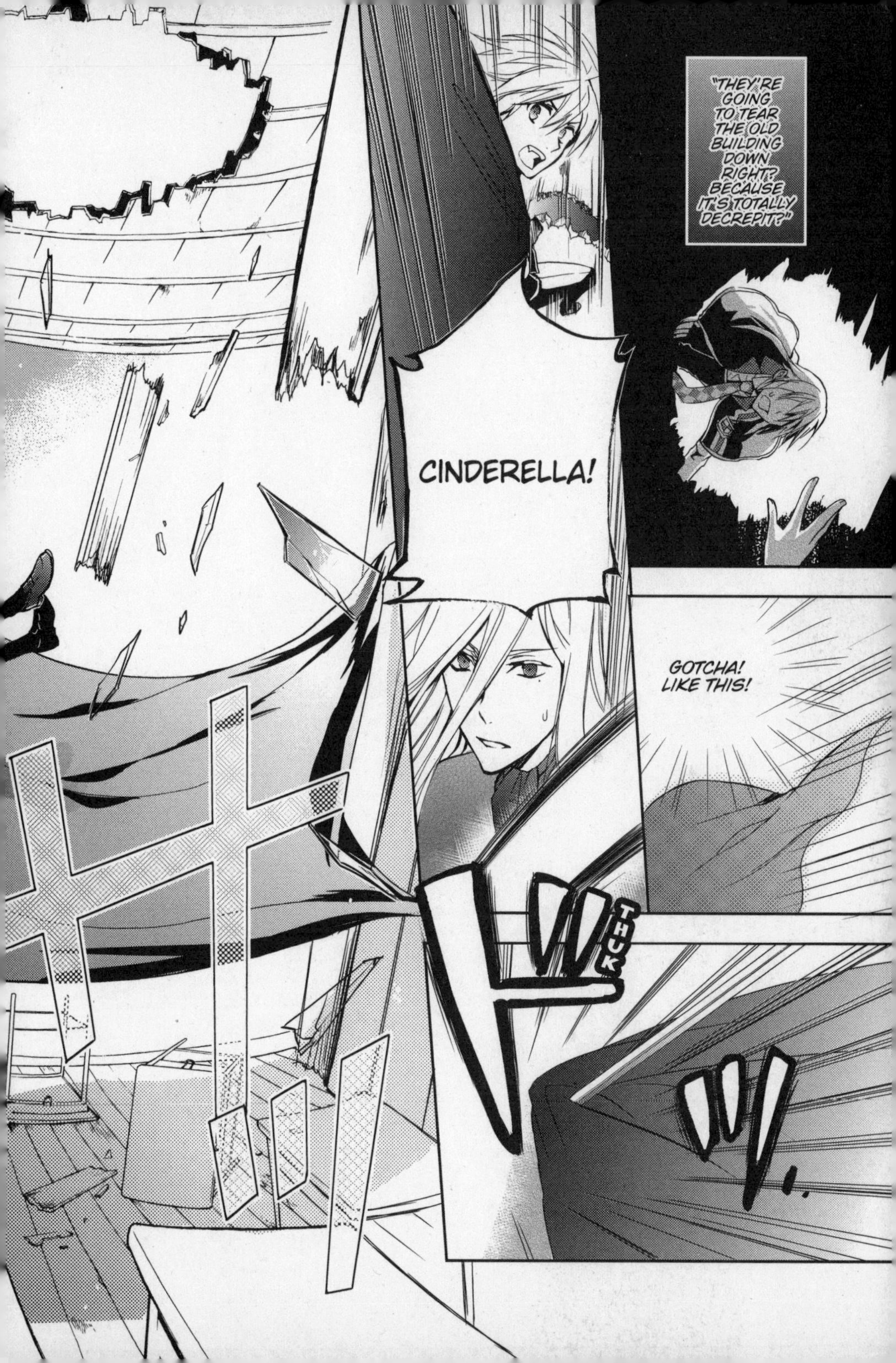
"THEY'RE GOING TO TEAR THE OLD BUILDING DOWN RIGHT? BECAUSE IT'S TOTALLY DECREPIT?"
CINDERELLA!
GOTCHA! LIKE THIS!
THUK

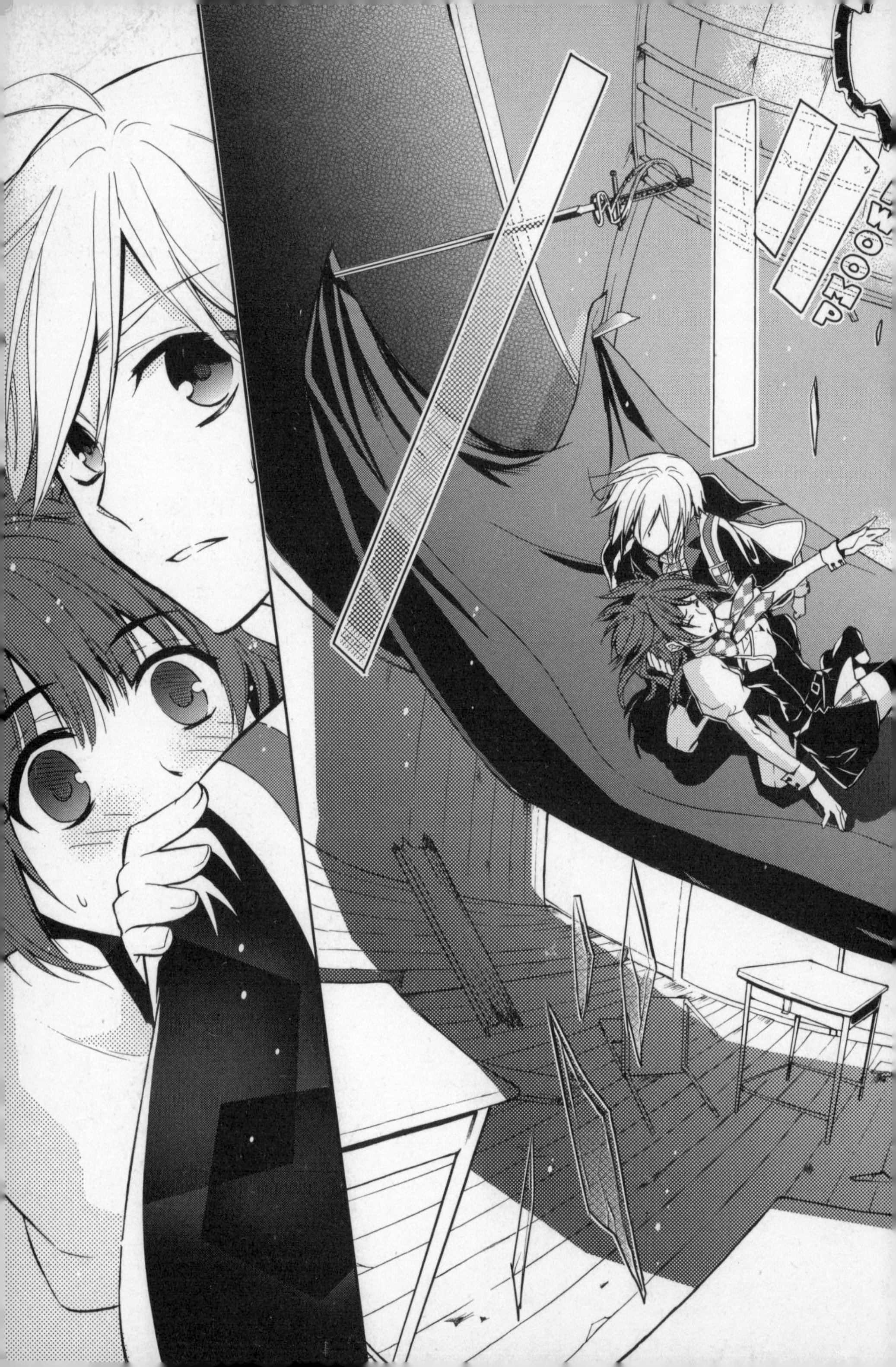
WOOMP

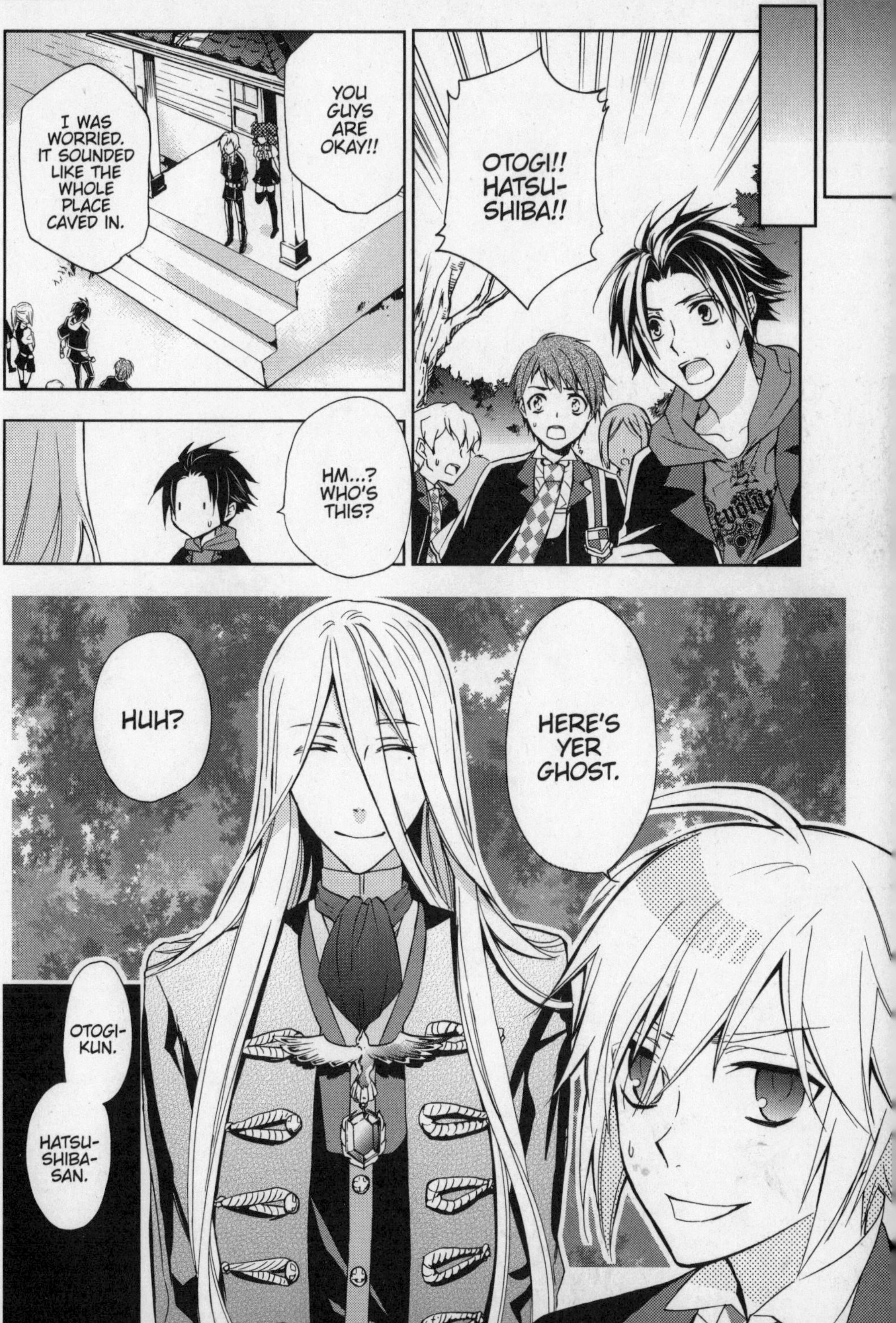
OTOGI!! HATSU-SHIBA!!
YOU GUYS ARE OKAY!!
I WAS WORRIED. IT SOUNDED LIKE THE WHOLE PLACE CAVED IN.
HM...? WHO'S THIS?
HERE'S YER GHOST.
HUH?
OTOGI-KUN.
HATSU-SHIBA-SAN.

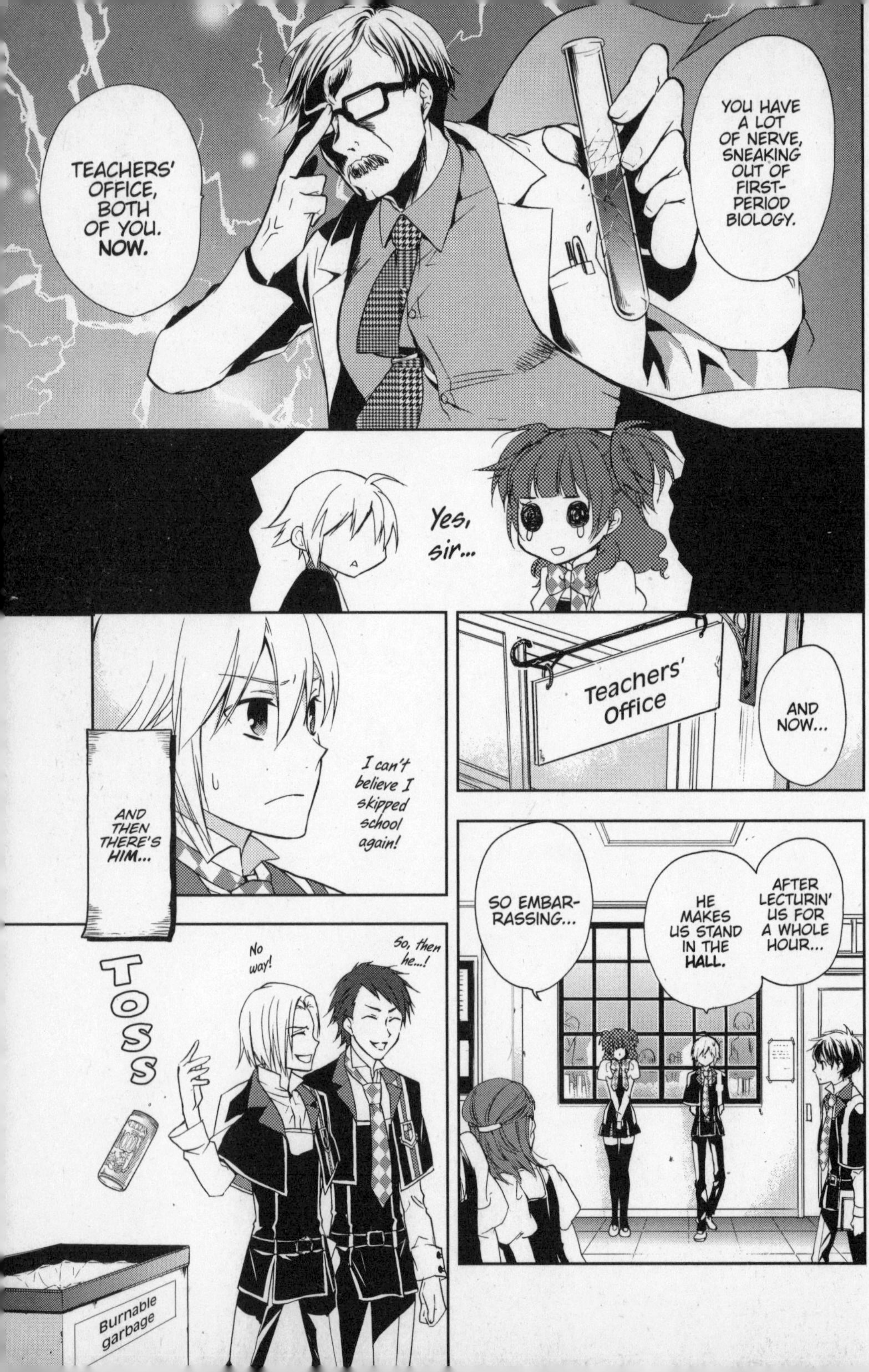
YOU HAVE A LOT OF NERVE, SNEAKING OUT OF FIRST-PERIOD BIOLOGY.
TEACHERS' OFFICE, BOTH OF YOU. NOW.
Yes, sir...
Teachers' Office
AND NOW...
AFTER LECTURIN' US FOR A WHOLE HOUR...
HE MAKES US STAND IN THE HALL.
SO EMBARRASSING...
I can't believe I skipped school again!
AND THEN THERE'S HIM...
So, then he...!
No way!
TOSS
Burnable garbage

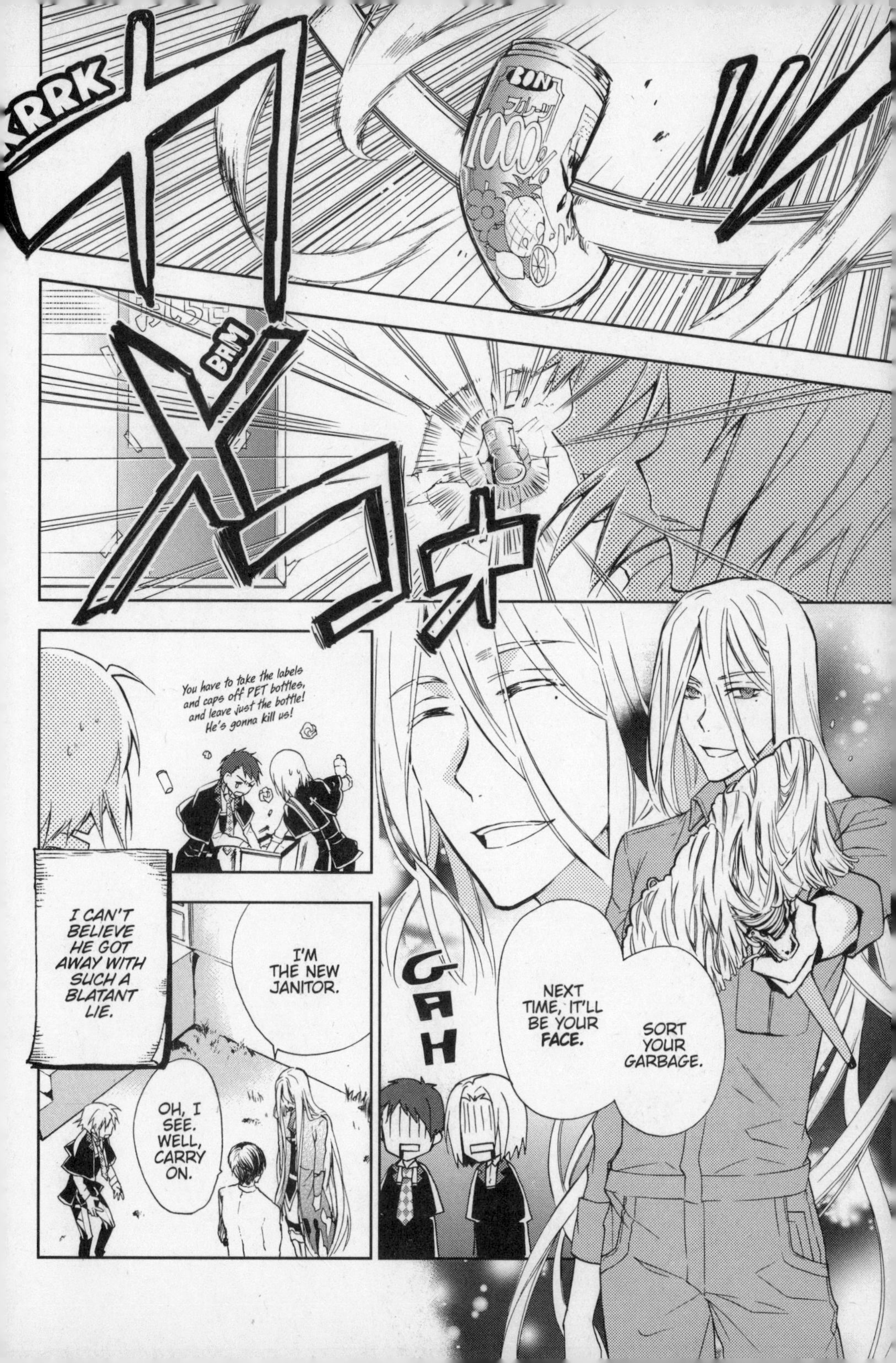
KRRK
BON
BAM
SORT YOUR GARBAGE.
NEXT TIME, IT'LL BE YOUR FACE.
GAH
You have to take the labels and caps off PET bottles, and leave just the bottle! He's gonna kill us!
I'M THE NEW JANITOR.
I CAN'T BELIEVE HE GOT AWAY WITH SUCH A BLATANT LIE.
OH, I SEE. WELL, CARRY ON.

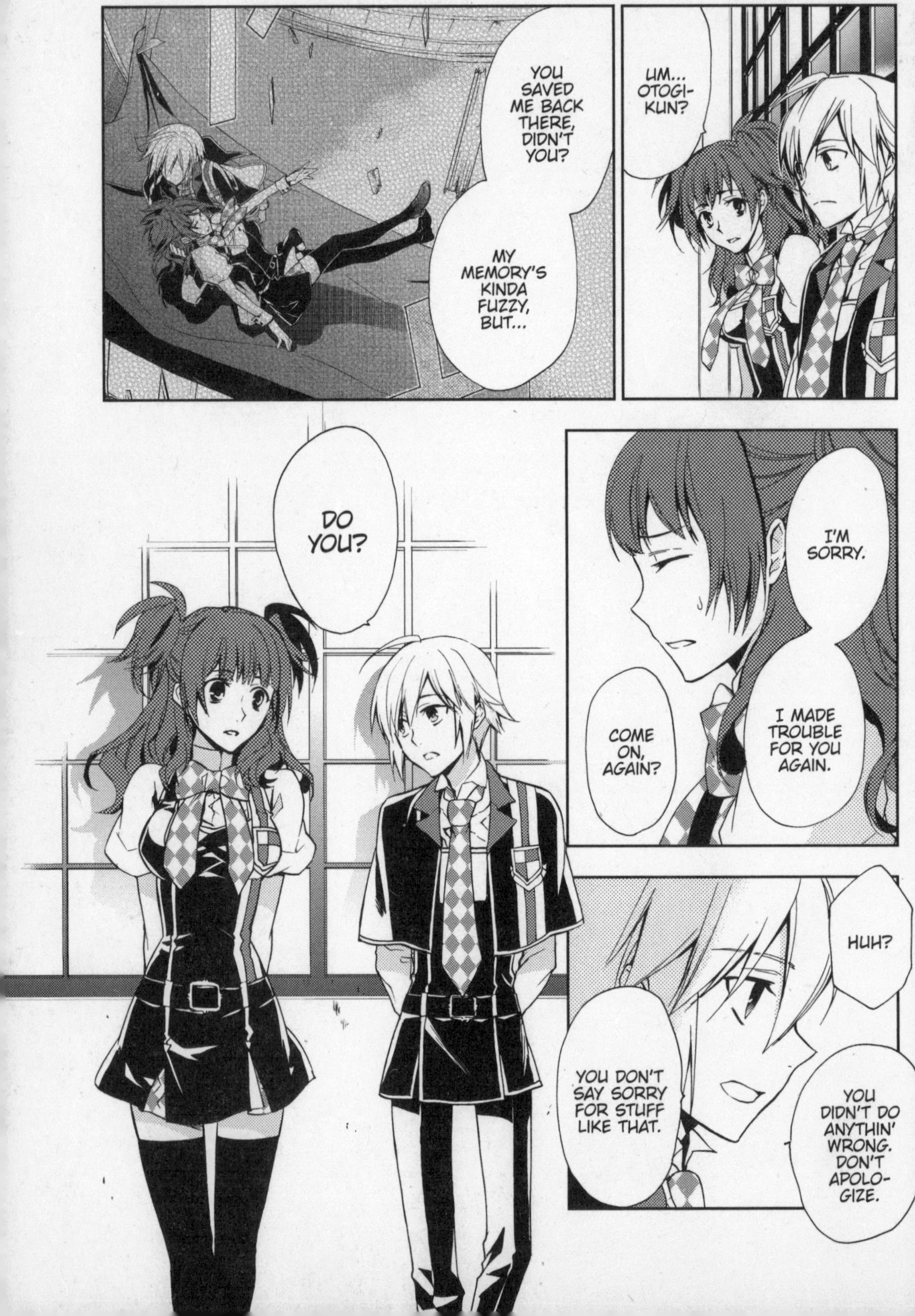
UM... OTOGI-KUN?
YOU SAVED ME BACK THERE, DIDN'T YOU?
MY MEMORY'S KINDA FUZZY, BUT...
I'M SORRY.
I MADE TROUBLE FOR YOU AGAIN.
COME ON, AGAIN?
HUH?
YOU DIDN'T DO ANYTHIN' WRONG. DON'T APOLO-GIZE.
YOU DON'T SAY SORRY FOR STUFF LIKE THAT.
DO YOU?

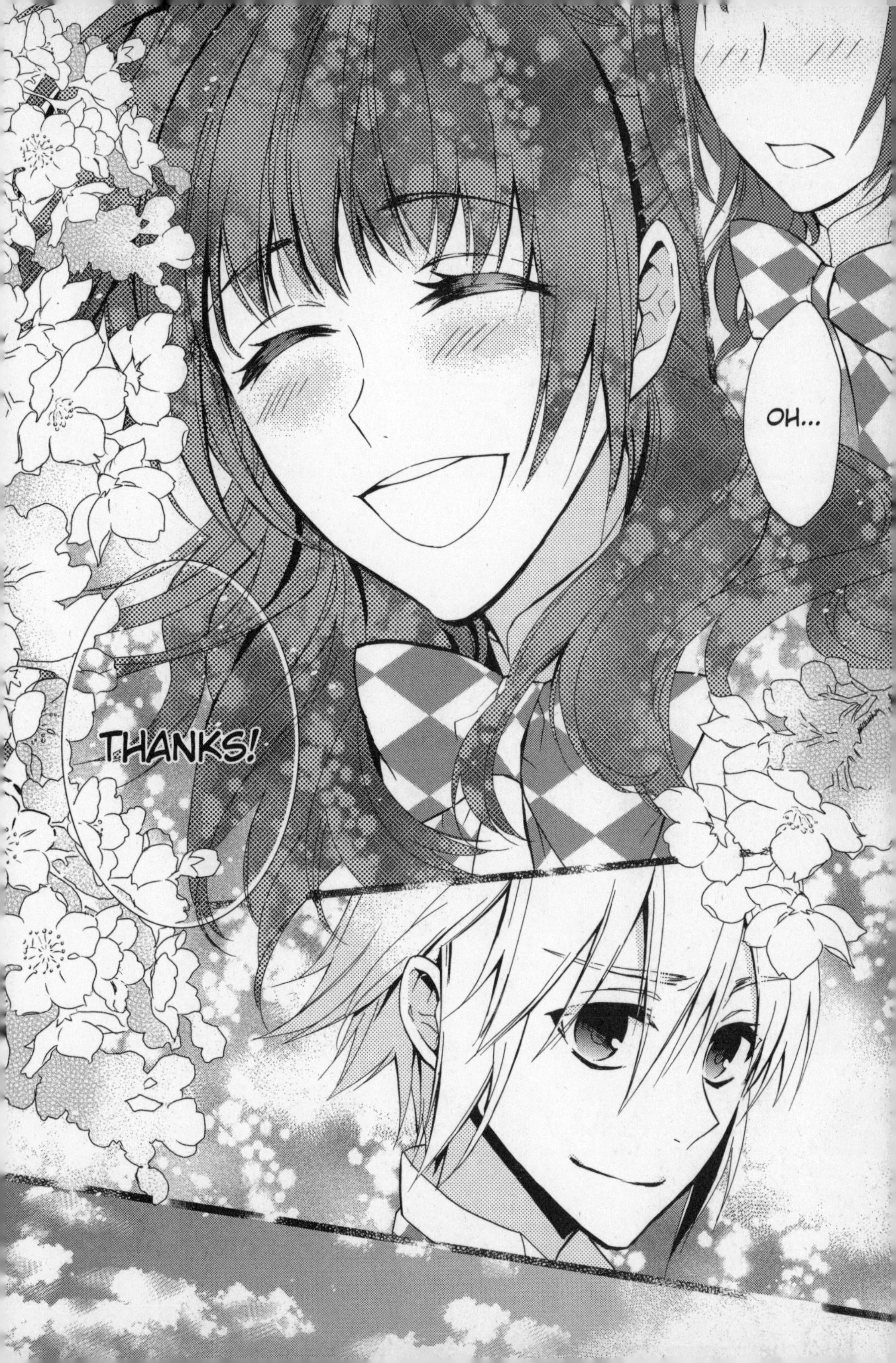
OH...
THANKS!

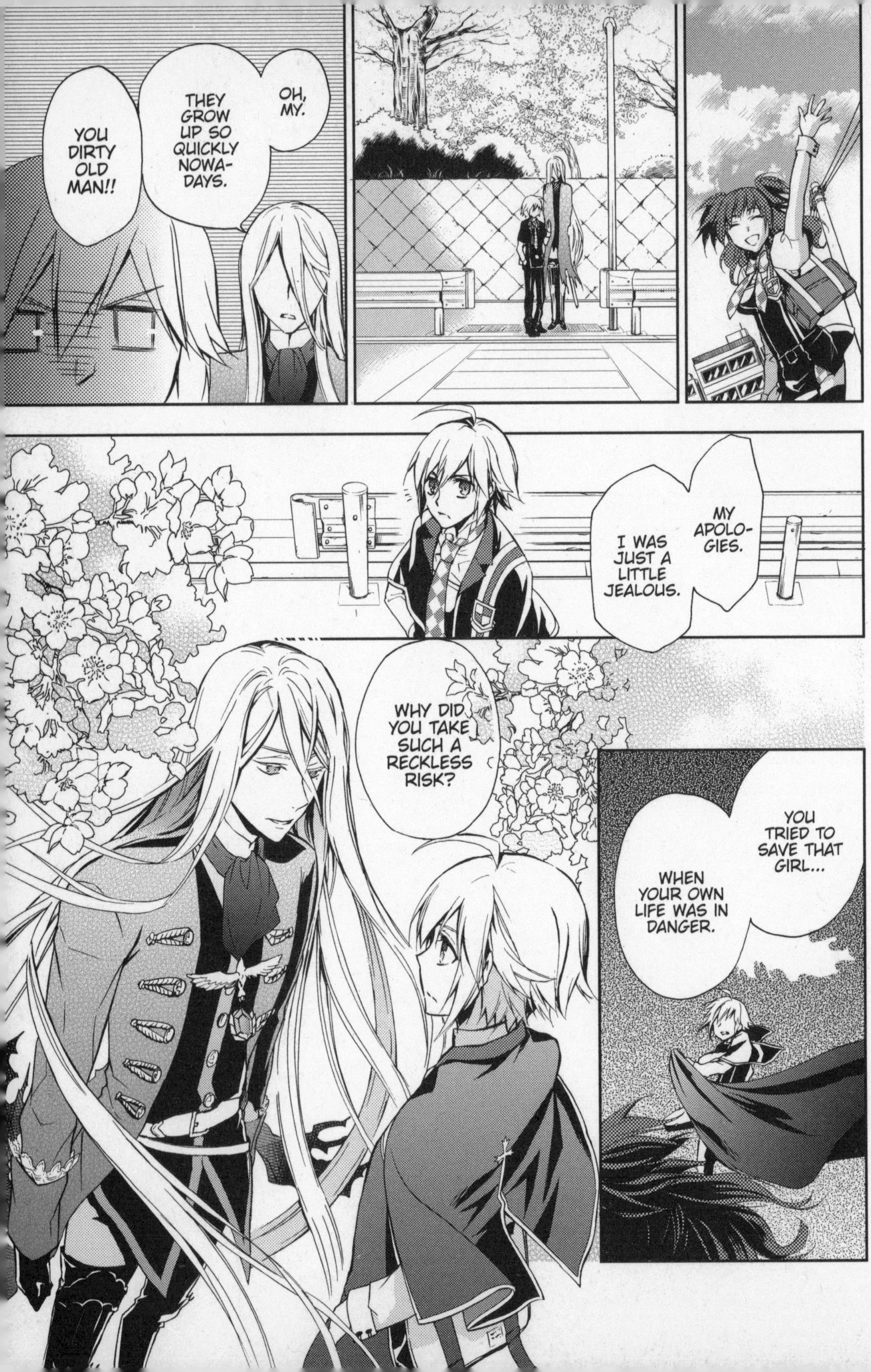
OH, MY.
THEY GROW UP SO QUICKLY NOWADAYS.
YOU DIRTY OLD MAN!!
MY APOLOGIES.
I WAS JUST A LITTLE JEALOUS.
YOU TRIED TO SAVE THAT GIRL...
WHEN YOUR OWN LIFE WAS IN DANGER.
WHY DID YOU TAKE SUCH A RECKLESS RISK?

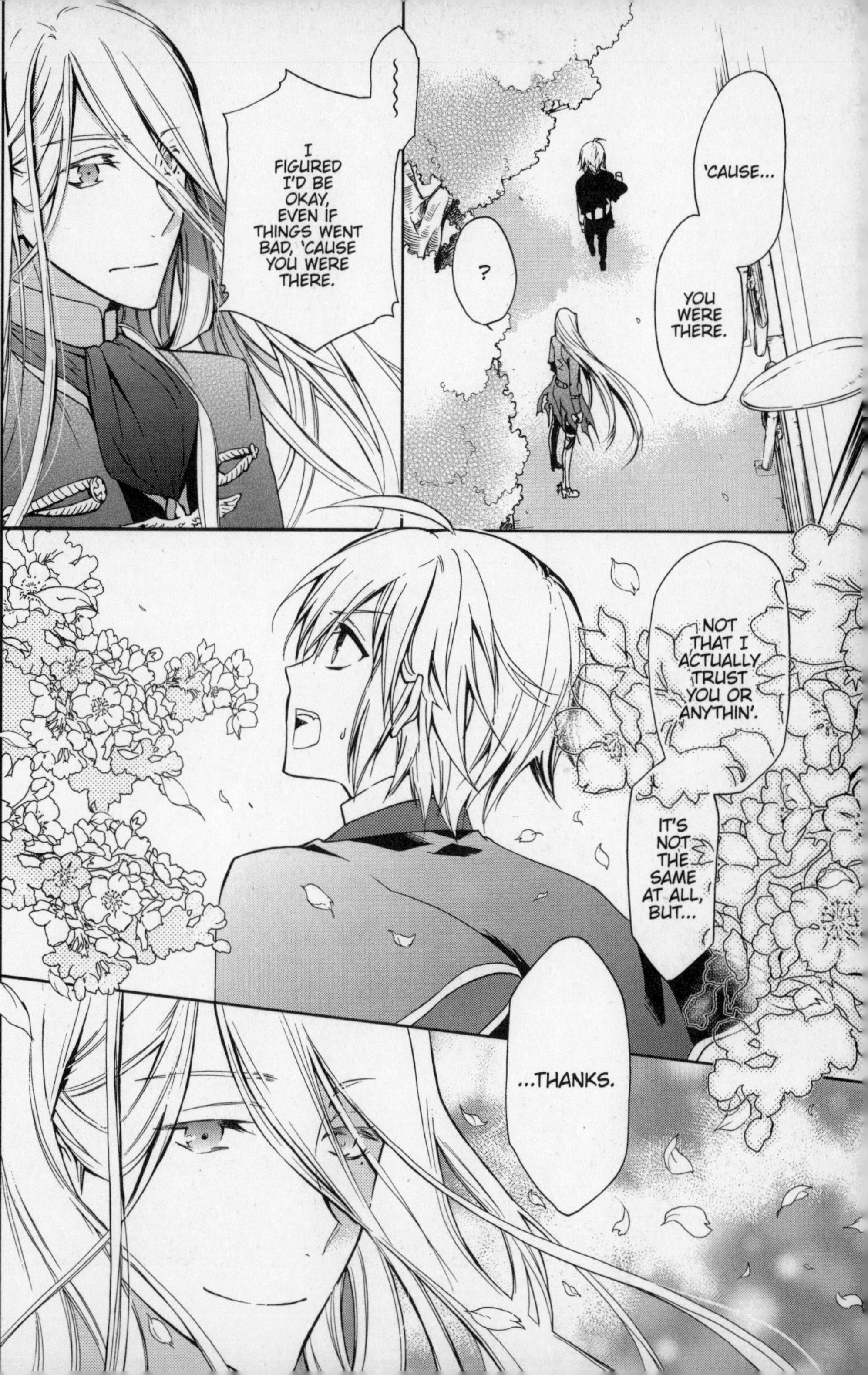
'CAUSE...
YOU WERE THERE.
?
I FIGURED I'D BE OKAY, EVEN IF THINGS WENT BAD, 'CAUSE YOU WERE THERE.
NOT THAT I ACTUALLY TRUST YOU OR ANYTHIN'.
IT'S NOT THE SAME AT ALL, BUT...
...THANKS.

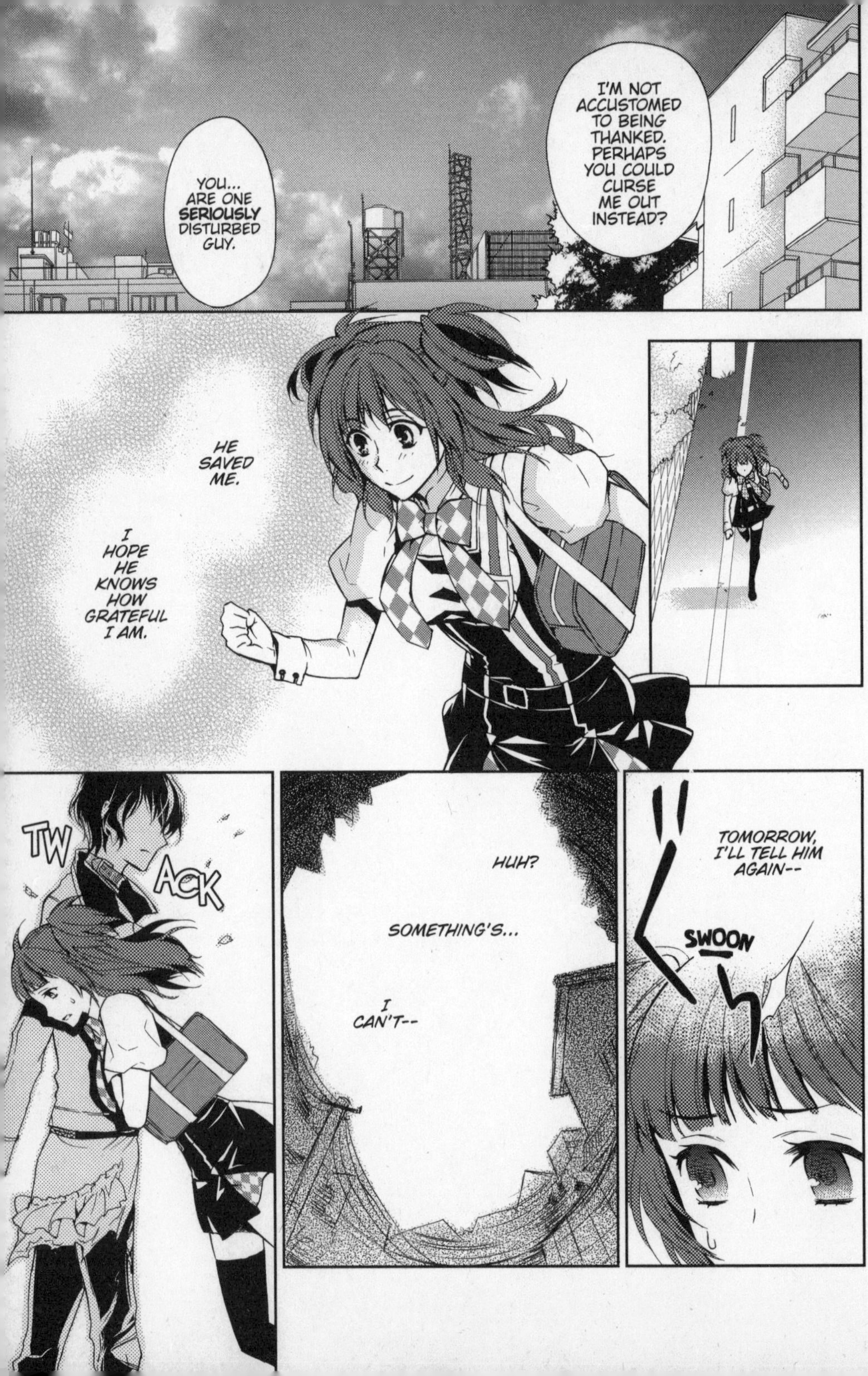
I'M NOT ACCUSTOMED TO BEING THANKED. PERHAPS YOU COULD CURSE ME OUT INSTEAD?
YOU... ARE ONE **SERIOUSLY** DISTURBED GUY.
HE SAVED ME.
I HOPE HE KNOWS HOW GRATEFUL I AM.
TOMORROW, I'LL TELL HIM AGAIN--
SWOON
HUH?
SOMETHING'S...
I CAN'T--
TWACK

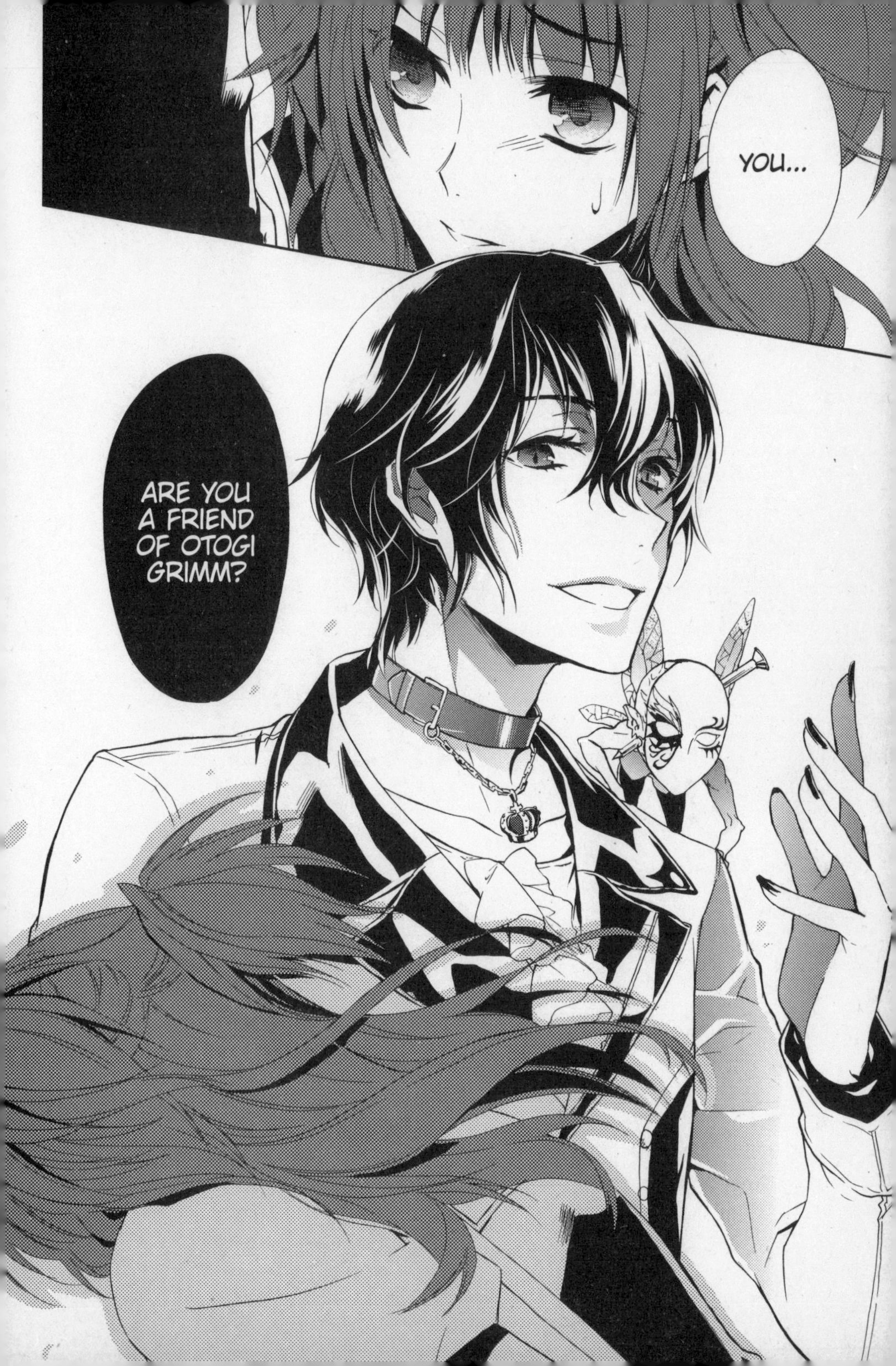
YOU...
ARE YOU A FRIEND OF OTOGI GRIMM?

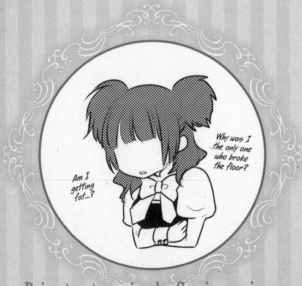

Why was I the only one who broke the floor?
Am I getting fat...?

Dictatorial Grimoire

独裁グリムワール
Dictatorial Grimoire

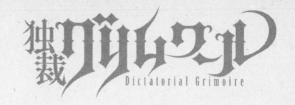

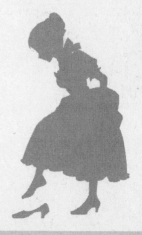

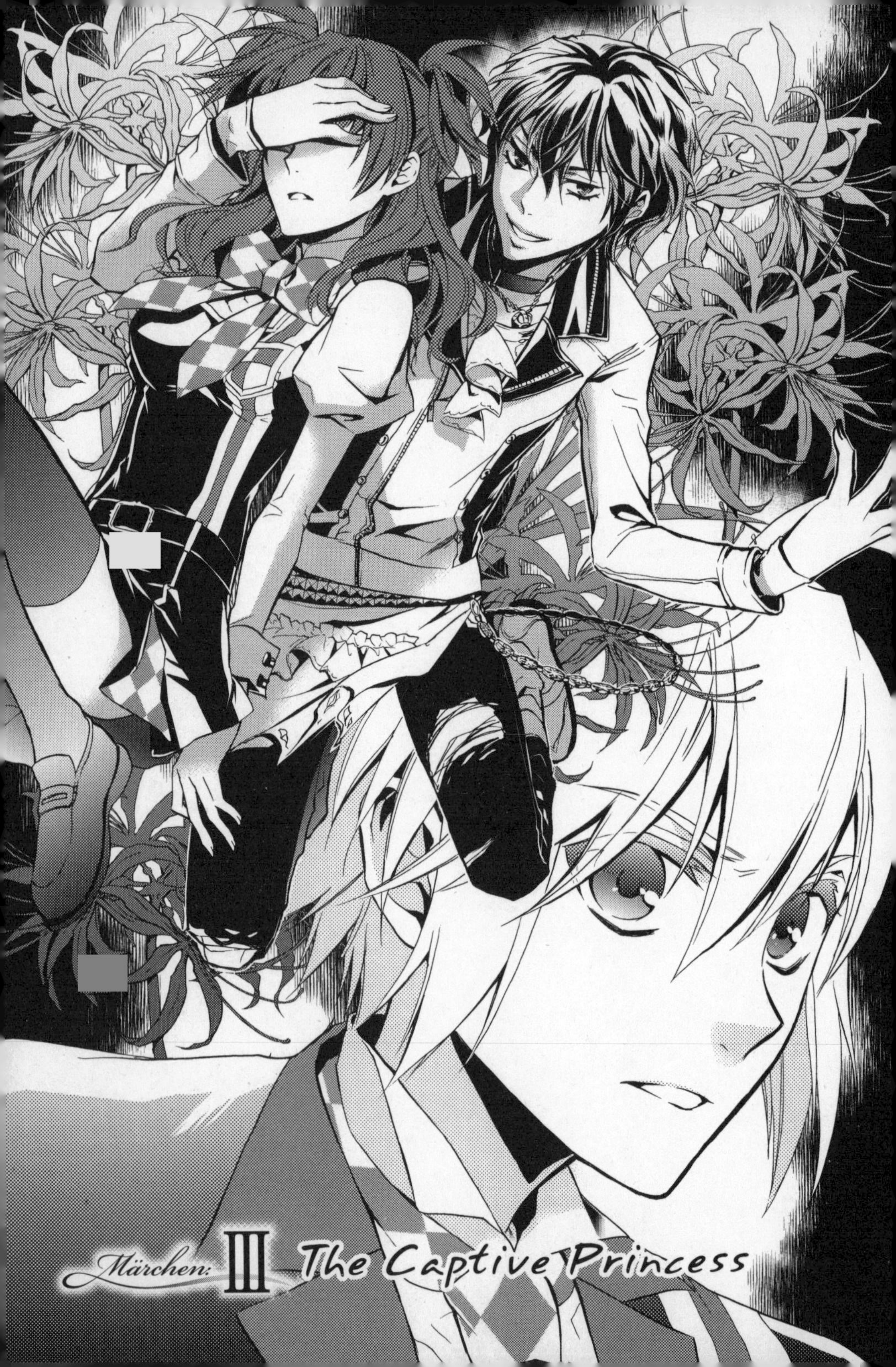
Märchen: III The Captive Princess

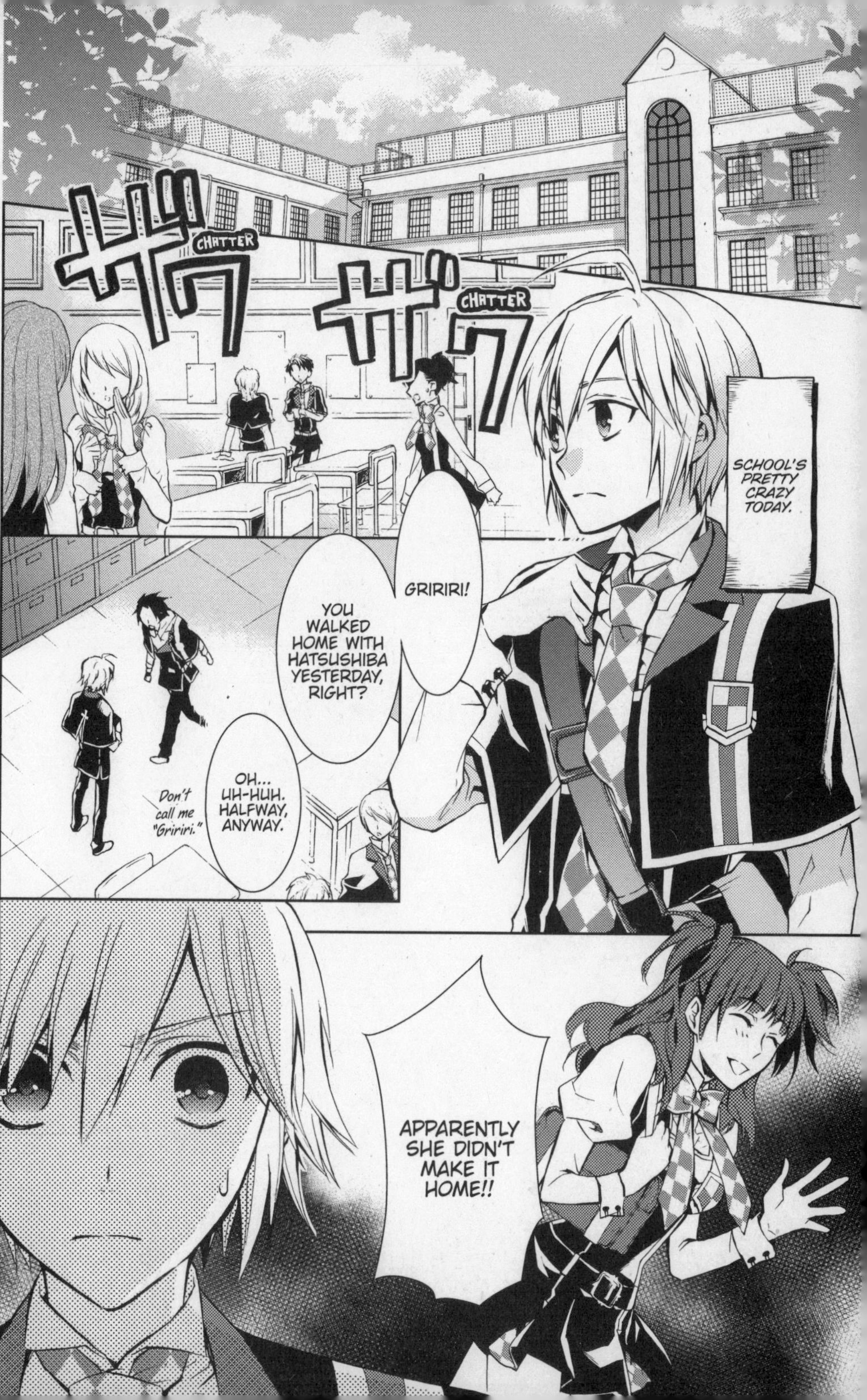
ザワ
CHATTER
ザワ
CHATTER
SCHOOL'S PRETTY CRAZY TODAY.
GRIRIRI!
YOU WALKED HOME WITH HATSUSHIBA YESTERDAY, RIGHT?
OH... UH-HUH. HALFWAY, ANYWAY.
Don't call me "Gririri."
APPARENTLY SHE DIDN'T MAKE IT HOME!!

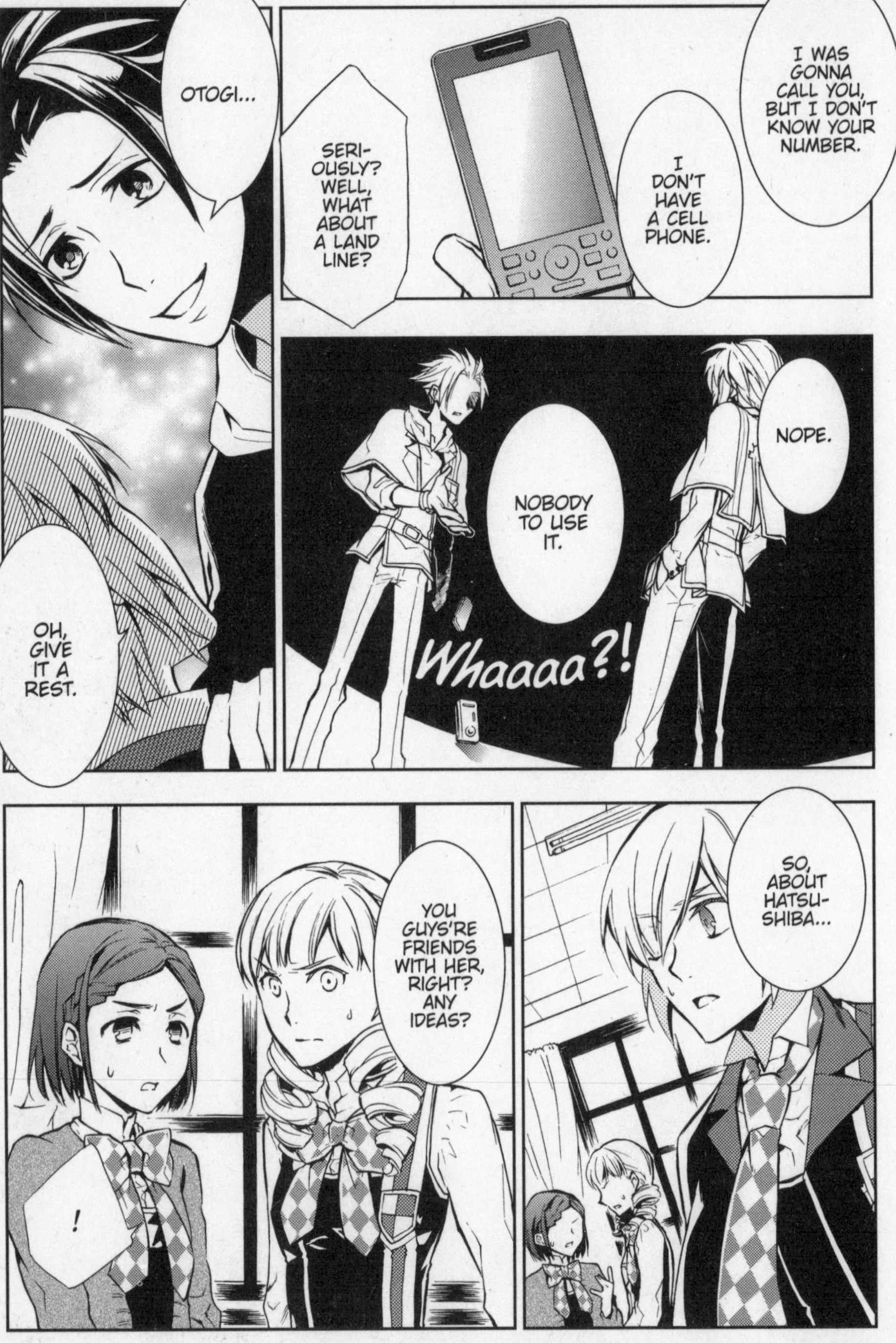
I WAS GONNA CALL YOU, BUT I DON'T KNOW YOUR NUMBER.
I DON'T HAVE A CELL PHONE.
SERI-OUSLY? WELL, WHAT ABOUT A LAND LINE?
NOPE.
NOBODY TO USE IT.
Whaaaa?!
OTOGI...
OH, GIVE IT A REST.
SO, ABOUT HATSU-SHIBA...
YOU GUYS'RE FRIENDS WITH HER, RIGHT? ANY IDEAS?
!

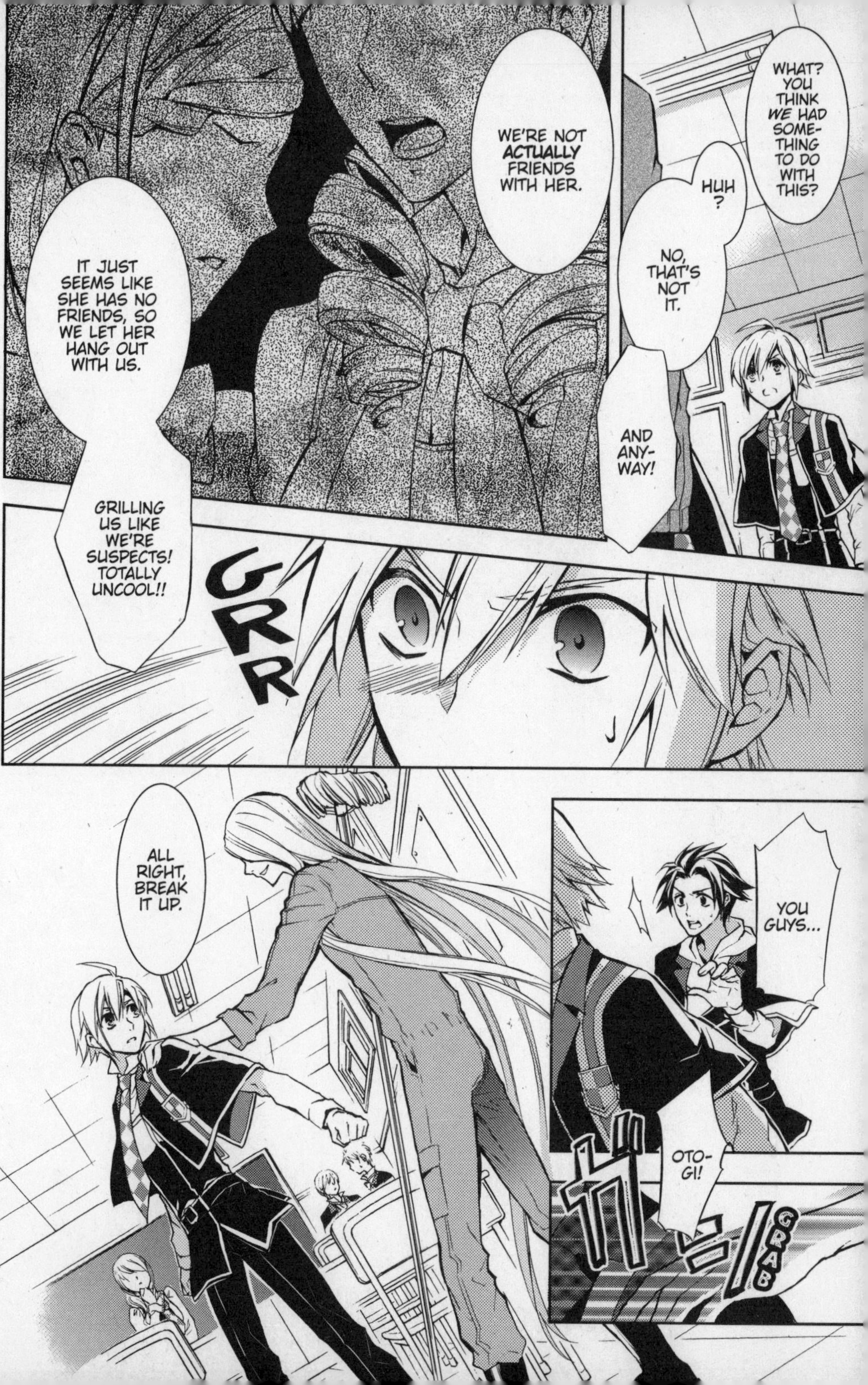
WHAT? YOU THINK *WE* HAD SOMETHING TO DO WITH THIS?
HUH?
NO, THAT'S NOT IT.
AND ANYWAY!
WE'RE NOT **ACTUALLY** FRIENDS WITH HER.
IT JUST SEEMS LIKE SHE HAS NO FRIENDS, SO WE LET HER HANG OUT WITH US.
GRILLING US LIKE WE'RE SUSPECTS! TOTALLY UNCOOL!!
GRR
YOU GUYS...
OTO-GI!
GRAB
ALL RIGHT, BREAK IT UP.

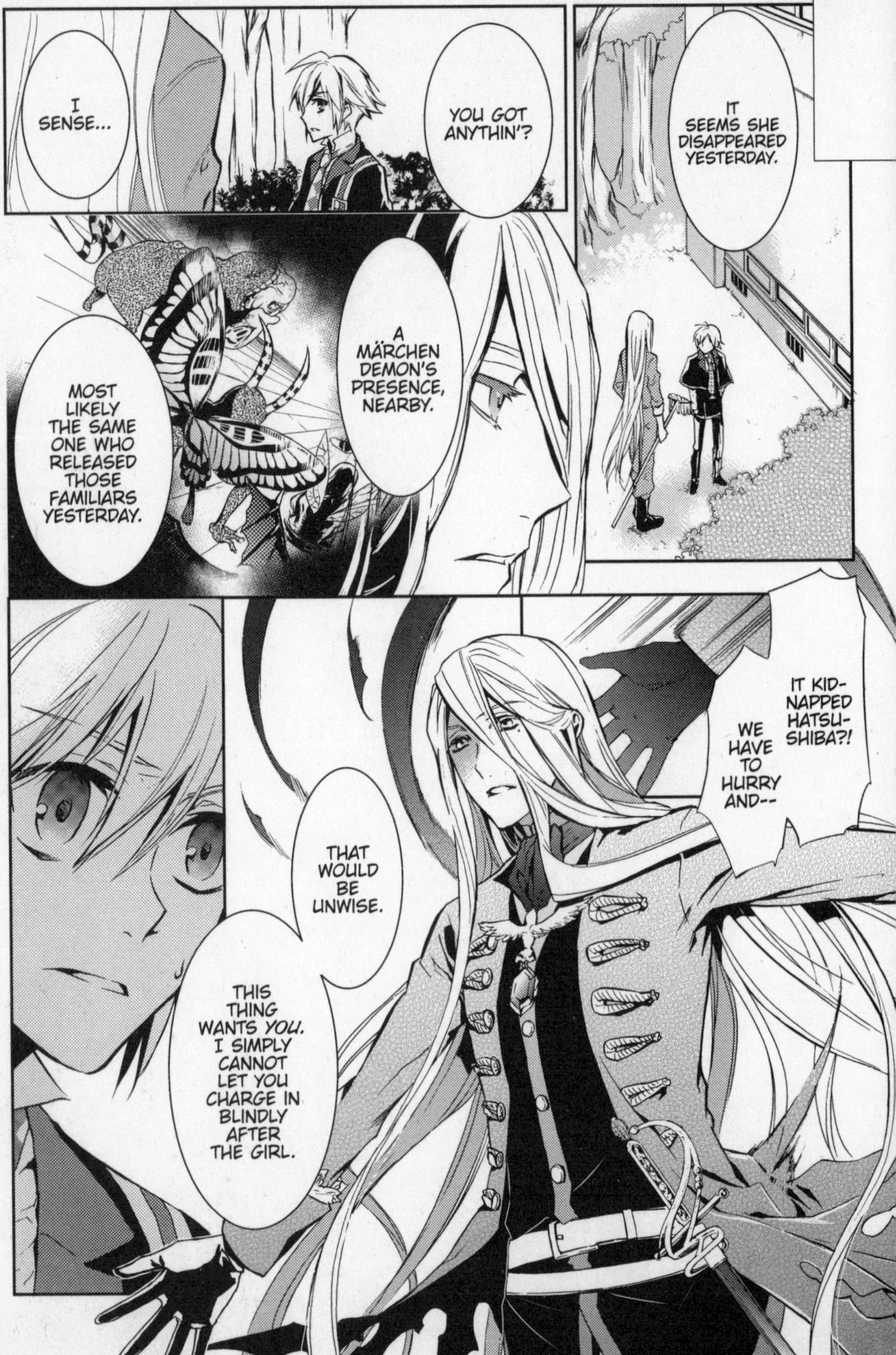
IT SEEMS SHE DISAPPEARED YESTERDAY.
YOU GOT ANYTHIN'?
I SENSE...
A MÄRCHEN DEMON'S PRESENCE, NEARBY.
MOST LIKELY THE SAME ONE WHO RELEASED THOSE FAMILIARS YESTERDAY.
IT KIDNAPPED HATSUSHIBA?! WE HAVE TO HURRY AND--
THAT WOULD BE UNWISE.
THIS THING WANTS *YOU*. I SIMPLY CANNOT LET YOU CHARGE IN BLINDLY AFTER THE GIRL.

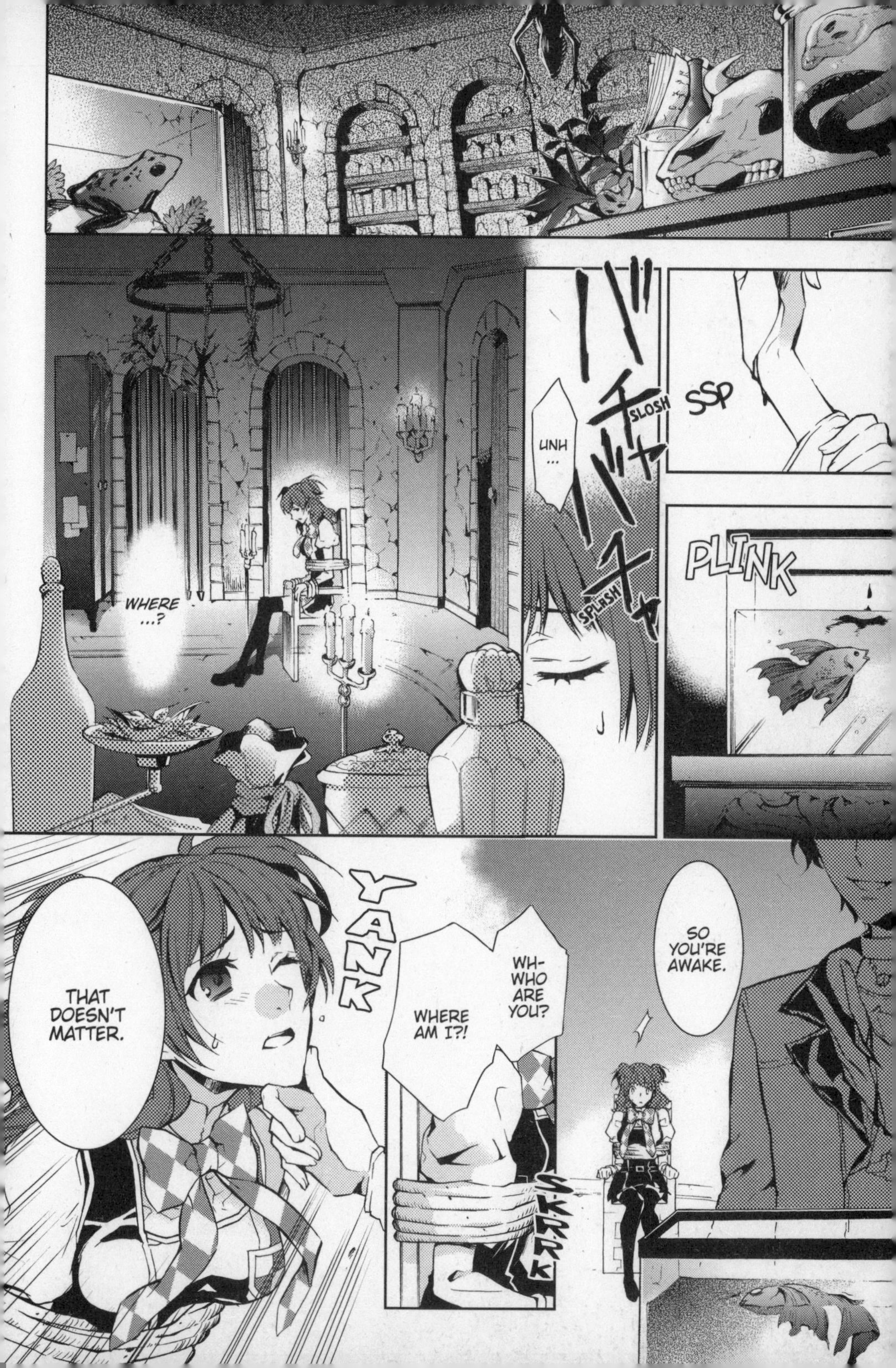
SSP
PLINK
UNH ...
SLOSH
SPLASH
WHERE ...?
SO YOU'RE AWAKE.
WH- WHO ARE YOU?
WHERE AM I?!
YANK
S-K-R-R-K
THAT DOESN'T MATTER.

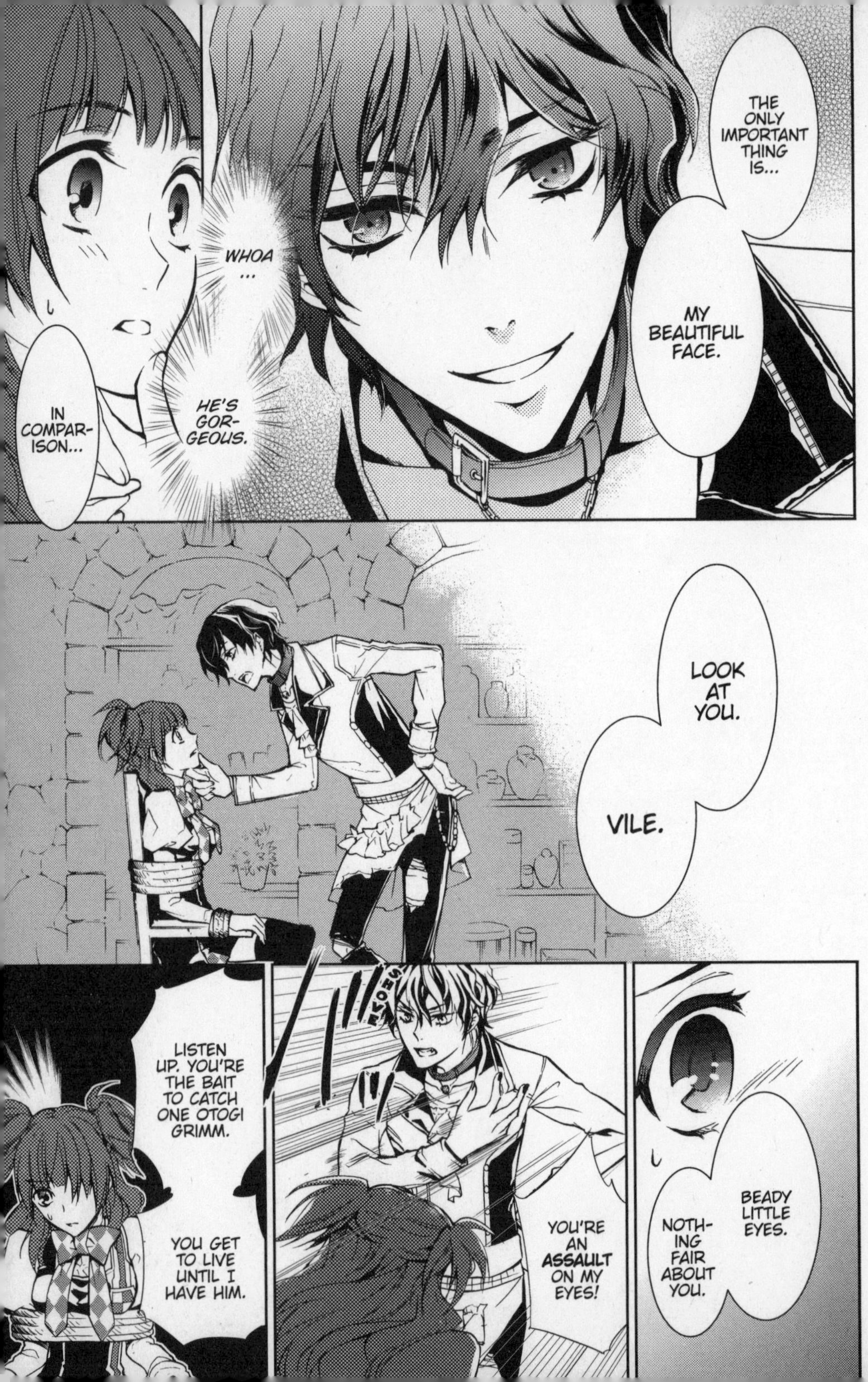
THE ONLY IMPORTANT THING IS...
MY BEAUTIFUL FACE.
WHOA...
HE'S GORGEOUS.
IN COMPARISON...
LOOK AT YOU.
VILE.
BEADY LITTLE EYES.
NOTHING FAIR ABOUT YOU.
SHOVE
YOU'RE AN **ASSAULT** ON MY EYES!
LISTEN UP. YOU'RE THE BAIT TO CATCH ONE OTOGI GRIMM.
YOU GET TO LIVE UNTIL I HAVE HIM.

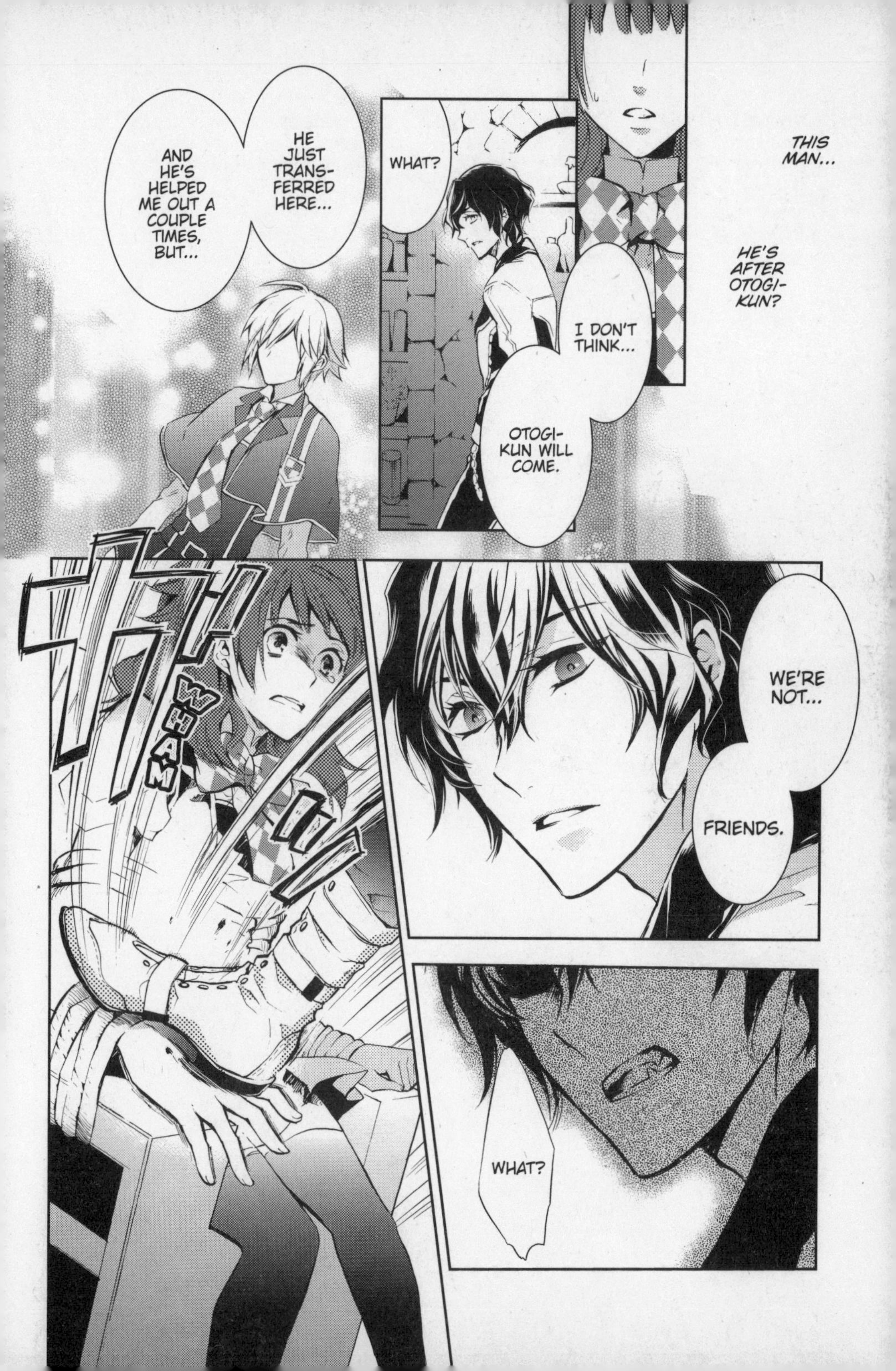
THIS MAN...
HE'S AFTER OTOGI-KUN?
WHAT?
I DON'T THINK...
OTOGI-KUN WILL COME.
HE JUST TRANSFERRED HERE...
AND HE'S HELPED ME OUT A COUPLE TIMES, BUT...
WE'RE NOT...
FRIENDS.
WHAT?
WHAM

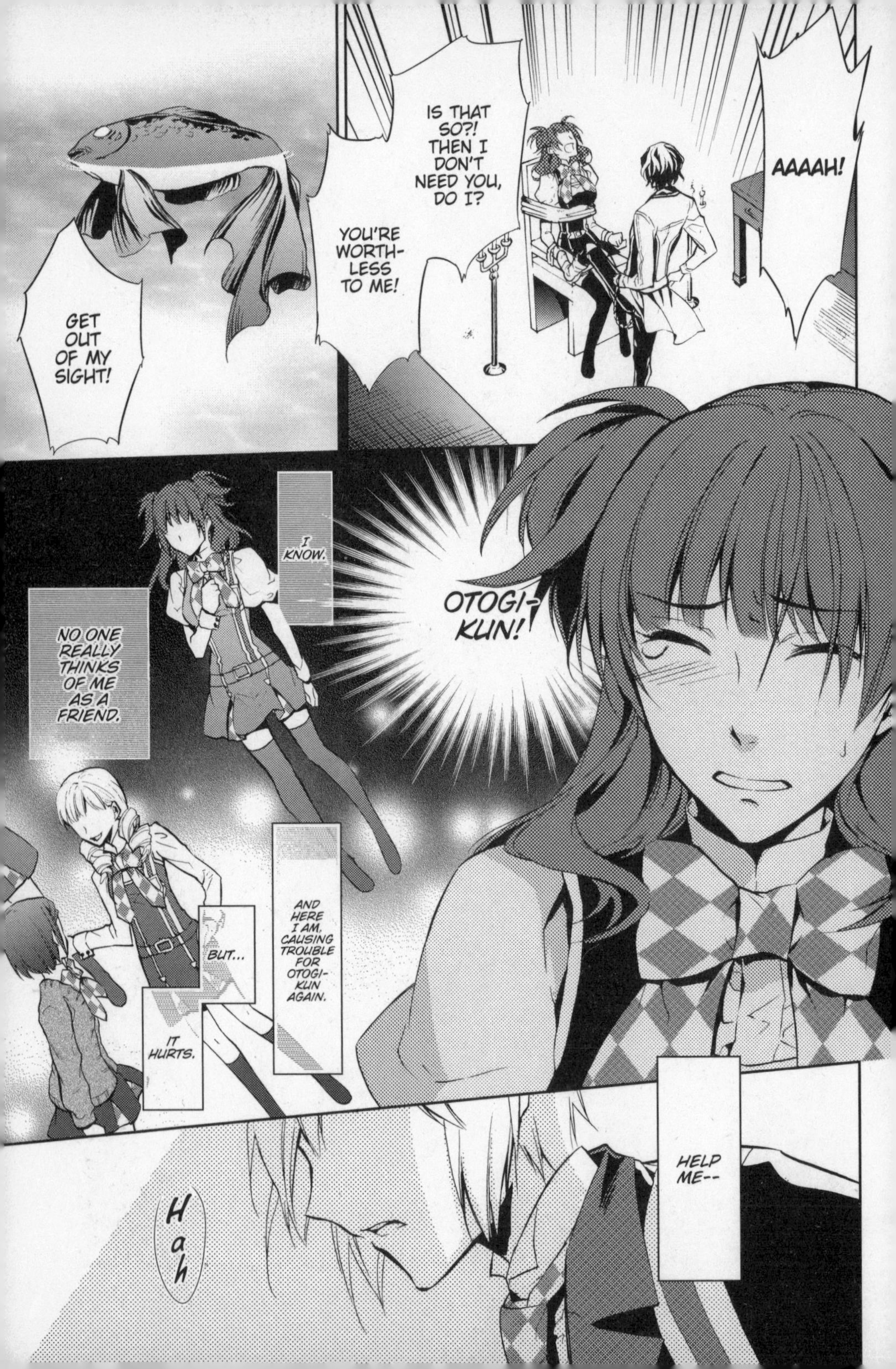
AAAAH!
IS THAT SO?! THEN I DON'T NEED YOU, DO I?
YOU'RE WORTH-LESS TO ME!
GET OUT OF MY SIGHT!
OTOGI-KUN!
I KNOW.
NO ONE REALLY THINKS OF ME AS A FRIEND.
AND HERE I AM, CAUSING TROUBLE FOR OTOGI-KUN AGAIN.
BUT...
IT HURTS.
HELP ME--
Hah

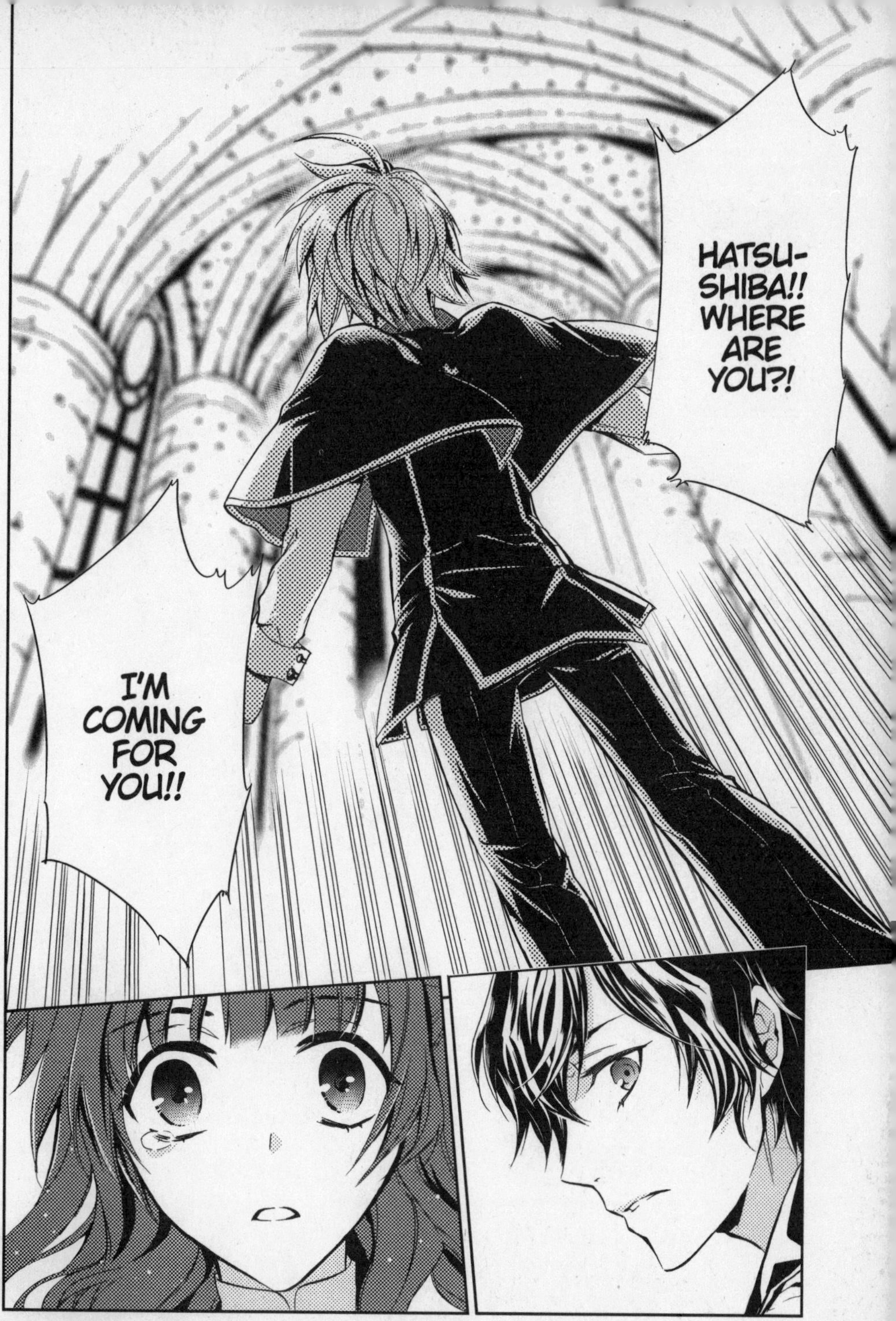
HATSU-SHIBA!! WHERE ARE YOU?!
I'M COMING FOR YOU!!

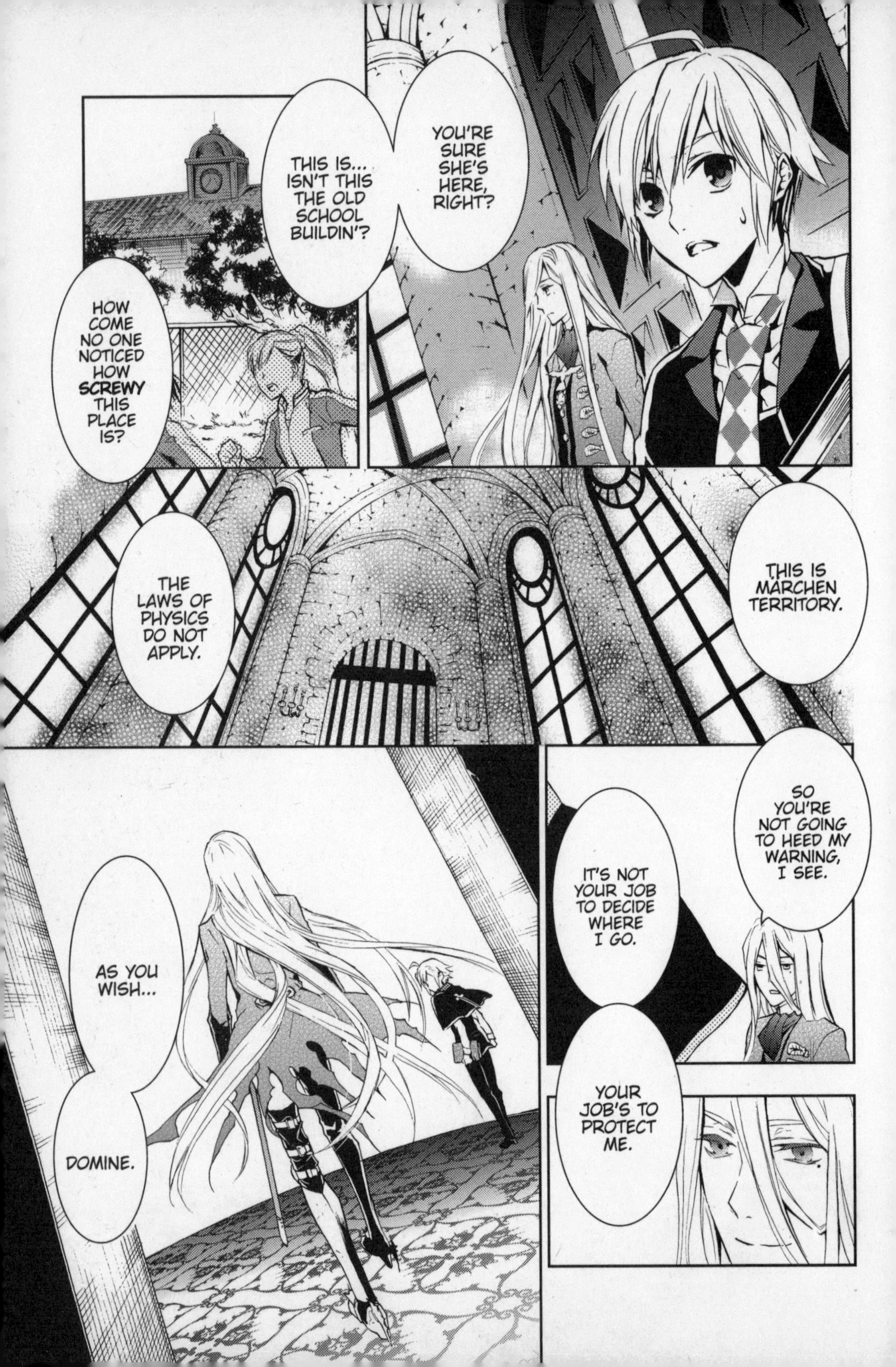
YOU'RE SURE SHE'S HERE, RIGHT?
THIS IS... ISN'T THIS THE OLD SCHOOL BUILDIN'?
HOW COME NO ONE NOTICED HOW **SCREWY** THIS PLACE IS?
THIS IS MARCHEN TERRITORY.
THE LAWS OF PHYSICS DO NOT APPLY.
SO YOU'RE NOT GOING TO HEED MY WARNING, I SEE.
IT'S NOT YOUR JOB TO DECIDE WHERE I GO.
YOUR JOB'S TO PROTECT ME.
AS YOU WISH...
DOMINE.

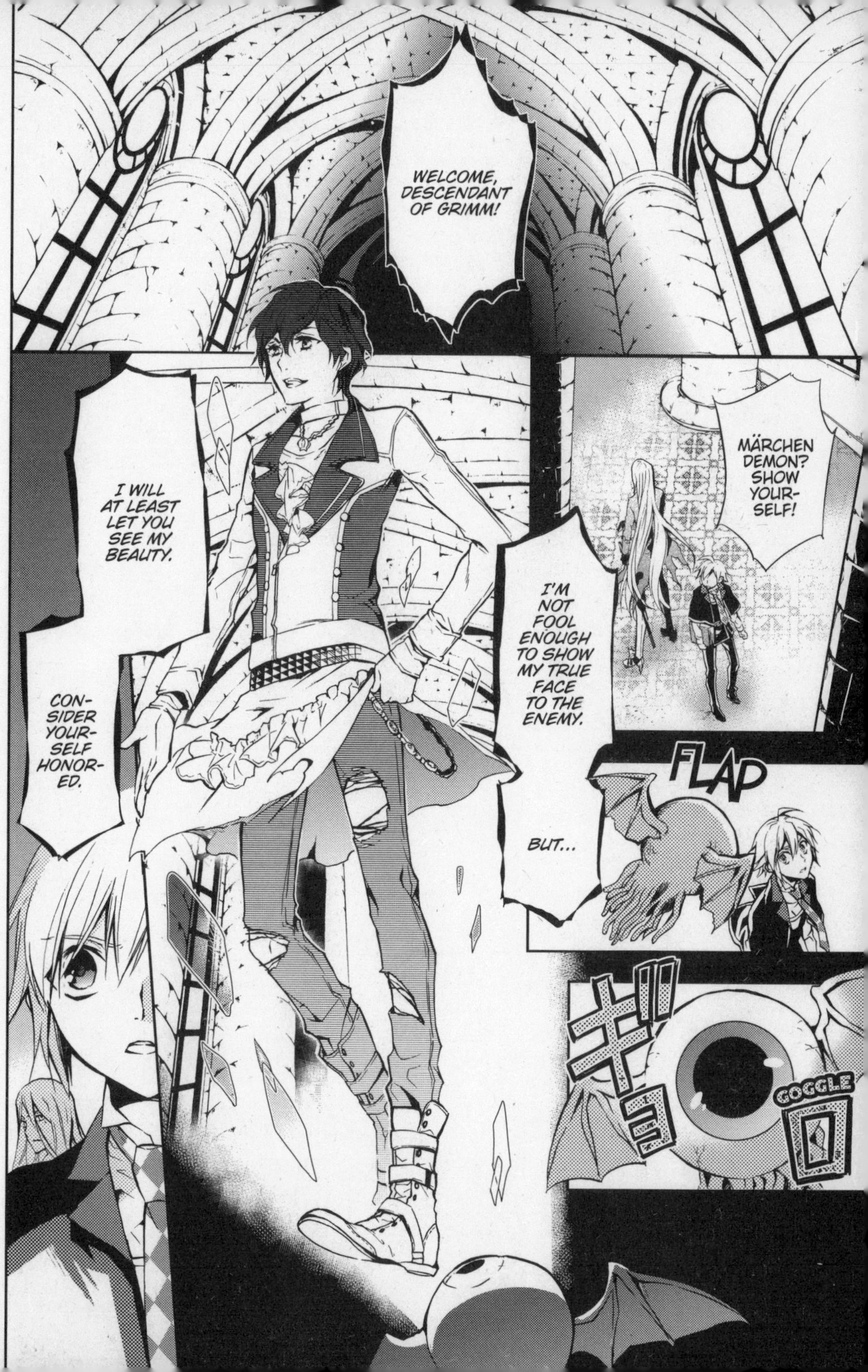
WELCOME, DESCENDANT OF GRIMM!
MÄRCHEN DEMON? SHOW YOUR-SELF!
I'M NOT FOOL ENOUGH TO SHOW MY TRUE FACE TO THE ENEMY.
FLAP
BUT...
ギョロ
GOGGLE
I WILL AT LEAST LET YOU SEE MY BEAUTY.
CON-SIDER YOUR-SELF HONOR-ED.

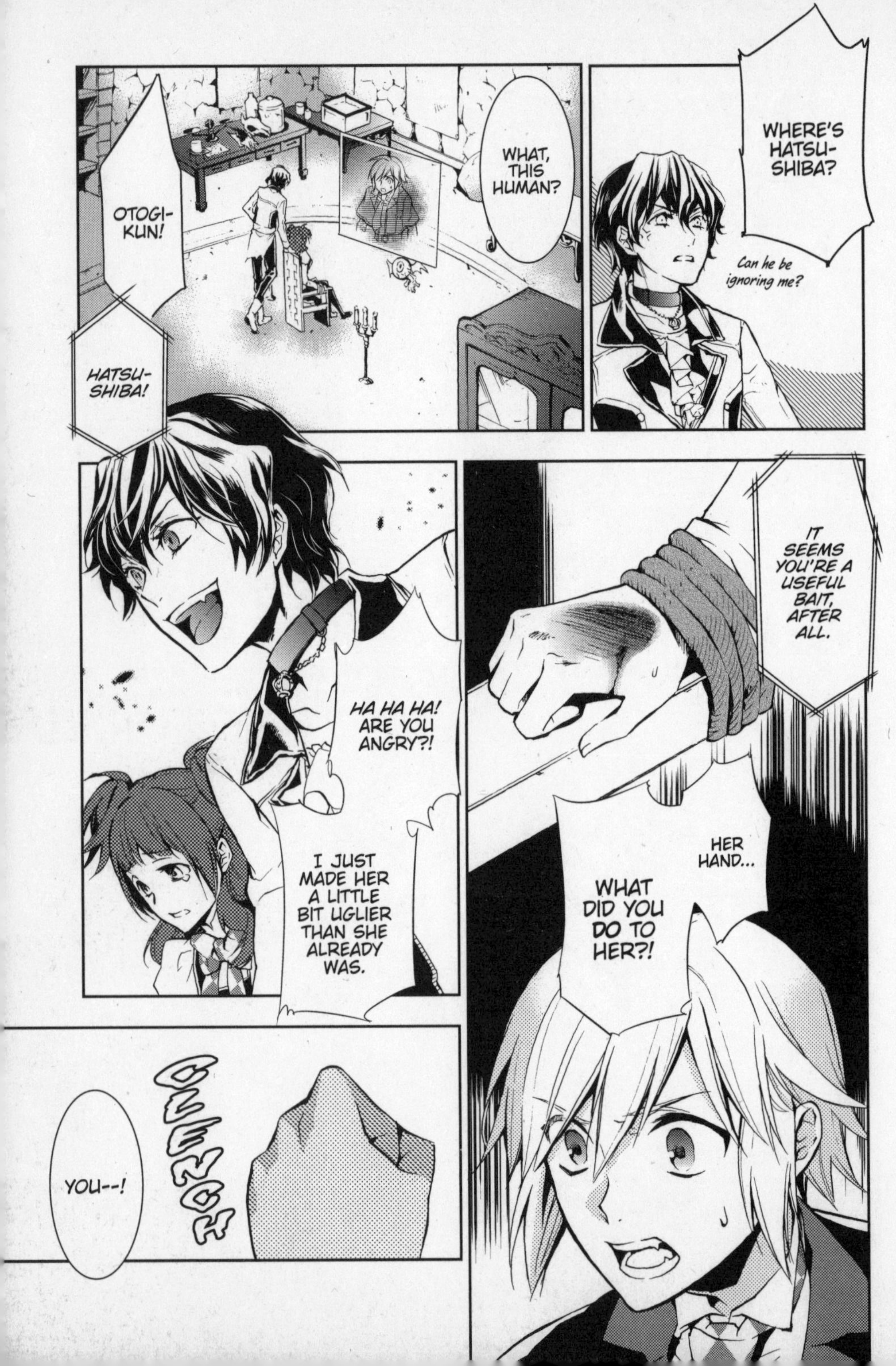
WHERE'S HATSU-SHIBA?
Can he be ignoring me?
WHAT, THIS HUMAN?
OTOGI-KUN!
HATSU-SHIBA!
IT SEEMS YOU'RE A USEFUL BAIT, AFTER ALL.
HER HAND...
WHAT DID YOU DO TO HER?!
HA HA HA! ARE YOU ANGRY?!
I JUST MADE HER A LITTLE BIT UGLIER THAN SHE ALREADY WAS.
CLENCH
YOU--!

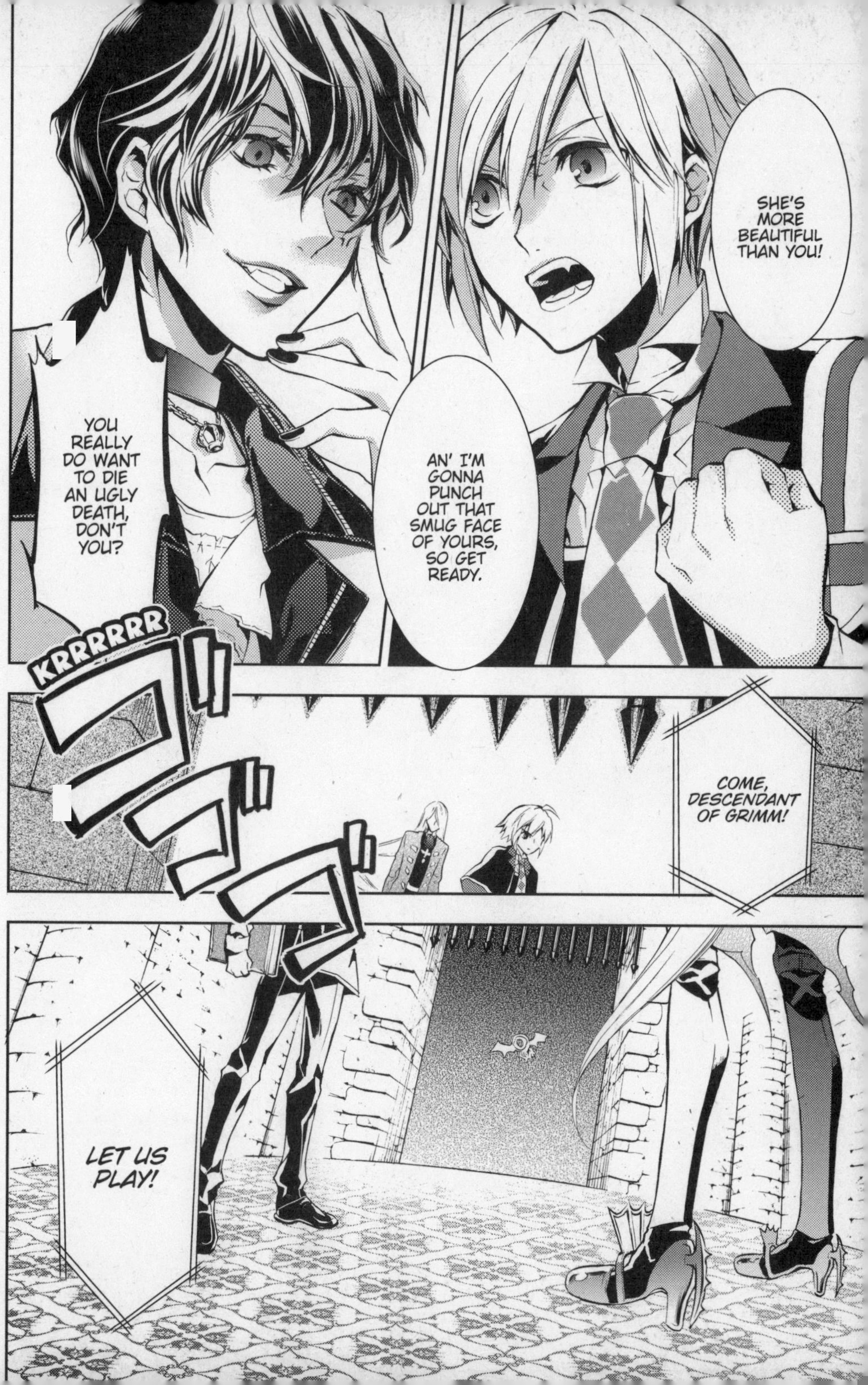
SHE'S MORE BEAUTIFUL THAN YOU!
AN' I'M GONNA PUNCH OUT THAT SMUG FACE OF YOURS, SO GET READY.
YOU REALLY DO WANT TO DIE AN UGLY DEATH, DON'T YOU?
KRRRRRR
COME, DESCENDANT OF GRIMM!
LET US PLAY!

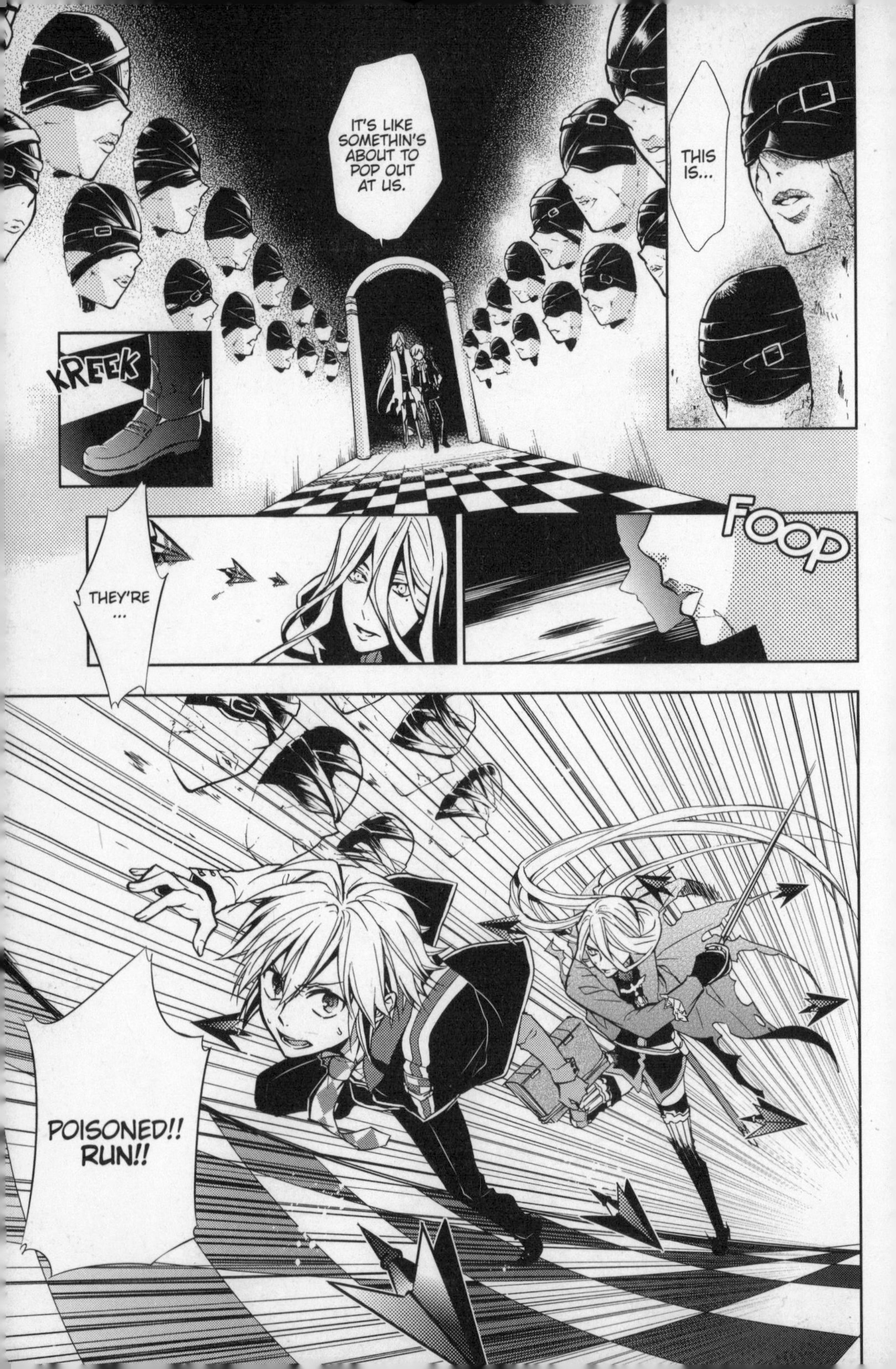
THIS IS...
IT'S LIKE SOMETHIN'S ABOUT TO POP OUT AT US.
KREEK
FOOP
THEY'RE ...
POISONED!! RUN!!

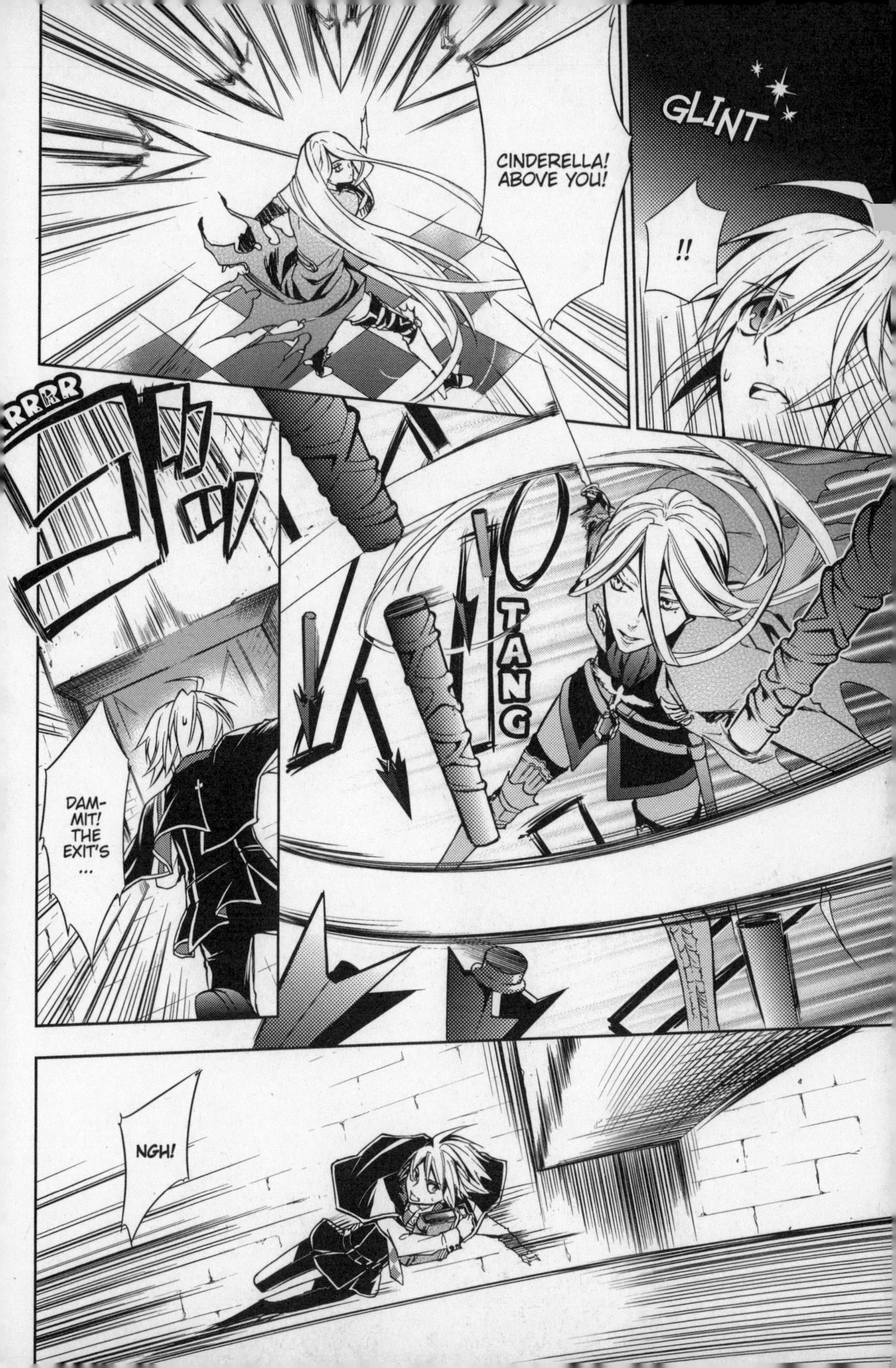
GLINT
!!
CINDERELLA! ABOVE YOU!
TANG
RRRR
DAM-MIT! THE EXIT'S ...
NGH!

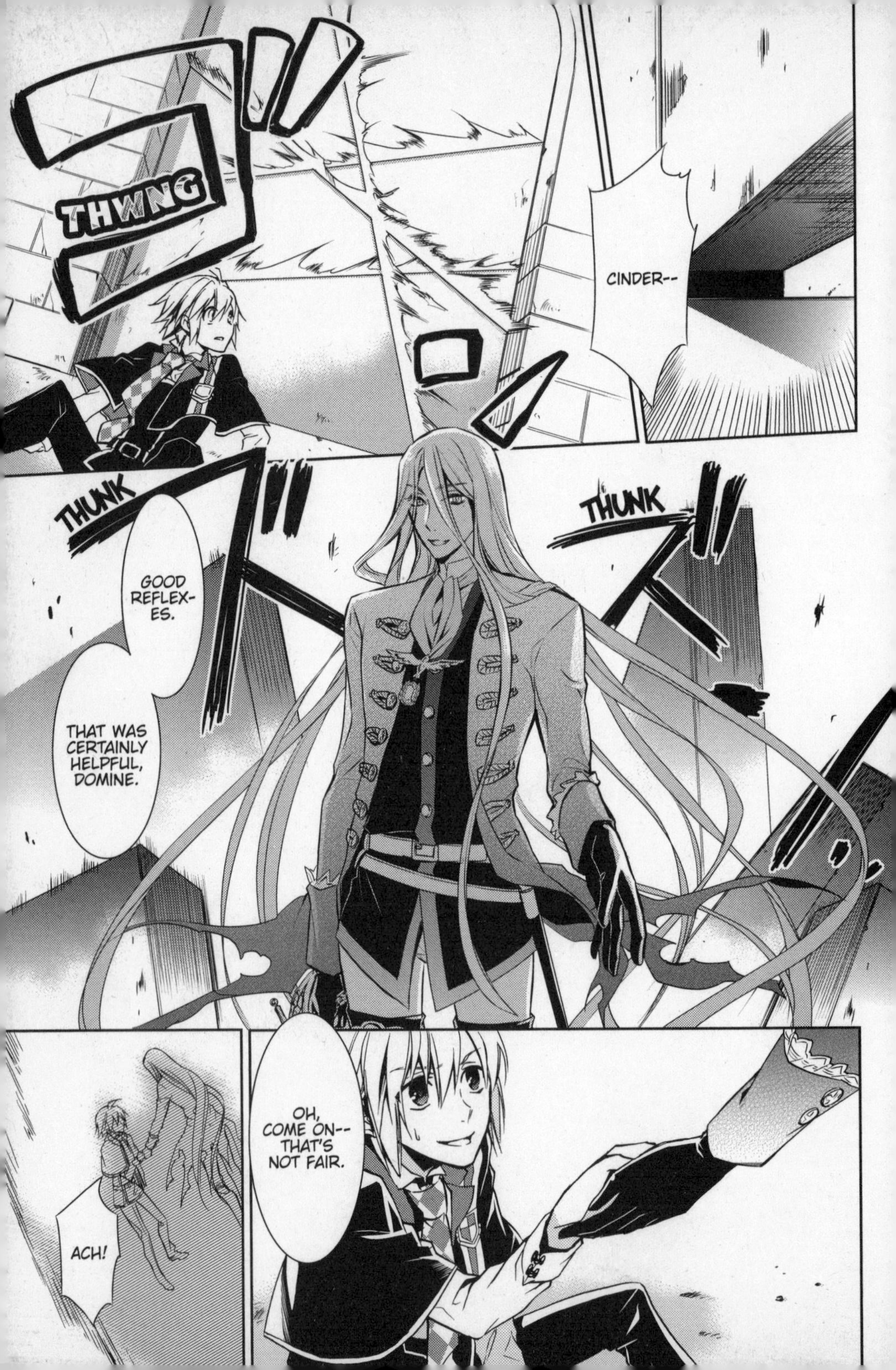
CINDER--
THWNG
THUNK
THUNK
GOOD REFLEX-ES.
THAT WAS CERTAINLY HELPFUL, DOMINE.
OH, COME ON-- THAT'S NOT FAIR.
ACH!

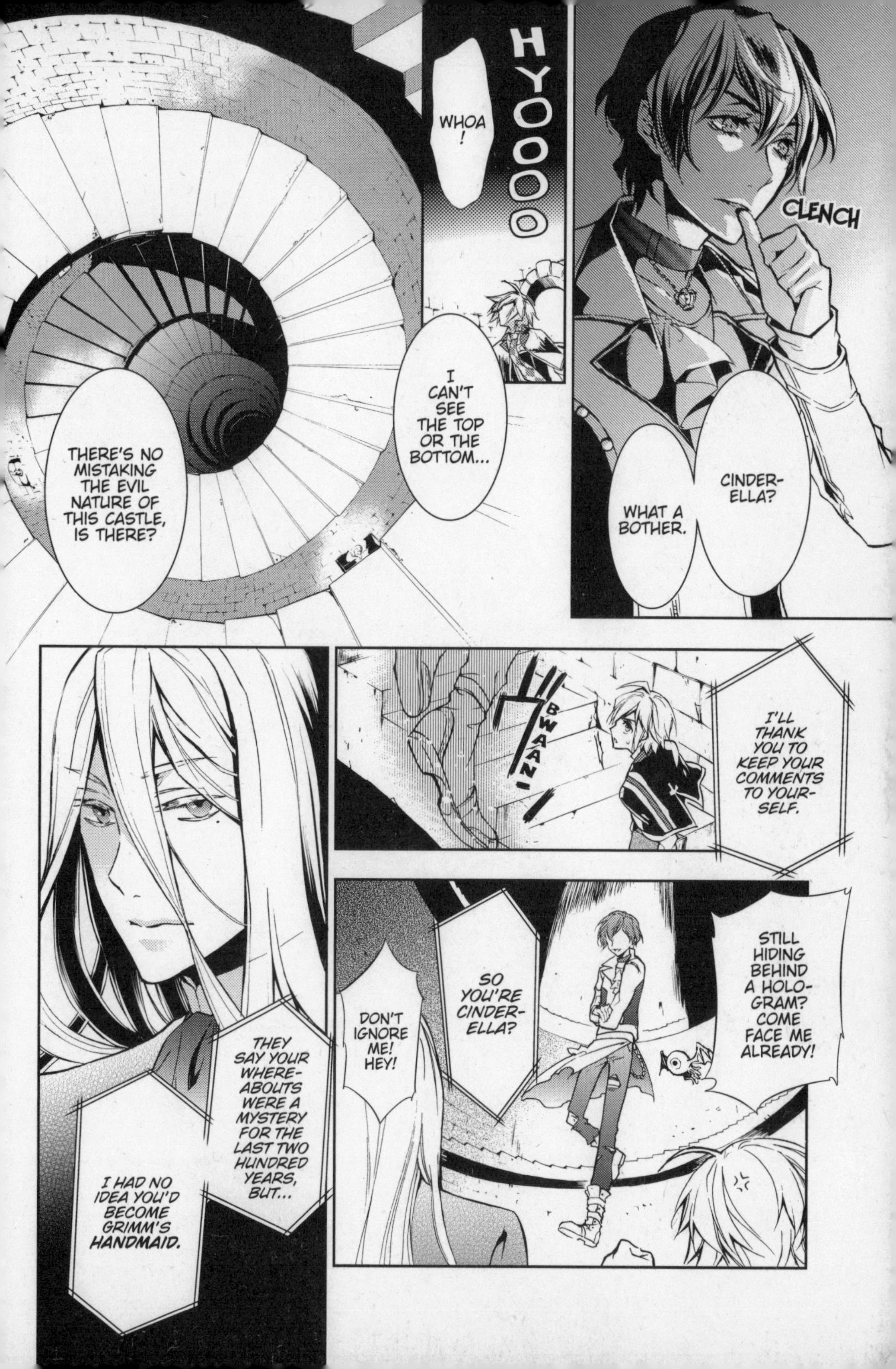
CLENCH
CINDERELLA?
WHAT A BOTHER.
HYOOOO
WHOA!
I CAN'T SEE THE TOP OR THE BOTTOM...
THERE'S NO MISTAKING THE EVIL NATURE OF THIS CASTLE, IS THERE?
BWAAAN
I'LL THANK YOU TO KEEP YOUR COMMENTS TO YOURSELF.
STILL HIDING BEHIND A HOLOGRAM? COME FACE ME ALREADY!
SO YOU'RE CINDERELLA?
DON'T IGNORE ME! HEY!
THEY SAY YOUR WHEREABOUTS WERE A MYSTERY FOR THE LAST TWO HUNDRED YEARS, BUT...
I HAD NO IDEA YOU'D BECOME GRIMM'S HANDMAID.

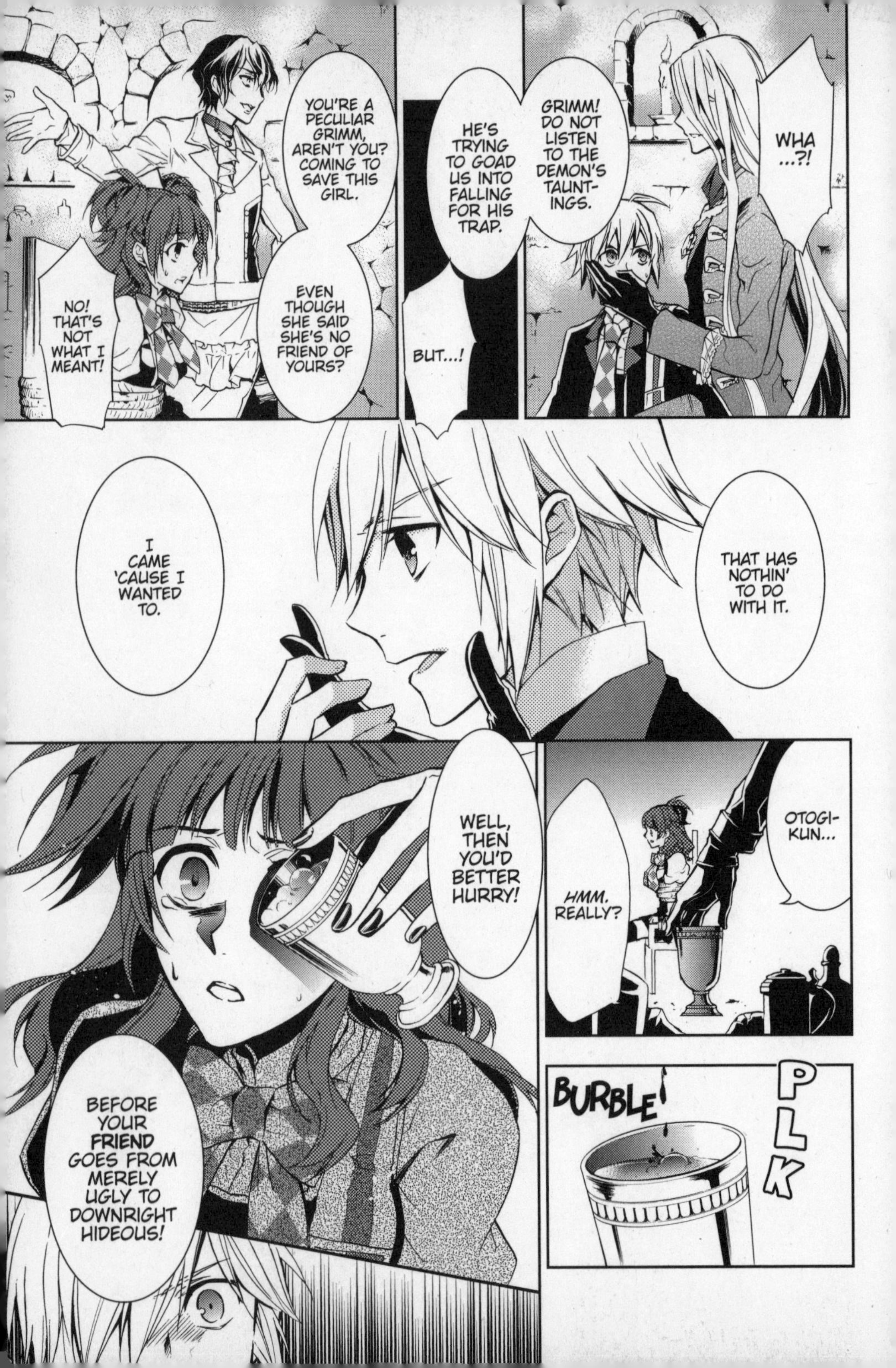
WHA ...?!
GRIMM! DO NOT LISTEN TO THE DEMON'S TAUNT-INGS.
HE'S TRYING TO GOAD US INTO FALLING FOR HIS TRAP.
BUT...!
YOU'RE A PECULIAR GRIMM, AREN'T YOU? COMING TO SAVE THIS GIRL.
EVEN THOUGH SHE SAID SHE'S NO FRIEND OF YOURS?
NO! THAT'S NOT WHAT I MEANT!
THAT HAS NOTHIN' TO DO WITH IT.
I CAME 'CAUSE I WANTED TO.
OTOGI-KUN...
HMM. REALLY?
PLK
BURBLE
WELL, THEN YOU'D BETTER HURRY!
BEFORE YOUR FRIEND GOES FROM MERELY UGLY TO DOWNRIGHT HIDEOUS!

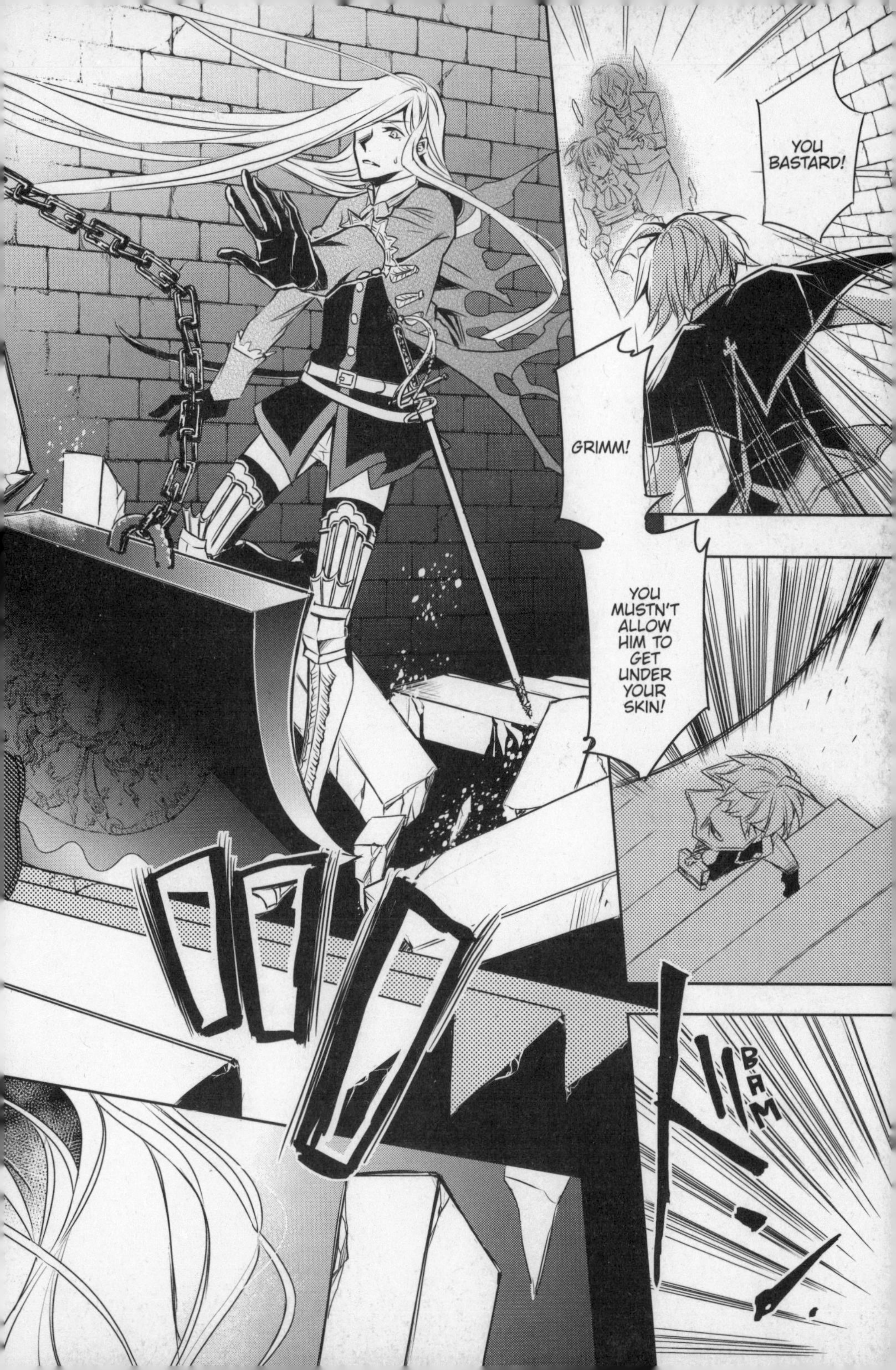
YOU BASTARD!
GRIMM!
YOU MUSTN'T ALLOW HIM TO GET UNDER YOUR SKIN!
BAM

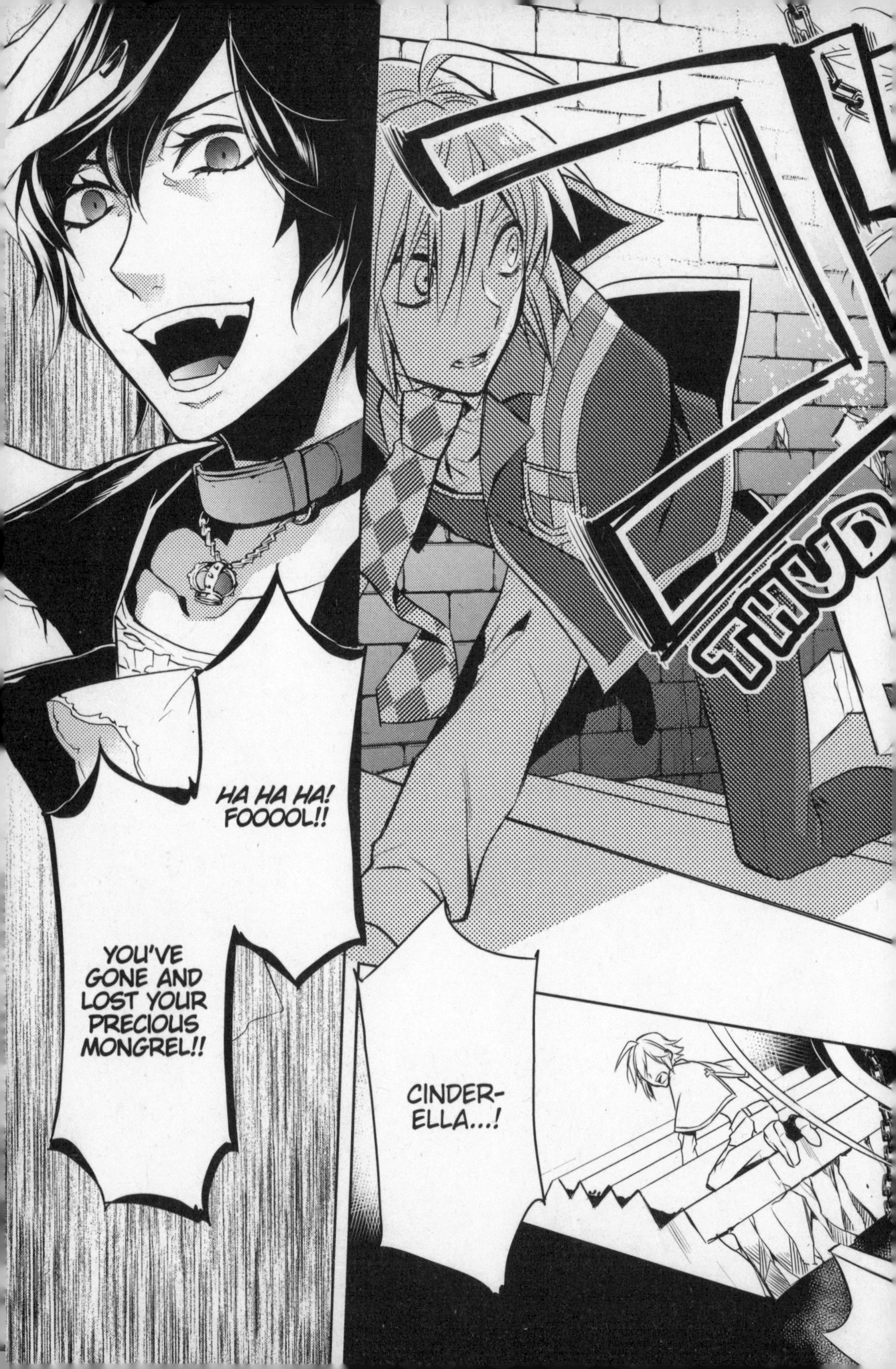
THUD
CINDER-ELLA...!
HA HA HA! FOOOOL!!
YOU'VE GONE AND LOST YOUR PRECIOUS MONGREL!!

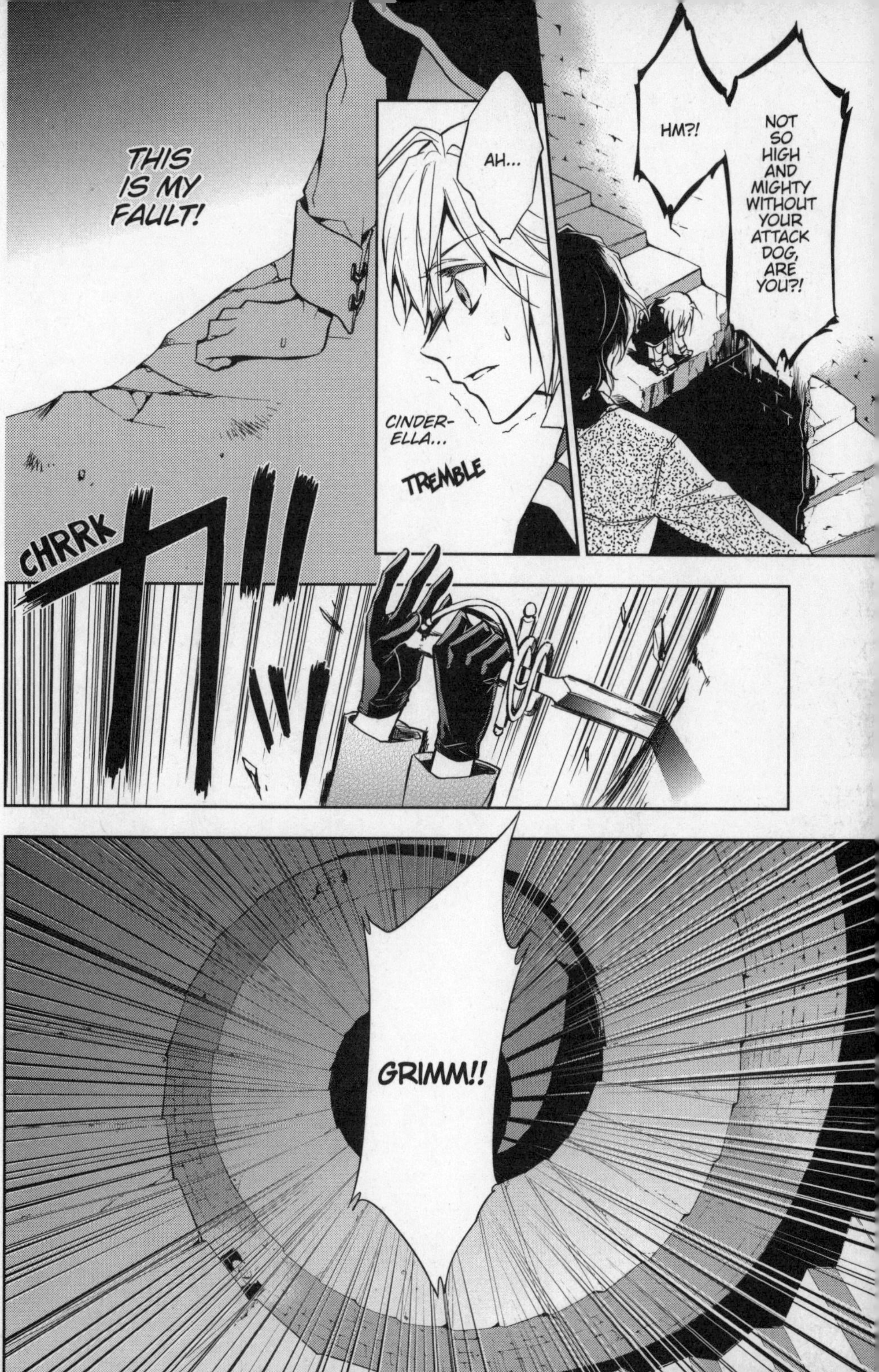
NOT SO HIGH AND MIGHTY WITHOUT YOUR ATTACK DOG, ARE YOU?!
HM?!
AH...
CINDER-ELLA...
TREMBLE
THIS IS MY FAULT!
CHRRK
GRIMM!!

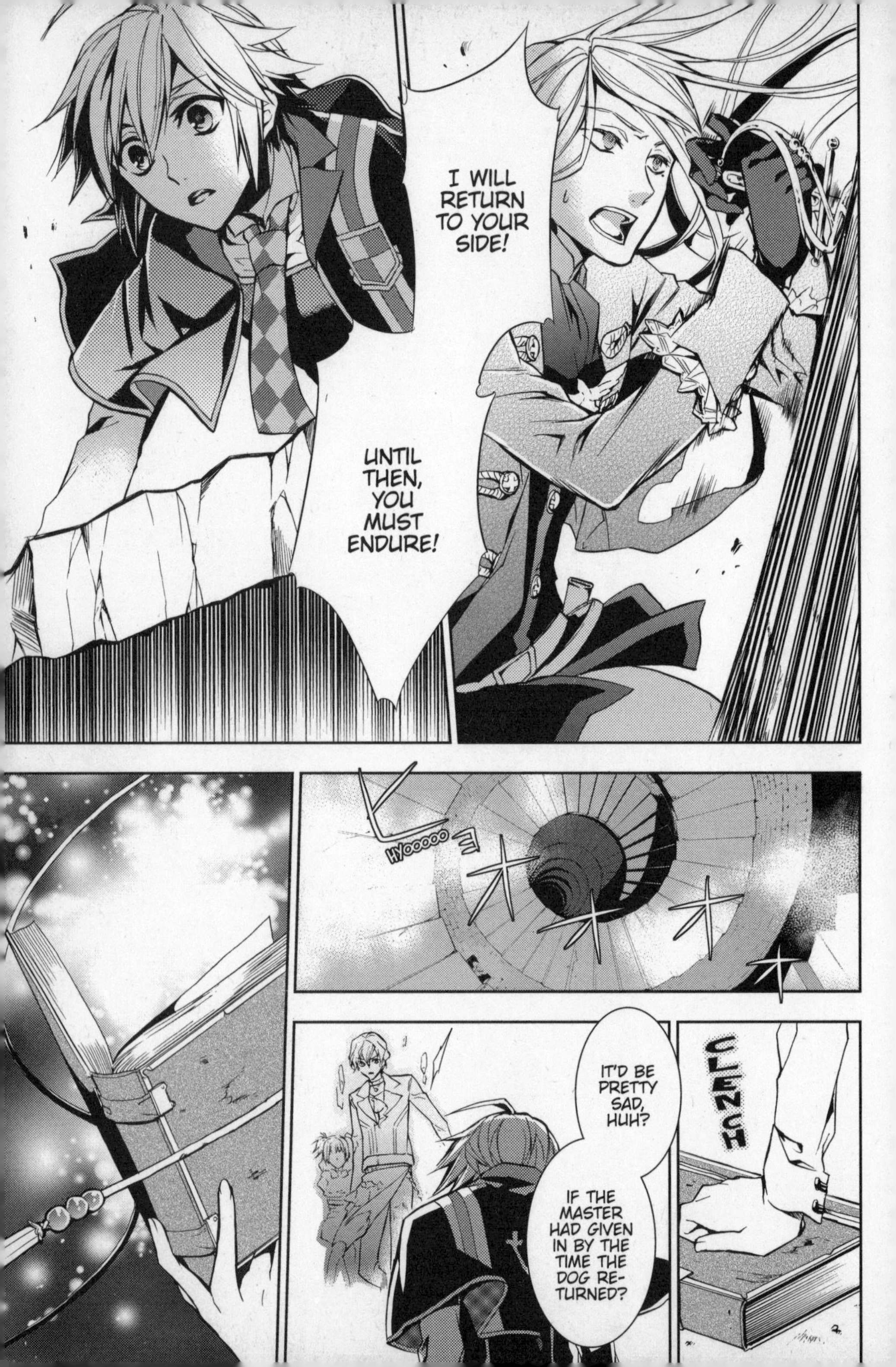
I WILL RETURN TO YOUR SIDE!
UNTIL THEN, YOU MUST ENDURE!
HYOOOOO
CLENCH
IT'D BE PRETTY SAD, HUH?
IF THE MASTER HAD GIVEN IN BY THE TIME THE DOG RE-TURNED?

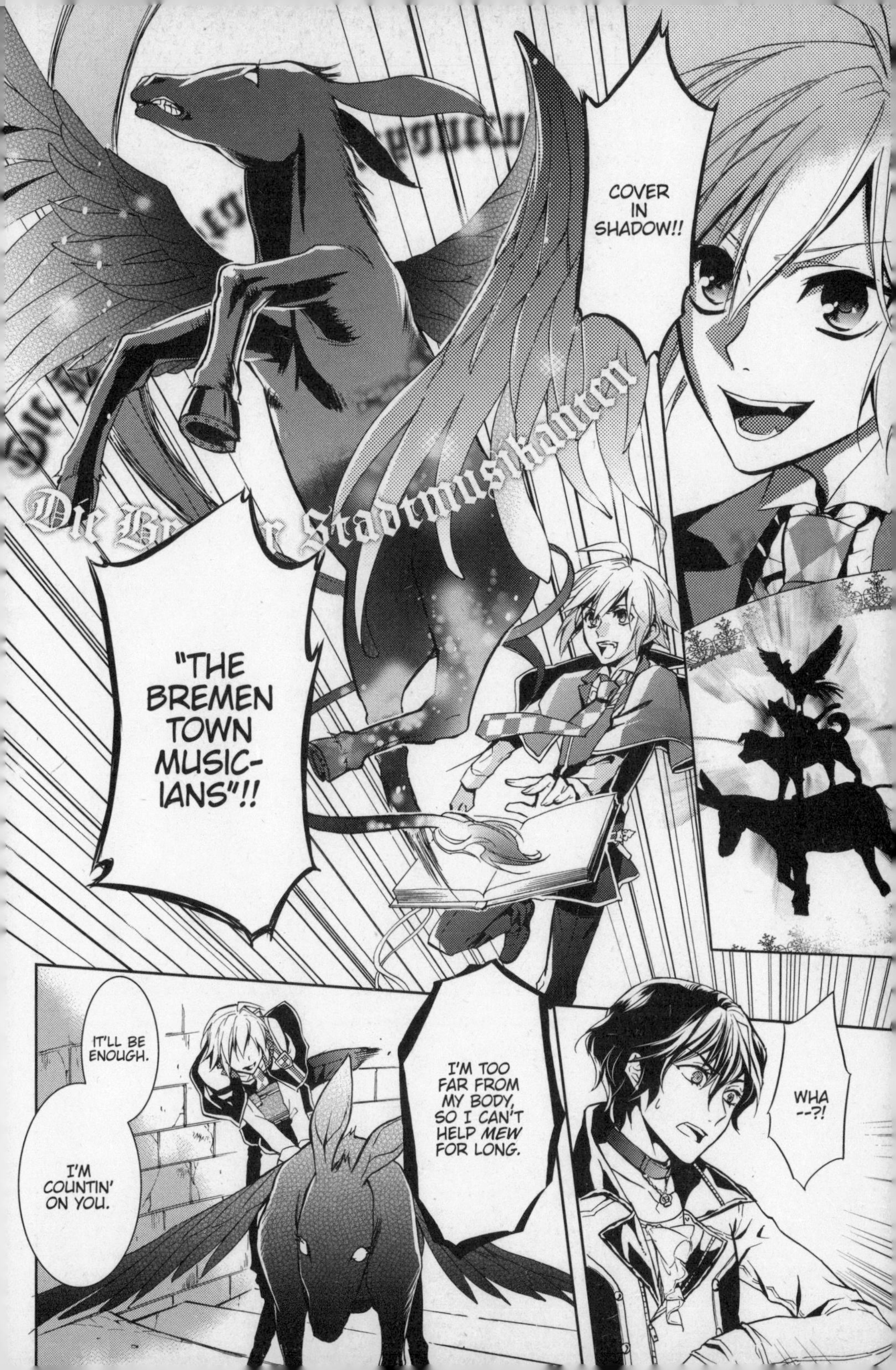
COVER IN SHADOW!!
"THE BREMEN TOWN MUSIC-IANS"!!
WHA--?!
I'M TOO FAR FROM MY BODY, SO I CAN'T HELP *MEW* FOR LONG.
IT'LL BE ENOUGH.
I'M COUNTIN' ON YOU.

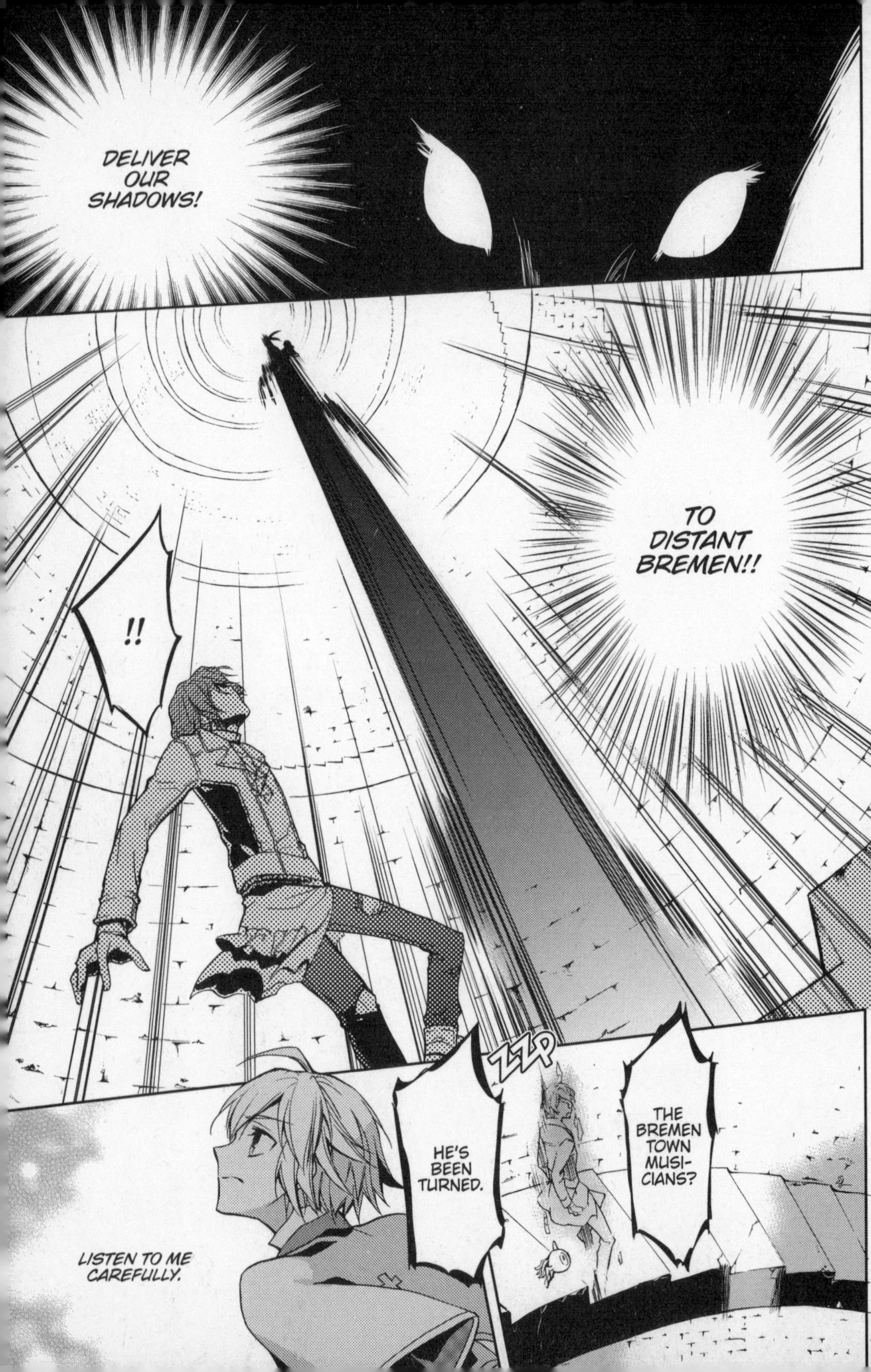
DELIVER OUR SHADOWS!
TO DISTANT BREMEN!!
!!
THE BREMEN TOWN MUSI-CIANS?
ZZP
HE'S BEEN TURNED.
LISTEN TO ME CAREFULLY.

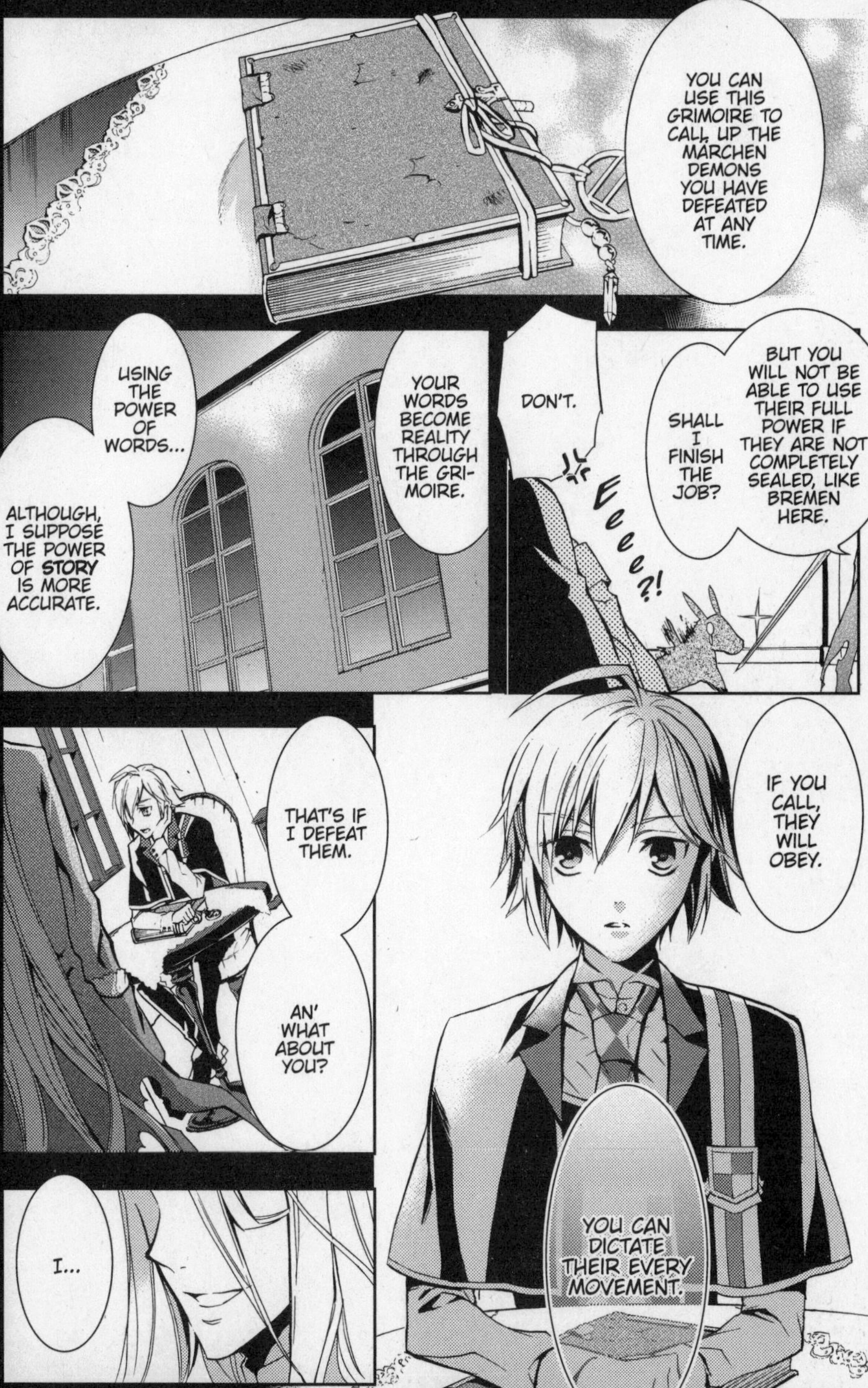
YOU CAN USE THIS GRIMOIRE TO CALL UP THE MÄRCHEN DEMONS YOU HAVE DEFEATED AT ANY TIME.
BUT YOU WILL NOT BE ABLE TO USE THEIR FULL POWER IF THEY ARE NOT COMPLETELY SEALED, LIKE BREMEN HERE.
SHALL I FINISH THE JOB?
DON'T.
Eeee?!
YOUR WORDS BECOME REALITY THROUGH THE GRI-MOIRE.
USING THE POWER OF WORDS...
ALTHOUGH, I SUPPOSE THE POWER OF **STORY** IS MORE ACCURATE.
IF YOU CALL, THEY WILL OBEY.
YOU CAN DICTATE THEIR EVERY MOVEMENT.
THAT'S IF I DEFEAT THEM.
AN' WHAT ABOUT YOU?
I...

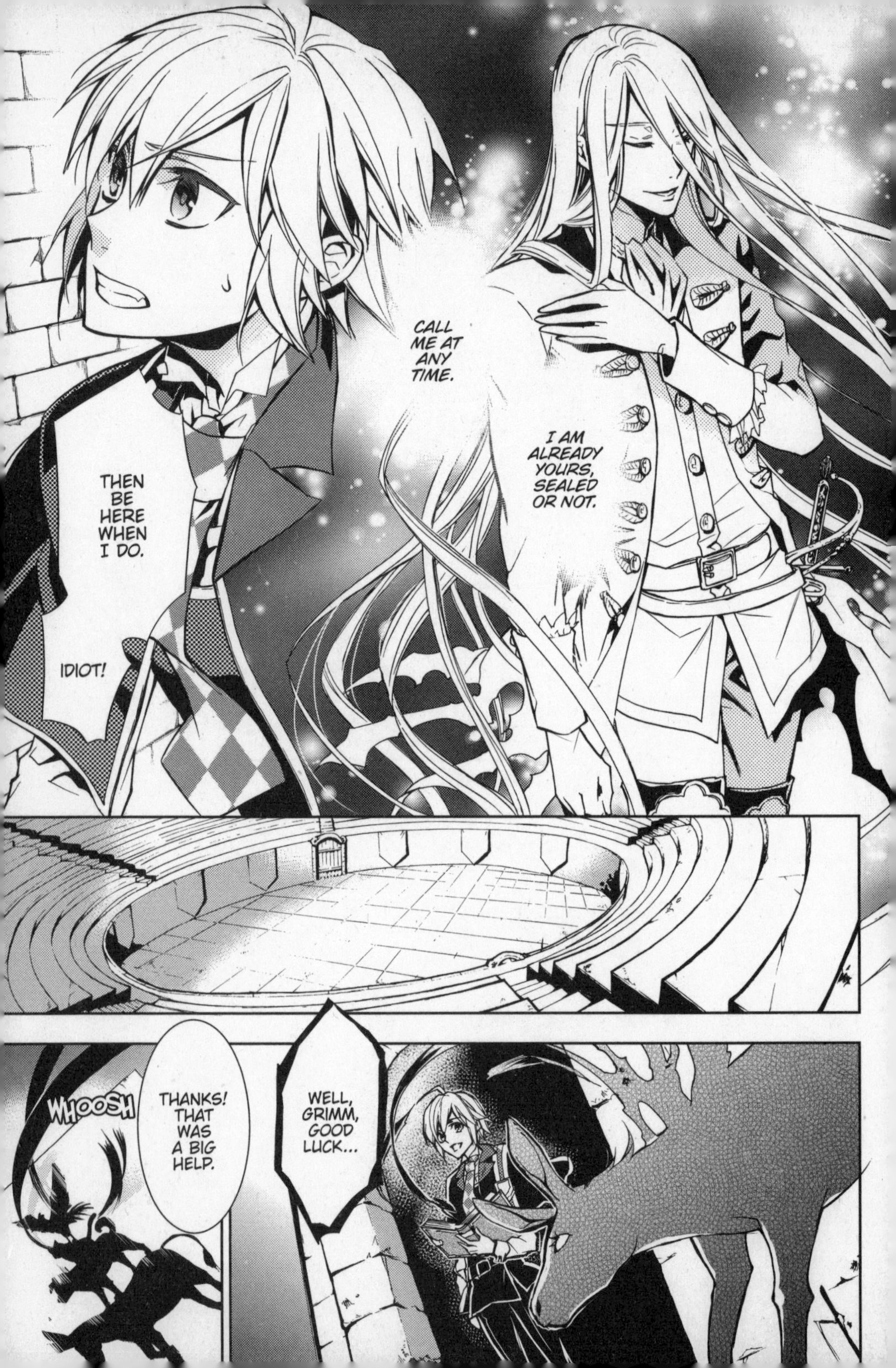
CALL ME AT ANY TIME.
I AM ALREADY YOURS, SEALED OR NOT.
THEN BE HERE WHEN I DO.
IDIOT!
WELL, GRIMM, GOOD LUCK...
THANKS! THAT WAS A BIG HELP.
WHOOSH

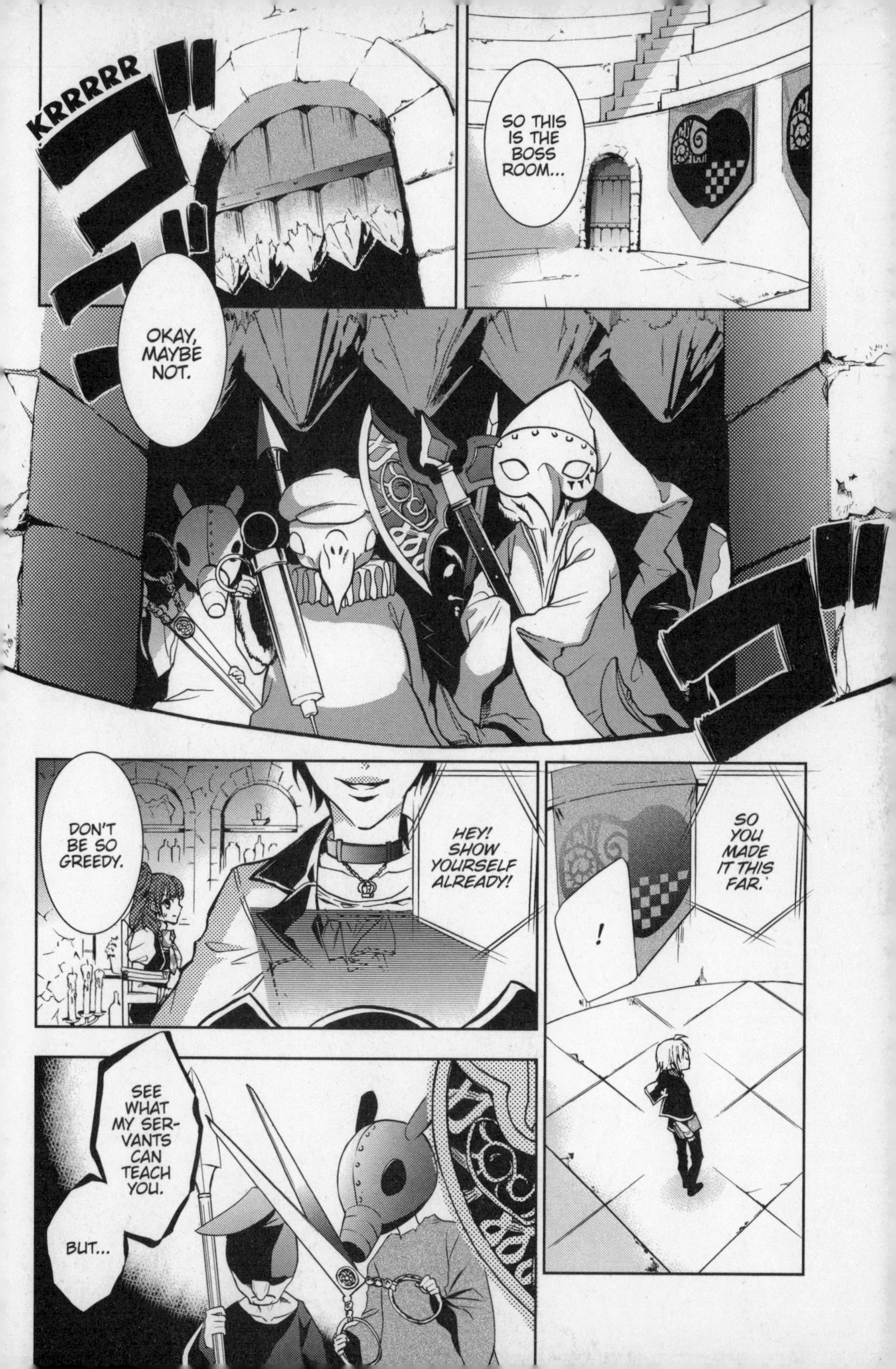
SO THIS IS THE BOSS ROOM...
KRRRRR
OKAY, MAYBE NOT.
SO YOU MADE IT THIS FAR.
!
HEY! SHOW YOURSELF ALREADY!
DON'T BE SO GREEDY.
SEE WHAT MY SER-VANTS CAN TEACH YOU.
BUT...

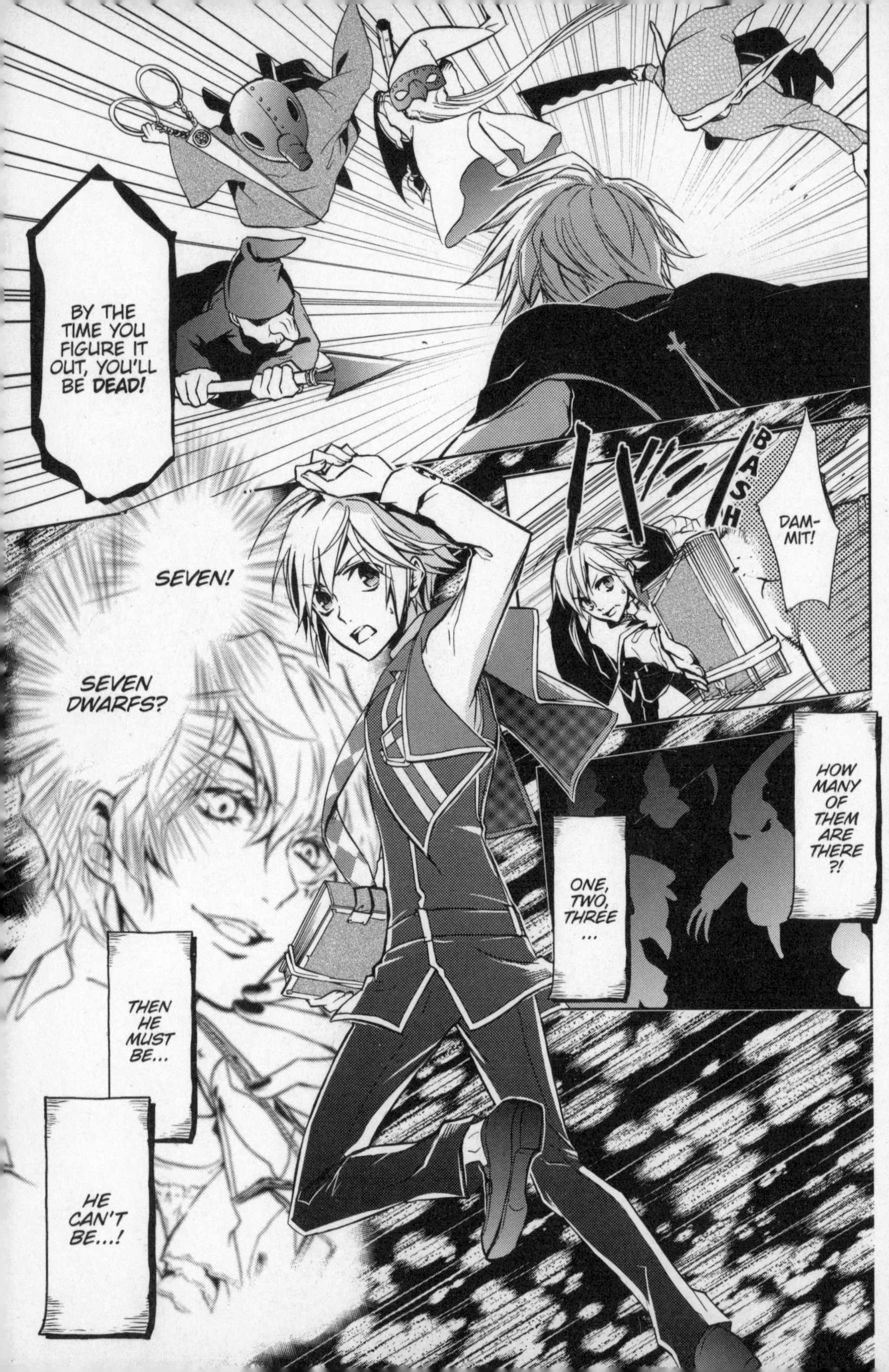

BY THE TIME YOU FIGURE IT OUT, YOU'LL BE DEAD!
BASH
DAM-MIT!
HOW MANY OF THEM ARE THERE?!
ONE, TWO, THREE...
SEVEN!
SEVEN DWARFS?
THEN HE MUST BE...
HE CAN'T BE...!

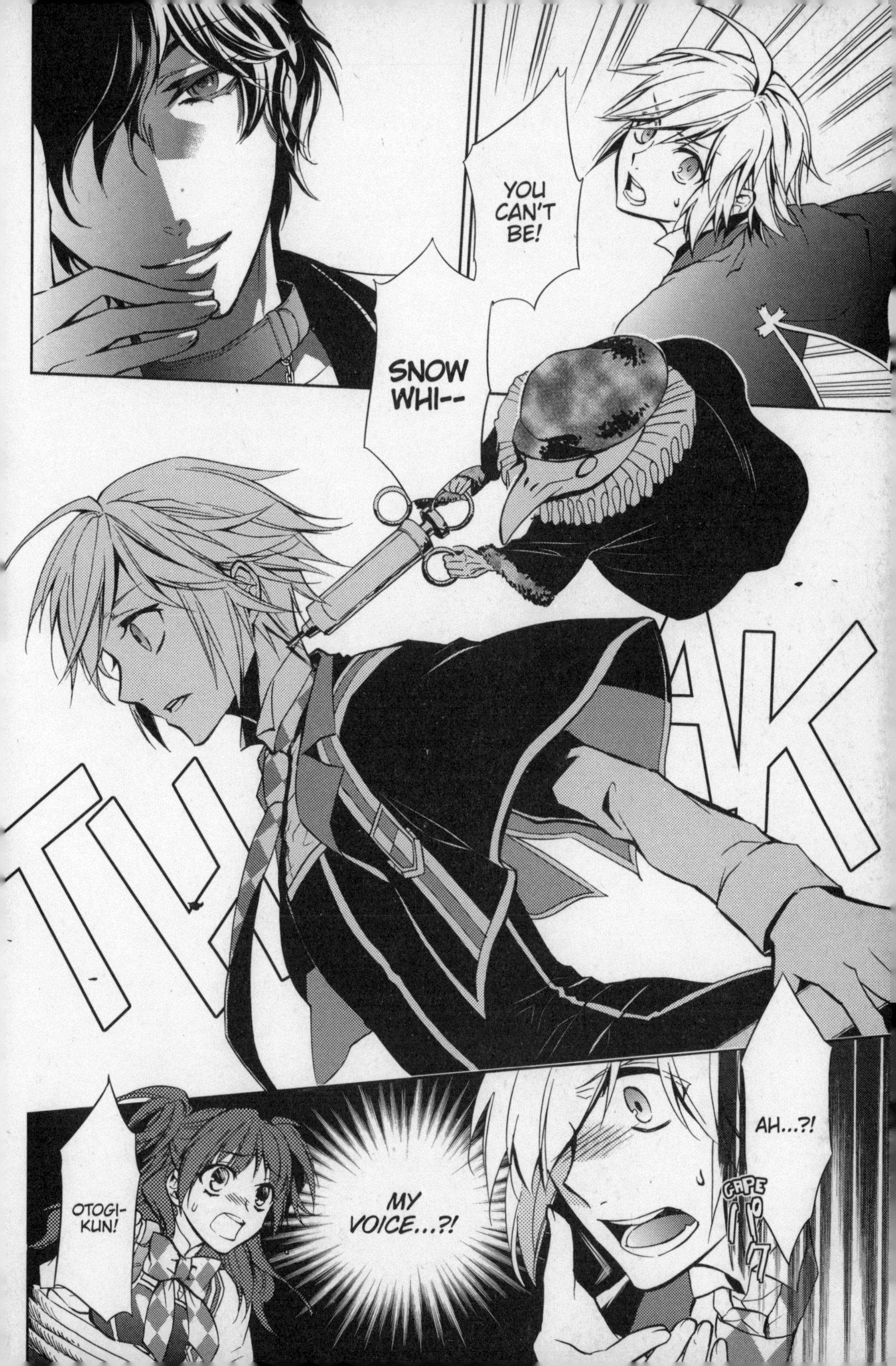
YOU CAN'T BE!
SNOW WHI--
AH...?!
GAPE
MY VOICE...?!
OTOGI-KUN!

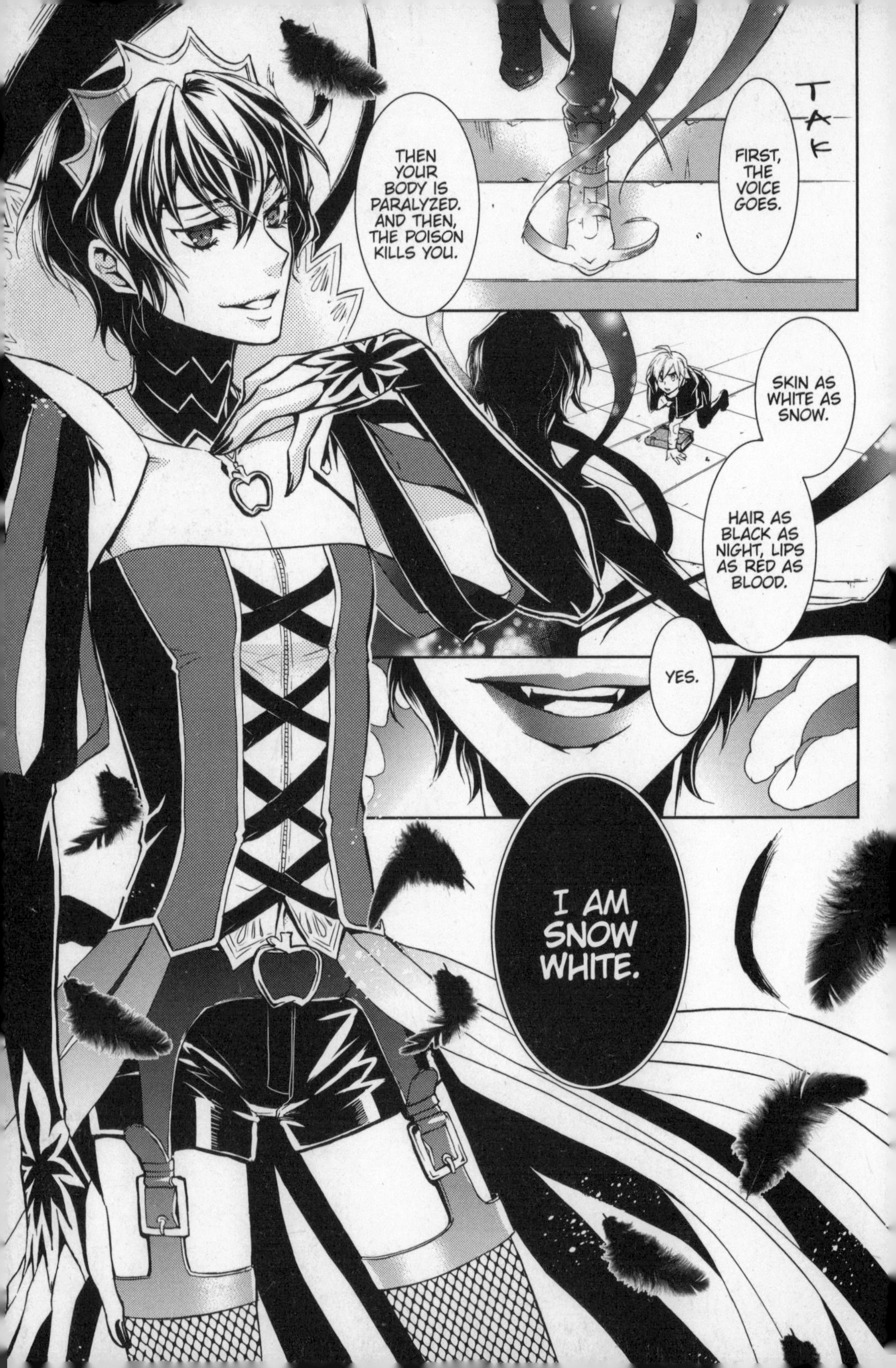
TAK
FIRST, THE VOICE GOES.
THEN YOUR BODY IS PARALYZED. AND THEN, THE POISON KILLS YOU.
SKIN AS WHITE AS SNOW.
HAIR AS BLACK AS NIGHT, LIPS AS RED AS BLOOD.
YES.
I AM SNOW WHITE.

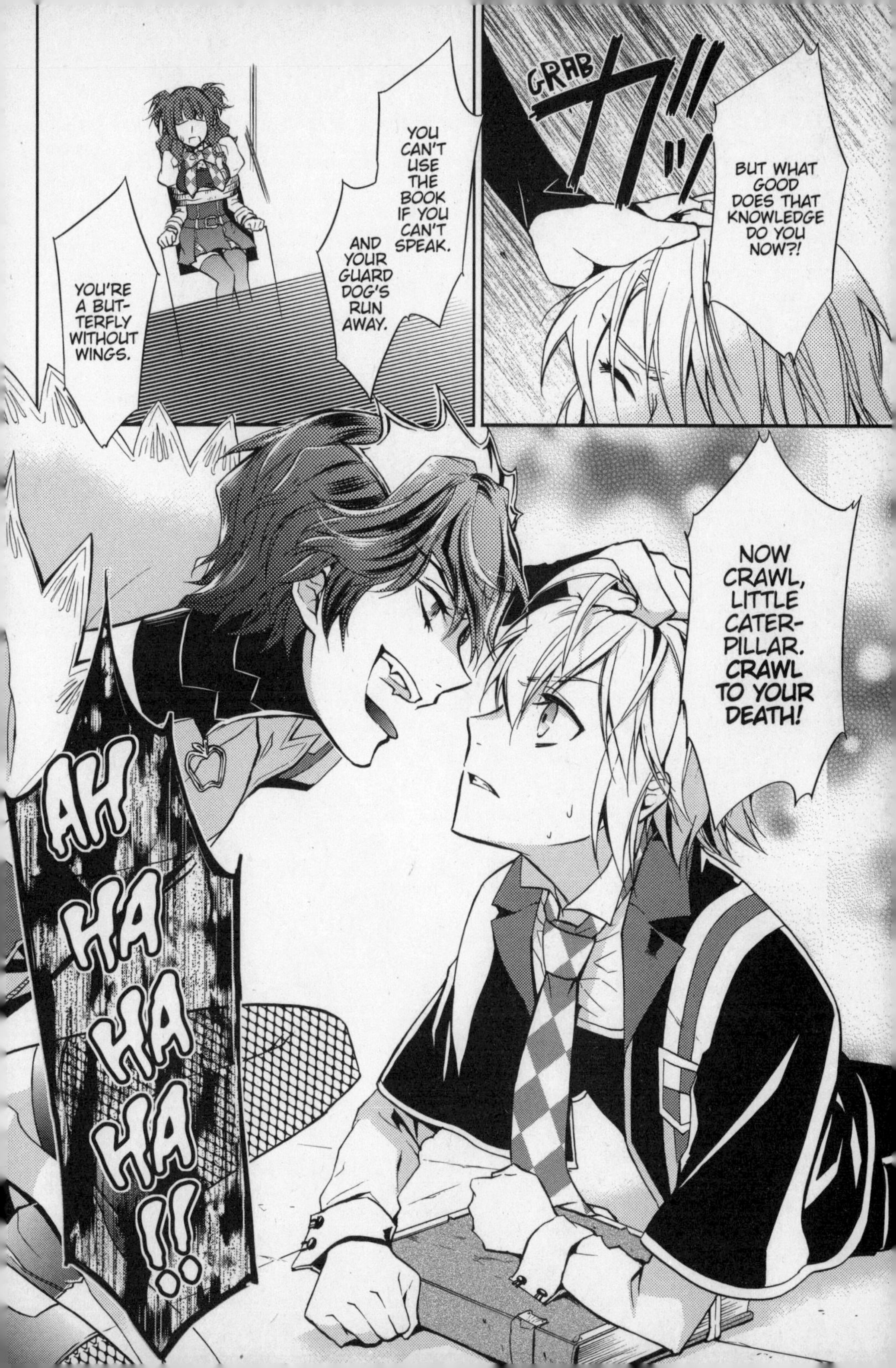
GRAB
BUT WHAT GOOD DOES THAT KNOWLEDGE DO YOU NOW?!
YOU CAN'T USE THE BOOK IF YOU CAN'T SPEAK.
AND YOUR GUARD DOG'S RUN AWAY.
YOU'RE A BUTTERFLY WITHOUT WINGS.
NOW CRAWL, LITTLE CATERPILLAR. CRAWL TO YOUR DEATH!
AH HA HA HA!!

Dictatorial Grimoire

独裁グリムワール

Dictatorial Grimoire

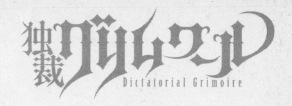

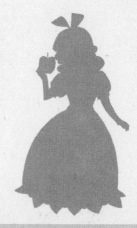

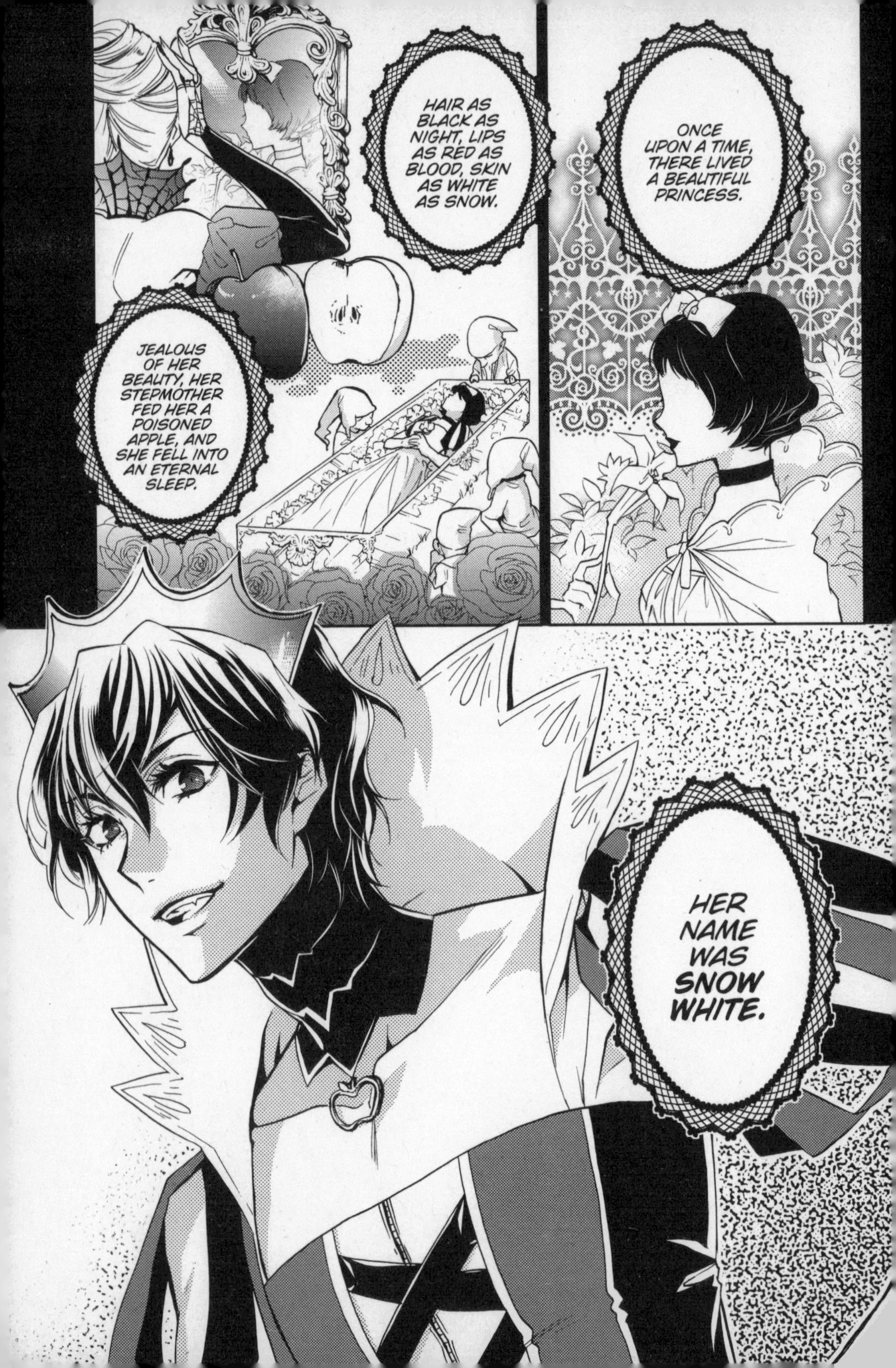
ONCE UPON A TIME, THERE LIVED A BEAUTIFUL PRINCESS.
HAIR AS BLACK AS NIGHT, LIPS AS RED AS BLOOD, SKIN AS WHITE AS SNOW.
JEALOUS OF HER BEAUTY, HER STEPMOTHER FED HER A POISONED APPLE, AND SHE FELL INTO AN ETERNAL SLEEP.
HER NAME WAS SNOW WHITE.

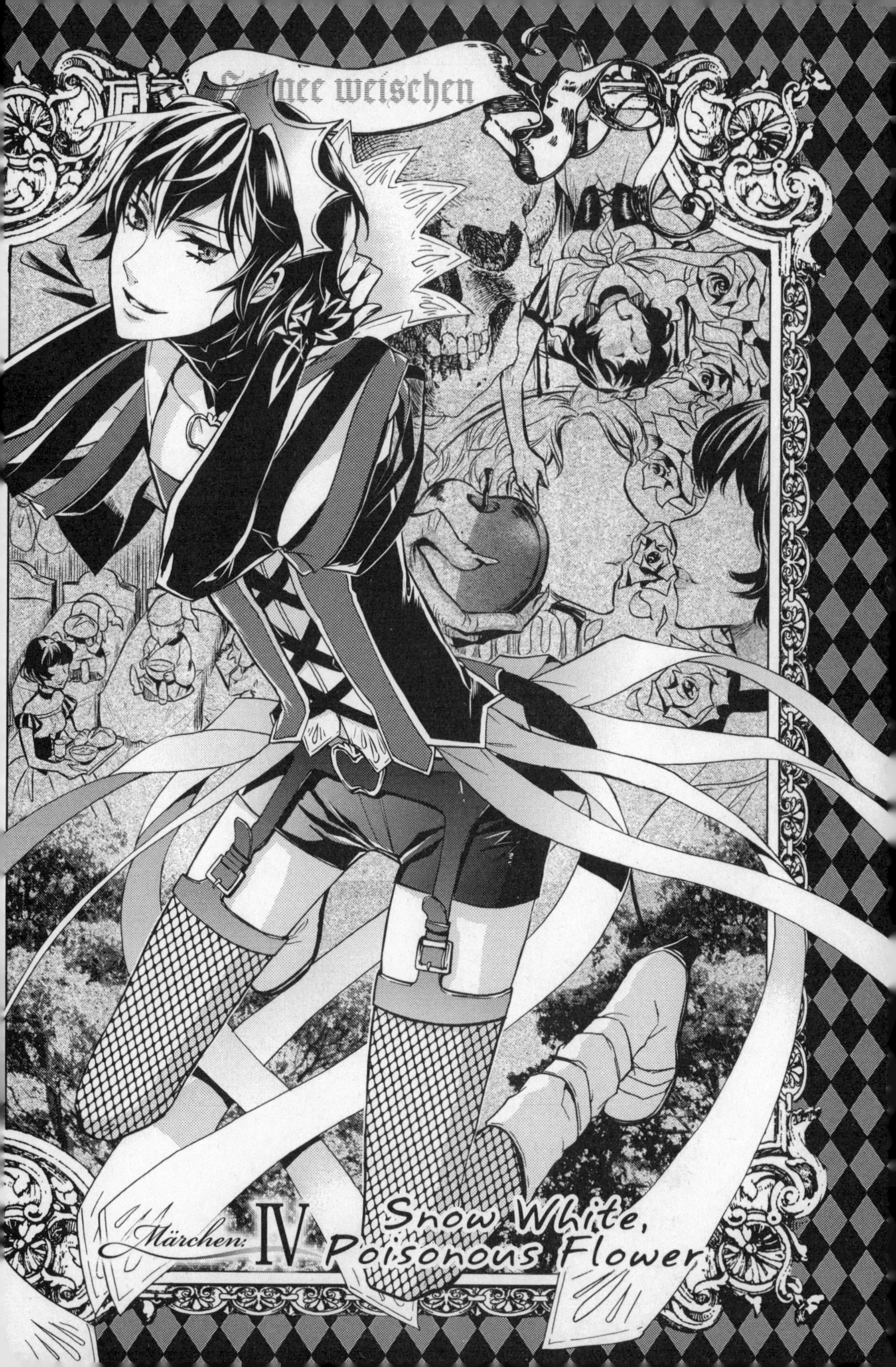

nee weischen
Märchen: IV
Snow White,
Poisonous Flower

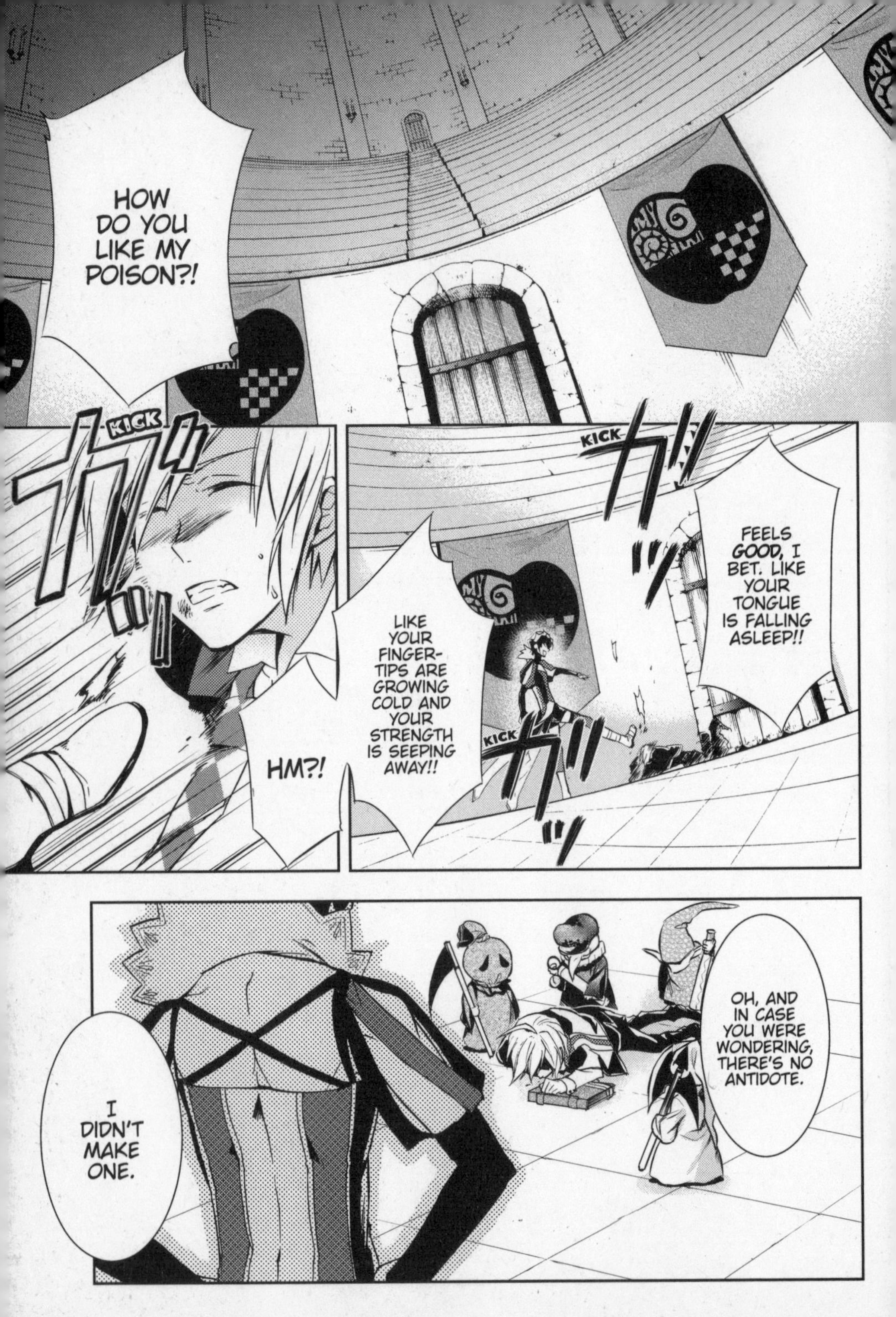
HOW DO YOU LIKE MY POISON?!
KICK
FEELS GOOD, I BET. LIKE YOUR TONGUE IS FALLING ASLEEP!!
LIKE YOUR FINGER-TIPS ARE GROWING COLD AND YOUR STRENGTH IS SEEPING AWAY!!
KICK
KICK
HM?!
OH, AND IN CASE YOU WERE WONDERING, THERE'S NO ANTIDOTE.
I DIDN'T MAKE ONE.

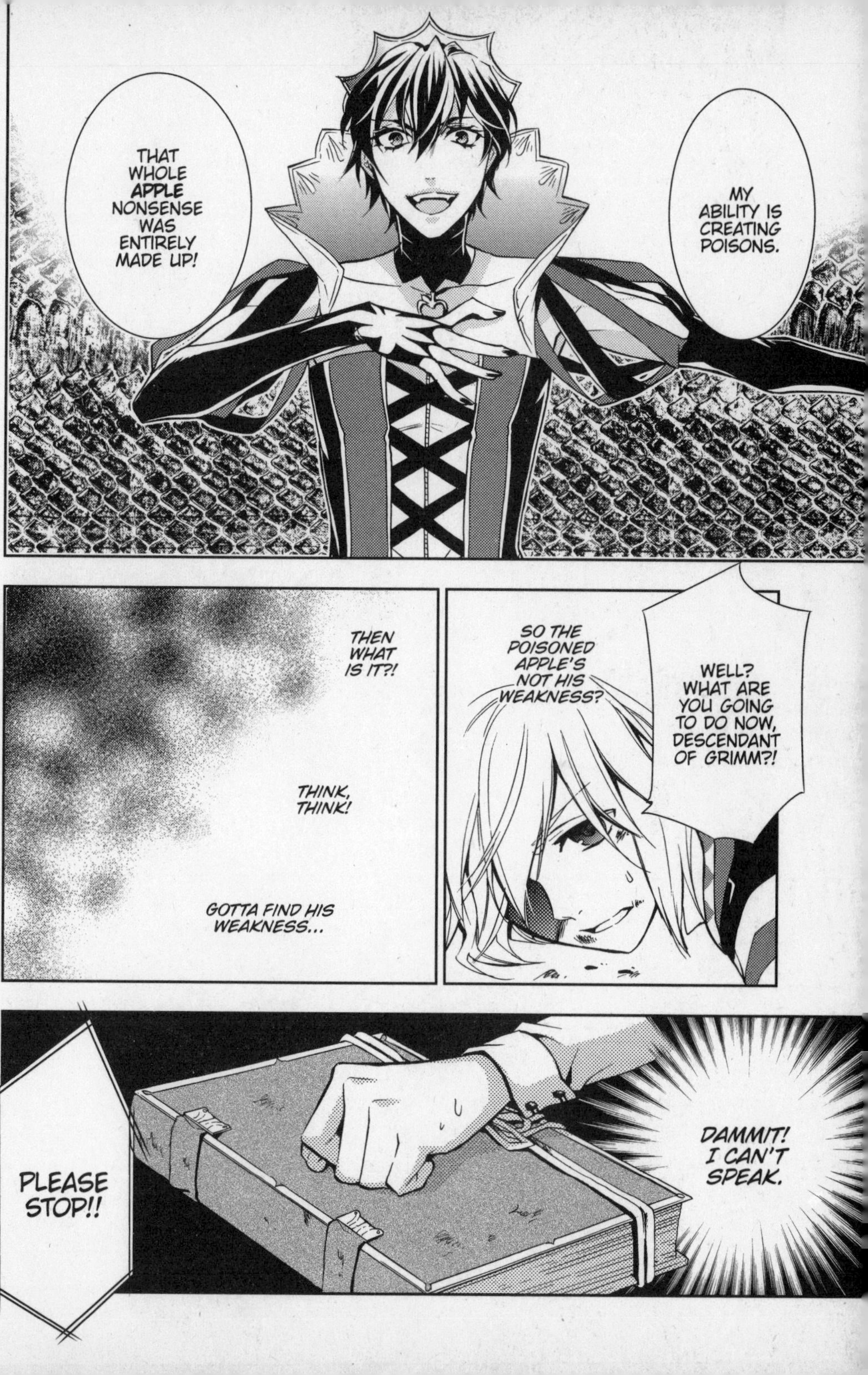
MY ABILITY IS CREATING POISONS.
THAT WHOLE APPLE NONSENSE WAS ENTIRELY MADE UP!
WELL? WHAT ARE YOU GOING TO DO NOW, DESCENDANT OF GRIMM?!
SO THE POISONED APPLE'S NOT HIS WEAKNESS?
THEN WHAT IS IT?!
THINK, THINK!
GOTTA FIND HIS WEAKNESS...
DAMMIT! I CAN'T SPEAK.
PLEASE STOP!!

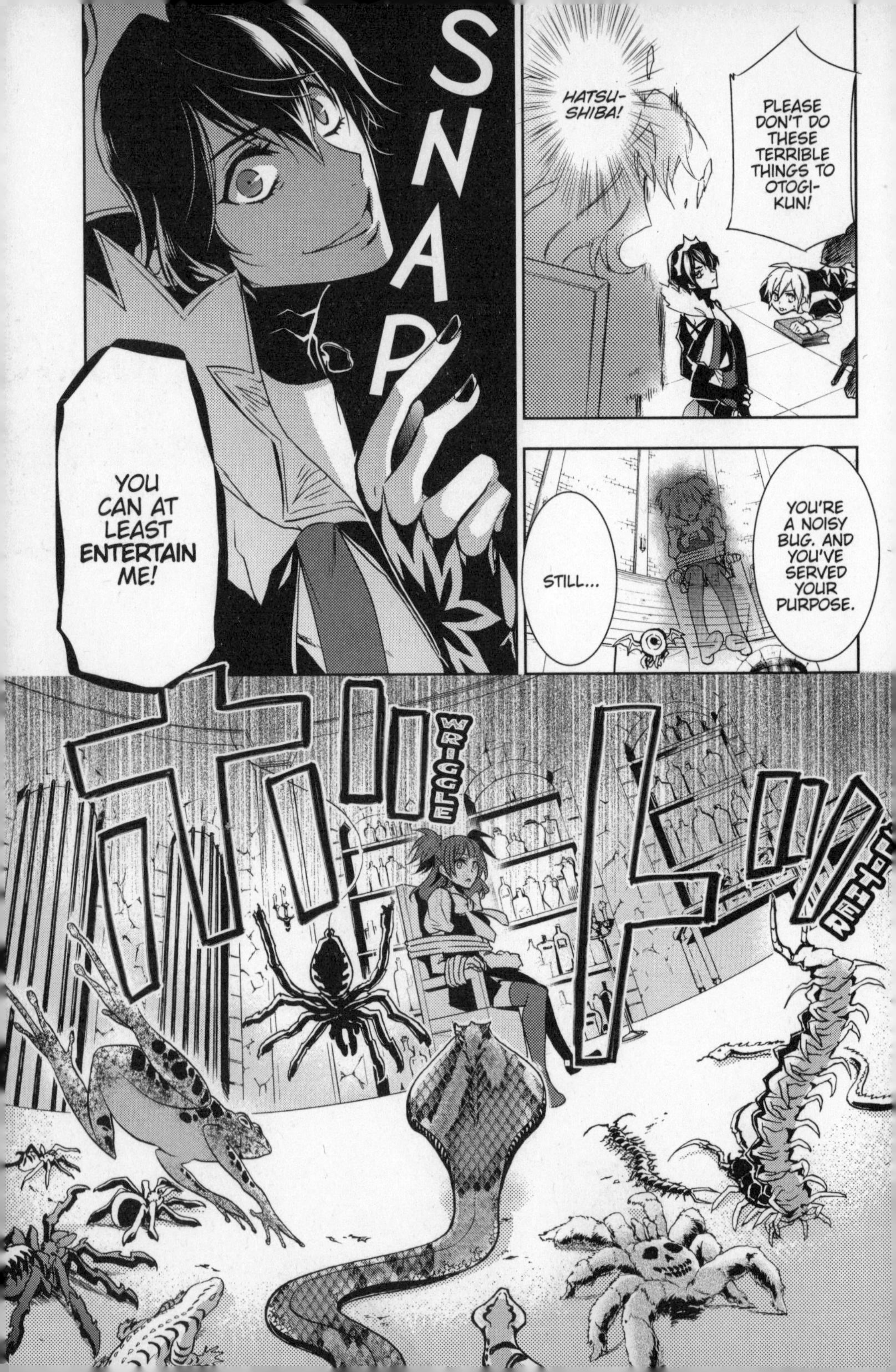
PLEASE DON'T DO THESE TERRIBLE THINGS TO OTOGI-KUN!
HATSU-SHIBA!
YOU'RE A NOISY BUG. AND YOU'VE SERVED YOUR PURPOSE.
STILL...
SNAP
YOU CAN AT LEAST ENTERTAIN ME!
WRIGGLE

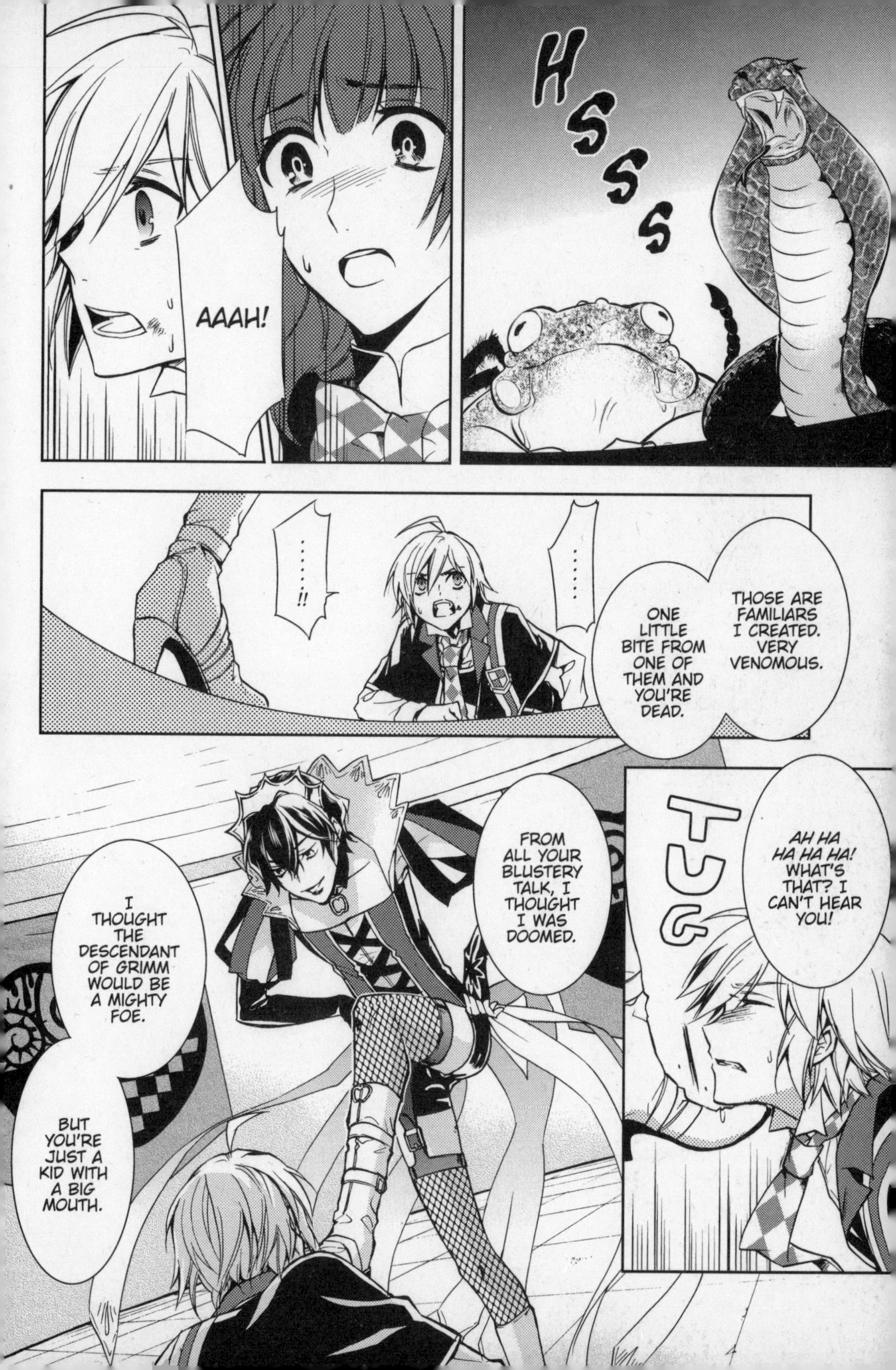
HSSSS
AAAH!
THOSE ARE FAMILIARS I CREATED. VERY VENOMOUS.
ONE LITTLE BITE FROM ONE OF THEM AND YOU'RE DEAD.
......
......!!
AH HA HA HA HA! WHAT'S THAT? I CAN'T HEAR YOU!
TUG
FROM ALL YOUR BLUSTERY TALK, I THOUGHT I WAS DOOMED.
I THOUGHT THE DESCENDANT OF GRIMM WOULD BE A MIGHTY FOE.
BUT YOU'RE JUST A KID WITH A BIG MOUTH.

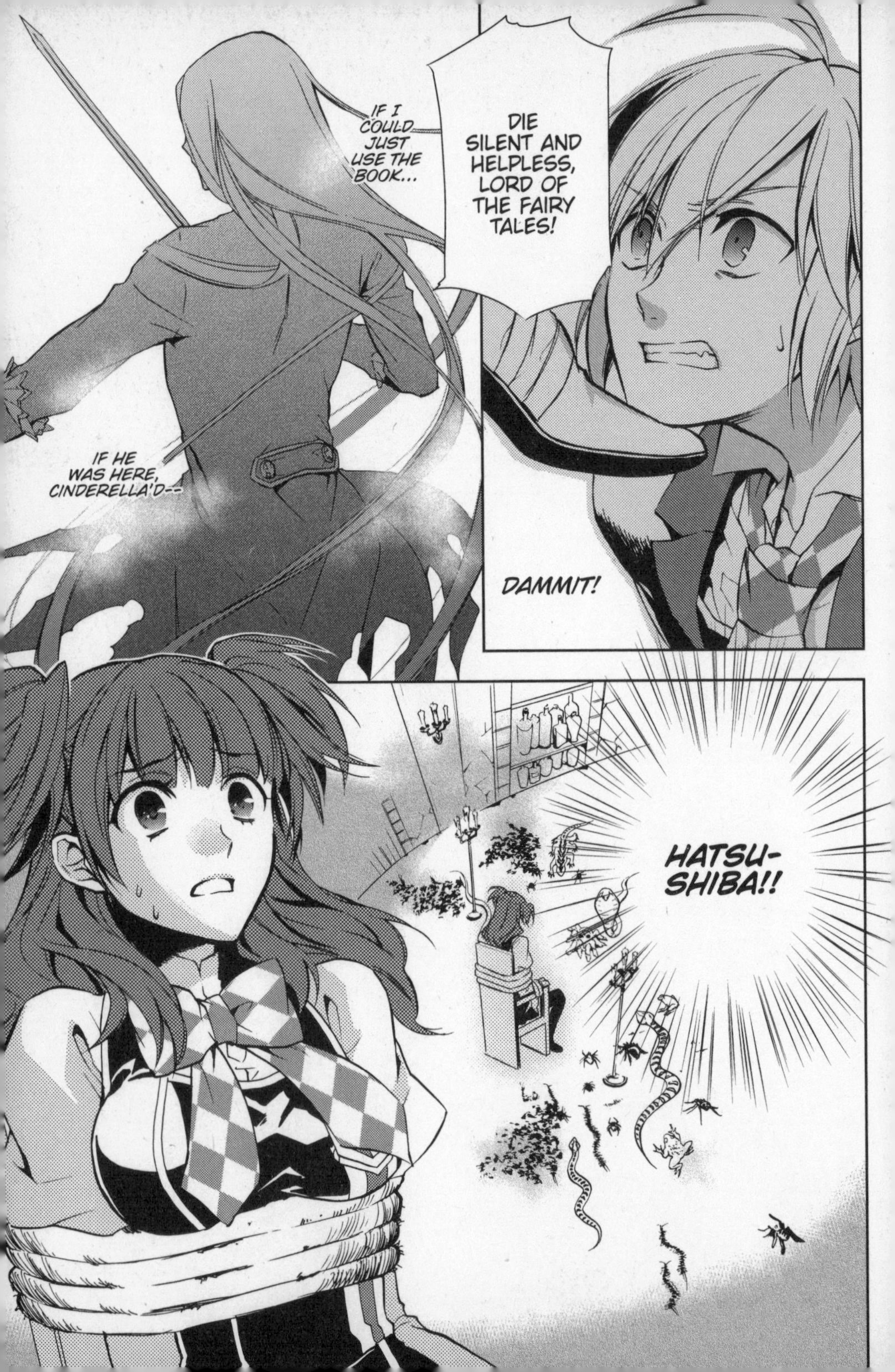
DIE SILENT AND HELPLESS, LORD OF THE FAIRY TALES!
DAMMIT!
IF I COULD JUST USE THE BOOK...
IF HE WAS HERE, CINDERELLA'D--
HATSU-SHIBA!!

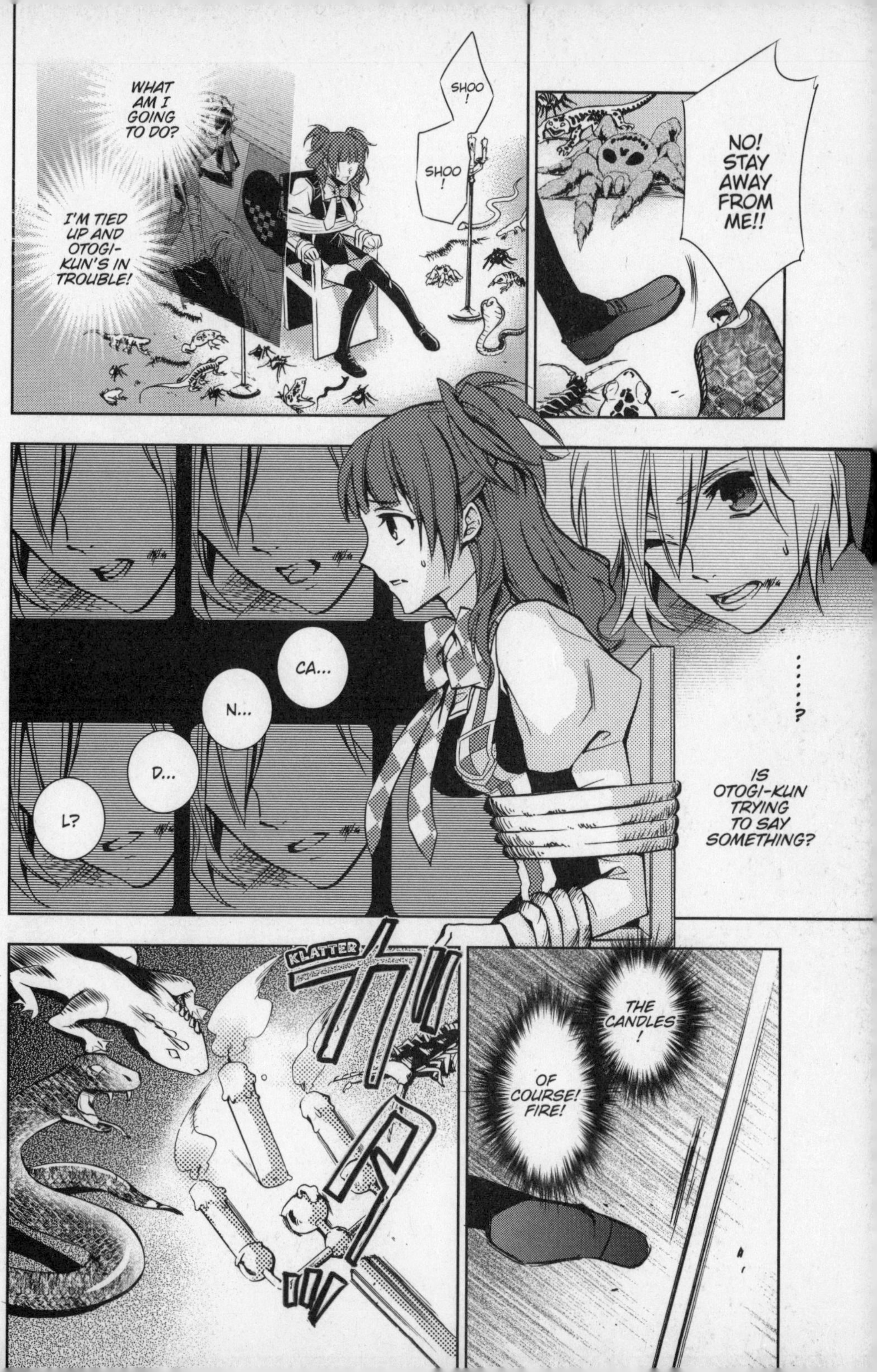
NO! STAY AWAY FROM ME!!
SHOO!
SHOO!
WHAT AM I GOING TO DO?
I'M TIED UP AND OTOGI-KUN'S IN TROUBLE!
......?
IS OTOGI-KUN TRYING TO SAY SOMETHING?
CA...
N...
D...
L?
THE CANDLES!
OF COURSE! FIRE!
KLATTER

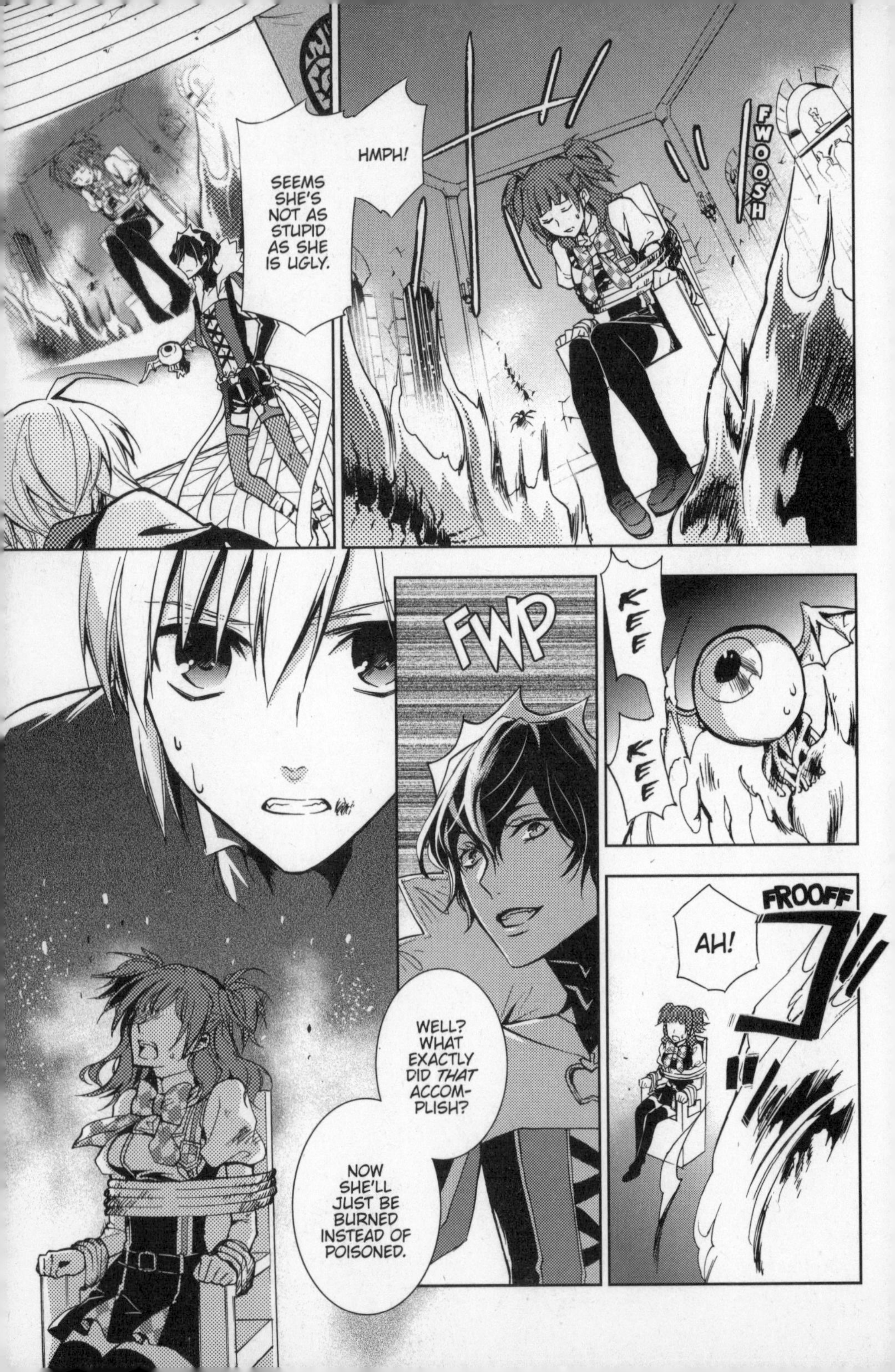
FWOOSH
HMPH!
SEEMS SHE'S NOT AS STUPID AS SHE IS UGLY.
KEE KEE
FROOFF
AH!
FWP
WELL? WHAT EXACTLY DID *THAT* ACCOMPLISH?
NOW SHE'LL JUST BE BURNED INSTEAD OF POISONED.

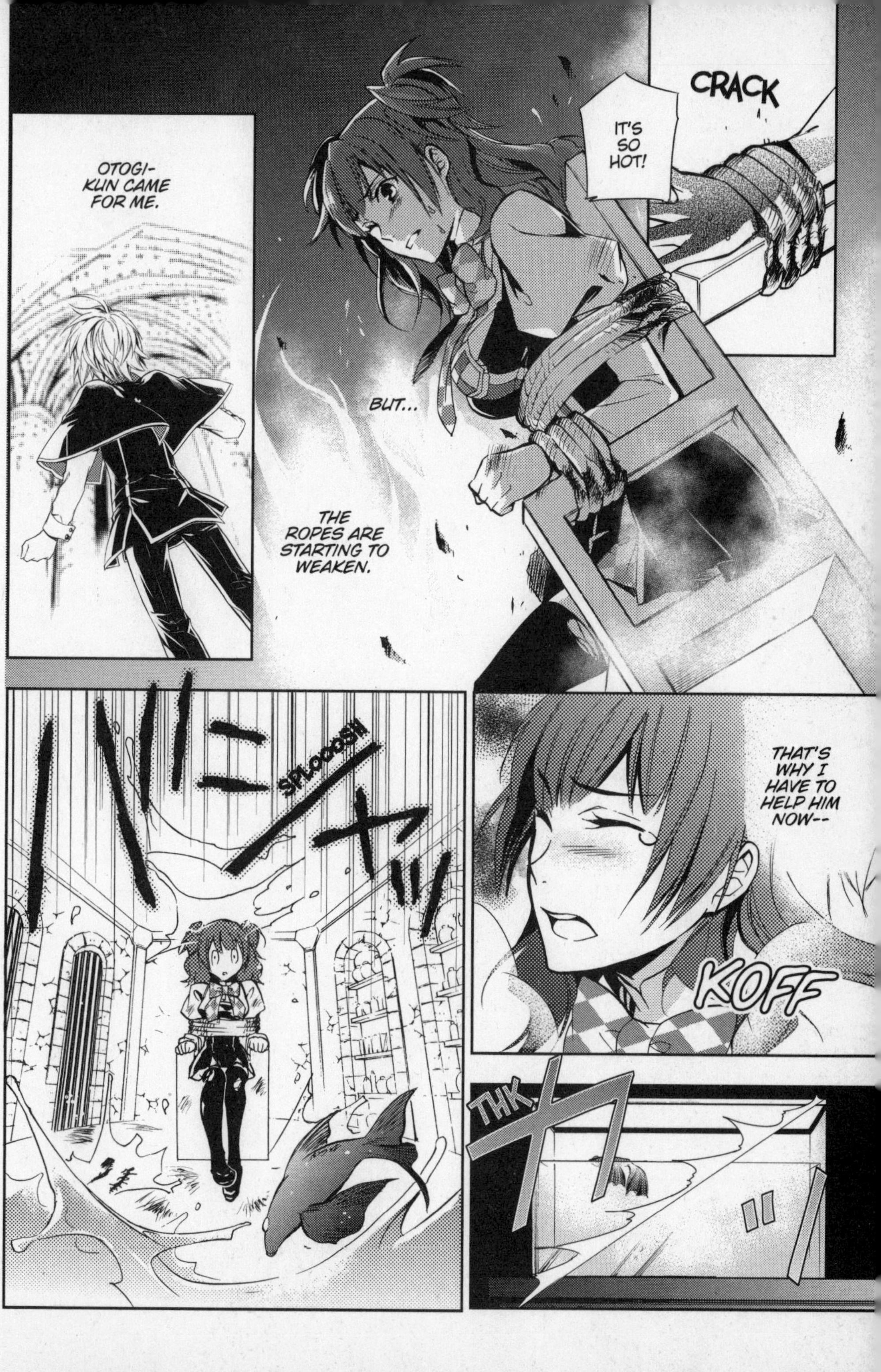
CRACK
IT'S SO HOT!
BUT...
THE ROPES ARE STARTING TO WEAKEN.
OTOGI-KUN CAME FOR ME.
THAT'S WHY I HAVE TO HELP HIM NOW--
KOFF
THK
SPLOOOSH

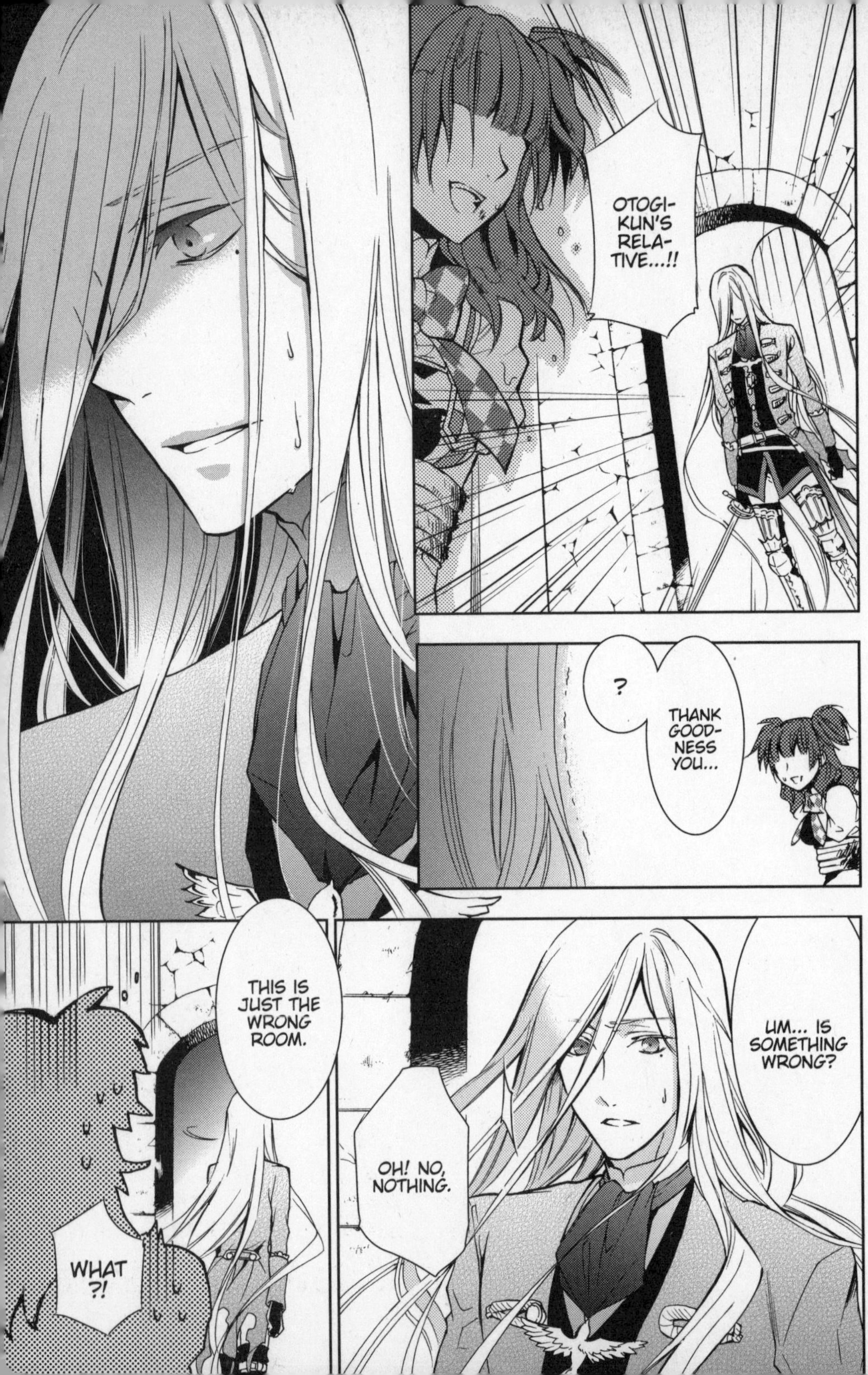
OTOGI-KUN'S RELATIVE...!!
?
THANK GOODNESS YOU...
UM... IS SOMETHING WRONG?
OH! NO, NOTHING.
THIS IS JUST THE WRONG ROOM.
WHAT?!

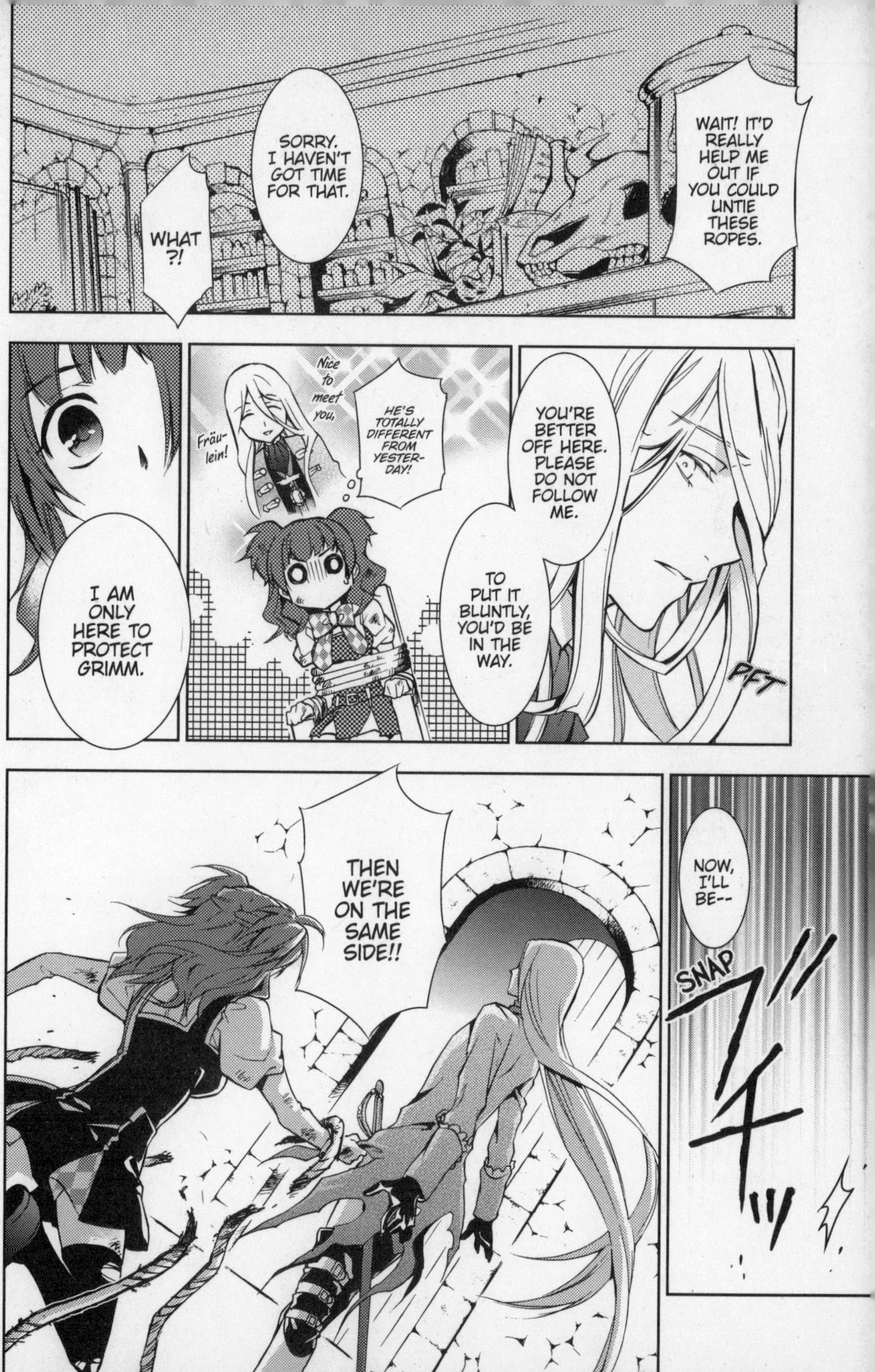
WAIT! IT'D REALLY HELP ME OUT IF YOU COULD UNTIE THESE ROPES.
SORRY. I HAVEN'T GOT TIME FOR THAT.
WHAT?!
YOU'RE BETTER OFF HERE. PLEASE DO NOT FOLLOW ME.
TO PUT IT BLUNTLY, YOU'D BE IN THE WAY.
PFFT
Nice to meet you, Fräulein!
HE'S TOTALLY DIFFERENT FROM YESTERDAY!
I AM ONLY HERE TO PROTECT GRIMM.
NOW, I'LL BE--
SNAP
THEN WE'RE ON THE SAME SIDE!!

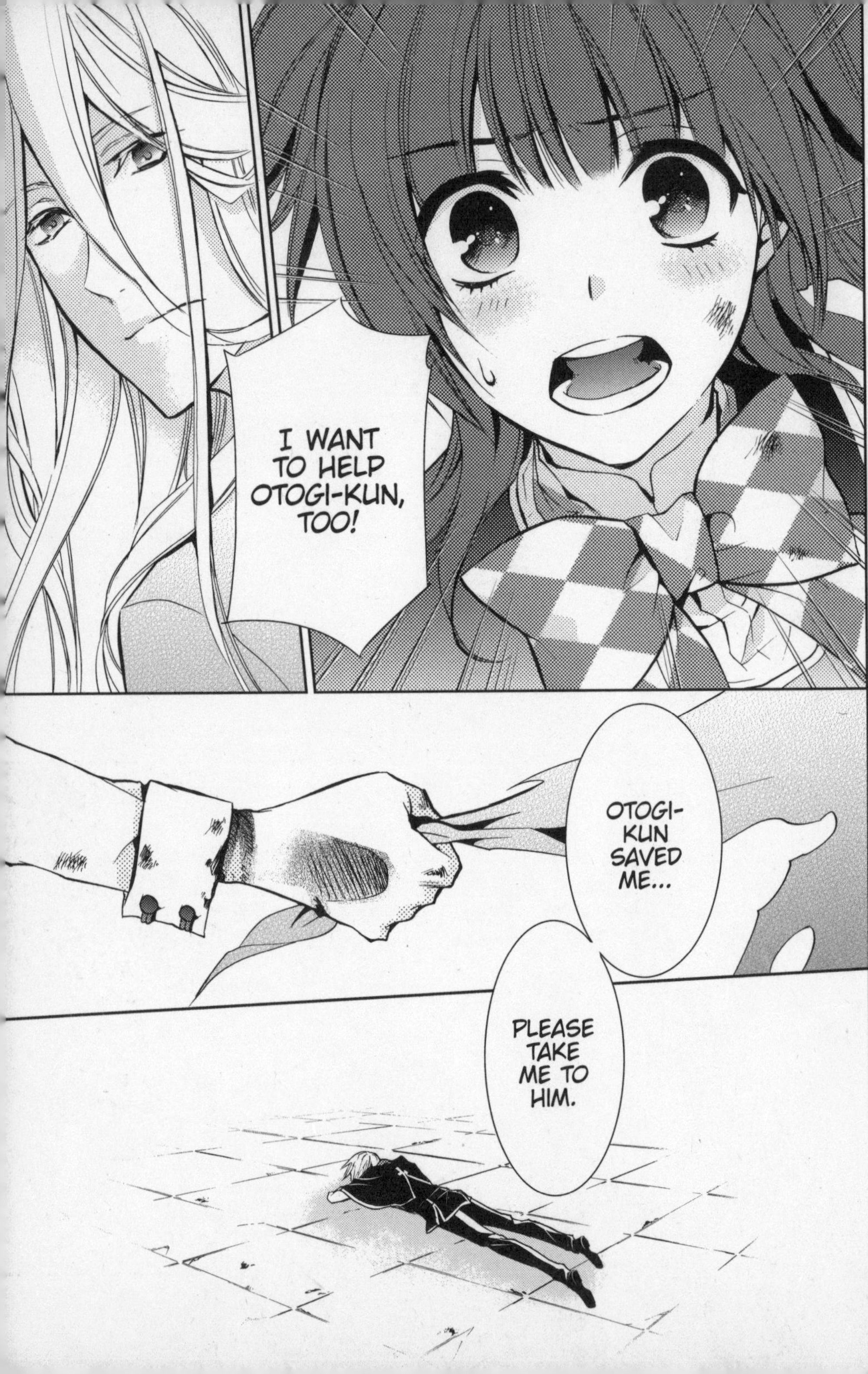
I WANT TO HELP OTOGI-KUN, TOO!
OTOGI-KUN SAVED ME...
PLEASE TAKE ME TO HIM.

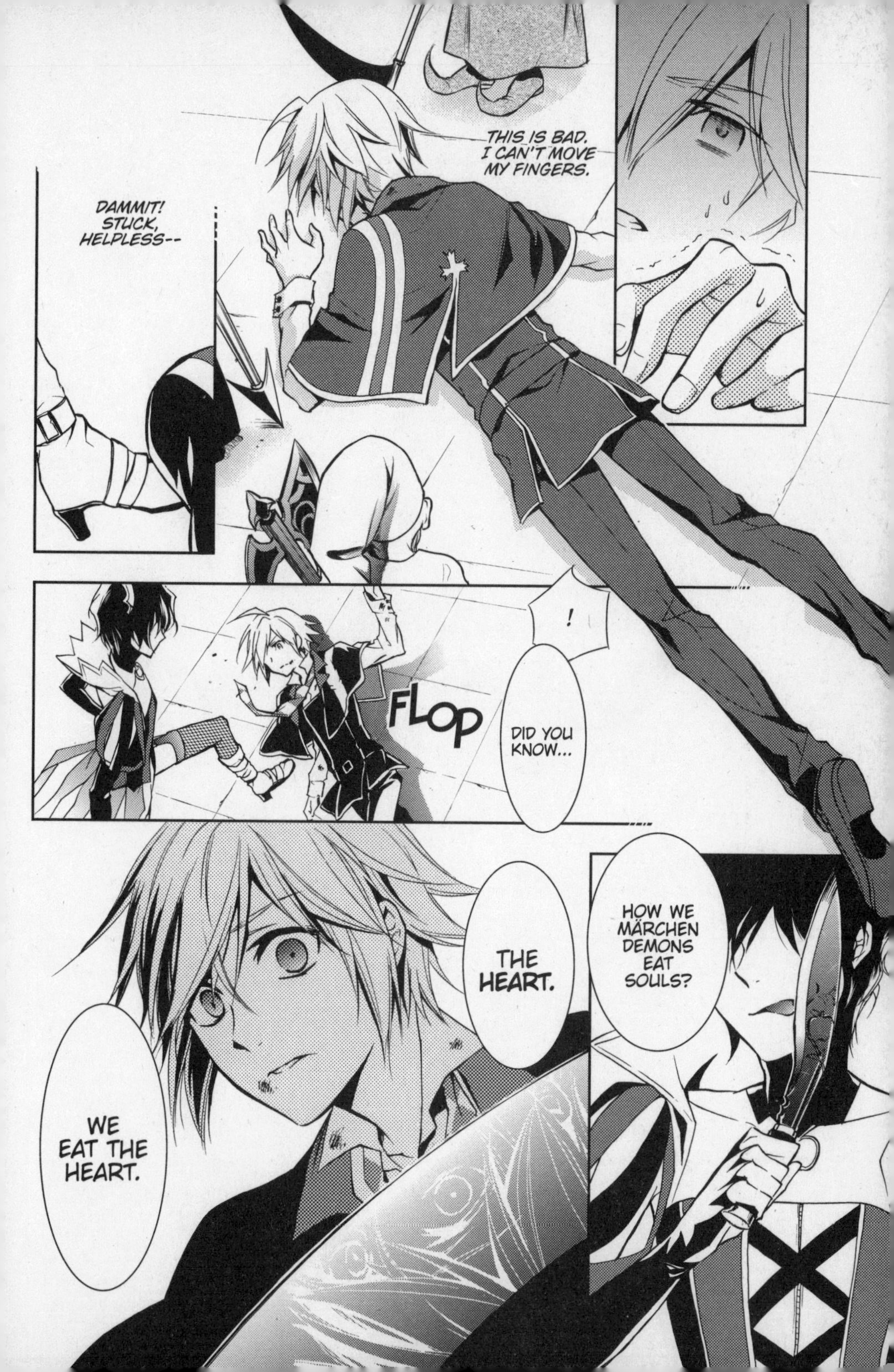
THIS IS BAD. I CAN'T MOVE MY FINGERS.
DAMMIT! STUCK, HELPLESS--
!
DID YOU KNOW...
FLOP
HOW WE MÄRCHEN DEMONS EAT SOULS?
THE HEART.
WE EAT THE HEART.

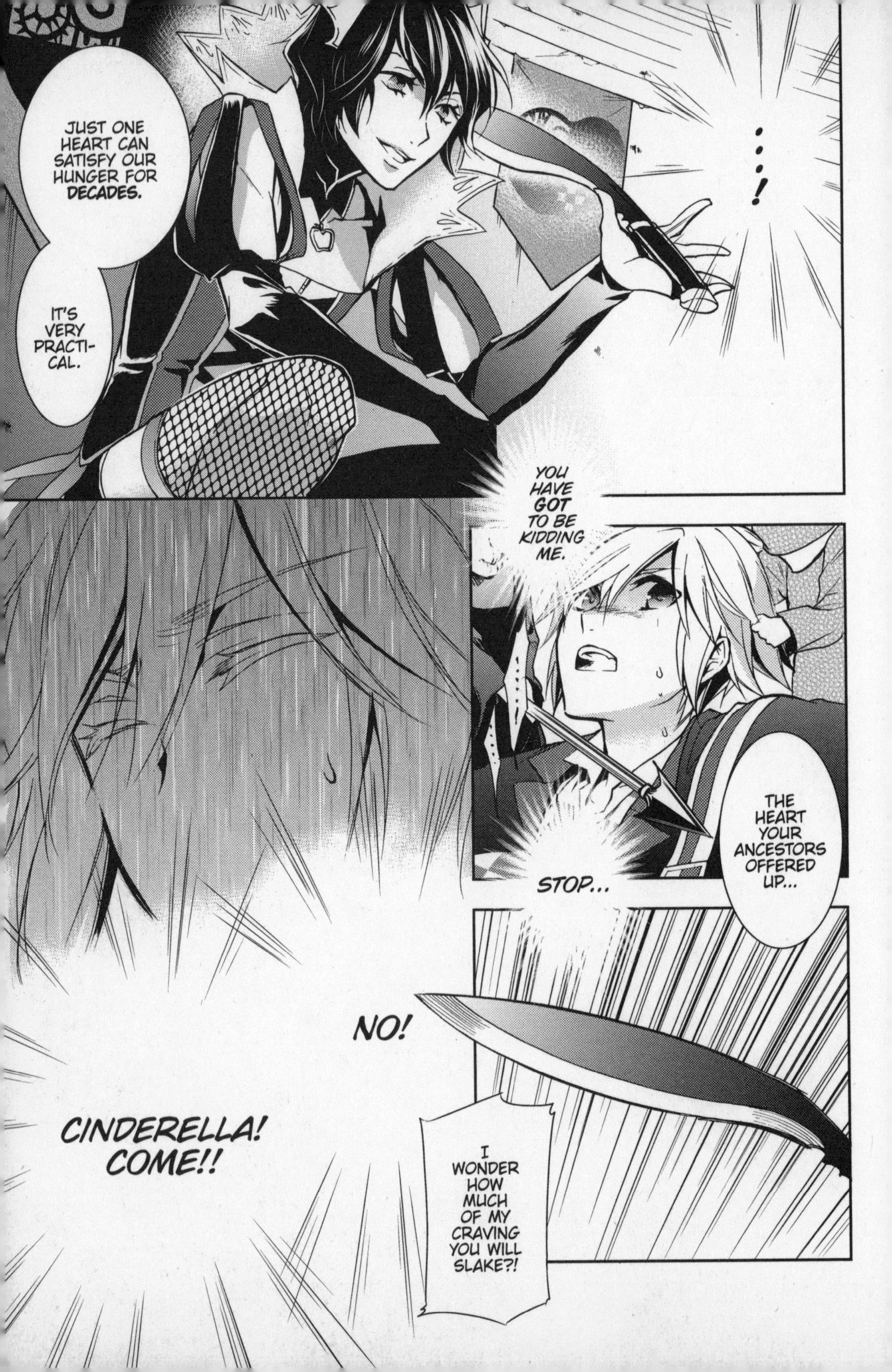
...!
JUST ONE HEART CAN SATISFY OUR HUNGER FOR DECADES.
IT'S VERY PRACTICAL.
YOU HAVE GOT TO BE KIDDING ME.
THE HEART YOUR ANCESTORS OFFERED UP...
STOP...
I WONDER HOW MUCH OF MY CRAVING YOU WILL SLAKE?!
NO!
CINDERELLA! COME!!

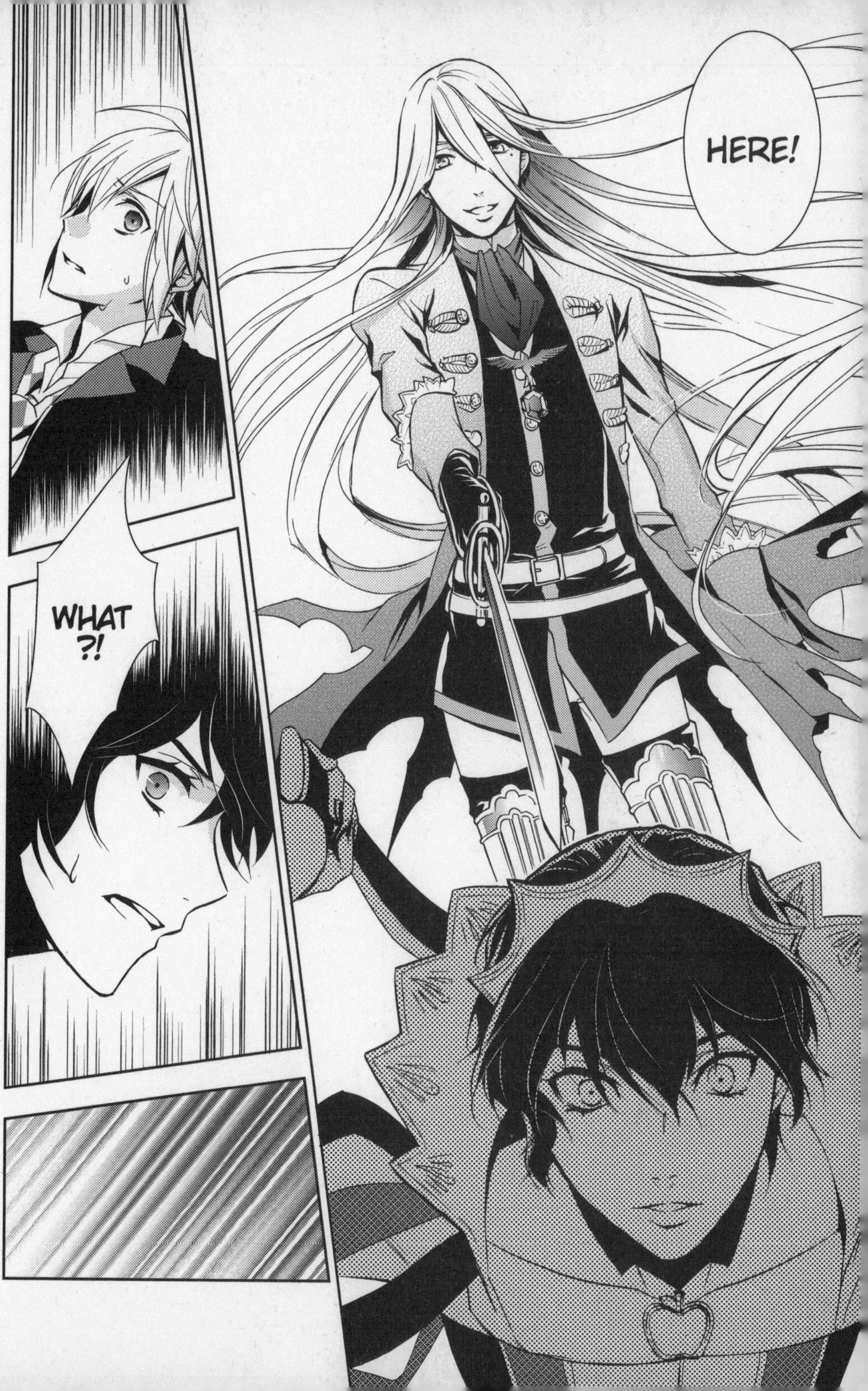
HERE!
WHAT ?!

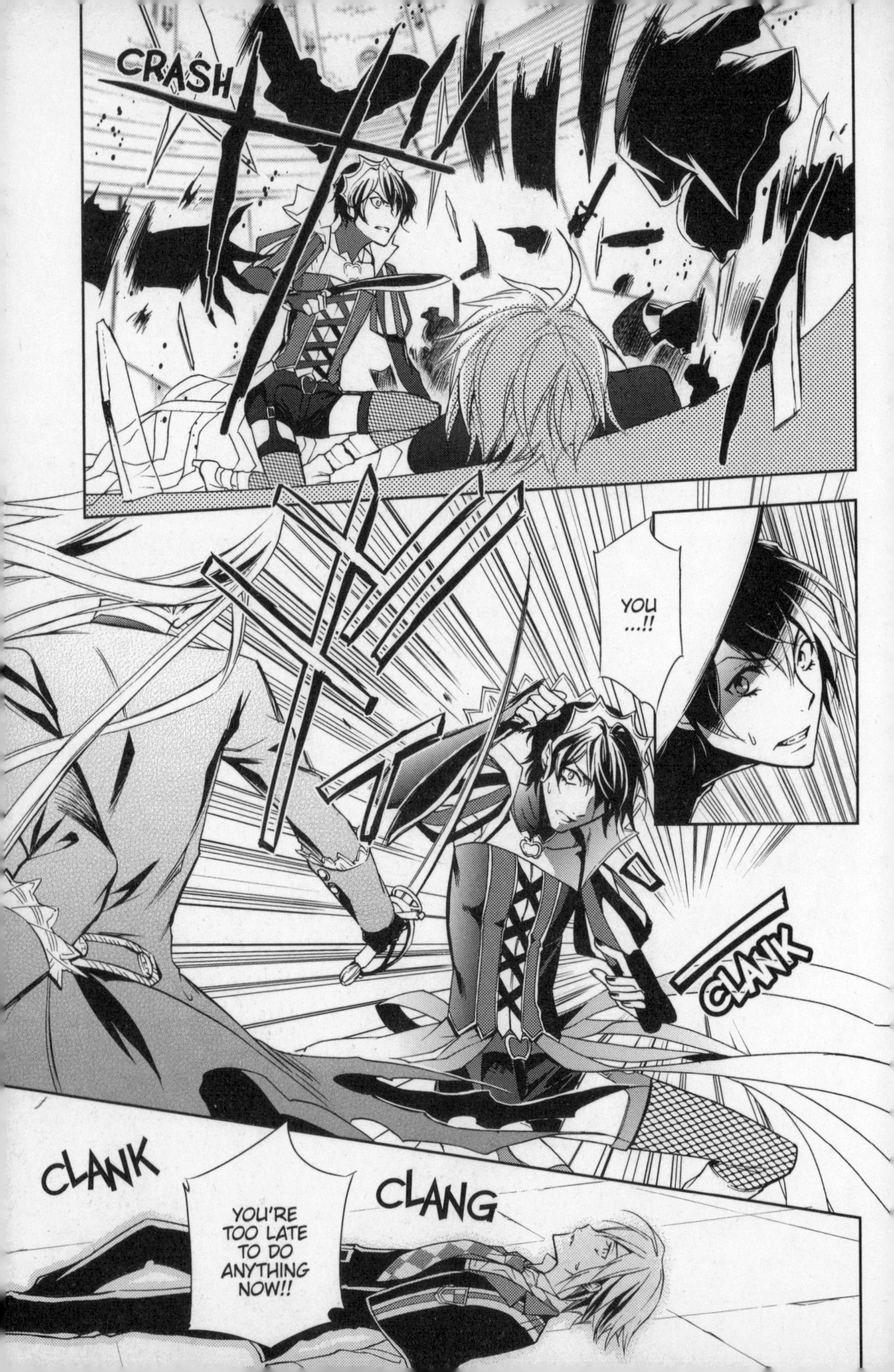
CRASH
YOU ...!!
CLANK
CLANG
YOU'RE TOO LATE TO DO ANYTHING NOW!!
CLANK

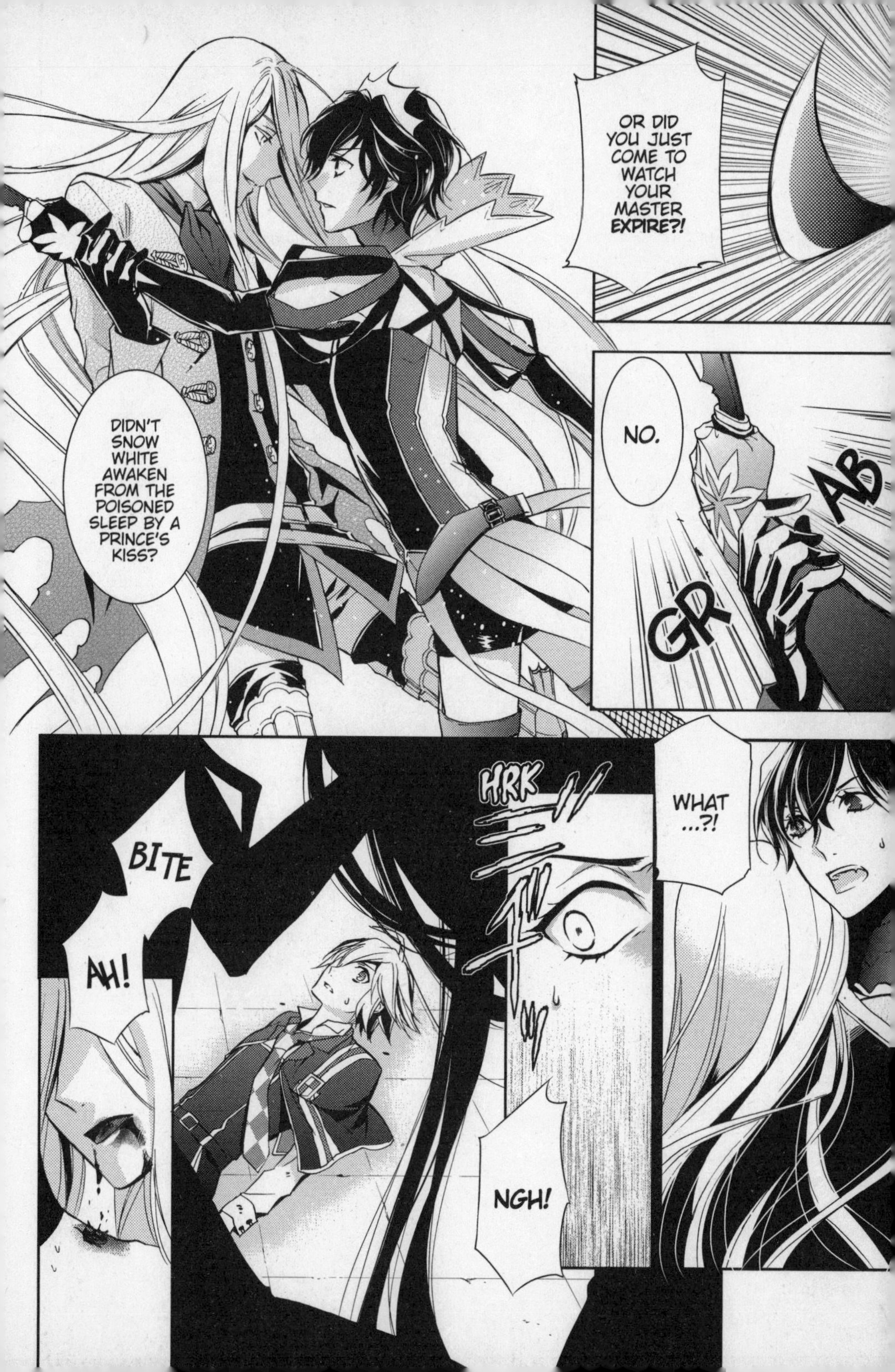

OR DID YOU JUST COME TO WATCH YOUR MASTER EXPIRE?!
NO.
GRAB
DIDN'T SNOW WHITE AWAKEN FROM THE POISONED SLEEP BY A PRINCE'S KISS?
WHAT ...?!
HRK
NGH!
BITE
AH!

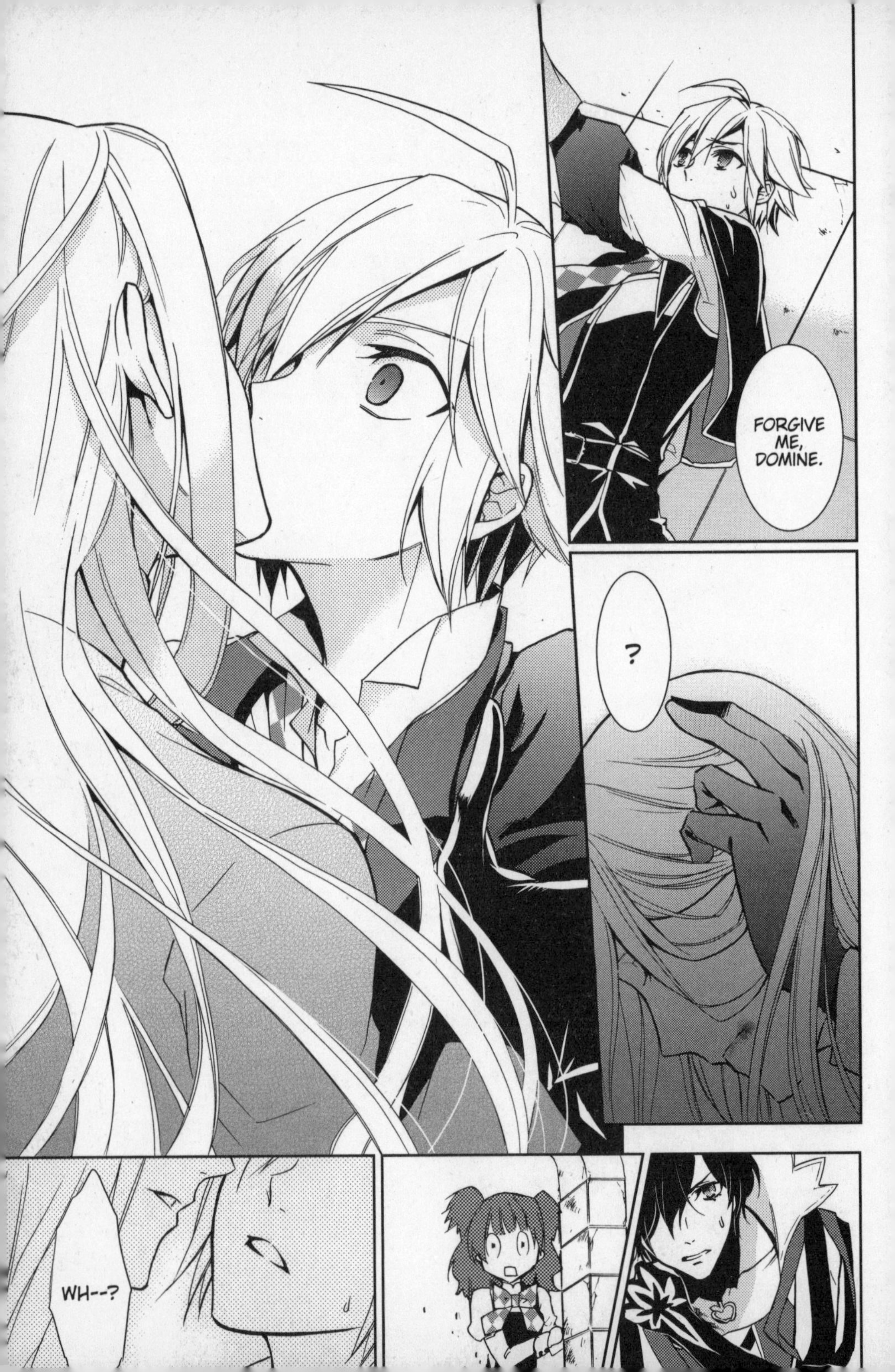
FORGIVE ME, DOMINE.
?
WH--?

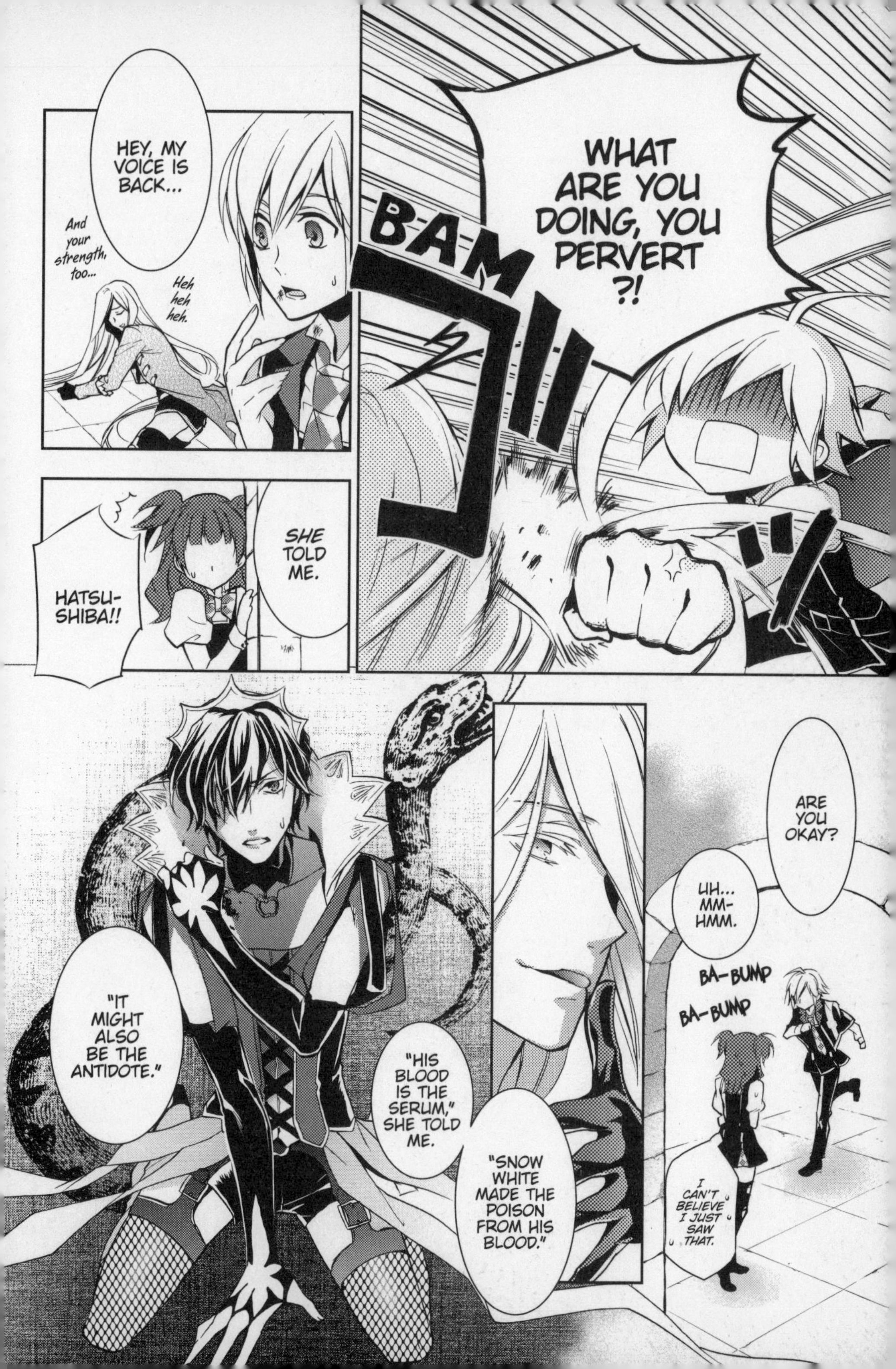
WHAT ARE YOU DOING, YOU PERVERT ?!
BAM
HEY, MY VOICE IS BACK...
And your strength, too...
Heh heh heh.
SHE TOLD ME.
HATSU-SHIBA!!
ARE YOU OKAY?
UH... MM-HMM.
BA-BUMP
BA-BUMP
I CAN'T BELIEVE I JUST SAW THAT.
"SNOW WHITE MADE THE POISON FROM HIS BLOOD."
"HIS BLOOD IS THE SERUM," SHE TOLD ME.
"IT MIGHT ALSO BE THE ANTIDOTE."

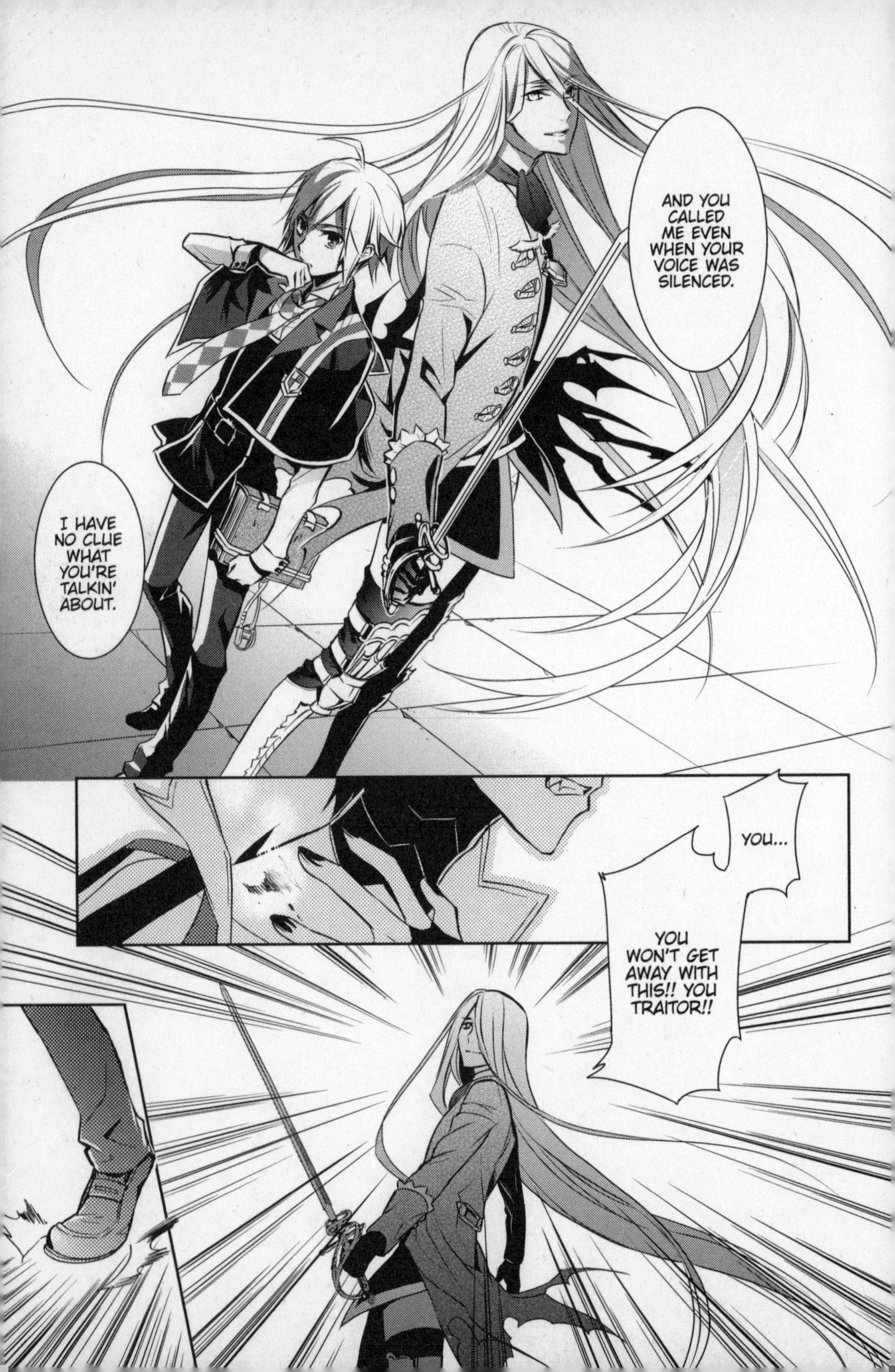
AND YOU CALLED ME EVEN WHEN YOUR VOICE WAS SILENCED.
I HAVE NO CLUE WHAT YOU'RE TALKIN' ABOUT.
YOU...
YOU WON'T GET AWAY WITH THIS!! YOU TRAITOR!!

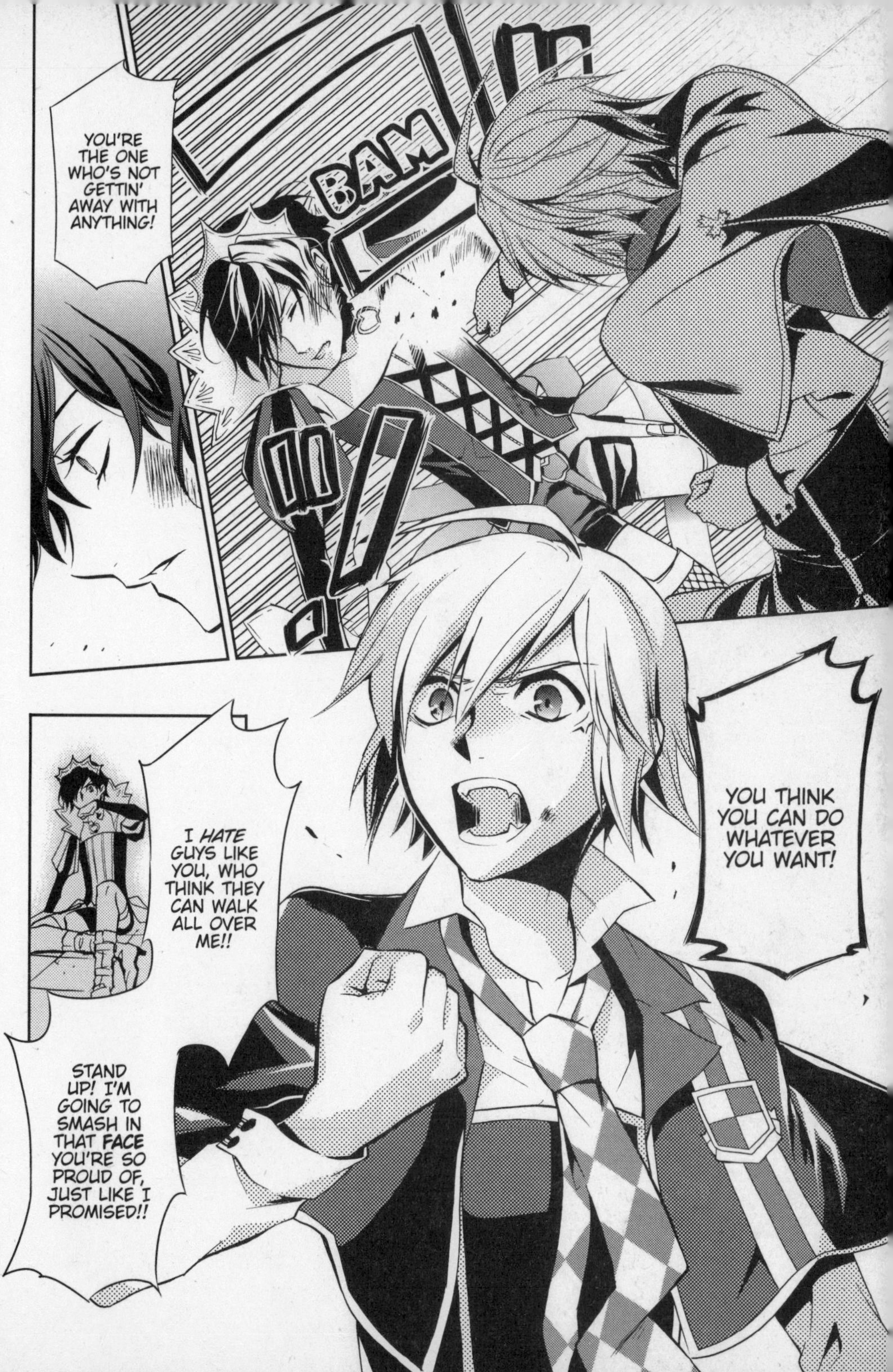
BAM
YOU'RE THE ONE WHO'S NOT GETTIN' AWAY WITH ANYTHING!
YOU THINK YOU CAN DO WHATEVER YOU WANT!
I *HATE* GUYS LIKE YOU, WHO THINK THEY CAN WALK ALL OVER ME!!
STAND UP! I'M GOING TO SMASH IN THAT **FACE** YOU'RE SO PROUD OF, JUST LIKE I PROMISED!!

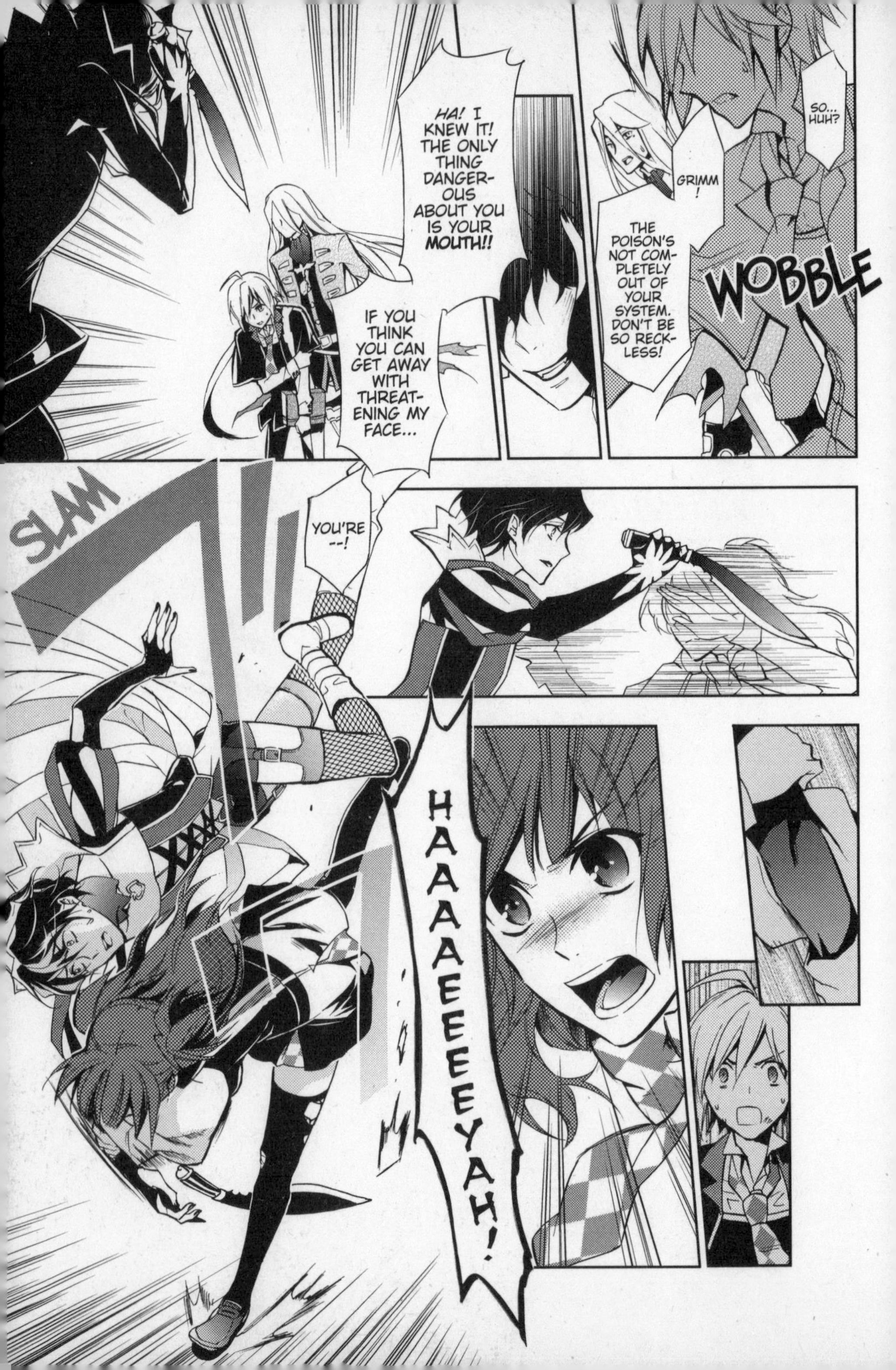

SO... HUH?
GRIMM!
THE POISON'S NOT COMPLETELY OUT OF YOUR SYSTEM. DON'T BE SO RECKLESS!
WOBBLE
HA! I KNEW IT! THE ONLY THING DANGEROUS ABOUT YOU IS YOUR **MOUTH!!**
IF YOU THINK YOU CAN GET AWAY WITH THREATENING MY FACE...
YOU'RE --!
SLAM
HAAAAEEEEYAH!

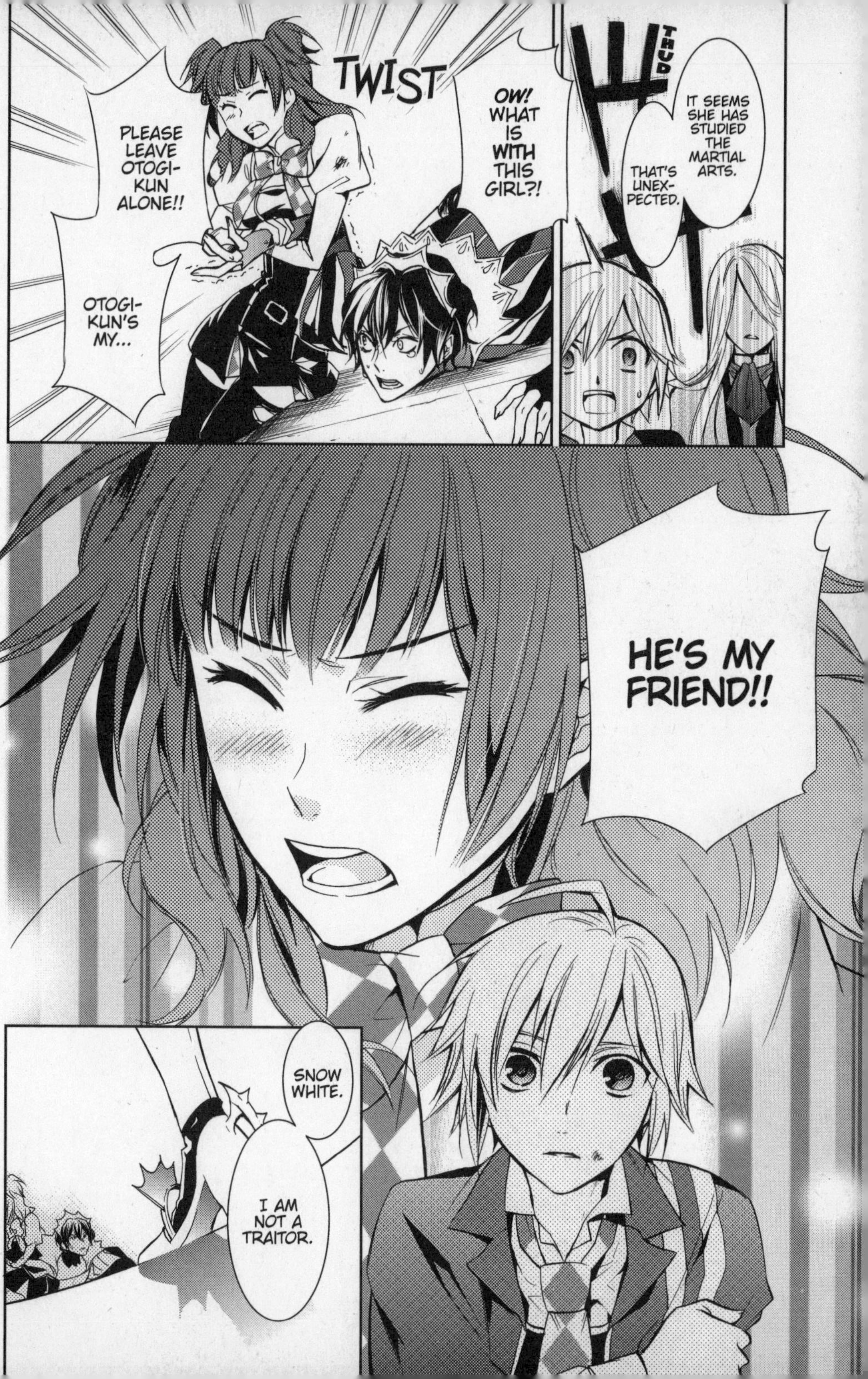
THUD
IT SEEMS SHE HAS STUDIED THE MARTIAL ARTS.
THAT'S UNEXPECTED.
OW! WHAT IS WITH THIS GIRL?!
TWIST
PLEASE LEAVE OTOGI-KUN ALONE!!
OTOGI-KUN'S MY...
HE'S MY FRIEND!!
SNOW WHITE.
I AM NOT A TRAITOR.

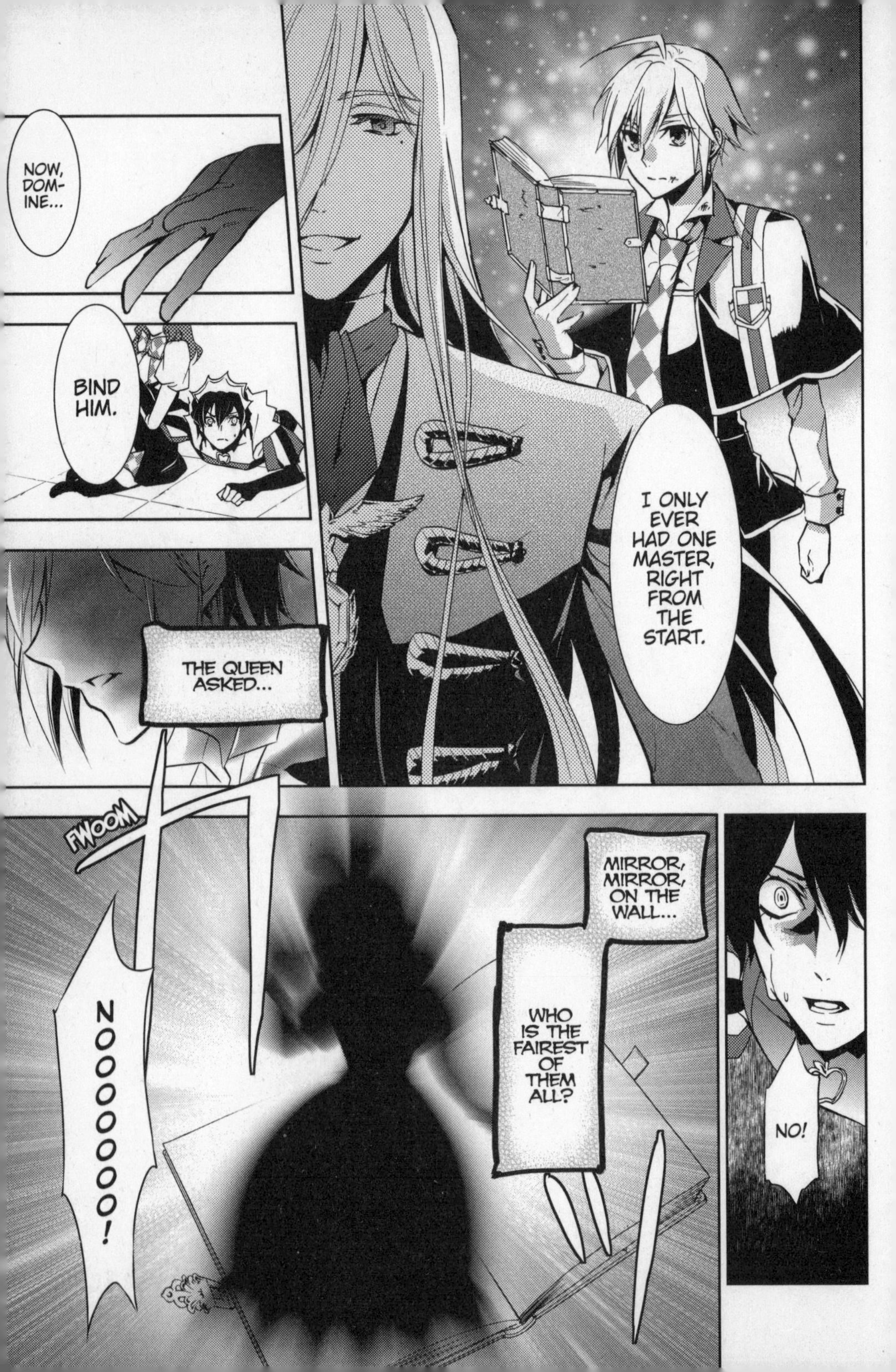
I ONLY EVER HAD ONE MASTER, RIGHT FROM THE START.
NOW, DOMINE...
BIND HIM.
THE QUEEN ASKED...
NO!
MIRROR, MIRROR, ON THE WALL...
WHO IS THE FAIREST OF THEM ALL?
FWOOM
NOOOOOOOO!

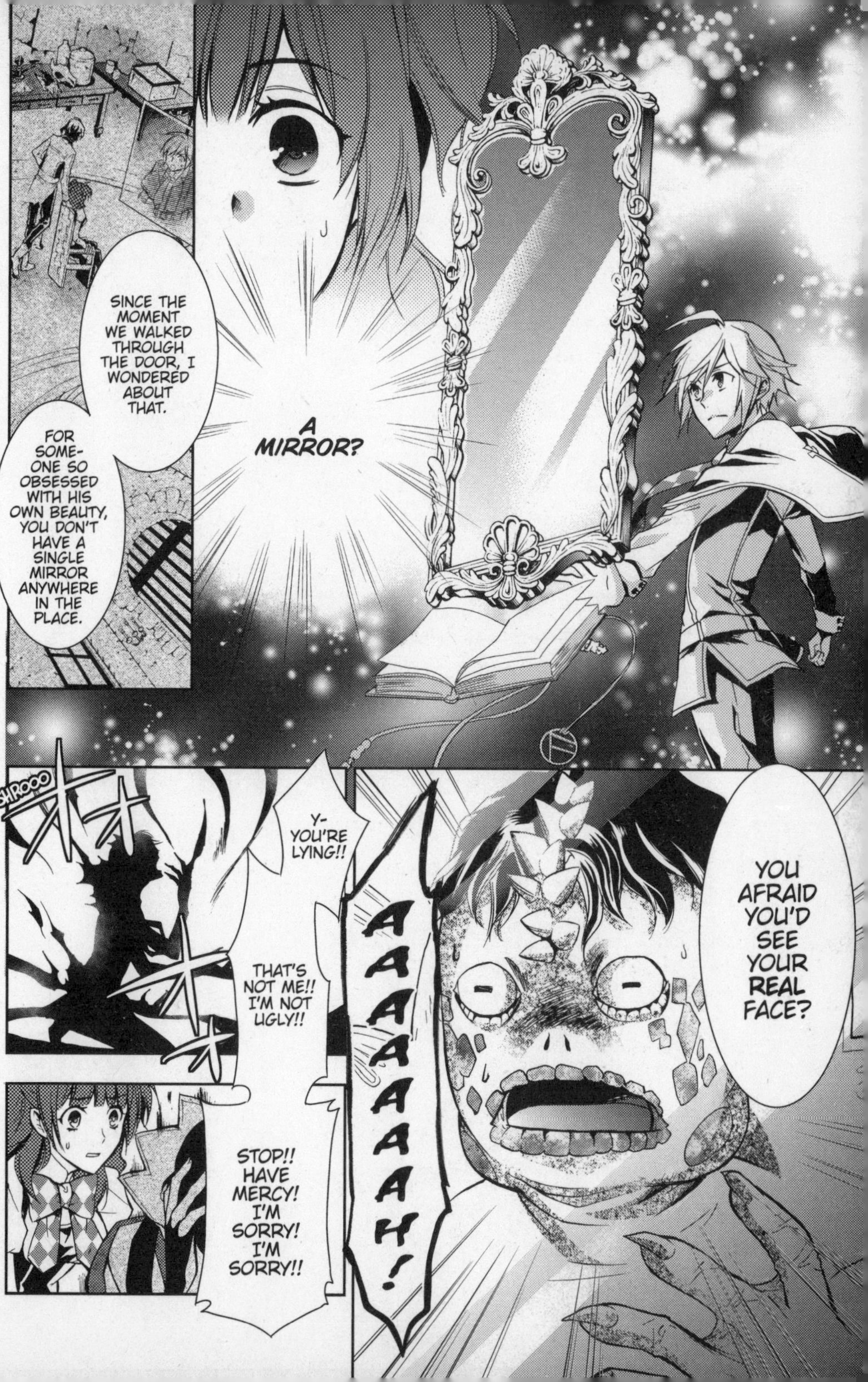
A MIRROR?
SINCE THE MOMENT WE WALKED THROUGH THE DOOR, I WONDERED ABOUT THAT.
FOR SOMEONE SO OBSESSED WITH HIS OWN BEAUTY, YOU DON'T HAVE A SINGLE MIRROR ANYWHERE IN THE PLACE.
YOU AFRAID YOU'D SEE YOUR REAL FACE?
AAAAAAAAH!
Y-YOU'RE LYING!!
THAT'S NOT ME!! I'M NOT UGLY!!
SHROOO
STOP!! HAVE MERCY! I'M SORRY! I'M SORRY!!

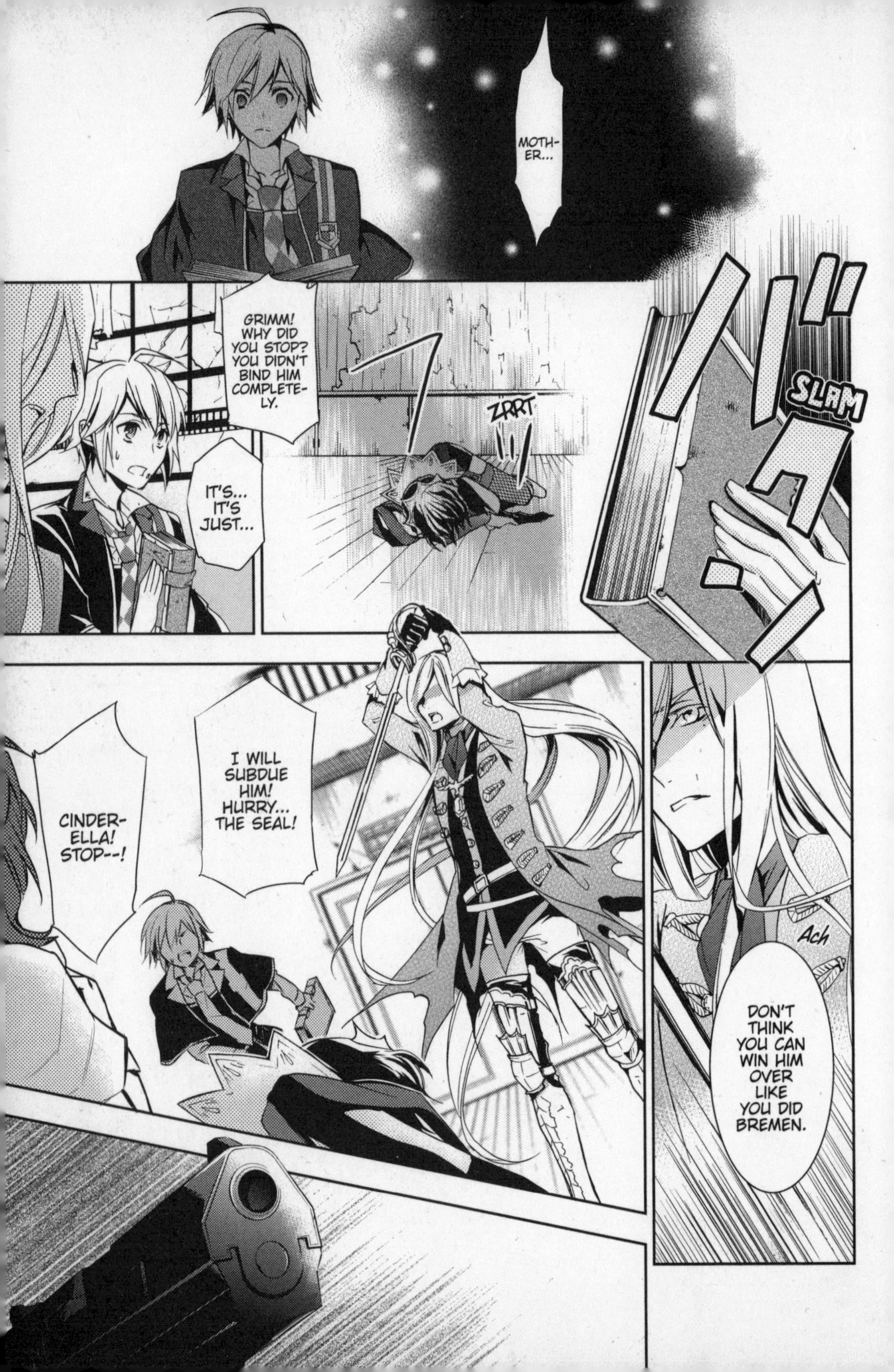
MOTH-
ER...
SLAM
ZRRT
GRIMM! WHY DID YOU STOP? YOU DIDN'T BIND HIM COMPLETE-LY.
IT'S... IT'S JUST...
Ach
DON'T THINK YOU CAN WIN HIM OVER LIKE YOU DID BREMEN.
I WILL SUBDUE HIM! HURRY... THE SEAL!
CINDER-ELLA! STOP--!

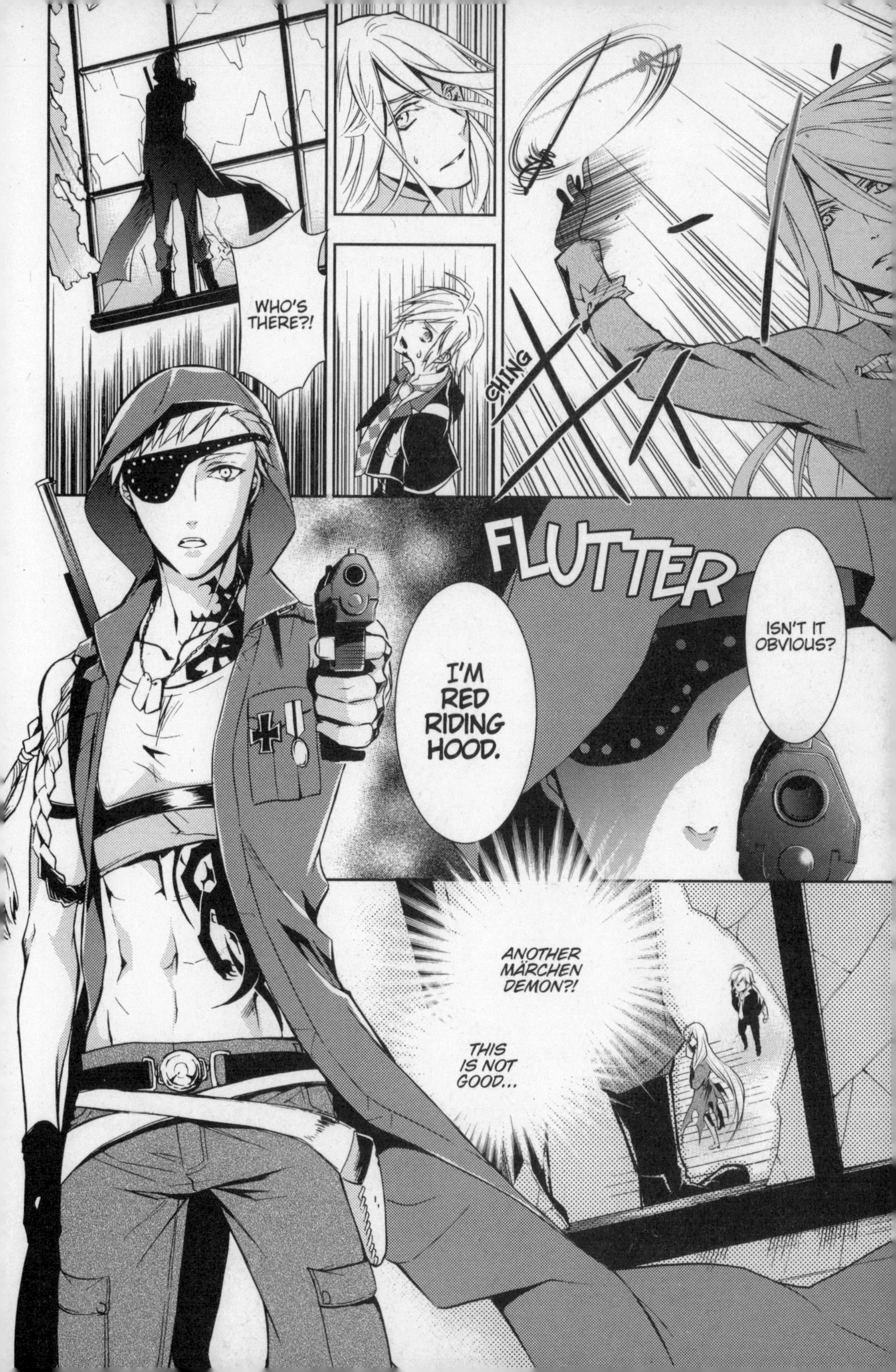
CHING
WHO'S THERE?!
FLUTTER
ISN'T IT OBVIOUS?
I'M RED RIDING HOOD.
ANOTHER MÄRCHEN DEMON?!
THIS IS NOT GOOD...

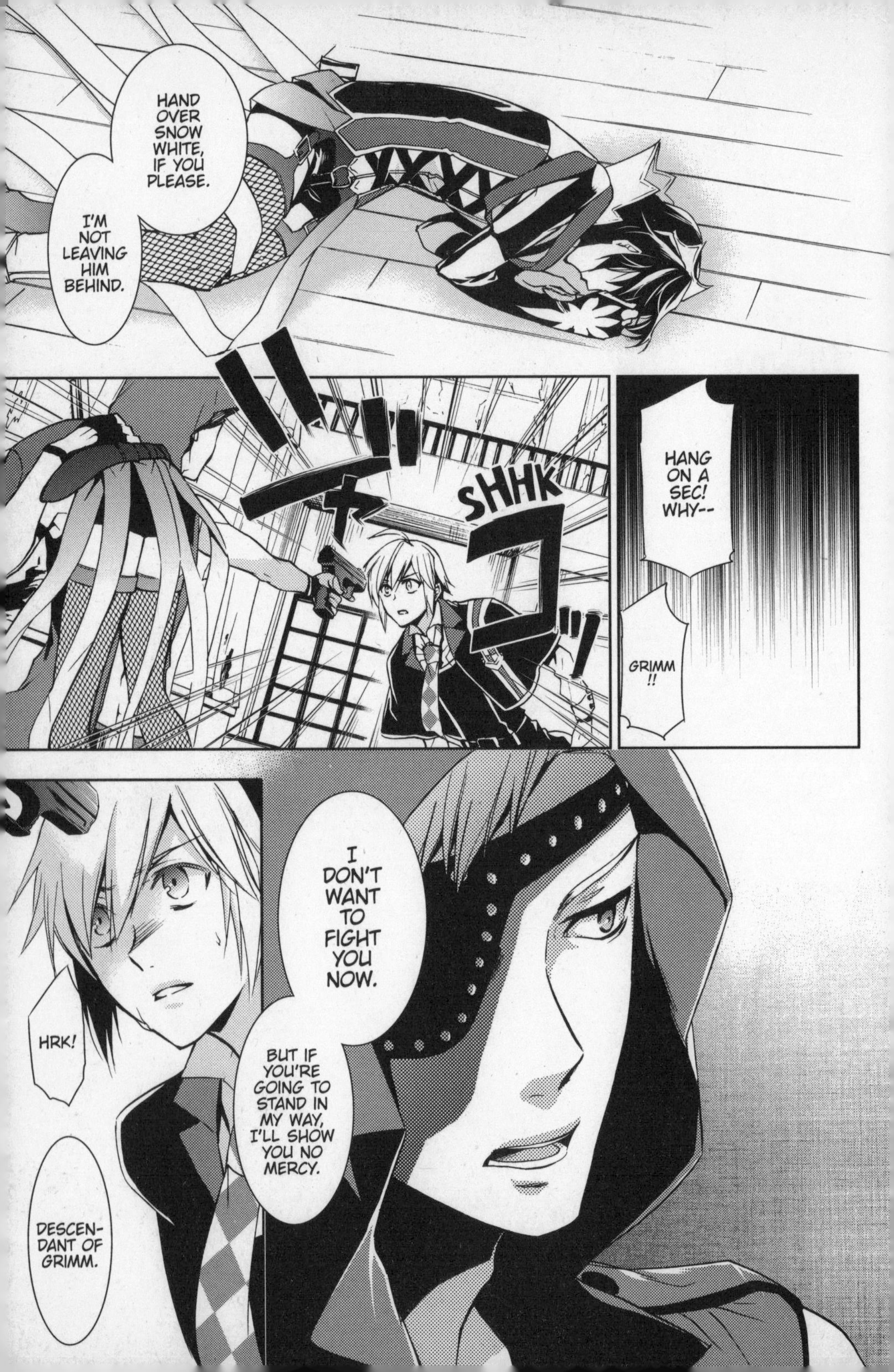
HAND OVER SNOW WHITE, IF YOU PLEASE.
I'M NOT LEAVING HIM BEHIND.
HANG ON A SEC! WHY--
GRIMM!!
SHHK
I DON'T WANT TO FIGHT YOU NOW.
BUT IF YOU'RE GOING TO STAND IN MY WAY, I'LL SHOW YOU NO MERCY.
HRK!
DESCENDANT OF GRIMM.

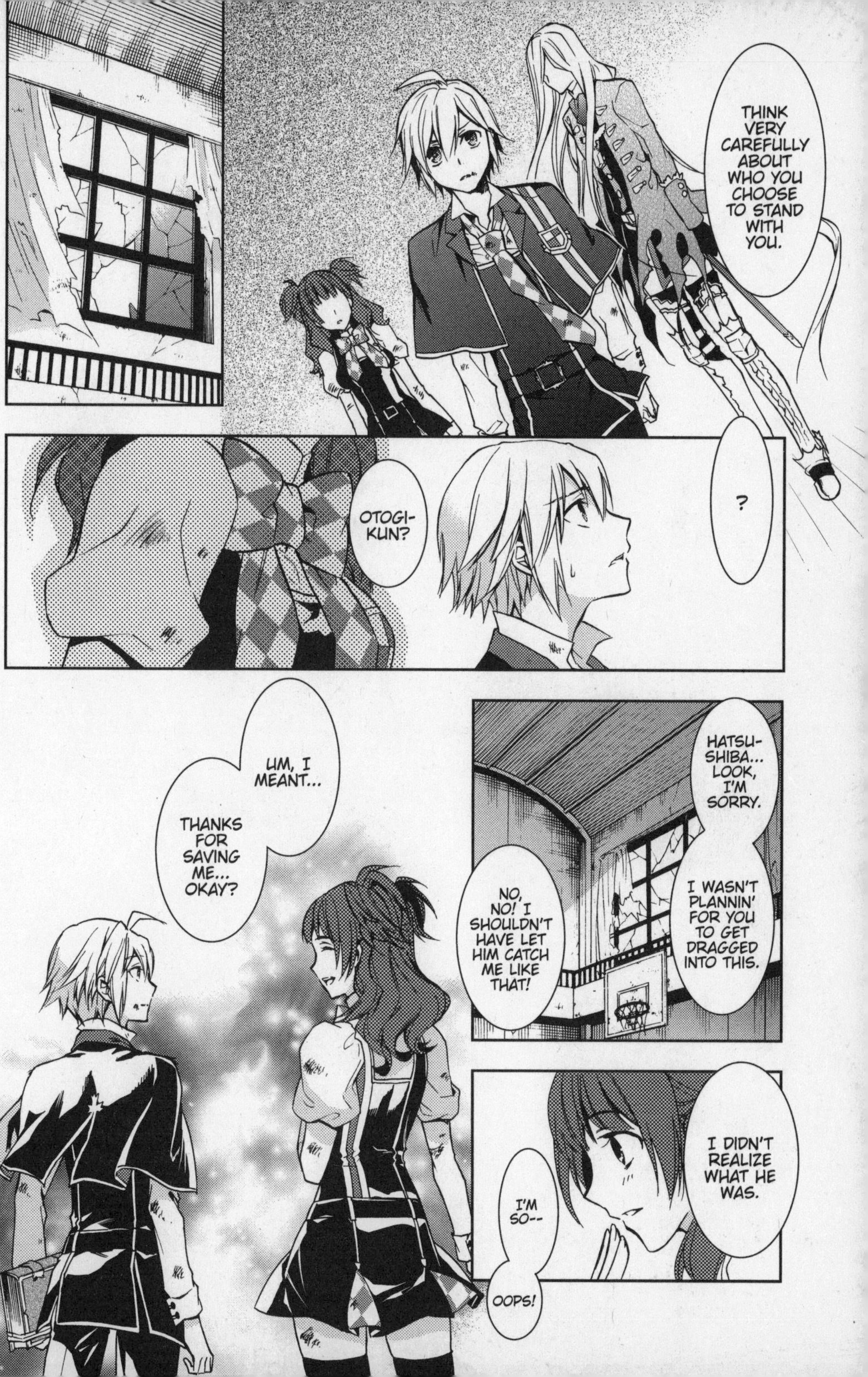
THINK VERY CAREFULLY ABOUT WHO YOU CHOOSE TO STAND WITH YOU.
?
OTOGI-KUN?
HATSU-SHIBA... LOOK, I'M SORRY.
I WASN'T PLANNIN' FOR YOU TO GET DRAGGED INTO THIS.
NO, NO! I SHOULDN'T HAVE LET HIM CATCH ME LIKE THAT!
I DIDN'T REALIZE WHAT HE WAS.
I'M SO--
OOPS!
UM, I MEANT...
THANKS FOR SAVING ME... OKAY?

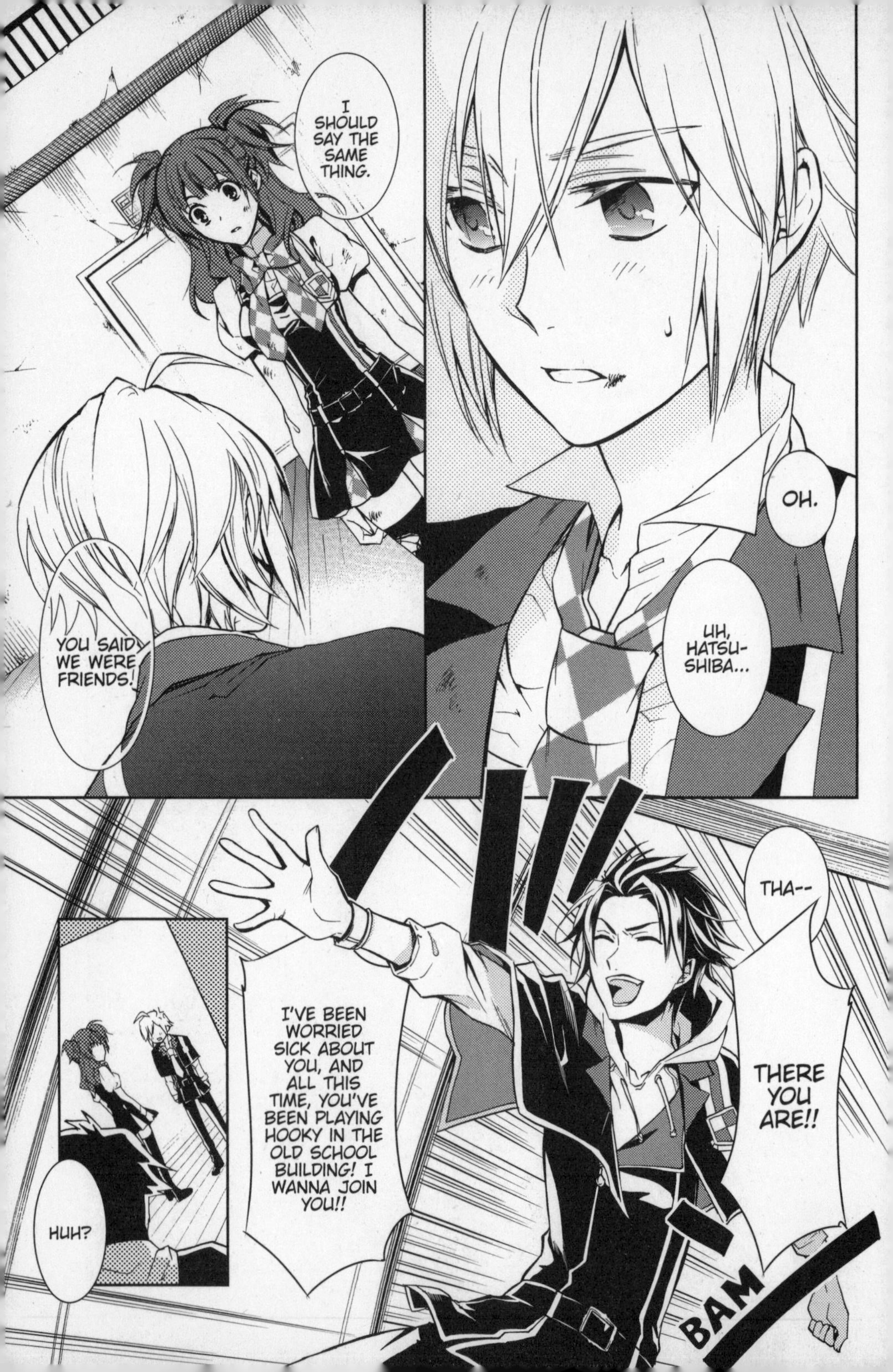
OH.
UH, HATSU-SHIBA...
I SHOULD SAY THE SAME THING.
YOU SAID WE WERE FRIENDS!
THA--
THERE YOU ARE!!
BAM
I'VE BEEN WORRIED SICK ABOUT YOU, AND ALL THIS TIME, YOU'VE BEEN PLAYING HOOKY IN THE OLD SCHOOL BUILDING! I WANNA JOIN YOU!!
HUH?

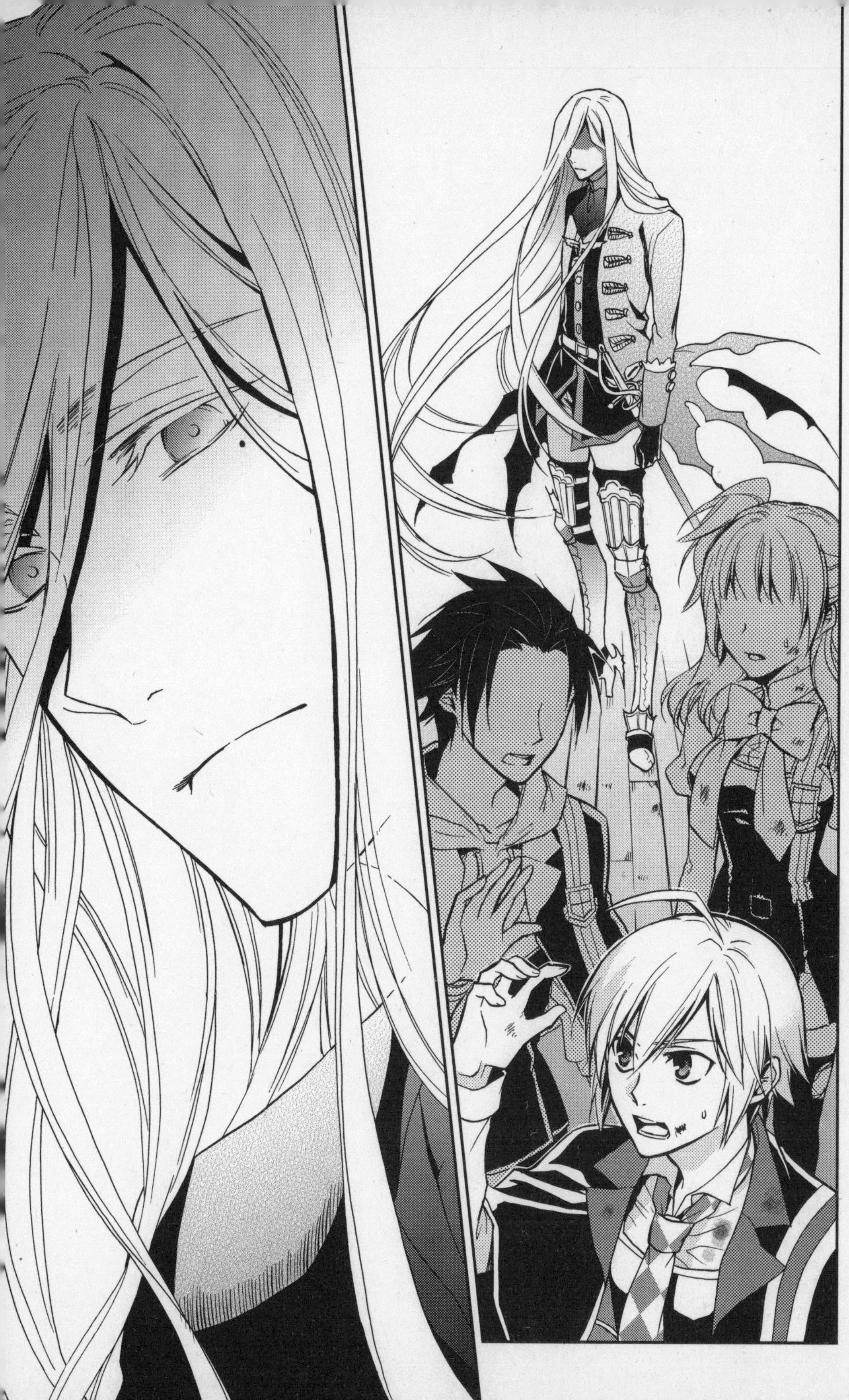

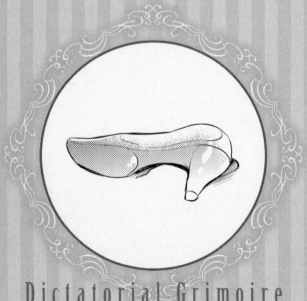

Dictatorial Grimoire

独裁グリムワール
Dictatorial Grimoire

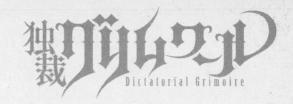

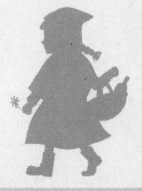

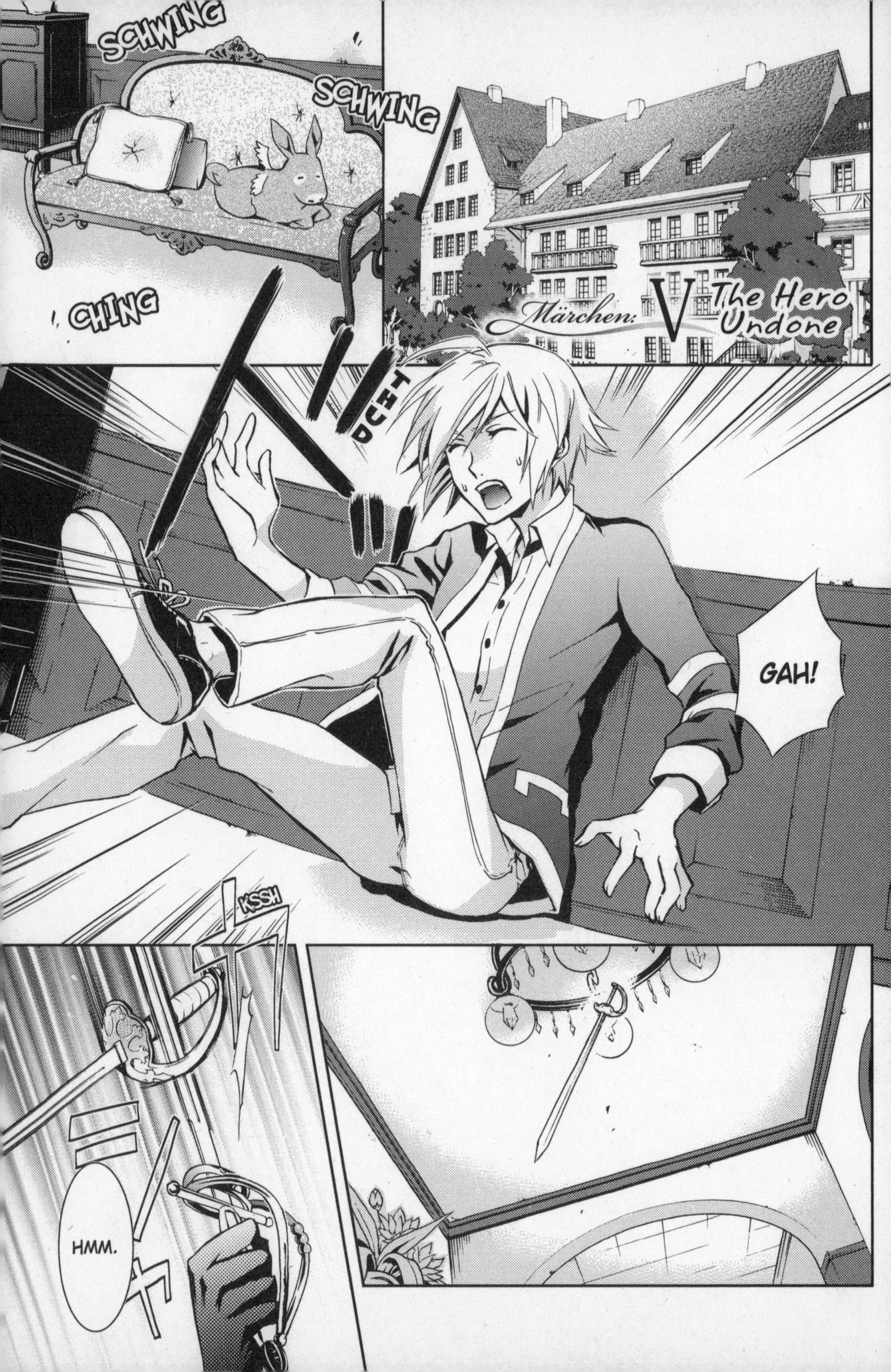
Märchen: V The Hero Undone
SCHWING
SCHWING
CHING
THUD
GAH!
KSSH
HMM.

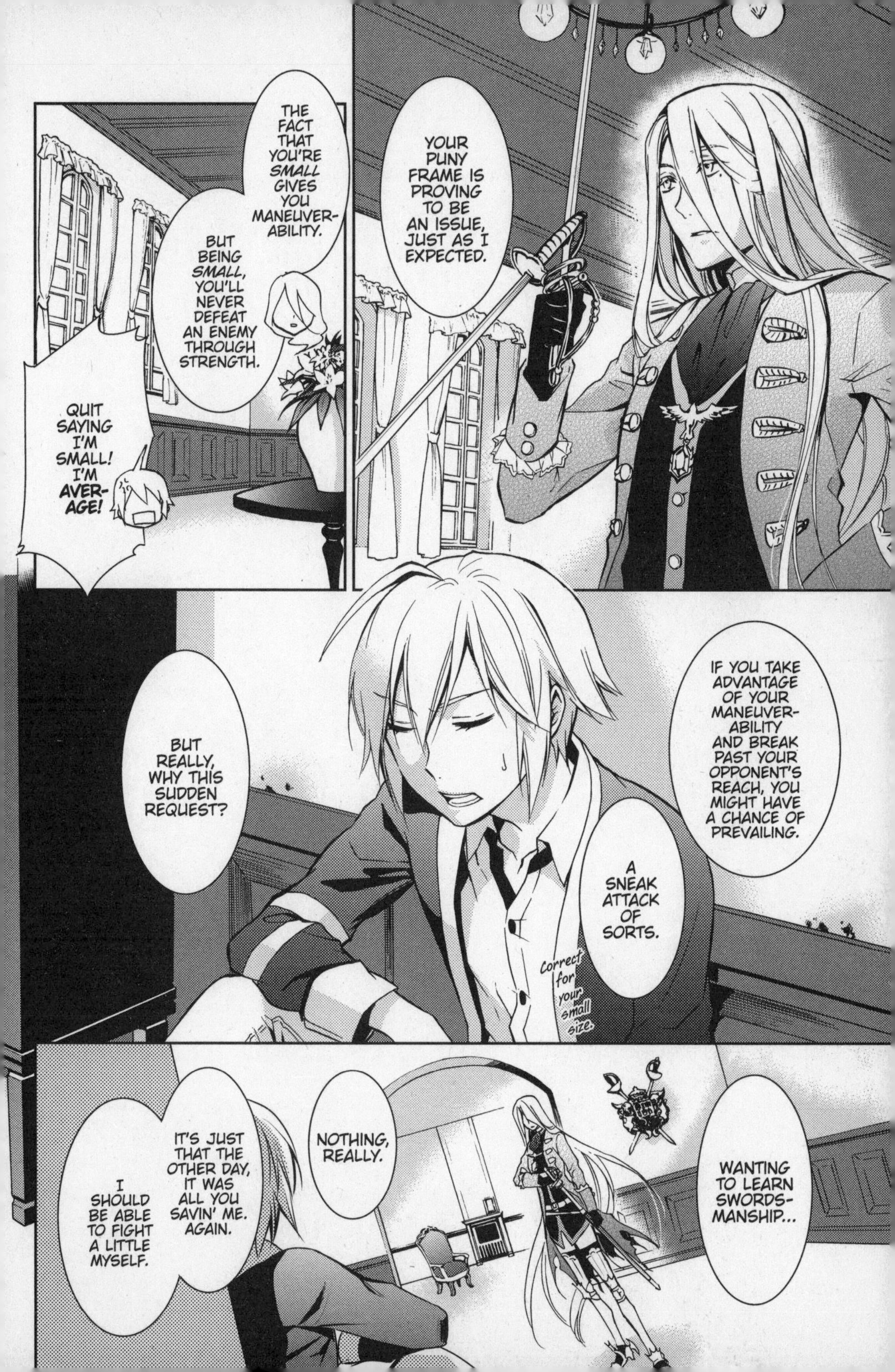
YOUR PUNY FRAME IS PROVING TO BE AN ISSUE, JUST AS I EXPECTED.
THE FACT THAT YOU'RE *SMALL* GIVES YOU MANEUVERABILITY.
BUT BEING *SMALL*, YOU'LL NEVER DEFEAT AN ENEMY THROUGH STRENGTH.
QUIT SAYING I'M SMALL! I'M **AVERAGE!**
IF YOU TAKE ADVANTAGE OF YOUR MANEUVERABILITY AND BREAK PAST YOUR OPPONENT'S REACH, YOU MIGHT HAVE A CHANCE OF PREVAILING.
A SNEAK ATTACK OF SORTS.
Correct for your small size.
BUT REALLY, WHY THIS SUDDEN REQUEST?
WANTING TO LEARN SWORDSMANSHIP...
NOTHING, REALLY.
IT'S JUST THAT THE OTHER DAY, IT WAS ALL YOU SAVIN' ME. AGAIN.
I SHOULD BE ABLE TO FIGHT A LITTLE MYSELF.

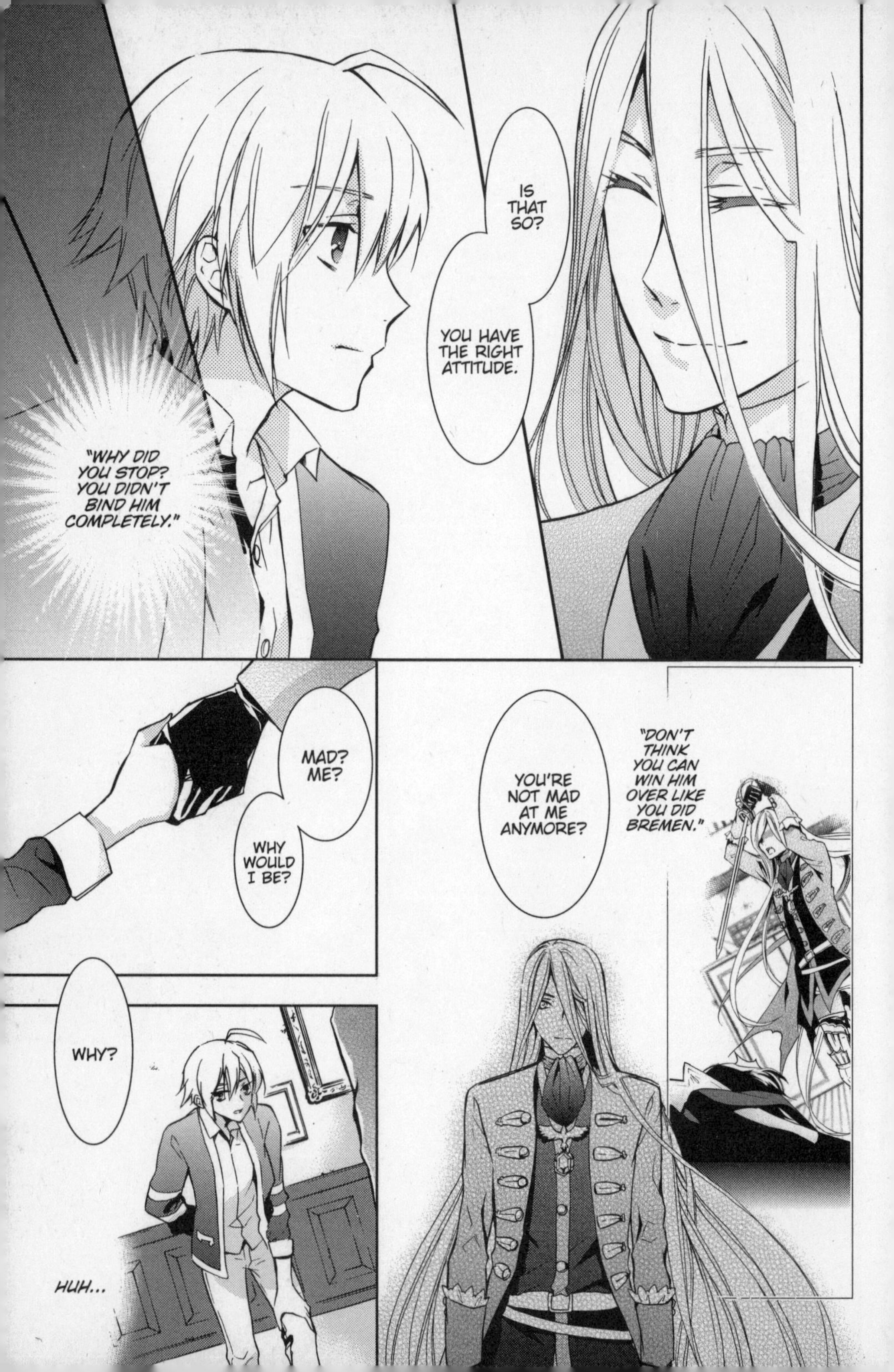
IS THAT SO?
YOU HAVE THE RIGHT ATTITUDE.
"WHY DID YOU STOP? YOU DIDN'T BIND HIM COMPLETELY."
"DON'T THINK YOU CAN WIN HIM OVER LIKE YOU DID BREMEN."
YOU'RE NOT MAD AT ME ANYMORE?
MAD? ME?
WHY WOULD I BE?
WHY?
HUH...

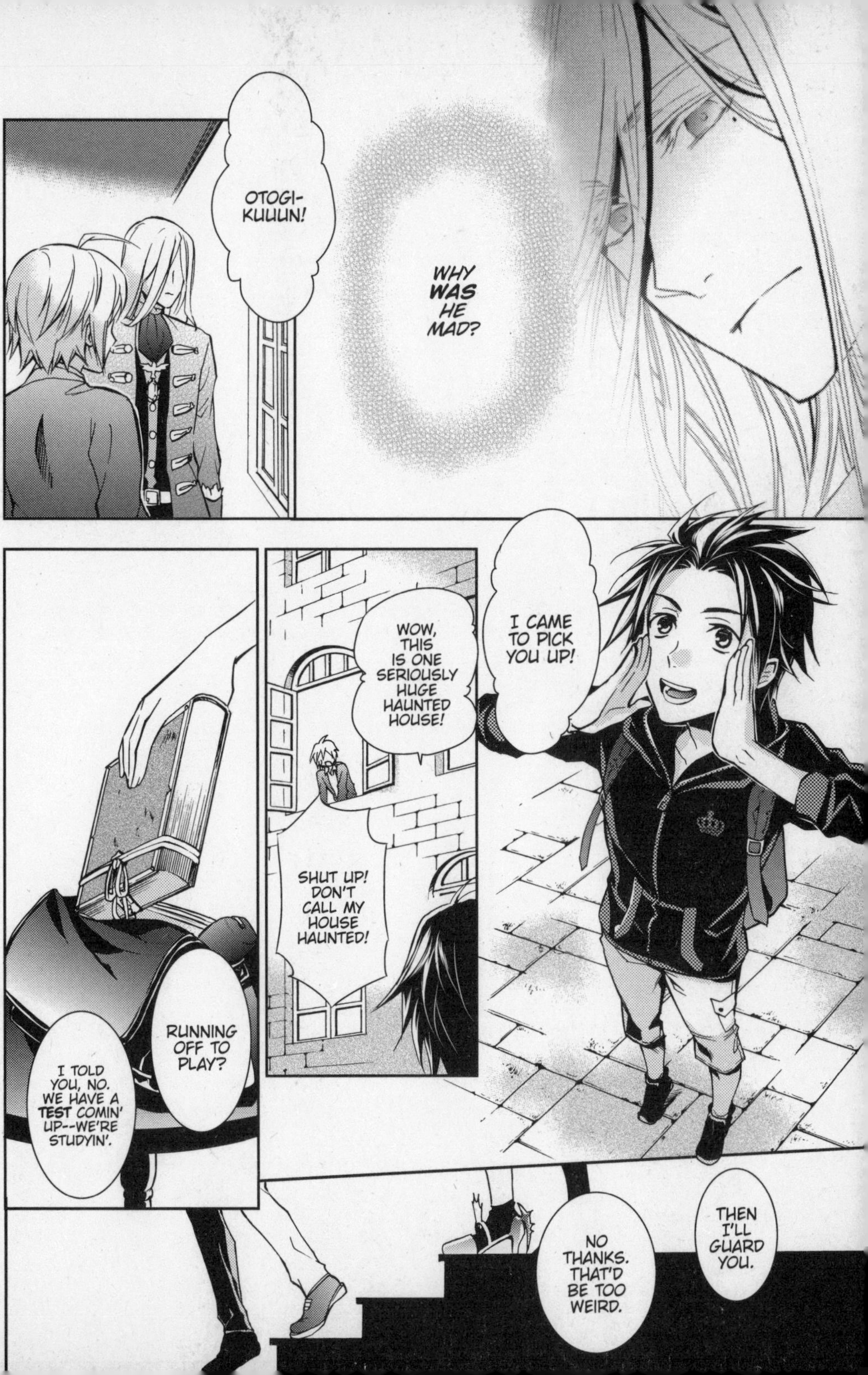
WHY WAS HE MAD?
OTOGI-KUUUN!
I CAME TO PICK YOU UP!
WOW, THIS IS ONE SERIOUSLY HUGE HAUNTED HOUSE!
SHUT UP! DON'T CALL MY HOUSE HAUNTED!
RUNNING OFF TO PLAY?
I TOLD YOU, NO. WE HAVE A TEST COMIN' UP--WE'RE STUDYIN'.
THEN I'LL GUARD YOU.
NO THANKS. THAT'D BE TOO WEIRD.

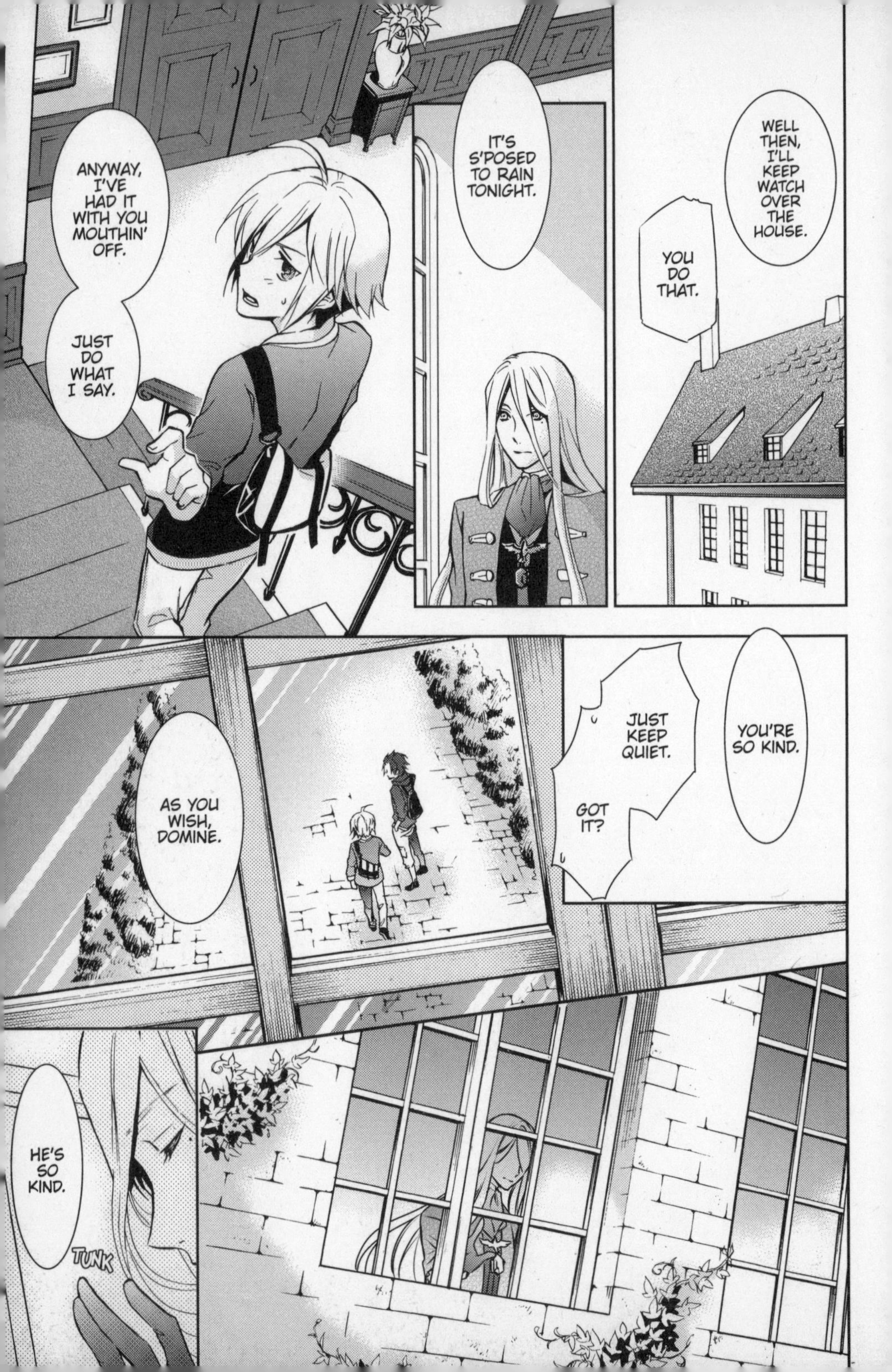

WELL THEN, I'LL KEEP WATCH OVER THE HOUSE.
YOU DO THAT.
IT'S S'POSED TO RAIN TONIGHT.
ANYWAY, I'VE HAD IT WITH YOU MOUTHIN' OFF.
JUST DO WHAT I SAY.
YOU'RE SO KIND.
JUST KEEP QUIET.
GOT IT?
AS YOU WISH, DOMINE.
HE'S SO KIND.
TUNK

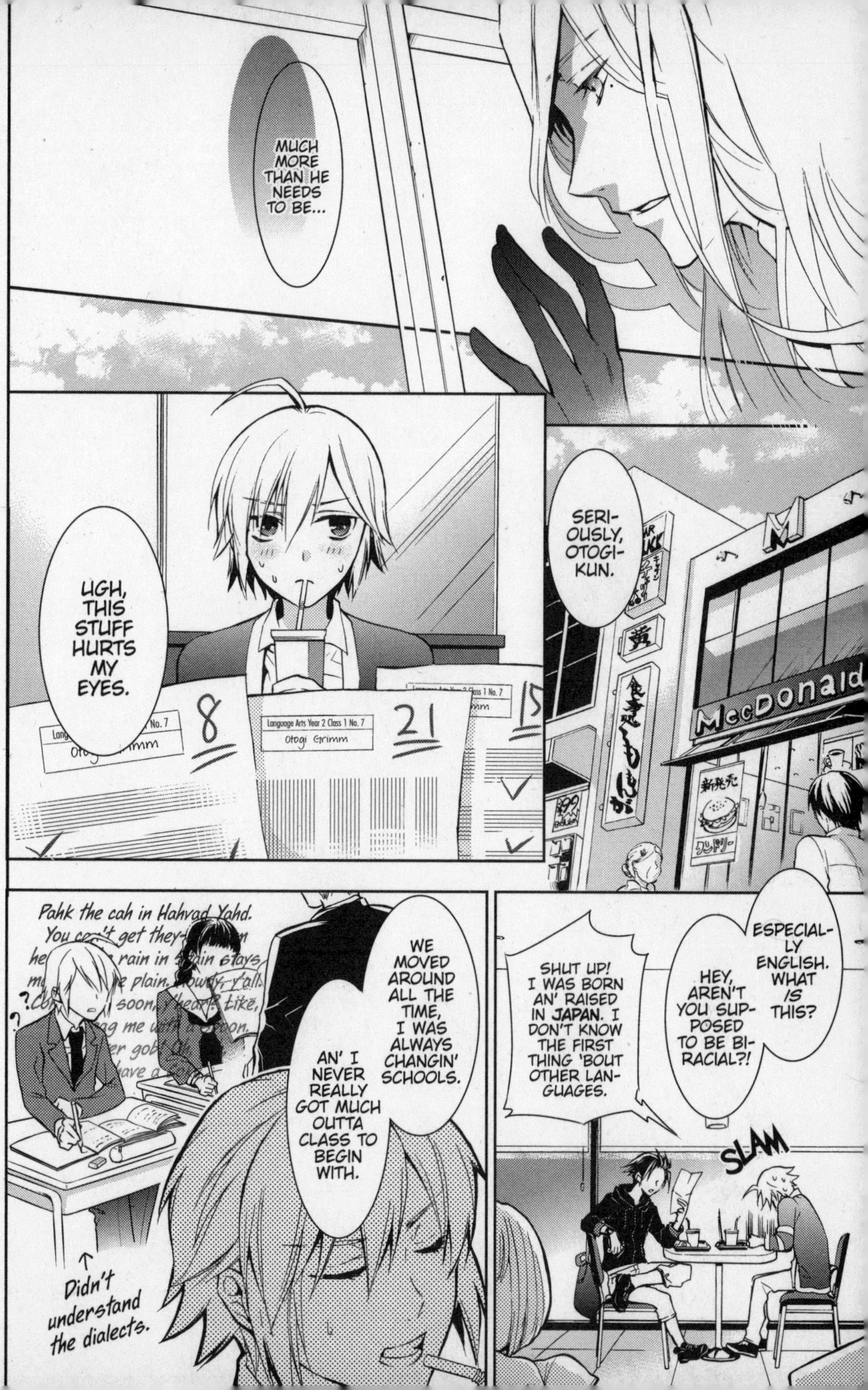
MUCH MORE THAN HE NEEDS TO BE...
SERI-OUSLY, OTOGI-KUN.
McDONALD
新発売
UGH, THIS STUFF HURTS MY EYES.
Language Arts Year 2 Class 1 No. 7
Otogi Grimm
21
8
15
ESPECIAL-LY ENGLISH. WHAT IS THIS?
HEY, AREN'T YOU SUP-POSED TO BE BI-RACIAL?!
SHUT UP! I WAS BORN AN' RAISED IN JAPAN. I DON'T KNOW THE FIRST THING 'BOUT OTHER LAN-GUAGES.
SLAM
WE MOVED AROUND ALL THE TIME, I WAS ALWAYS CHANGIN' SCHOOLS.
AN' I NEVER REALLY GOT MUCH OUTTA CLASS TO BEGIN WITH.
Pahk the cah in Hahvad Yahd.
Didn't understand the dialects.

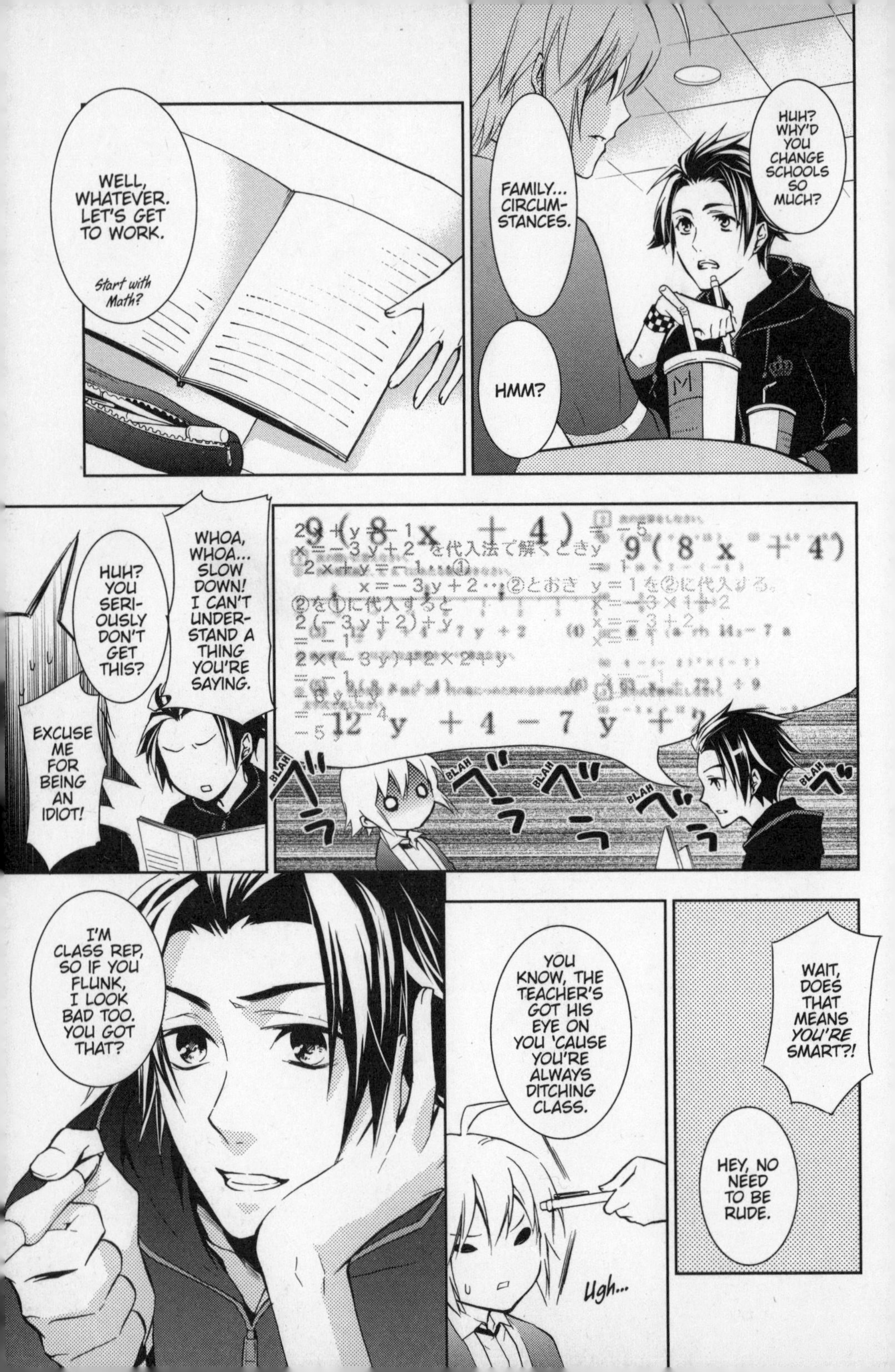
HUH? WHY'D YOU CHANGE SCHOOLS SO MUCH?
FAMILY... CIRCUM-STANCES.
HMM?
WELL, WHATEVER. LET'S GET TO WORK.
Start with Math?
BLAH
BLAH
BLAH
BLAH
BLAH
WHOA, WHOA... SLOW DOWN! I CAN'T UNDER-STAND A THING YOU'RE SAYING.
HUH? YOU SERI-OUSLY DON'T GET THIS?
EXCUSE ME FOR BEING AN IDIOT!
WAIT, DOES THAT MEANS YOU'RE SMART?!
HEY, NO NEED TO BE RUDE.
YOU KNOW, THE TEACHER'S GOT HIS EYE ON YOU 'CAUSE YOU'RE ALWAYS DITCHING CLASS.
Ugh...
I'M CLASS REP, SO IF YOU FLUNK, I LOOK BAD TOO. YOU GOT THAT?

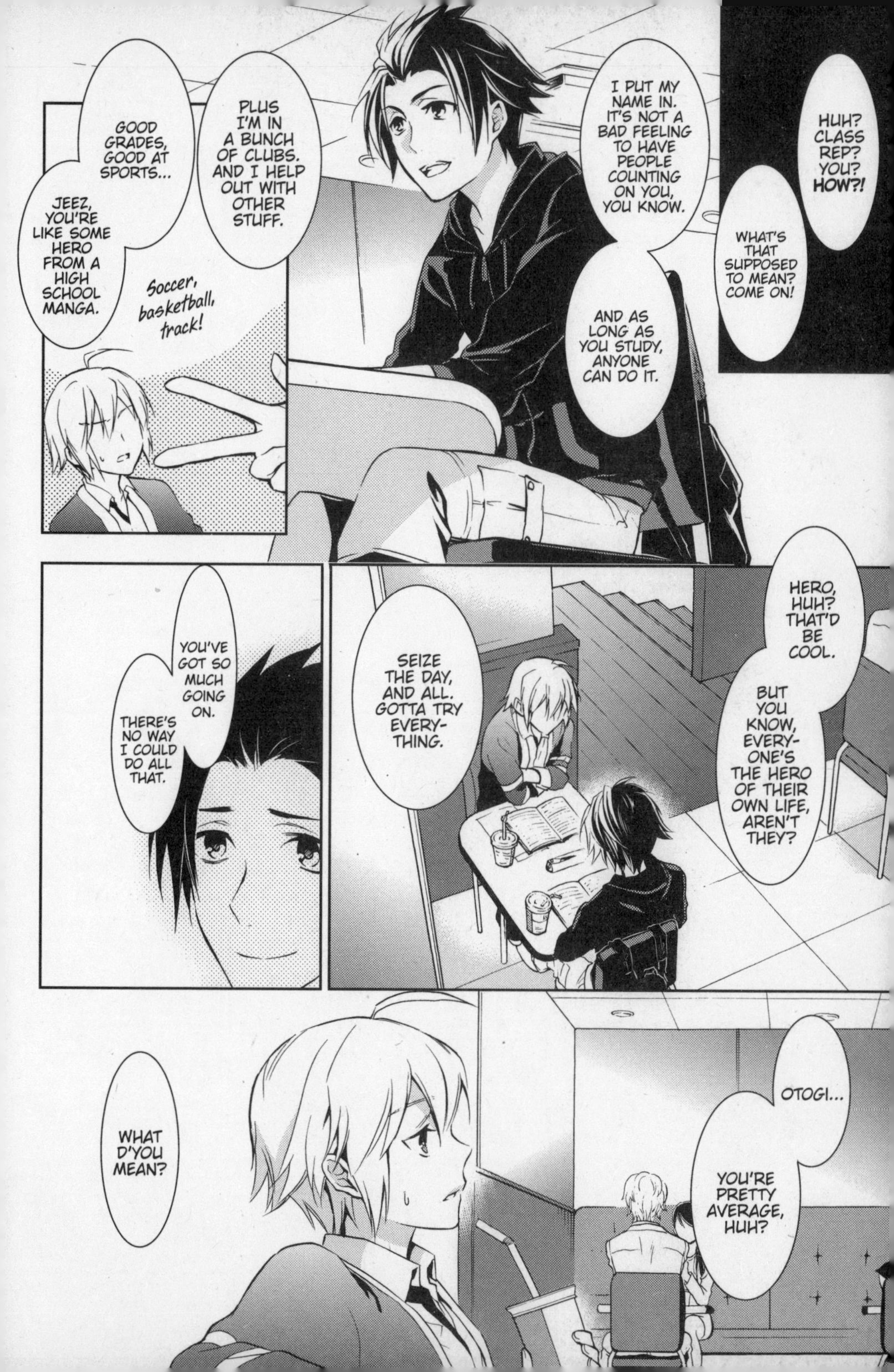
HUH? CLASS REP? YOU? **HOW?!**
WHAT'S THAT SUPPOSED TO MEAN? COME ON!
I PUT MY NAME IN. IT'S NOT A BAD FEELING TO HAVE PEOPLE COUNTING ON YOU, YOU KNOW.
AND AS LONG AS YOU STUDY, ANYONE CAN DO IT.
PLUS I'M IN A BUNCH OF CLUBS. AND I HELP OUT WITH OTHER STUFF.
GOOD GRADES, GOOD AT SPORTS...
JEEZ, YOU'RE LIKE SOME HERO FROM A HIGH SCHOOL MANGA.
Soccer, basketball, track!
HERO, HUH? THAT'D BE COOL.
BUT YOU KNOW, EVERYONE'S THE HERO OF THEIR OWN LIFE, AREN'T THEY?
SEIZE THE DAY, AND ALL. GOTTA TRY EVERYTHING.
YOU'VE GOT SO MUCH GOING ON.
THERE'S NO WAY I COULD DO ALL THAT.
OTOGI...
YOU'RE PRETTY AVERAGE, HUH?
WHAT D'YOU MEAN?

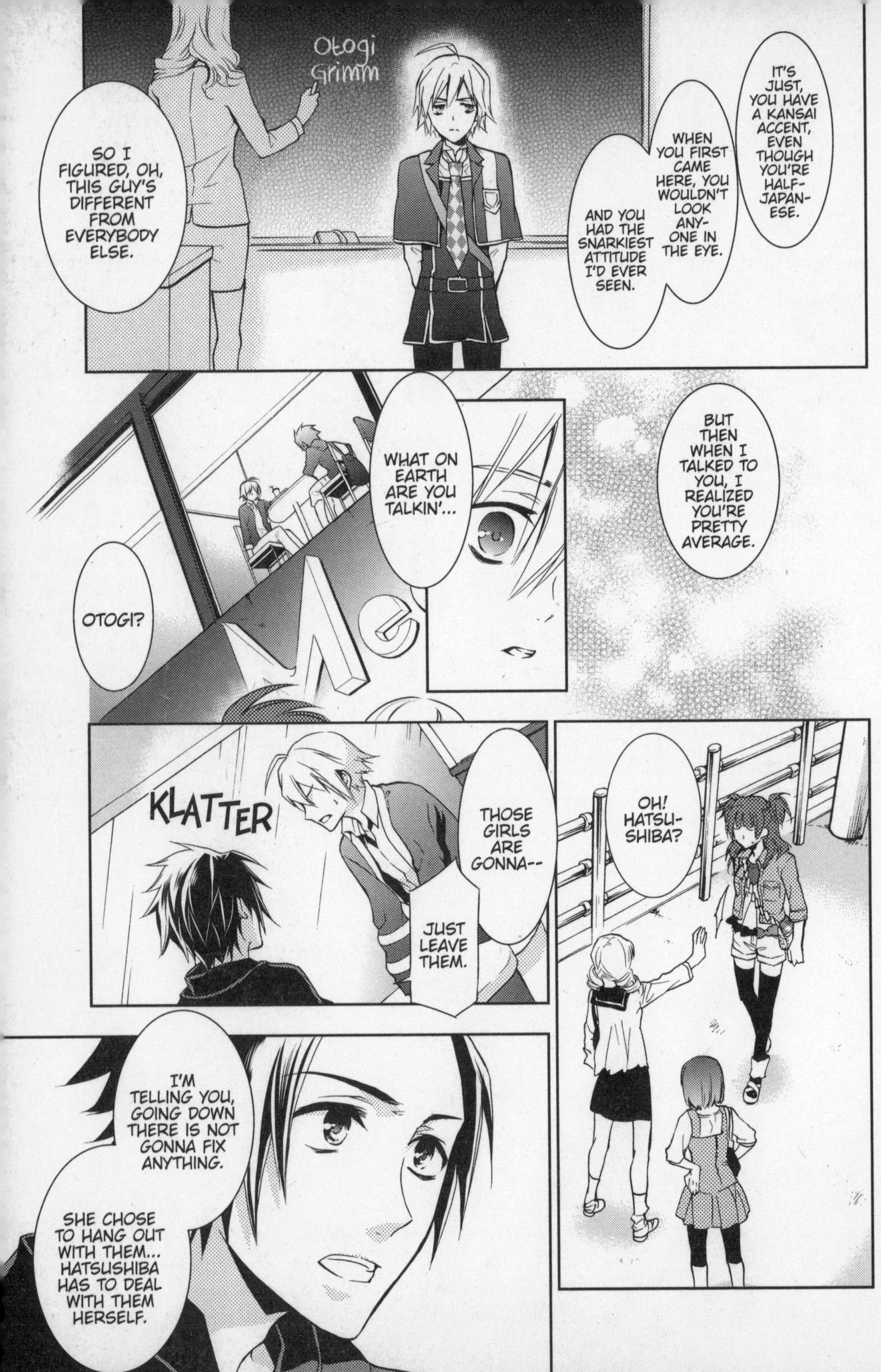

Otogi Grimm
IT'S JUST, YOU HAVE A KANSAI ACCENT, EVEN THOUGH YOU'RE HALF-JAPANESE.
WHEN YOU FIRST CAME HERE, YOU WOULDN'T LOOK ANYONE IN THE EYE.
AND YOU HAD THE SNARKIEST ATTITUDE I'D EVER SEEN.
SO I FIGURED, OH, THIS GUY'S DIFFERENT FROM EVERYBODY ELSE.
BUT THEN WHEN I TALKED TO YOU, I REALIZED YOU'RE PRETTY AVERAGE.
WHAT ON EARTH ARE YOU TALKIN'...
OTOGI?
OH! HATSUSHIBA?
KLATTER
THOSE GIRLS ARE GONNA--
JUST LEAVE THEM.
I'M TELLING YOU, GOING DOWN THERE IS NOT GONNA FIX ANYTHING.
SHE CHOSE TO HANG OUT WITH THEM... HATSUSHIBA HAS TO DEAL WITH THEM HERSELF.

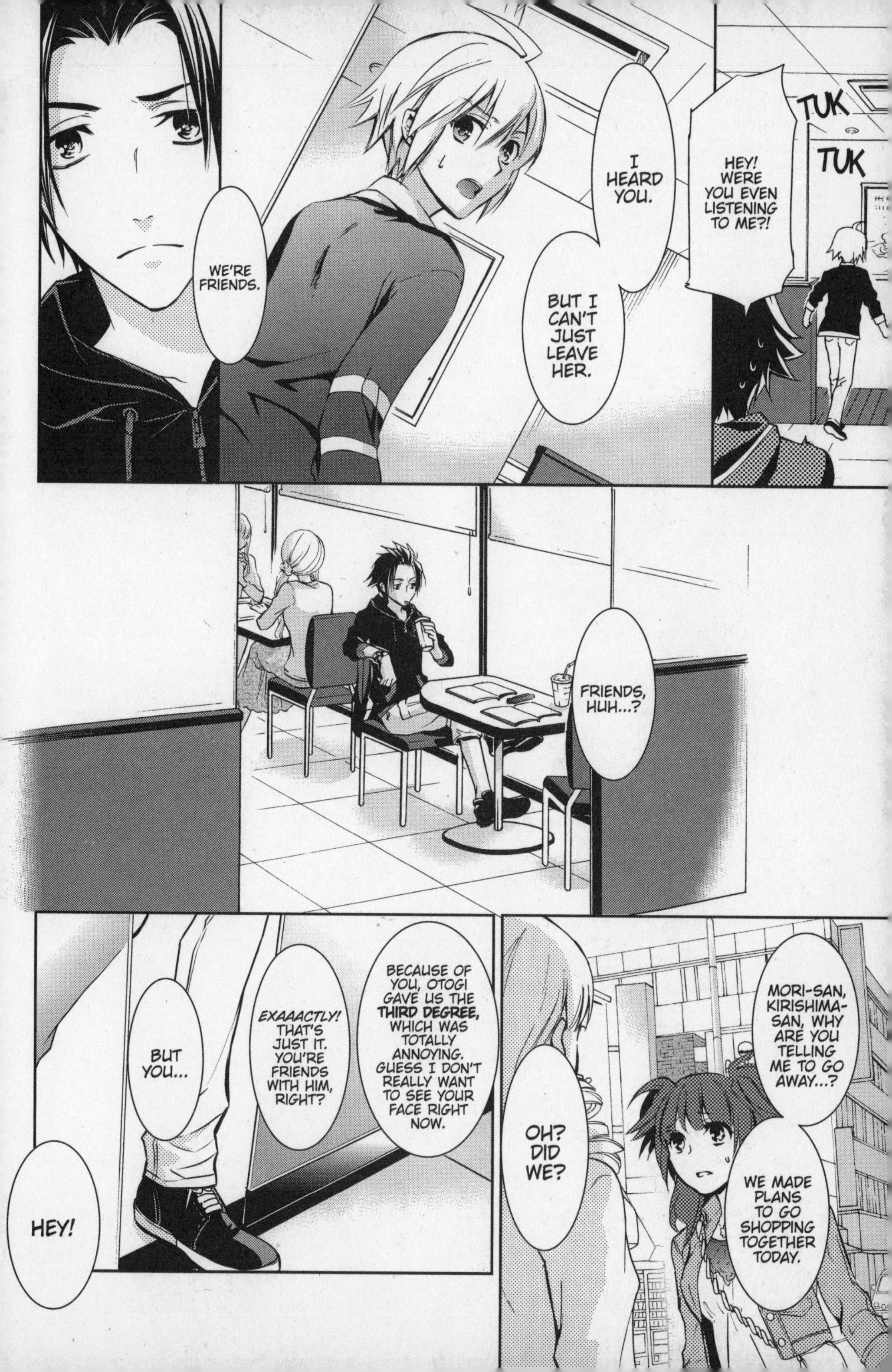
TUK
TUK
HEY! WERE YOU EVEN LISTENING TO ME?!
I HEARD YOU.
BUT I CAN'T JUST LEAVE HER.
WE'RE FRIENDS.
FRIENDS, HUH...?
MORI-SAN, KIRISHIMA-SAN, WHY ARE YOU TELLING ME TO GO AWAY...?
WE MADE PLANS TO GO SHOPPING TOGETHER TODAY.
OH? DID WE?
BECAUSE OF YOU, OTOGI GAVE US THE THIRD DEGREE, WHICH WAS TOTALLY ANNOYING. GUESS I DON'T REALLY WANT TO SEE YOUR FACE RIGHT NOW.
EXAAACTLY! THAT'S JUST IT. YOU'RE FRIENDS WITH HIM, RIGHT?
BUT YOU...
HEY!

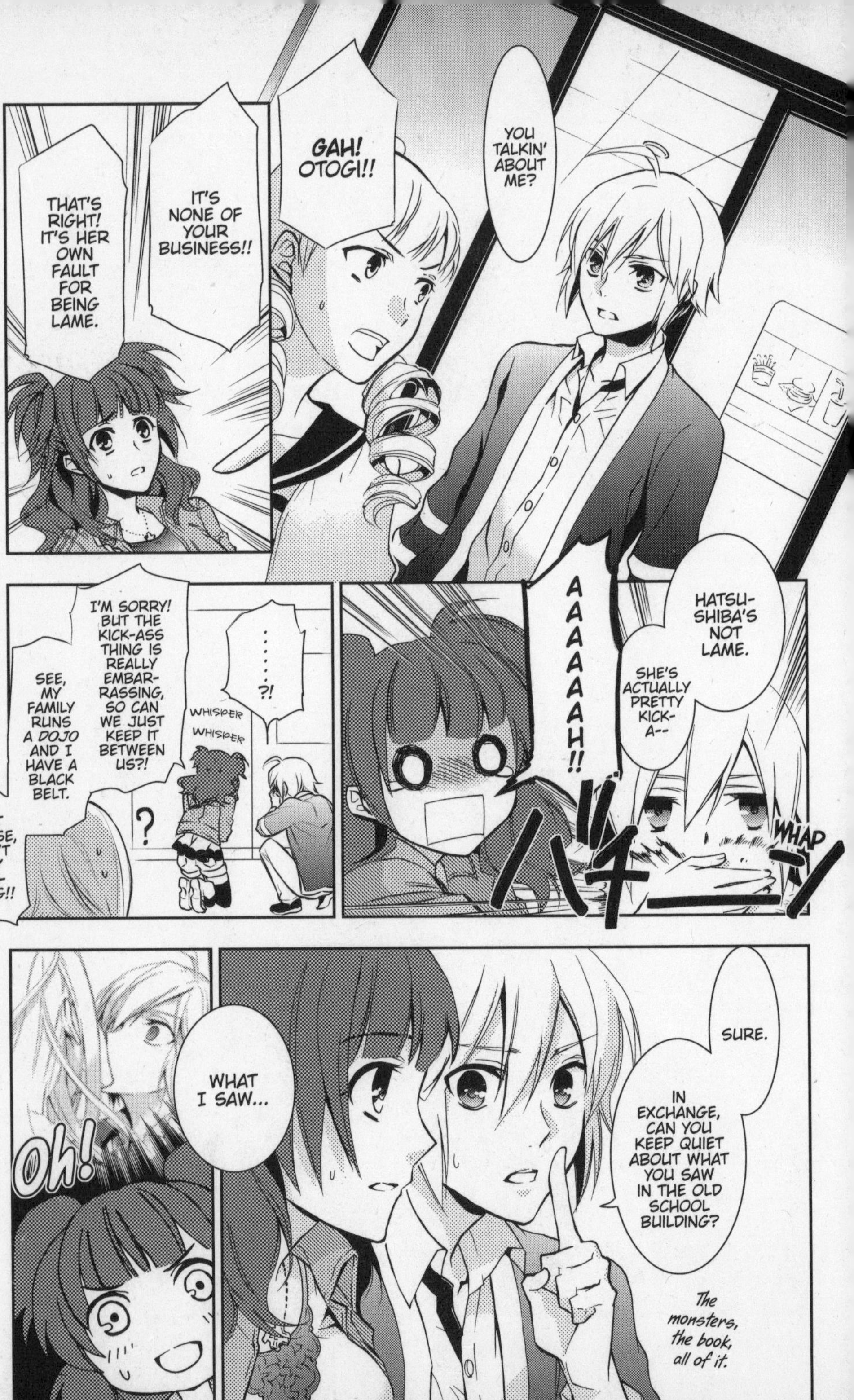
YOU TALKIN' ABOUT ME?
GAH! OTOGI!!
IT'S NONE OF YOUR BUSINESS!!
THAT'S RIGHT! IT'S HER OWN FAULT FOR BEING LAME.
HATSU-SHIBA'S NOT LAME.
SHE'S ACTUALLY PRETTY KICK-A--
AAAAAAAH!!
WHAP
......?!
WHISPER
WHISPER
I'M SORRY! BUT THE KICK-ASS THING IS REALLY EMBAR-RASSING, SO CAN WE JUST KEEP IT BETWEEN US?!
SEE, MY FAMILY RUNS A DOJO AND I HAVE A BLACK BELT.
?
BUT PLEASE, DON'T SAY ANY-THING!!
SURE.
IN EXCHANGE, CAN YOU KEEP QUIET ABOUT WHAT YOU SAW IN THE OLD SCHOOL BUILDING?
The monsters, the book, all of it.
WHAT I SAW...
Oh!

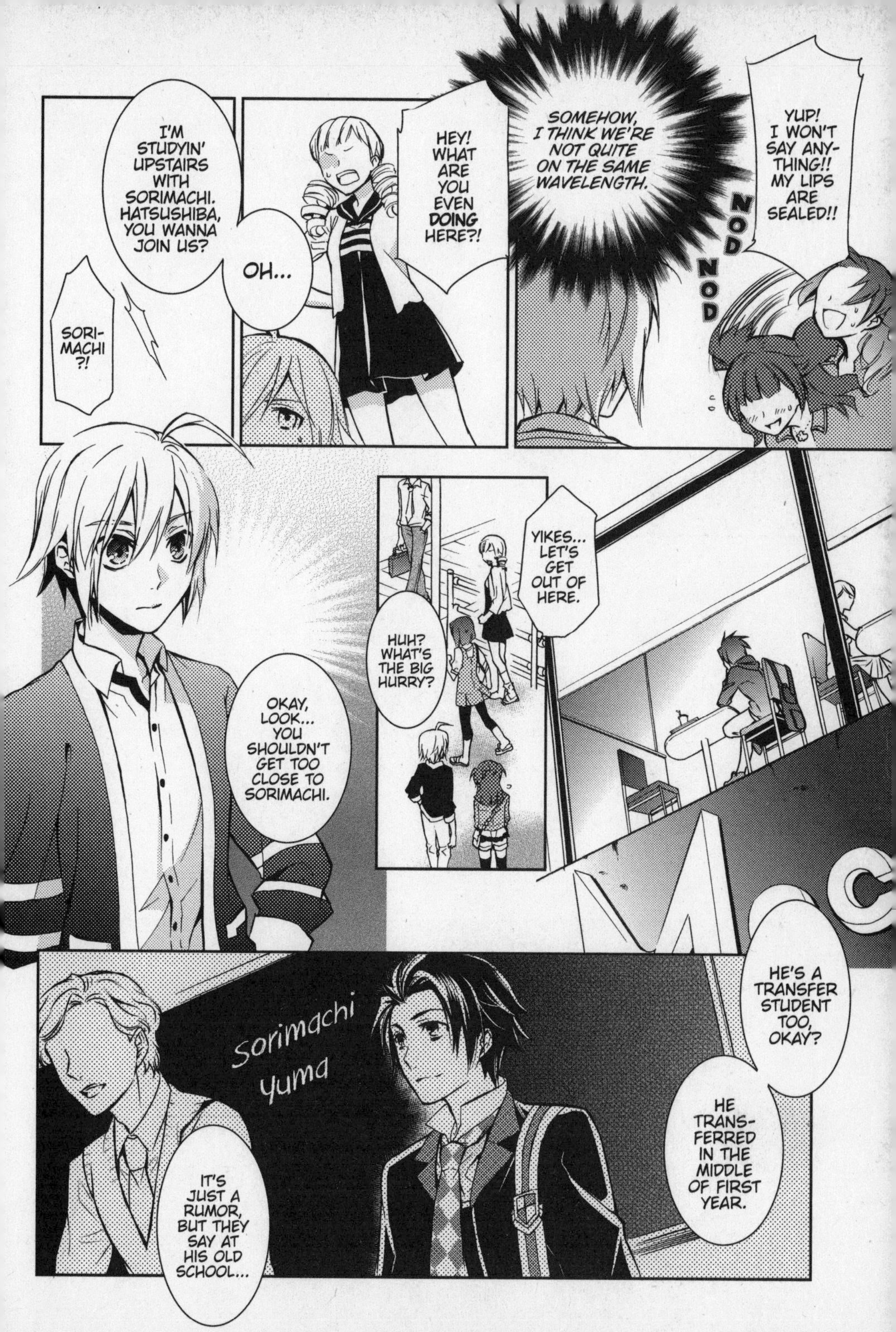
YUP! I WON'T SAY ANYTHING!! MY LIPS ARE SEALED!!
NOD NOD
SOMEHOW, I THINK WE'RE NOT QUITE ON THE SAME WAVELENGTH.
HEY! WHAT ARE YOU EVEN DOING HERE?!
OH...
I'M STUDYIN' UPSTAIRS WITH SORIMACHI. HATSUSHIBA, YOU WANNA JOIN US?
SORIMACHI?!
YIKES... LET'S GET OUT OF HERE.
HUH? WHAT'S THE BIG HURRY?
OKAY, LOOK... YOU SHOULDN'T GET TOO CLOSE TO SORIMACHI.
HE'S A TRANSFER STUDENT TOO, OKAY?
HE TRANSFERRED IN THE MIDDLE OF FIRST YEAR.
Sorimachi Yuma
IT'S JUST A RUMOR, BUT THEY SAY AT HIS OLD SCHOOL...

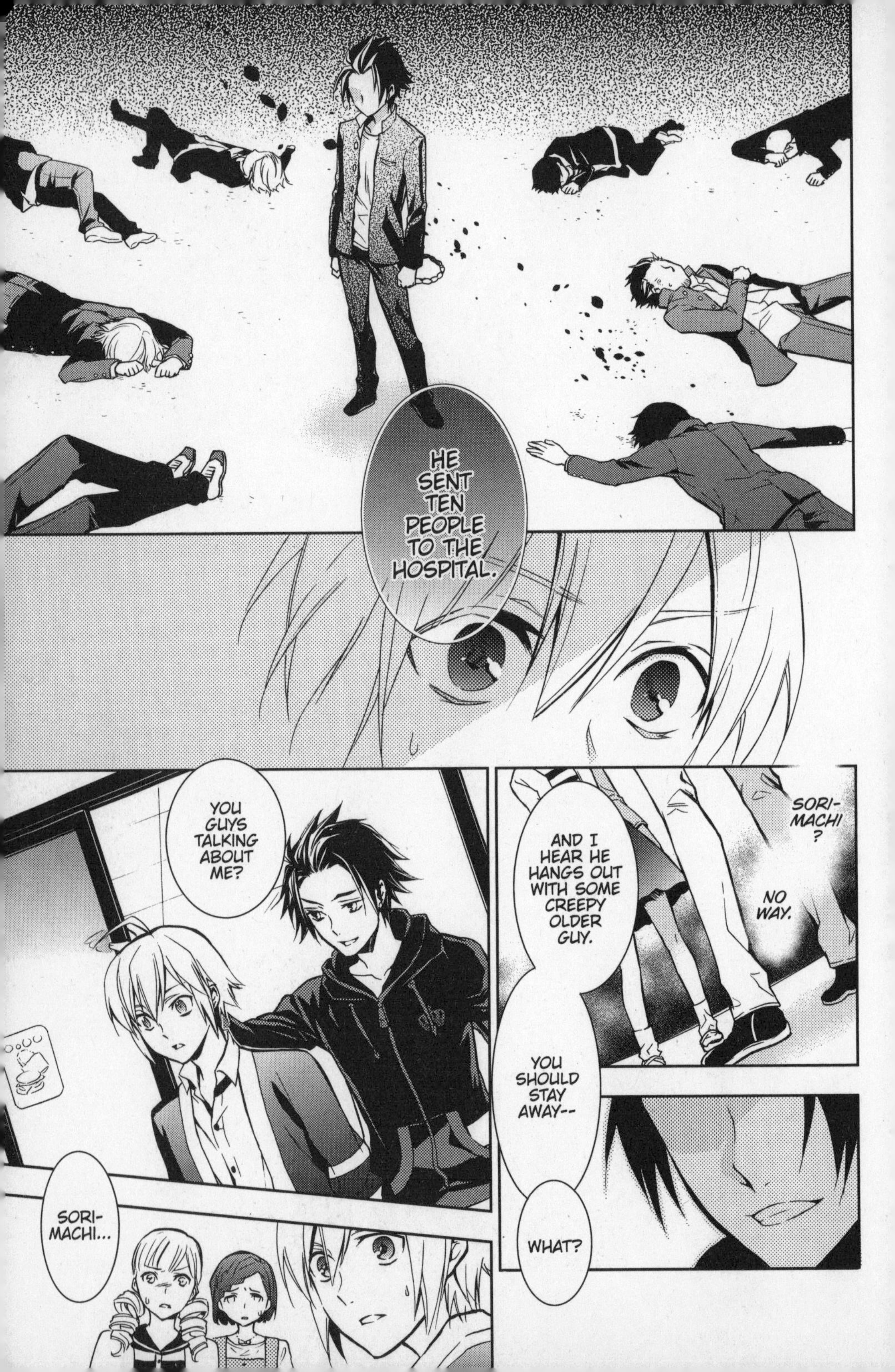

HE SENT TEN PEOPLE TO THE HOSPITAL.
SORI-MACHI?
NO WAY.
AND I HEAR HE HANGS OUT WITH SOME CREEPY OLDER GUY.
YOU SHOULD STAY AWAY--
WHAT?
YOU GUYS TALKING ABOUT ME?
SORI-MACHI...

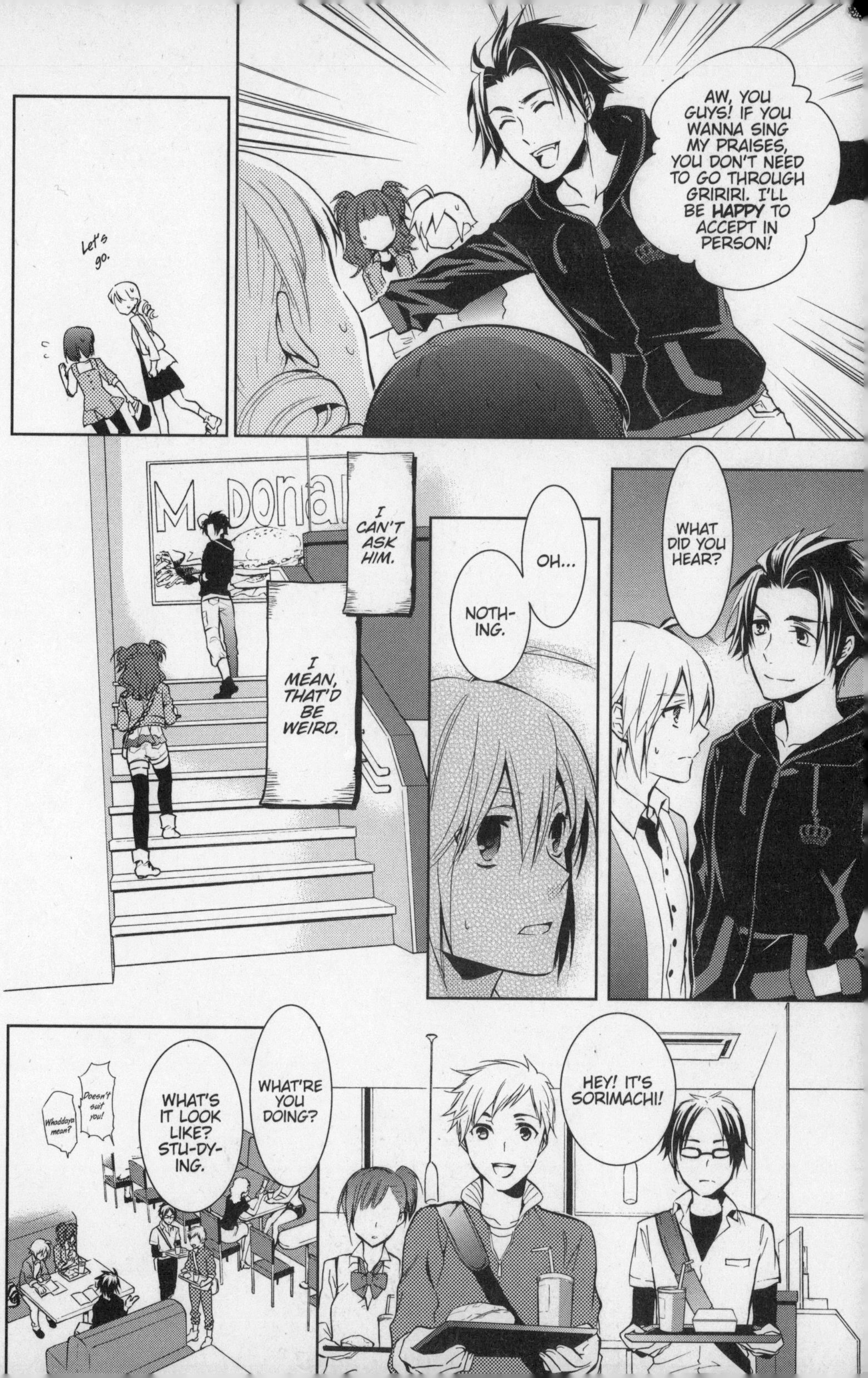
AW, YOU GUYS! IF YOU WANNA SING MY PRAISES, YOU DON'T NEED TO GO THROUGH GRIRIRI. I'LL BE **HAPPY** TO ACCEPT IN PERSON!
Let's go.
WHAT DID YOU HEAR?
OH...
NOTHING.
I CAN'T ASK HIM.
I MEAN, THAT'D BE WEIRD.
HEY! IT'S SORIMACHI!
WHAT'RE YOU DOING?
WHAT'S IT LOOK LIKE? STU-DY-ING.
Doesn't suit you!
Whaddaya mean?

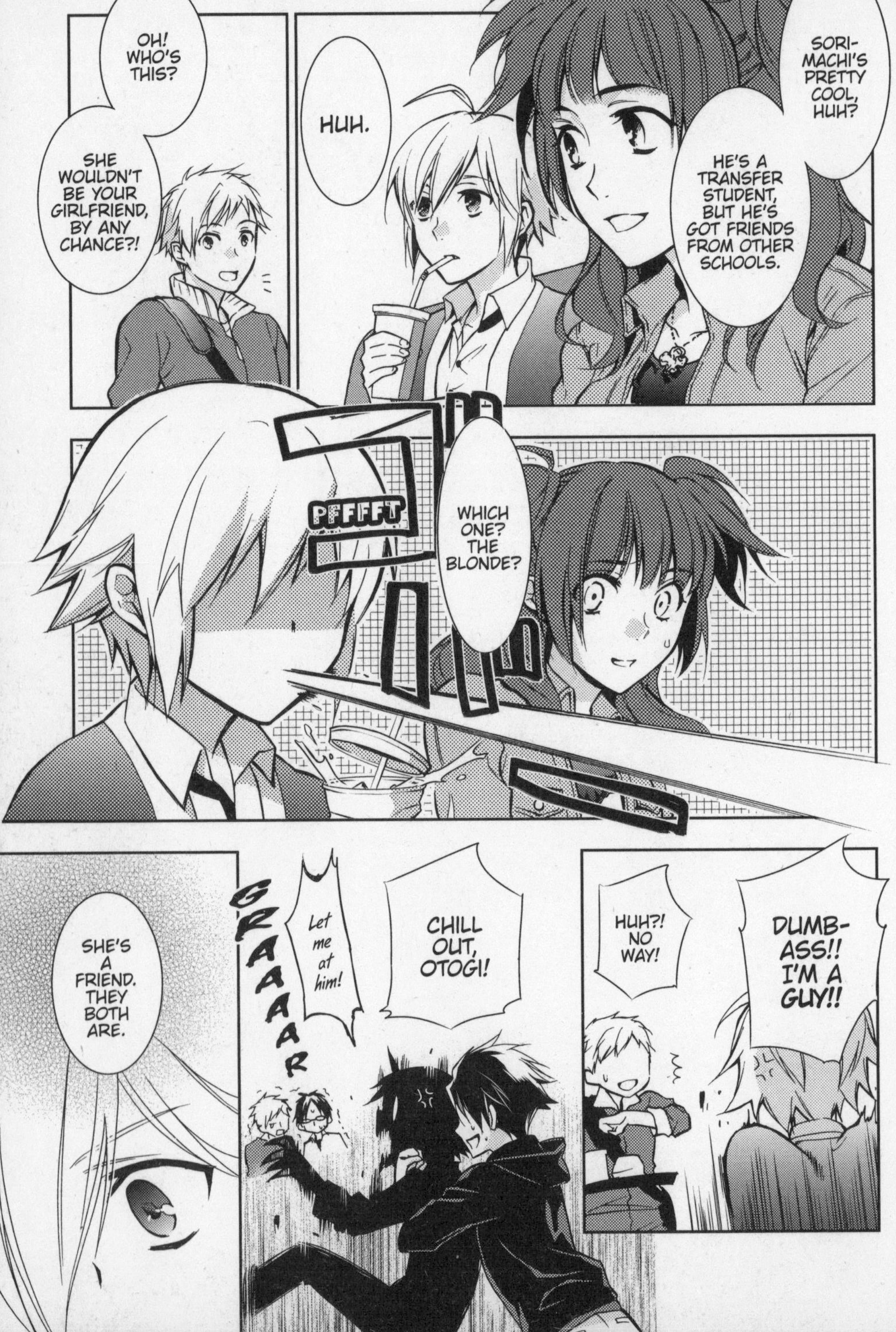
SORI-MACHI'S PRETTY COOL, HUH?
HE'S A TRANSFER STUDENT, BUT HE'S GOT FRIENDS FROM OTHER SCHOOLS.
HUH.
OH! WHO'S THIS?
SHE WOULDN'T BE YOUR GIRLFRIEND, BY ANY CHANCE?!
PFFFFT
WHICH ONE? THE BLONDE?
DUMB-ASS!! I'M A GUY!!
HUH?! NO WAY!
CHILL OUT, OTOGI!
Let me at him!
GRAAAAR
SHE'S A FRIEND. THEY BOTH ARE.

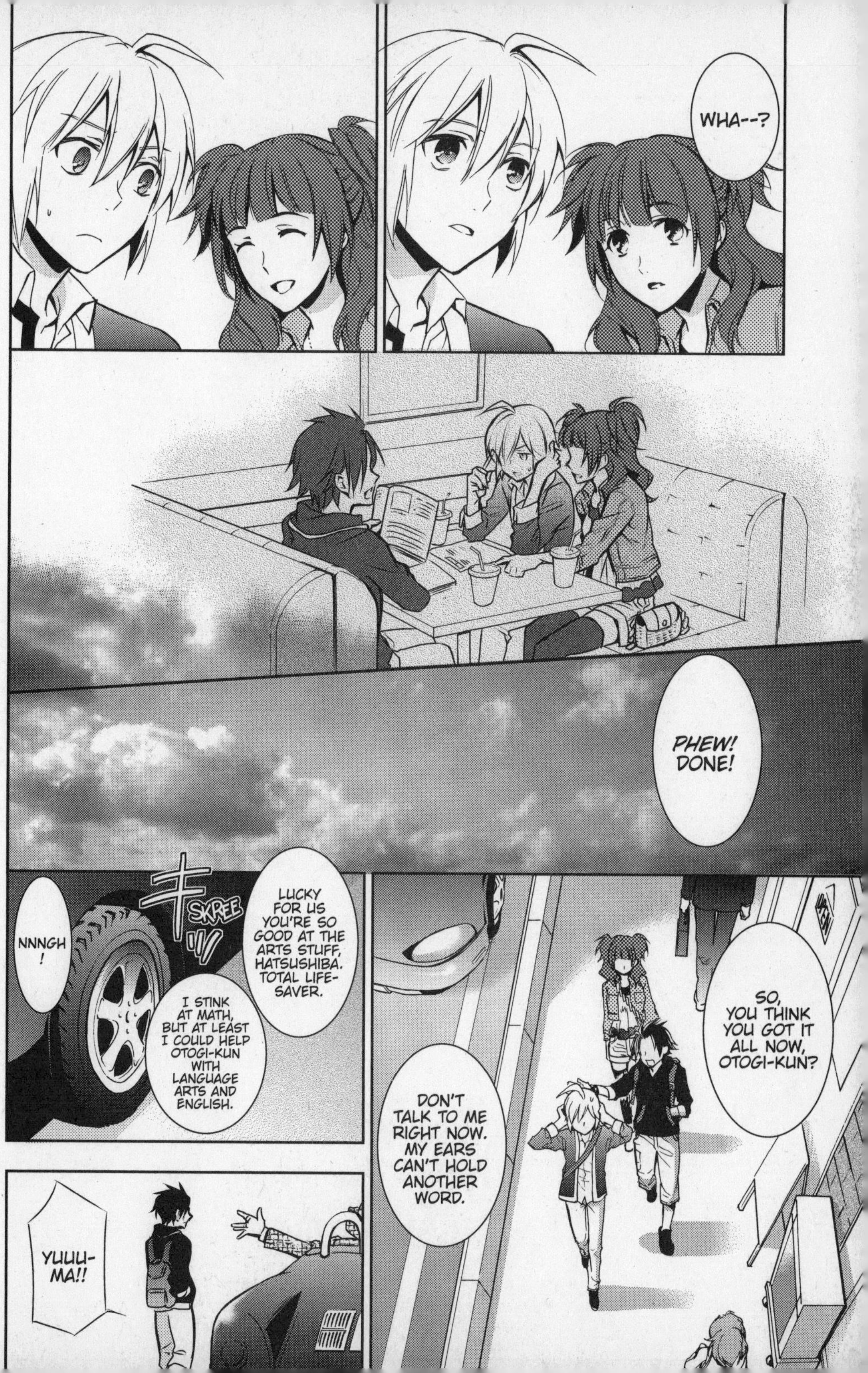
WHA--?
PHEW! DONE!
SO, YOU THINK YOU GOT IT ALL NOW, OTOGI-KUN?
DON'T TALK TO ME RIGHT NOW. MY EARS CAN'T HOLD ANOTHER WORD.
LUCKY FOR US YOU'RE SO GOOD AT THE ARTS STUFF, HATSUSHIBA. TOTAL LIFE-SAVER.
I STINK AT MATH, BUT AT LEAST I COULD HELP OTOGI-KUN WITH LANGUAGE ARTS AND ENGLISH.
SKREE
NNNGH!
YUUU-MA!!

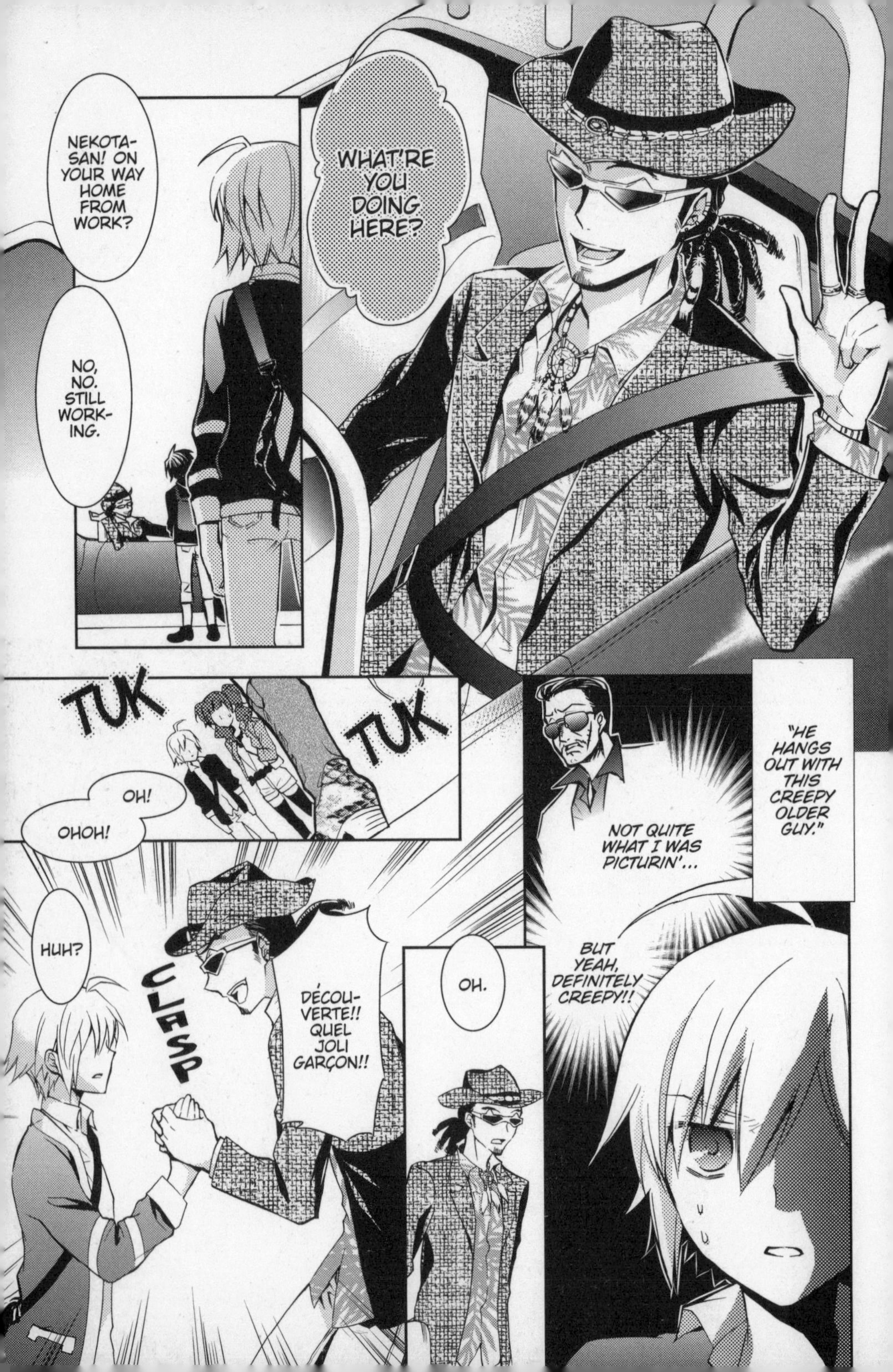
WHAT'RE YOU DOING HERE?
NEKOTA-SAN! ON YOUR WAY HOME FROM WORK?
NO, NO. STILL WORKING.
"HE HANGS OUT WITH THIS CREEPY OLDER GUY."
NOT QUITE WHAT I WAS PICTURIN'...
BUT YEAH, DEFINITELY CREEPY!!
TUK
TUK
OH!
OHOH!
OH.
DÉCOUVERTE!! QUEL JOLI GARÇON!!
CLASP
HUH?

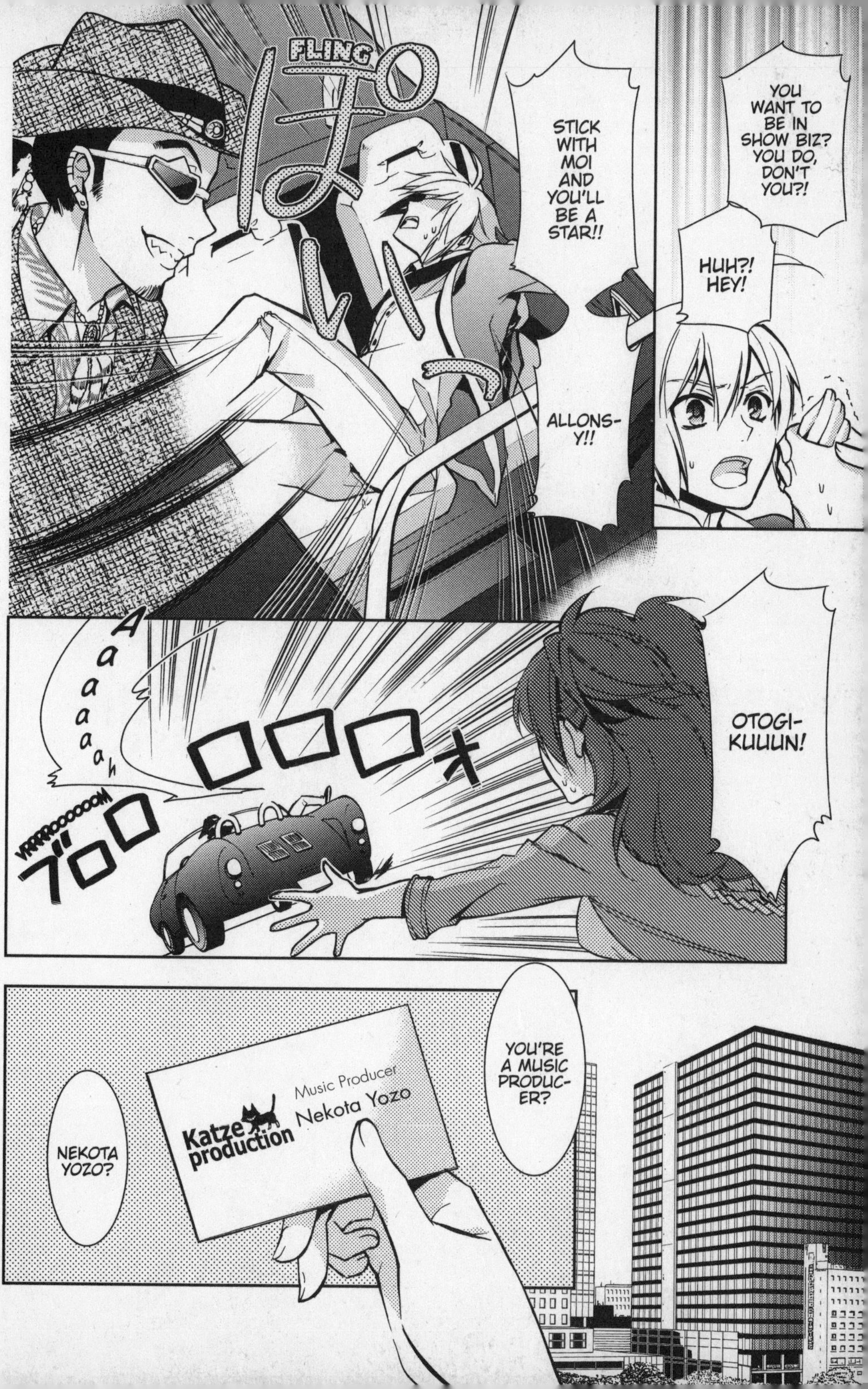
YOU WANT TO BE IN SHOW BIZ? YOU DO, DON'T YOU?!
HUH?! HEY!
FLING
STICK WITH MOI AND YOU'LL BE A STAR!!
ALLONS-Y!!
OTOGI-KUUUN!
Aaaaaaah
VRRRROOOOOOM
YOU'RE A MUSIC PRODUCER?
Music Producer
Nekota Yozo
Katze production
NEKOTA YOZO?

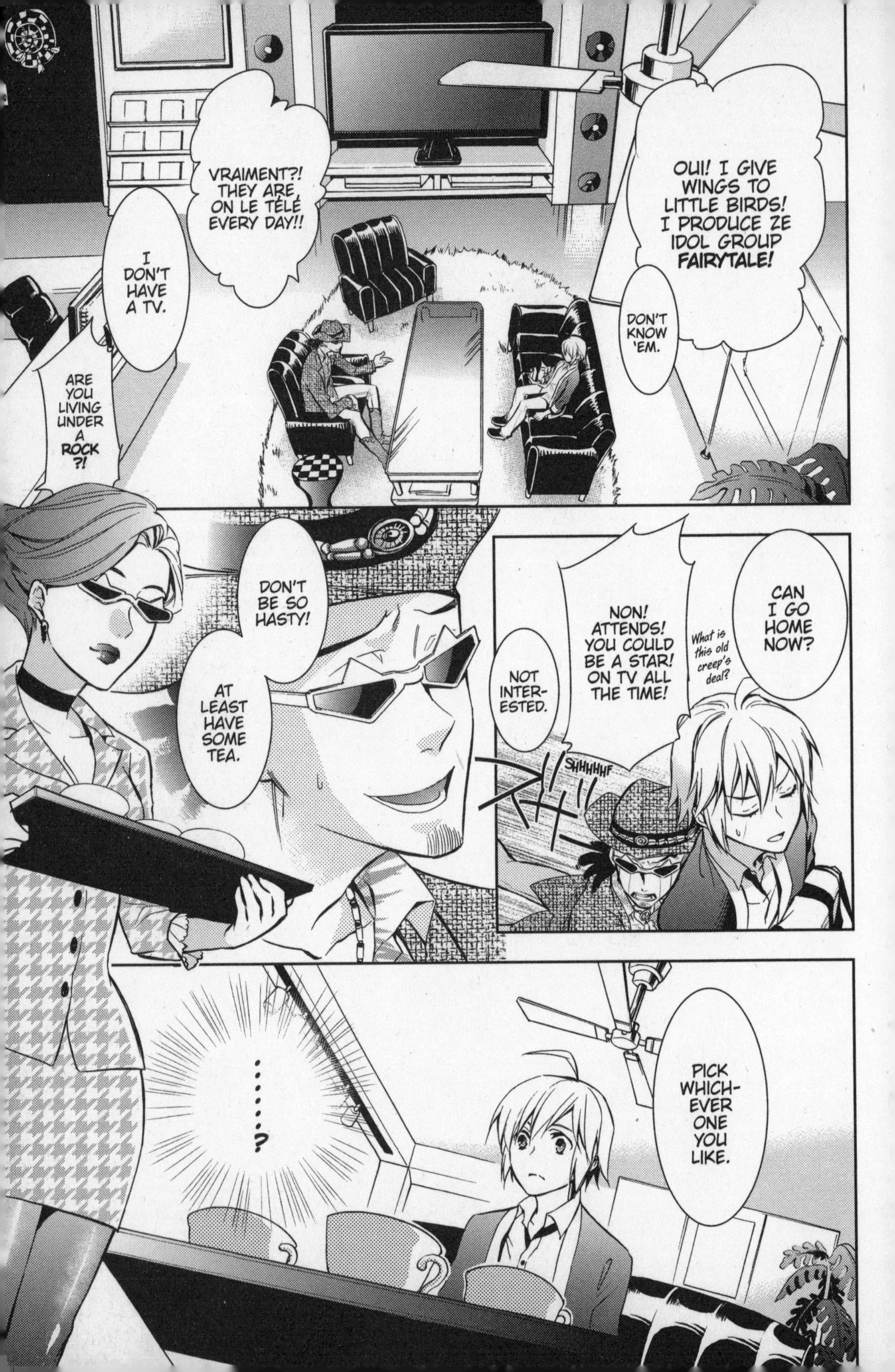
OUI! I GIVE WINGS TO LITTLE BIRDS! I PRODUCE ZE IDOL GROUP **FAIRYTALE!**
DON'T KNOW 'EM.
VRAIMENT?! THEY ARE ON LE TÉLÉ EVERY DAY!!
I DON'T HAVE A TV.
ARE YOU LIVING UNDER A **ROCK** ?!
CAN I GO HOME NOW?
What is this old creep's deal?
NON! ATTENDS! YOU COULD BE A STAR! ON TV ALL THE TIME!
NOT INTER-ESTED.
SHHHHHF
DON'T BE SO HASTY!
AT LEAST HAVE SOME TEA.
PICK WHICH-EVER ONE YOU LIKE.
......?

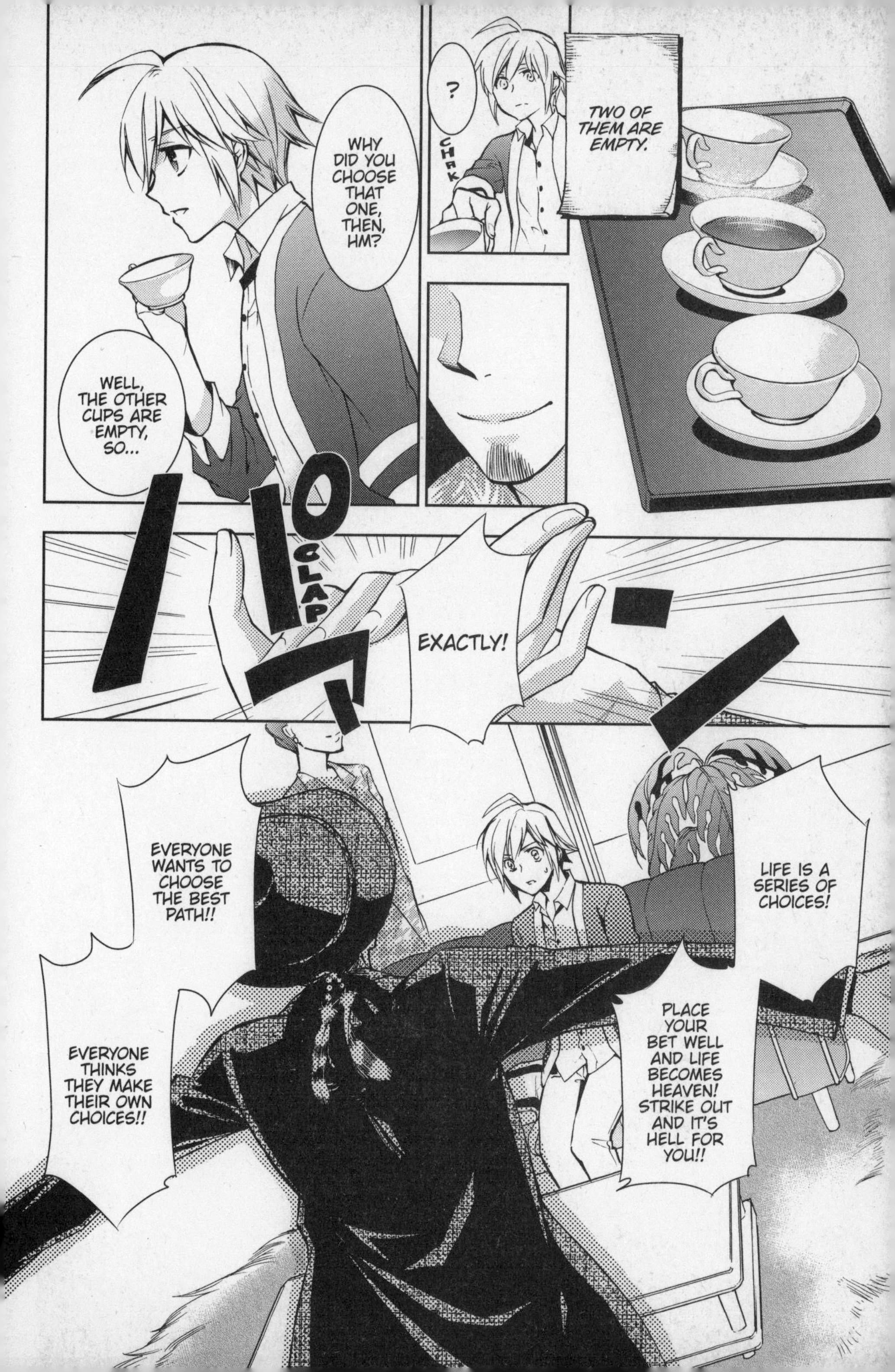

TWO OF THEM ARE EMPTY.
?
CHAK
WHY DID YOU CHOOSE THAT ONE, THEN, HM?
WELL, THE OTHER CUPS ARE EMPTY, SO...
CLAP
EXACTLY!
LIFE IS A SERIES OF CHOICES!
PLACE YOUR BET WELL AND LIFE BECOMES HEAVEN! STRIKE OUT AND IT'S HELL FOR YOU!!
EVERYONE WANTS TO CHOOSE THE BEST PATH!!
EVERYONE THINKS THEY MAKE THEIR OWN CHOICES!!

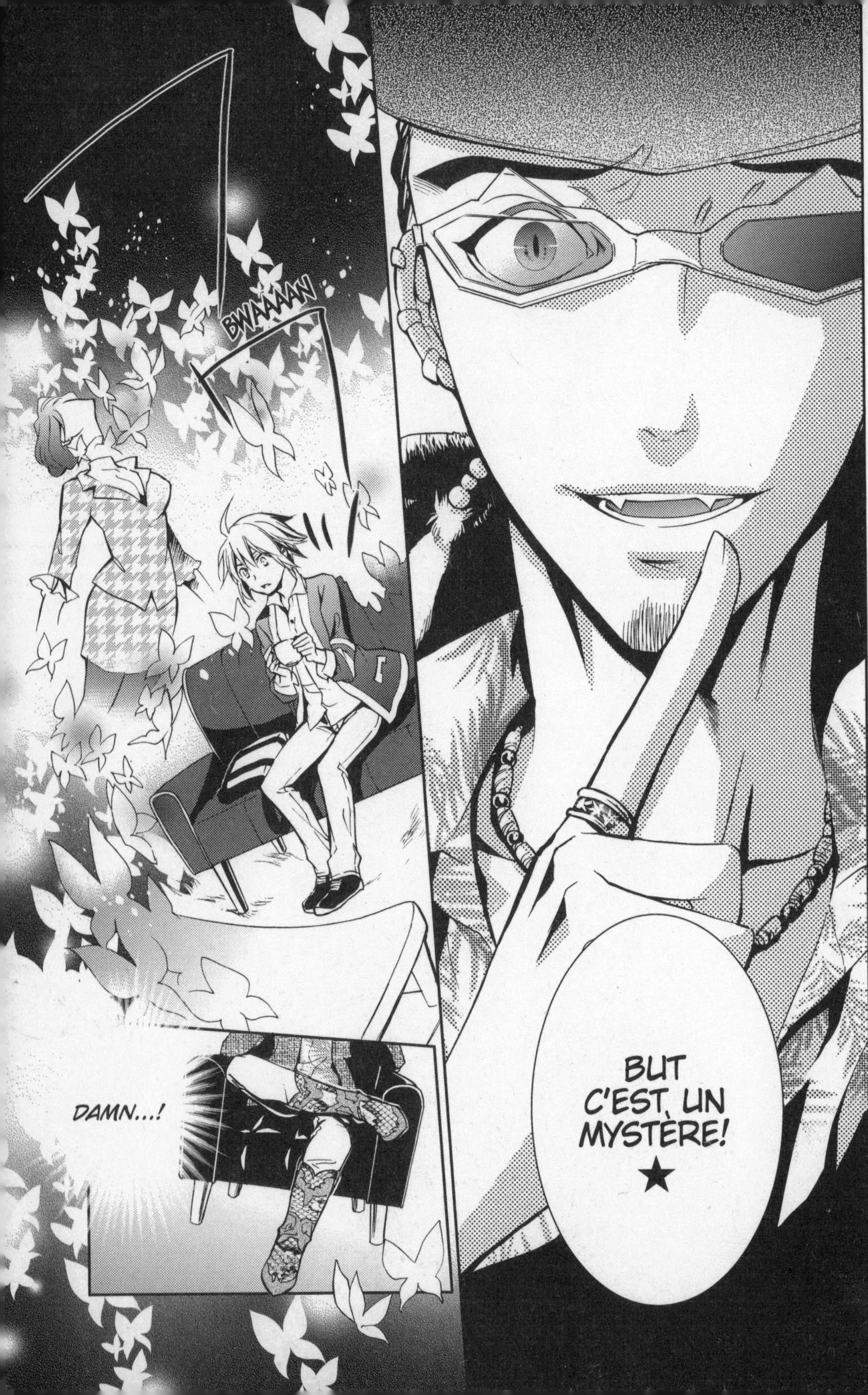
BUT C'EST, UN MYSTÈRE! ★
BWAAAAN
DAMN...!

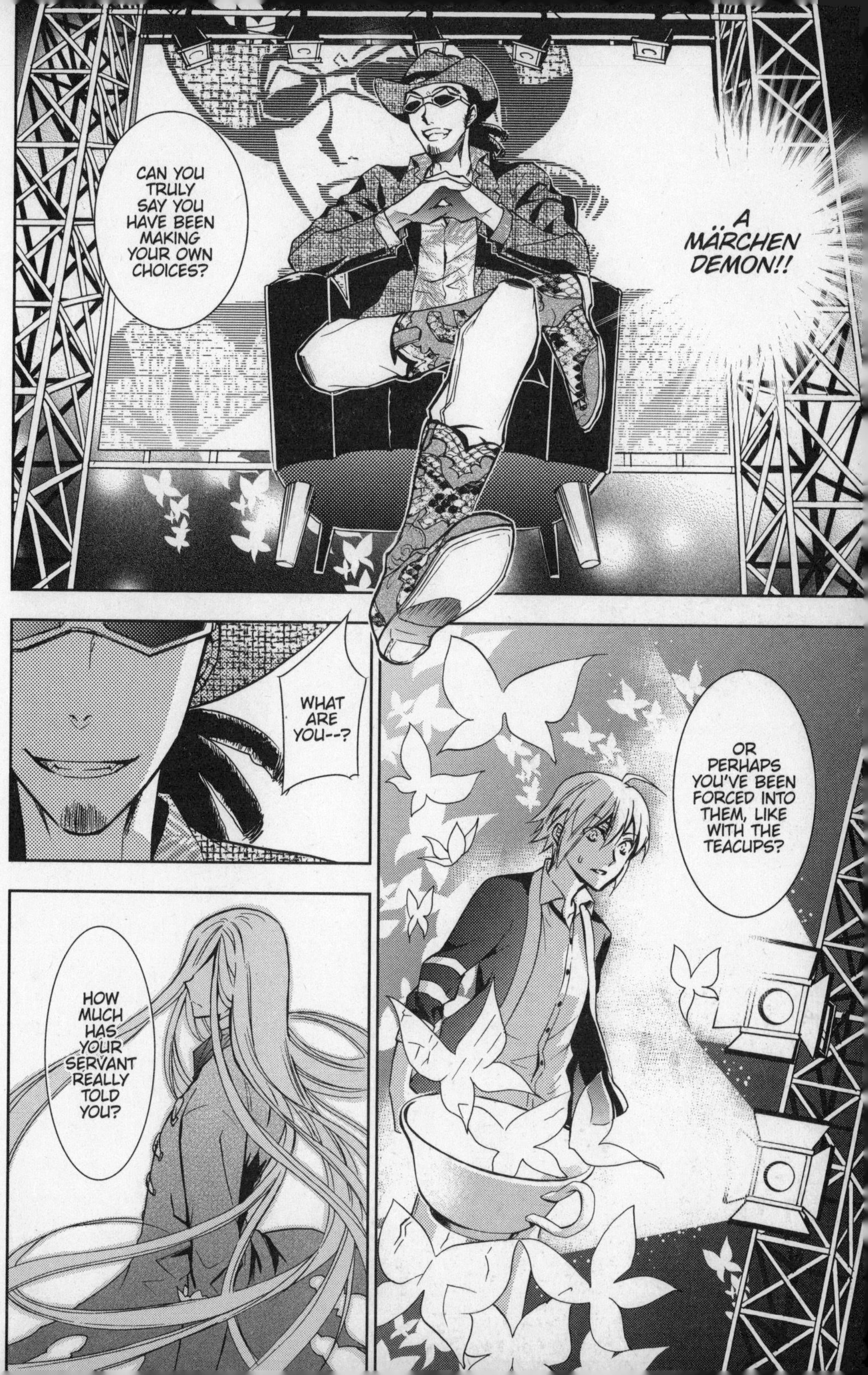
...A MÄRCHEN DEMON!!
CAN YOU TRULY SAY YOU HAVE BEEN MAKING YOUR OWN CHOICES?
OR PERHAPS YOU'VE BEEN FORCED INTO THEM, LIKE WITH THE TEACUPS?
WHAT ARE YOU--?
HOW MUCH HAS YOUR SERVANT REALLY TOLD YOU?

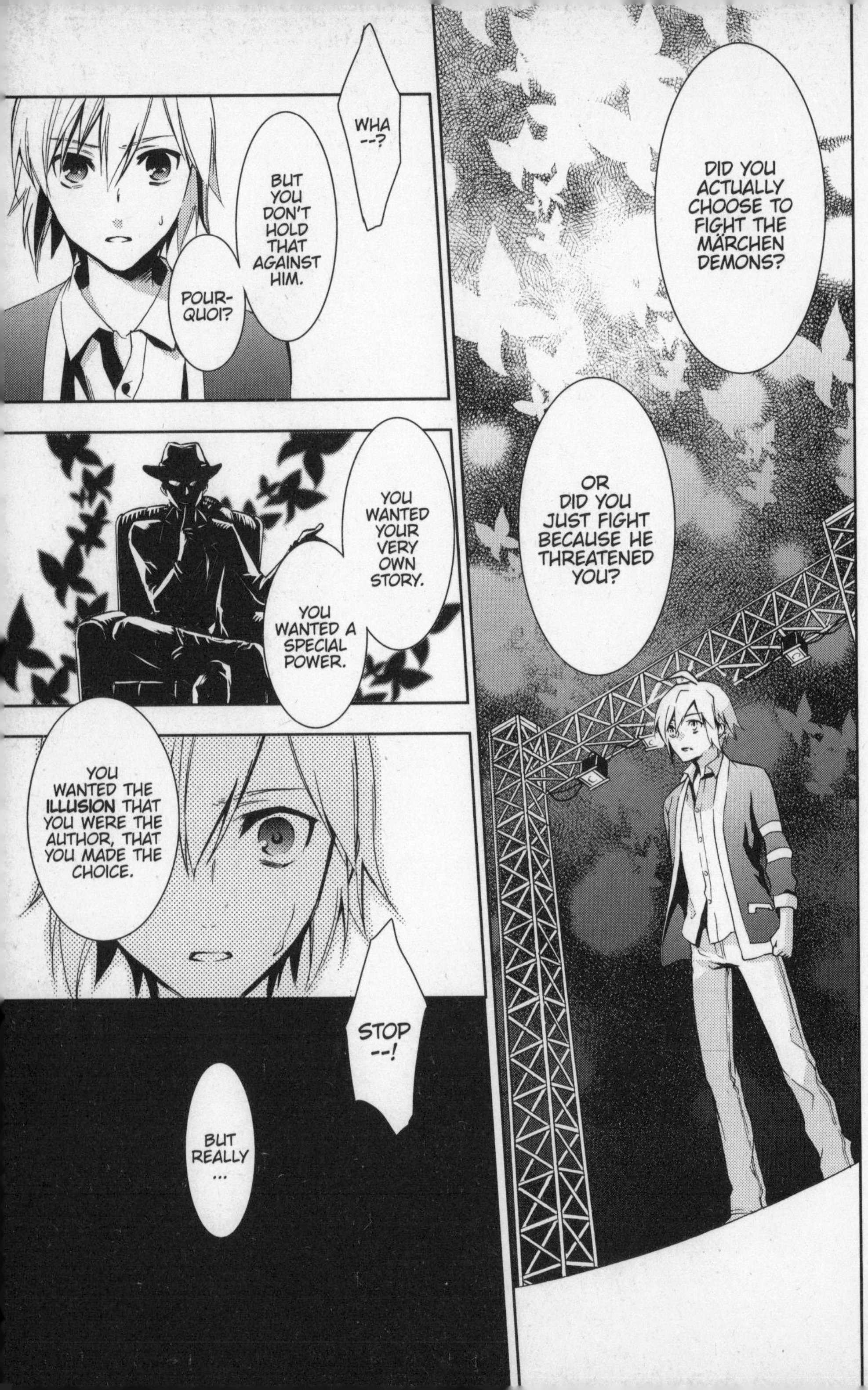
DID YOU ACTUALLY CHOOSE TO FIGHT THE MÄRCHEN DEMONS?
OR DID YOU JUST FIGHT BECAUSE HE THREATENED YOU?
WHA--?
BUT YOU DON'T HOLD THAT AGAINST HIM.
POURQUOI?
YOU WANTED YOUR VERY OWN STORY.
YOU WANTED A SPECIAL POWER.
YOU WANTED THE **ILLUSION** THAT YOU WERE THE AUTHOR, THAT YOU MADE THE CHOICE.
STOP--!
BUT REALLY...

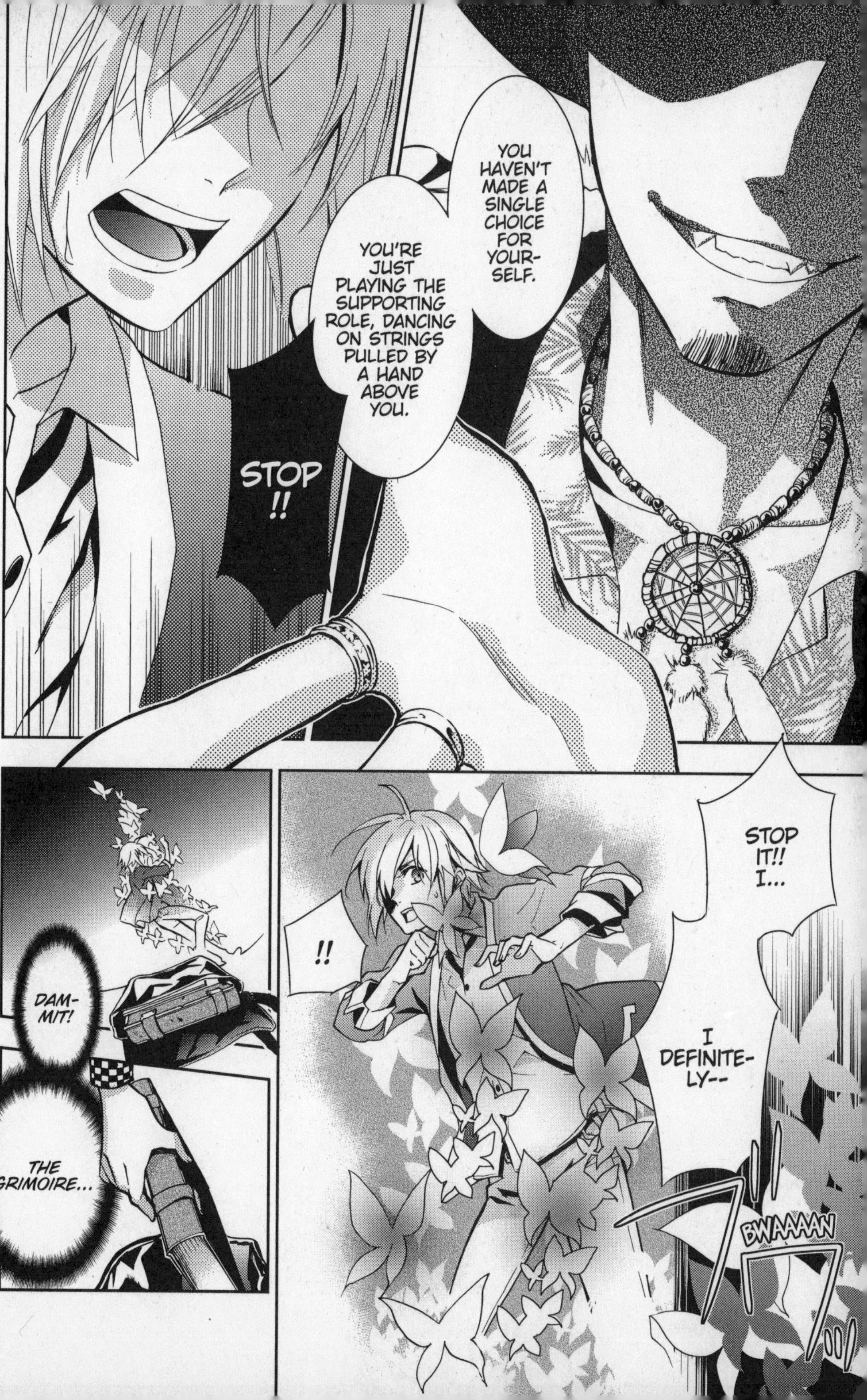
YOU HAVEN'T MADE A SINGLE CHOICE FOR YOUR-SELF.
YOU'RE JUST PLAYING THE SUPPORTING ROLE, DANCING ON STRINGS PULLED BY A HAND ABOVE YOU.
STOP !!
STOP IT!! I...
I DEFINITE-LY--
!!
BWAAAAN
DAM-MIT!
THE GRIMOIRE...

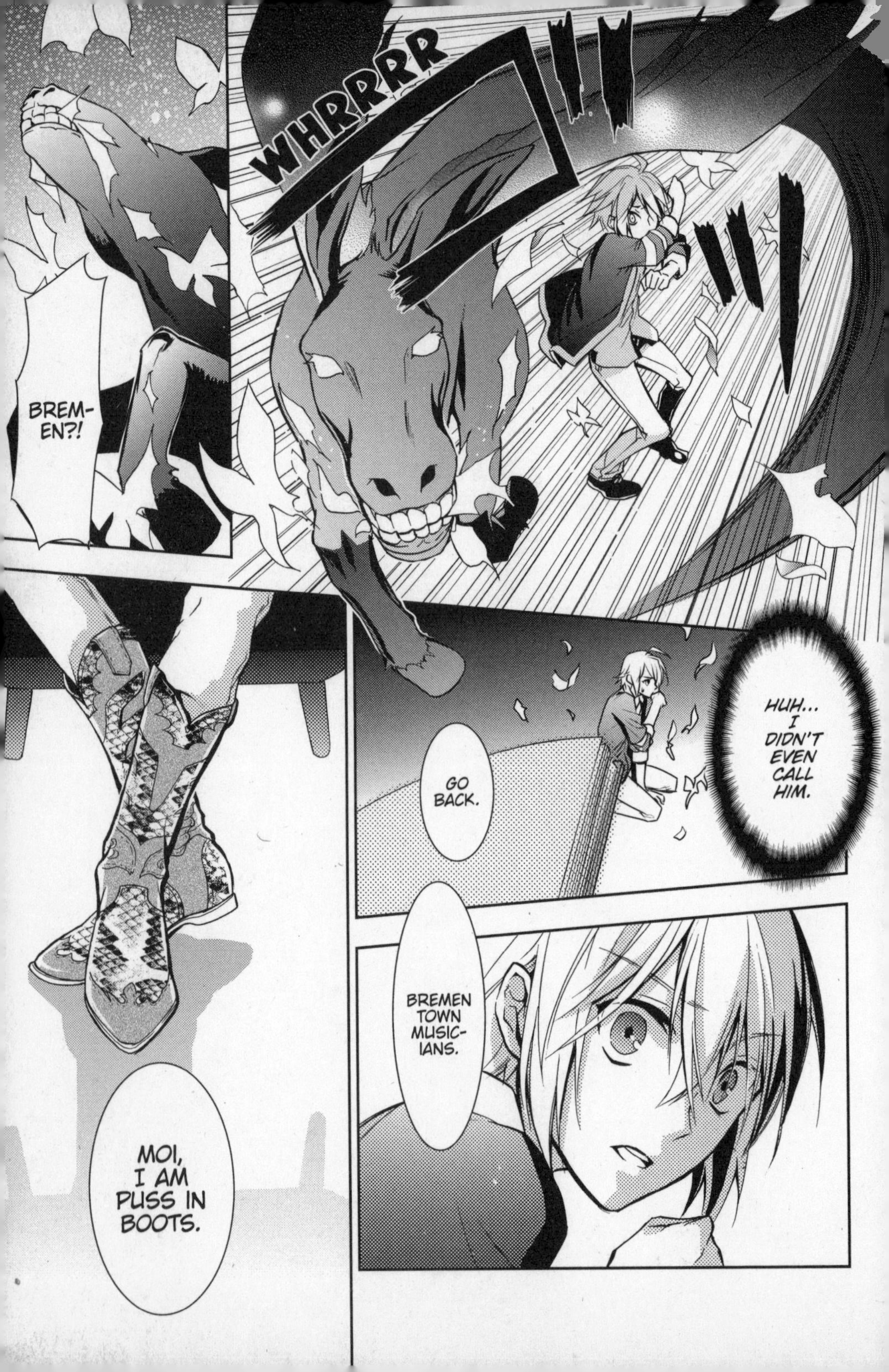
WHRRRR
BREMEN?!
HUH... I DIDN'T EVEN CALL HIM.
GO BACK.
BREMEN TOWN MUSIC-IANS.
MOI, I AM PUSS IN BOOTS.

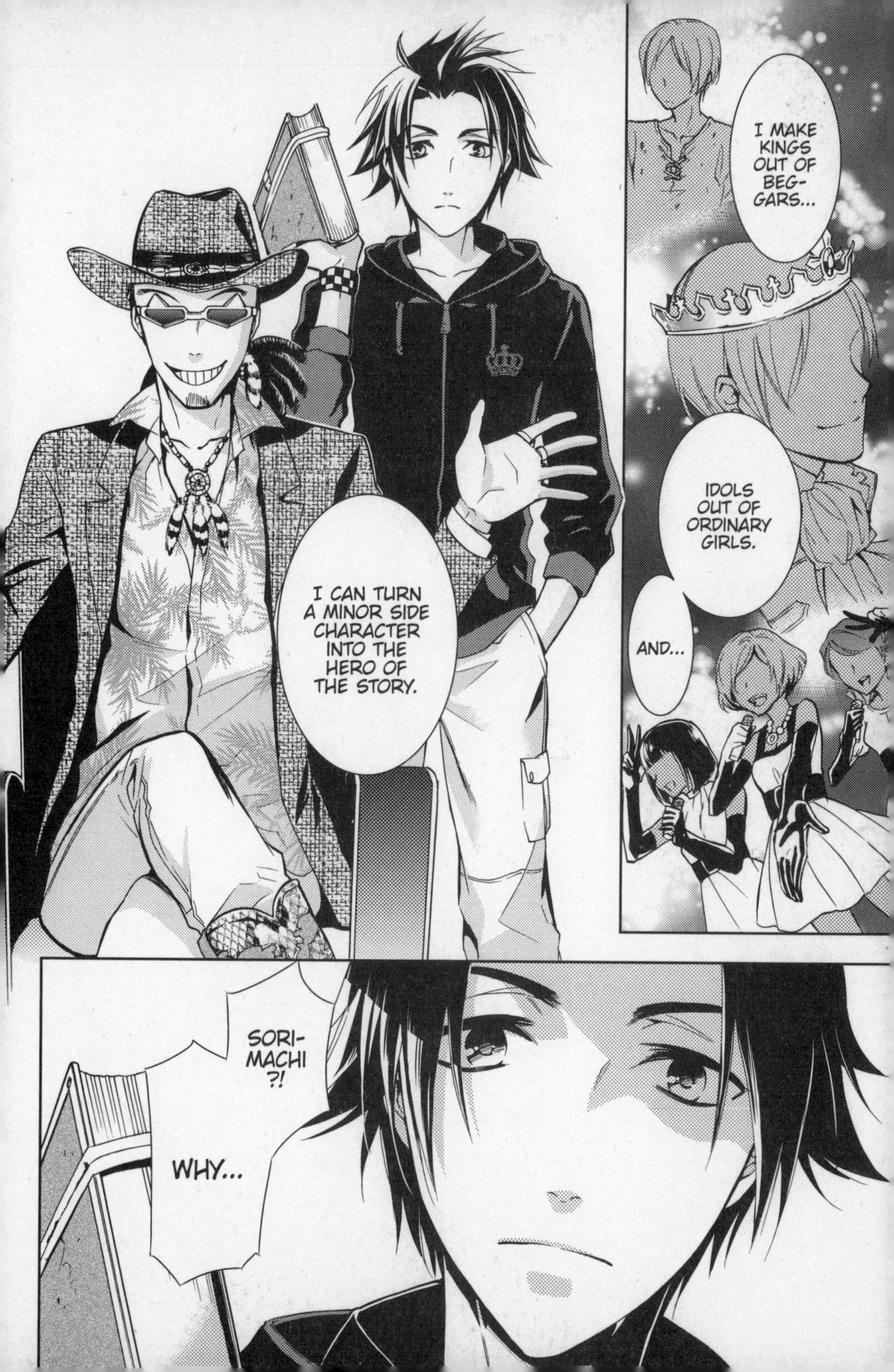
I MAKE KINGS OUT OF BEG-GARS...
IDOLS OUT OF ORDINARY GIRLS.
AND...
I CAN TURN A MINOR SIDE CHARACTER INTO THE HERO OF THE STORY.
SORI-MACHI ?!
WHY...

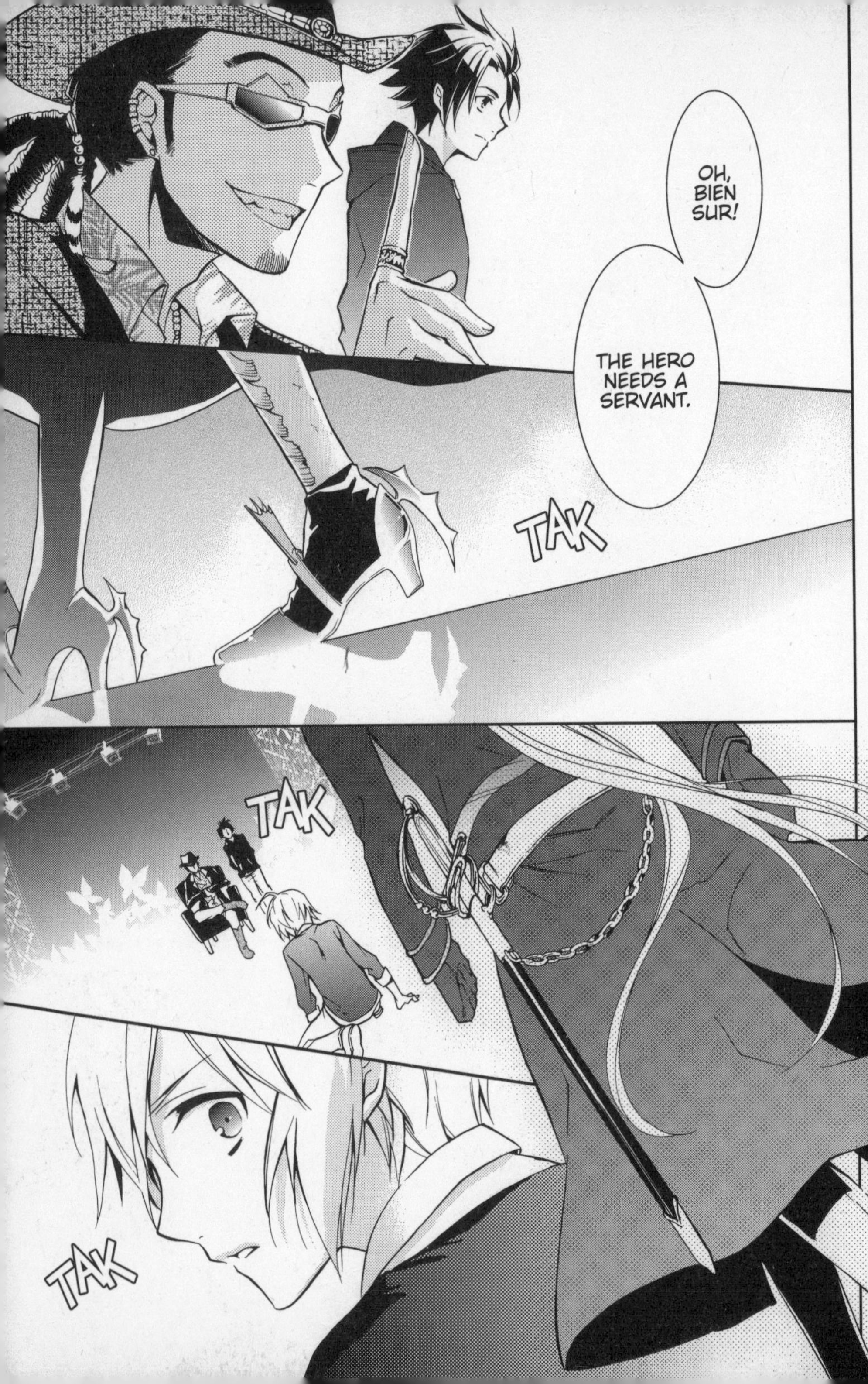
OH, BIEN SUR!
THE HERO NEEDS A SERVANT.
TAK
TAK
TAK

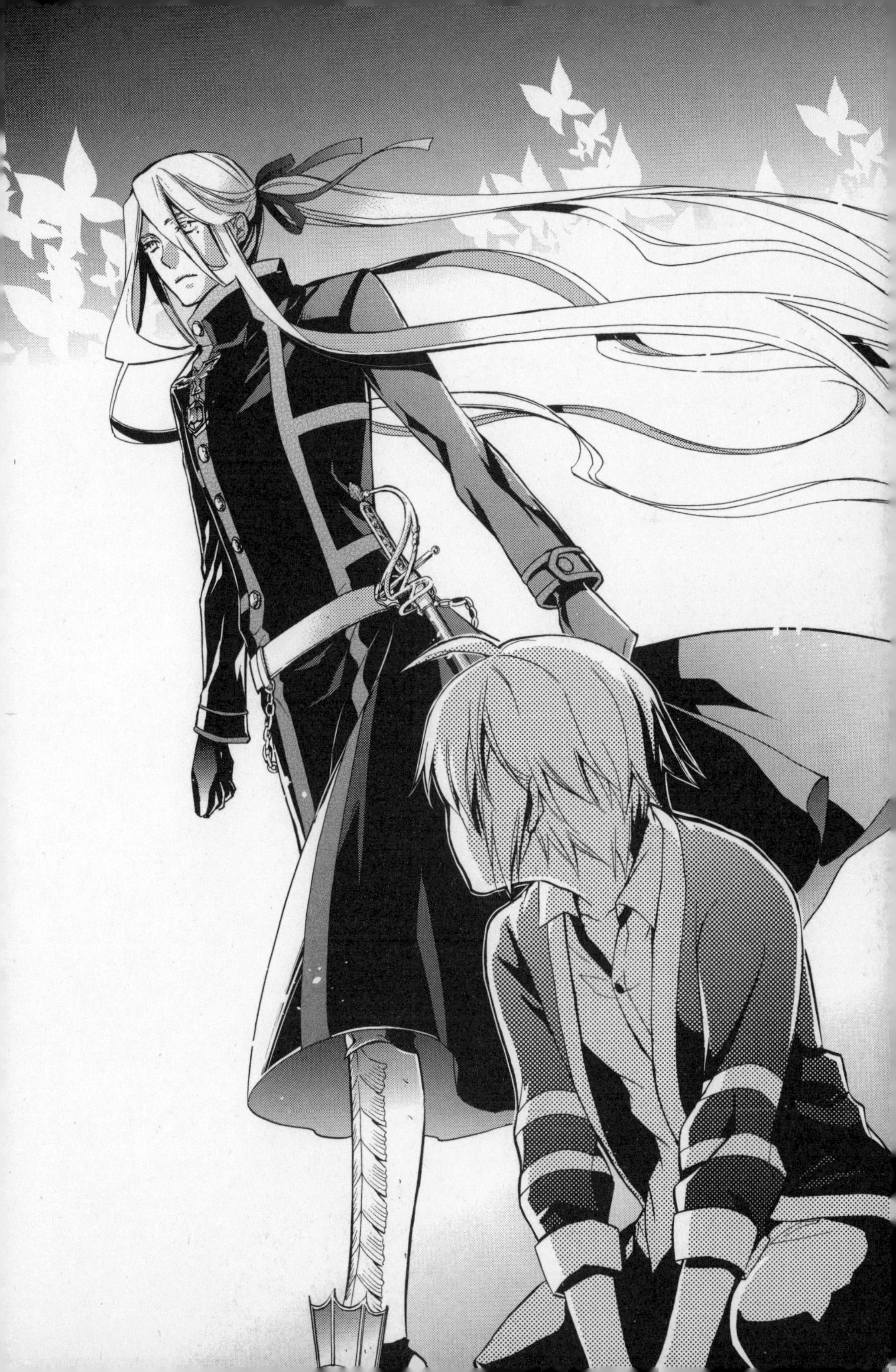

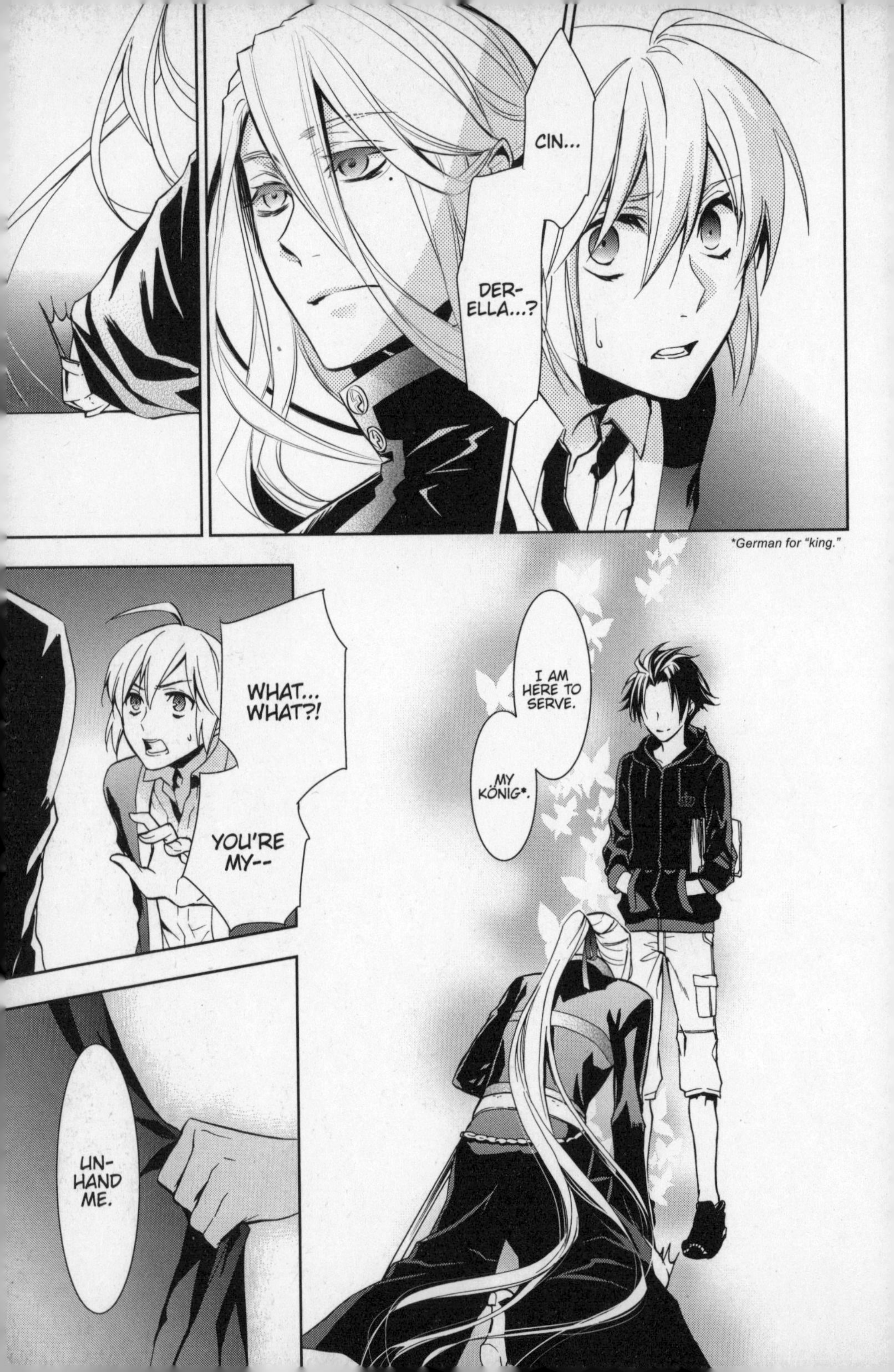
CIN...
DER-ELLA...?
I AM HERE TO SERVE.
MY KÖNIG*.
WHAT... WHAT?!
YOU'RE MY--
UN-HAND ME.
*German for "king."

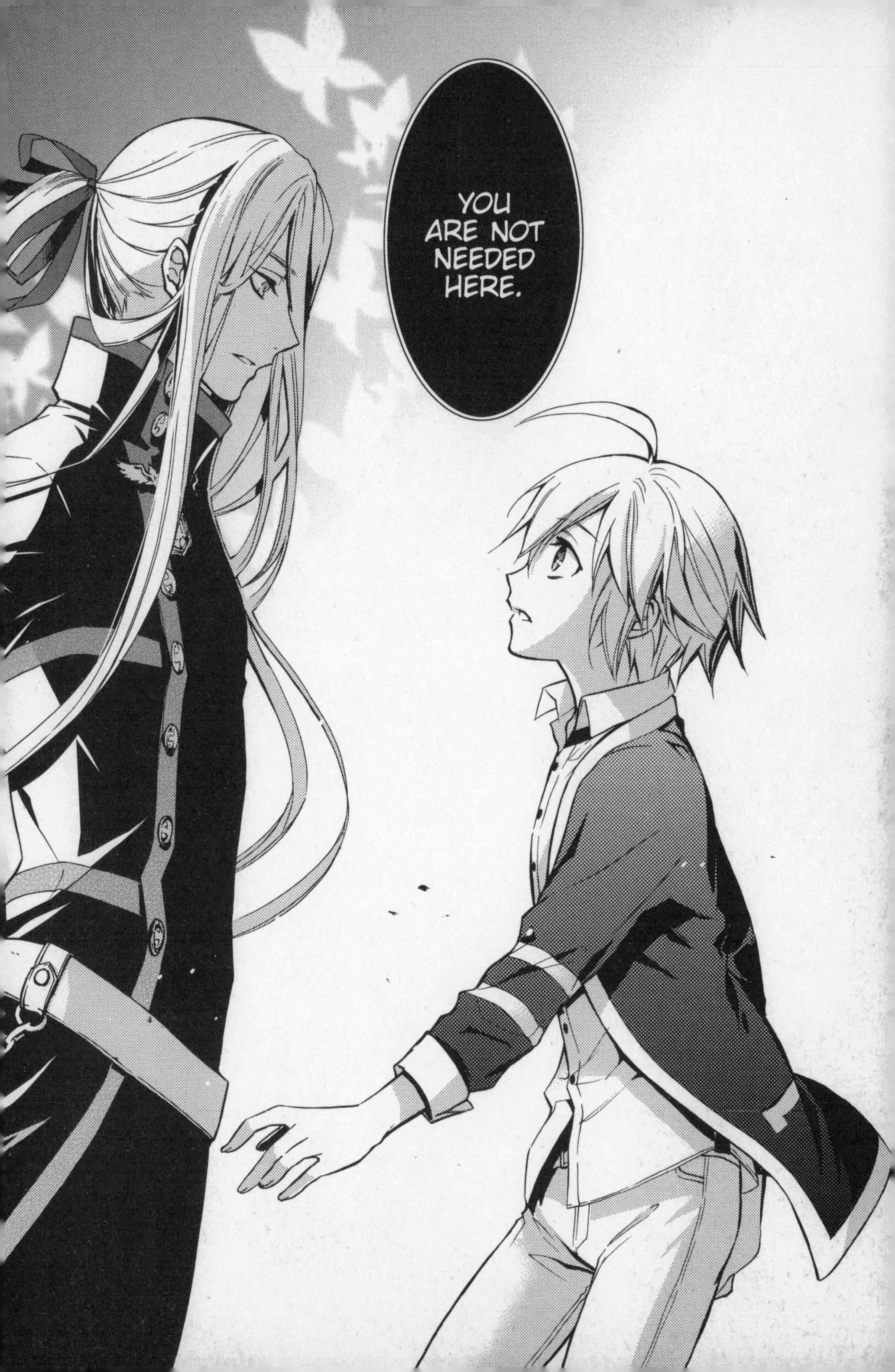
YOU ARE NOT NEEDED HERE.

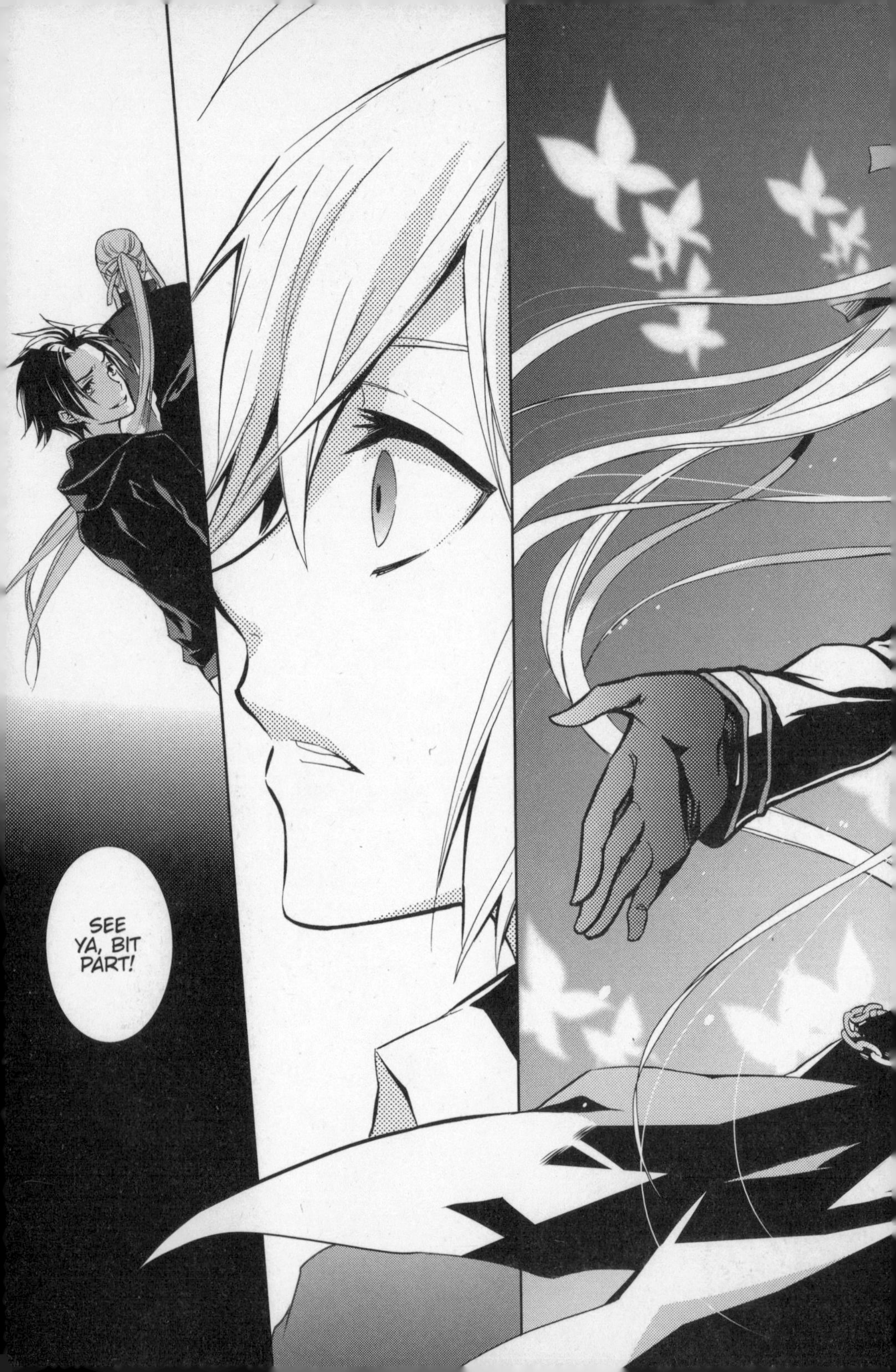
SEE YA, BIT PART!

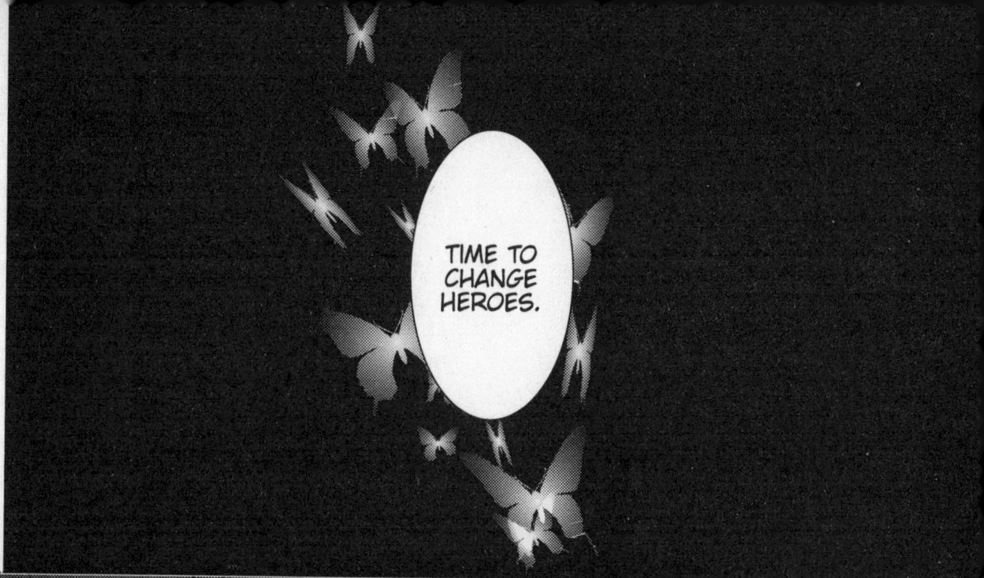
TIME TO CHANGE HEROES.
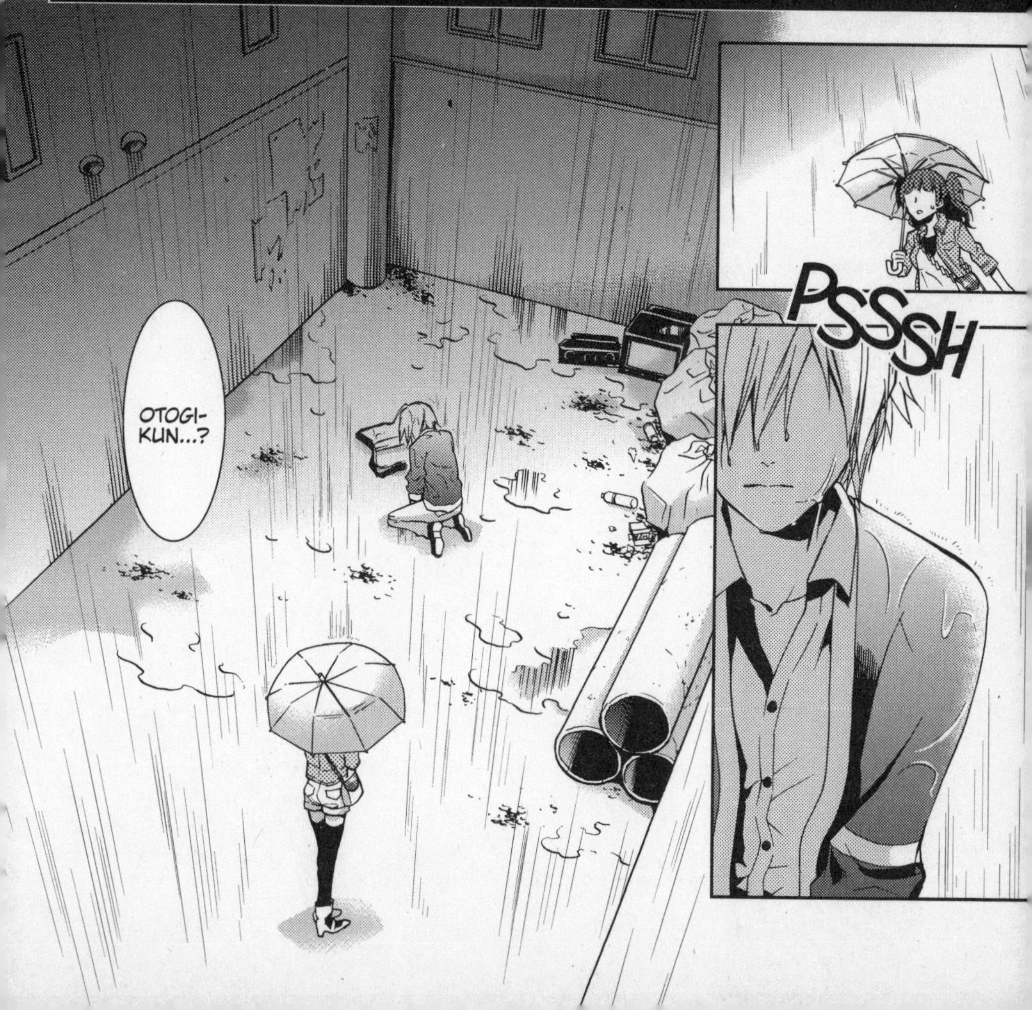
PSSSH
OTOGI-KUN...?

To be continued...

CHARACTERS

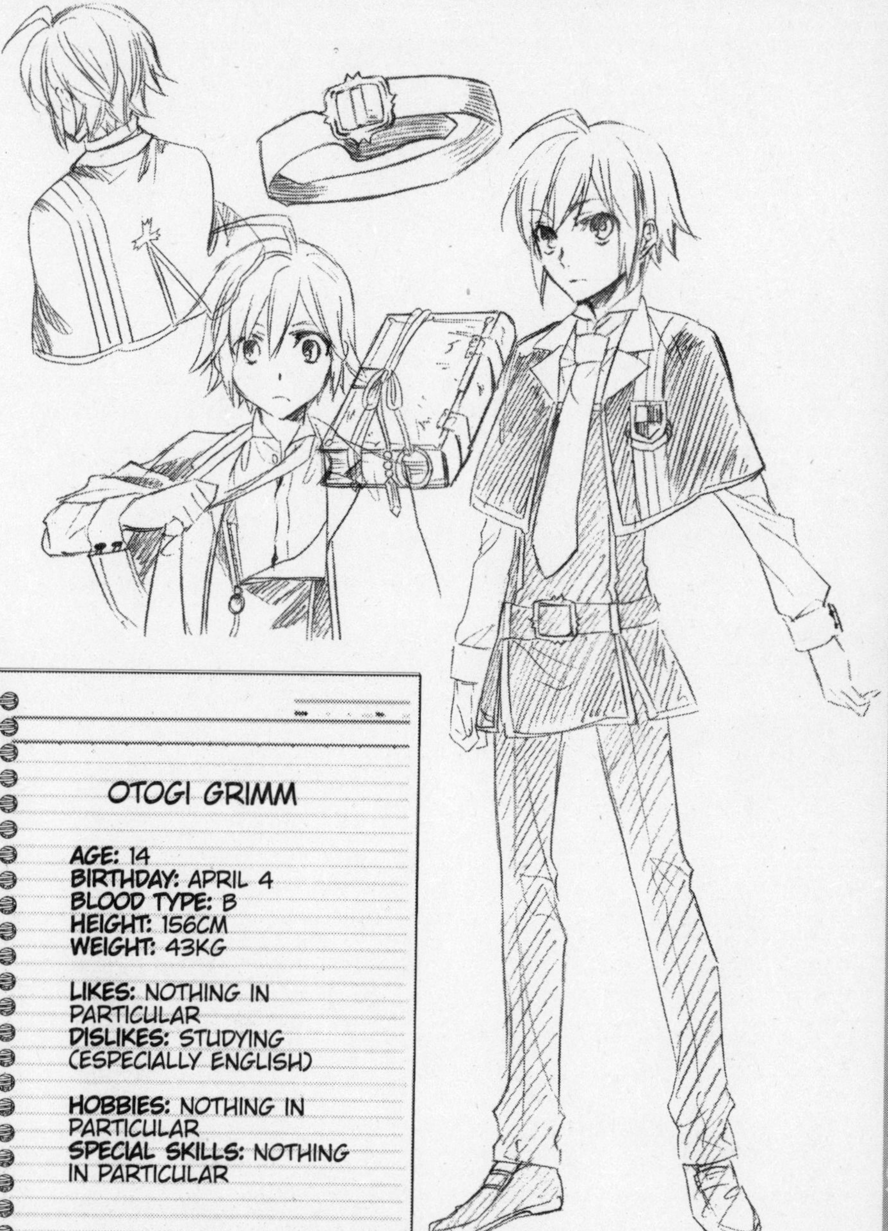

OTOGI GRIMM

AGE: 14
BIRTHDAY: APRIL 4
BLOOD TYPE: B
HEIGHT: 156CM
WEIGHT: 43KG

LIKES: NOTHING IN PARTICULAR
DISLIKES: STUDYING (ESPECIALLY ENGLISH)

HOBBIES: NOTHING IN PARTICULAR
SPECIAL SKILLS: NOTHING IN PARTICULAR

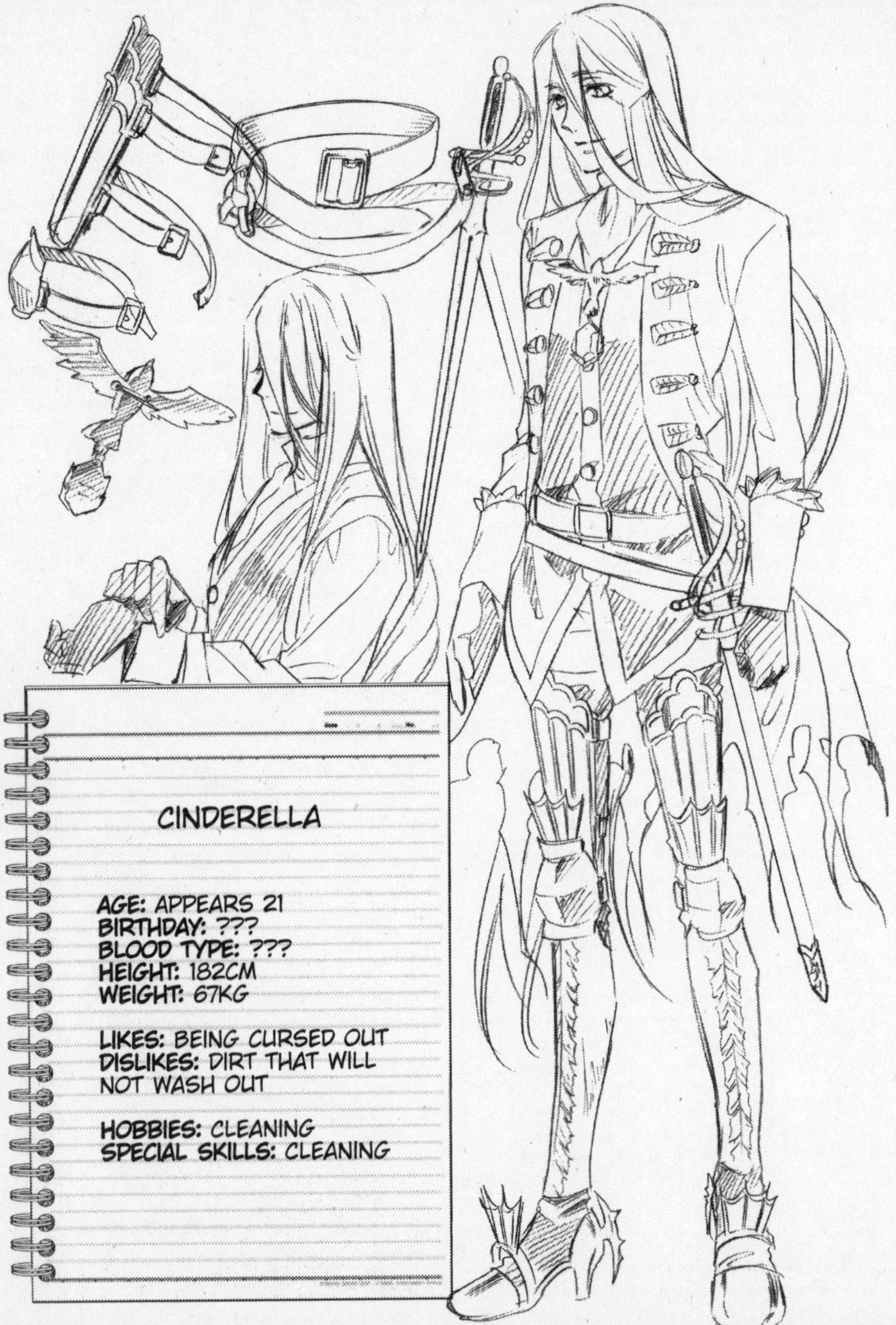

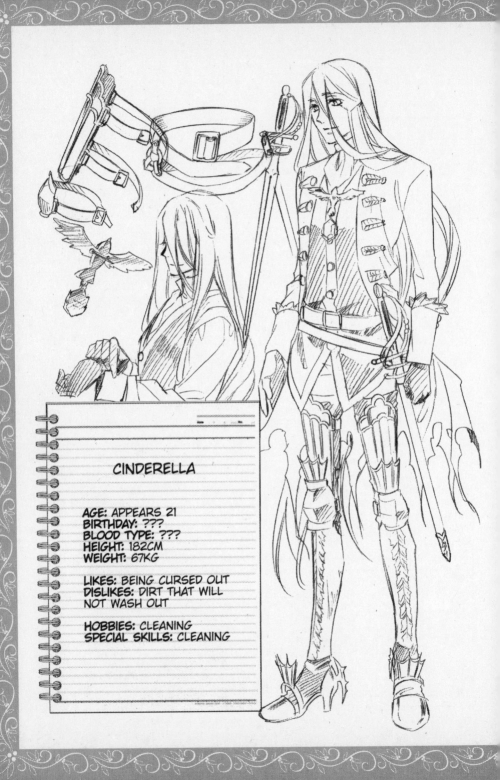

CINDERELLA

AGE: APPEARS 21
BIRTHDAY: ???
BLOOD TYPE: ???
HEIGHT: 182CM
WEIGHT: 67KG

LIKES: BEING CURSED OUT
DISLIKES: DIRT THAT WILL NOT WASH OUT

HOBBIES: CLEANING
SPECIAL SKILLS: CLEANING

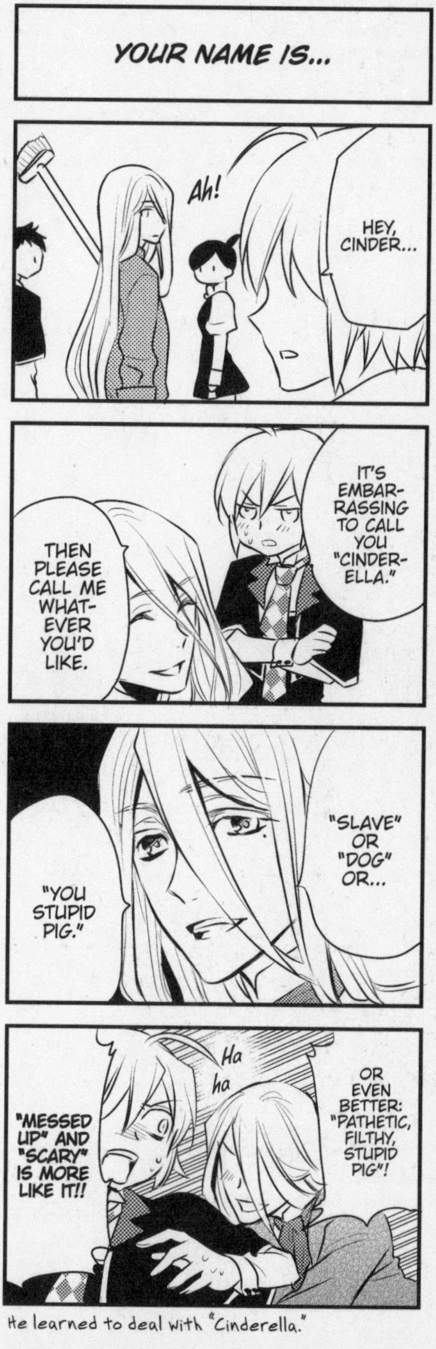
YOUR NAME IS...
HEY, CINDER...
Ah!
IT'S EMBARRASSING TO CALL YOU "CINDERELLA."
THEN PLEASE CALL ME WHATEVER YOU'D LIKE.
"SLAVE" OR "DOG" OR...
"YOU STUPID PIG."
OR EVEN BETTER: "PATHETIC, FILTHY, STUPID PIG"!
Ha ha
"MESSED UP" AND "SCARY" IS MORE LIKE IT!!

He learned to deal with "Cinderella."

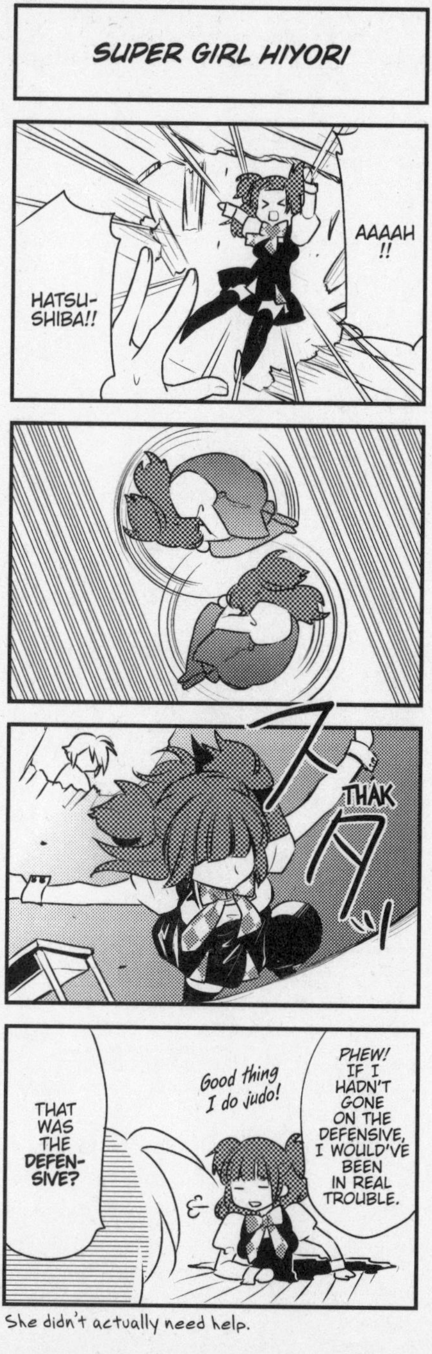
SUPER GIRL HIYORI
AAAAH!!
HATSUSHIBA!!
THAK
PHEW! IF I HADN'T GONE ON THE DEFENSIVE, I WOULD'VE BEEN IN REAL TROUBLE.
Good thing I do judo!
THAT WAS THE DEFENSIVE?

She didn't actually need help.

HELLO, NICE TO MEET YOU! MY NAME'S AYUMI KANOU. THANK YOU SO MUCH FOR PICKING UP VOLUME 1 OF *DICTATORIAL GRIMOIRE!!* IT'S MY FIRST ORIGINAL COMIC, SO I WAS A LITTLE NERVOUS, BUT I'LL BE HAPPY IF YOU ENJOYED READING IT.

I WAS SUPPOSED TO DRAW SOMETHING FOR THE MAGAZINE *COMIC GENE*, SO MY EDITOR AND I WERE RACKING OUR BRAINS FOR A GOOD IDEA. AND SO *DICTATORIAL GRIMOIRE* WAS BORN! "OKAY, SO THE CHARACTERS FROM GRIMM'S FAIRY TALES ATTACK." "THE PROTAGONIST'S TOTALLY FULL OF HIMSELF." "AND CINDERELLA'S A TOTAL MASOCHIST." I'M PRETTY SURE THOSE ARE ALL THINGS WE SAID IN THE MEETING. ROUGHLY SPEAKING... AND I'M SPEAKING ROUGHLY NOW, TOO, BUT I AM WORKING ON STORIES FOR NEXT TIME TO KEEP READERS ON THE EDGE OF THEIR SEATS.

YOU CAN LOOK FORWARD TO SEEING WHAT KIND OF FAIRY TALE DEMONS APPEAR NEXT TIME! I'M TRYING AS MUCH AS POSSIBLE TO REFERENCE STORIES THAT ARE VERY WELL KNOWN. AND I'D LOVE IT IF YOU'D TELL ME ABOUT ANY GRIMM'S FAIRY TALE CHARACTERS YOU'D LIKE TO SEE.

I'LL KEEP WORKING HARD SO THAT YOU'LL KEEP WANTING TO JOIN ME, SO I HOPE YOU WILL ALL ROOT FOR ME! I'LL SEE YOU IN THE NEXT BOOK! ENDING THIS WAY FEELS LIKE IT'S ALREADY THE LAST BOOK COMING UP... AND THIS IS ONLY VOLUME 1.

AYUMI KANOU

THIS BOOK CAME OUT THANKS TO THE KINDNESS OF:
EVERYONE IN THE EDITORIAL DEPARTMENT OF MEDIA FACTORY'S GENE
MY SUPERVISOR, IKG-SAN
SHIMA-SAN, YUKINA-SAN, ASAHINA-SAN, M-TA-SAN, HAZUKI-SAN
EVERYONE IN MY FAMILY, EVERYONE ELSE INVOLVED IN THIS BOOK
THANK YOU FOR EVERYTHING!

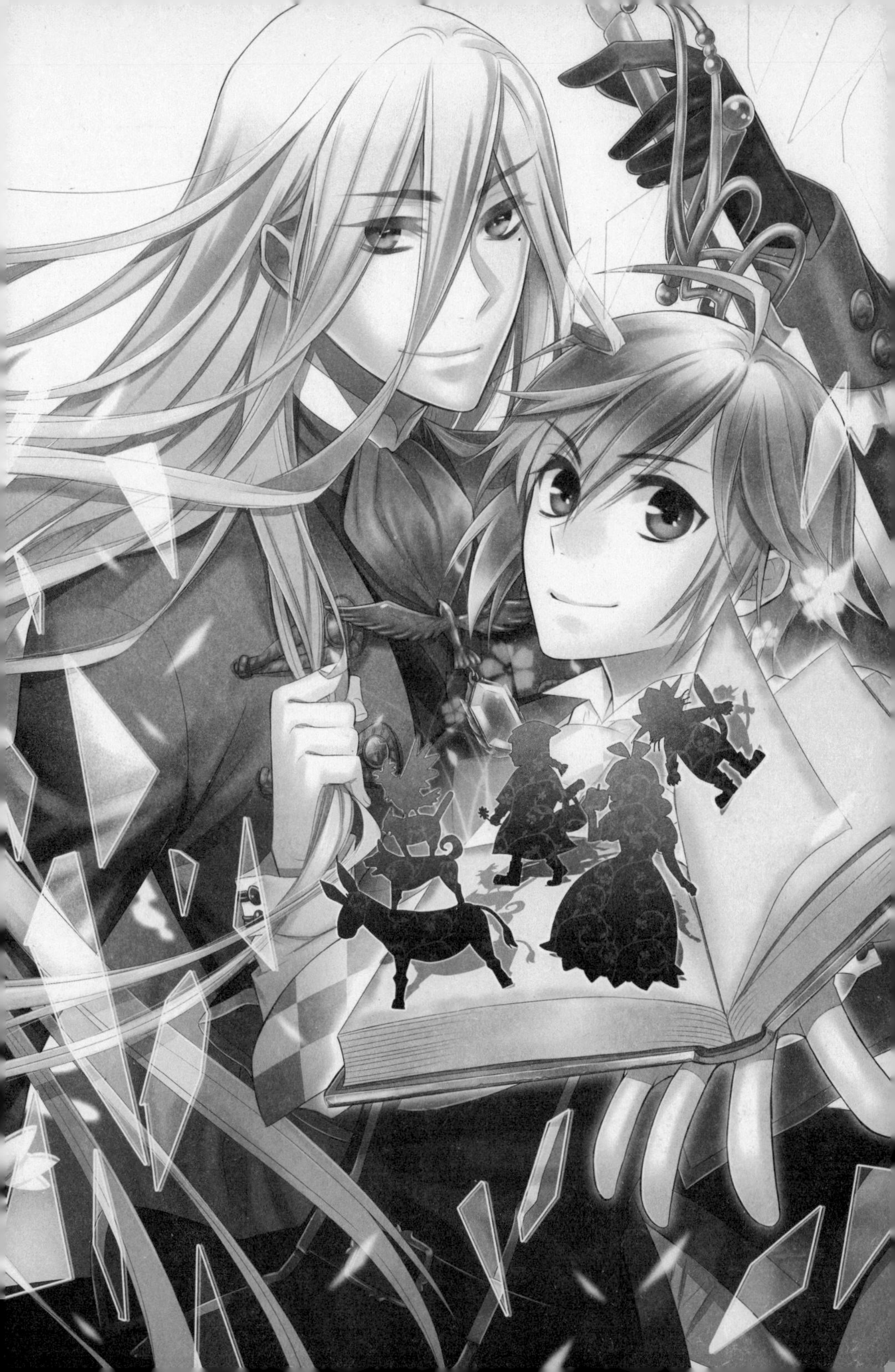

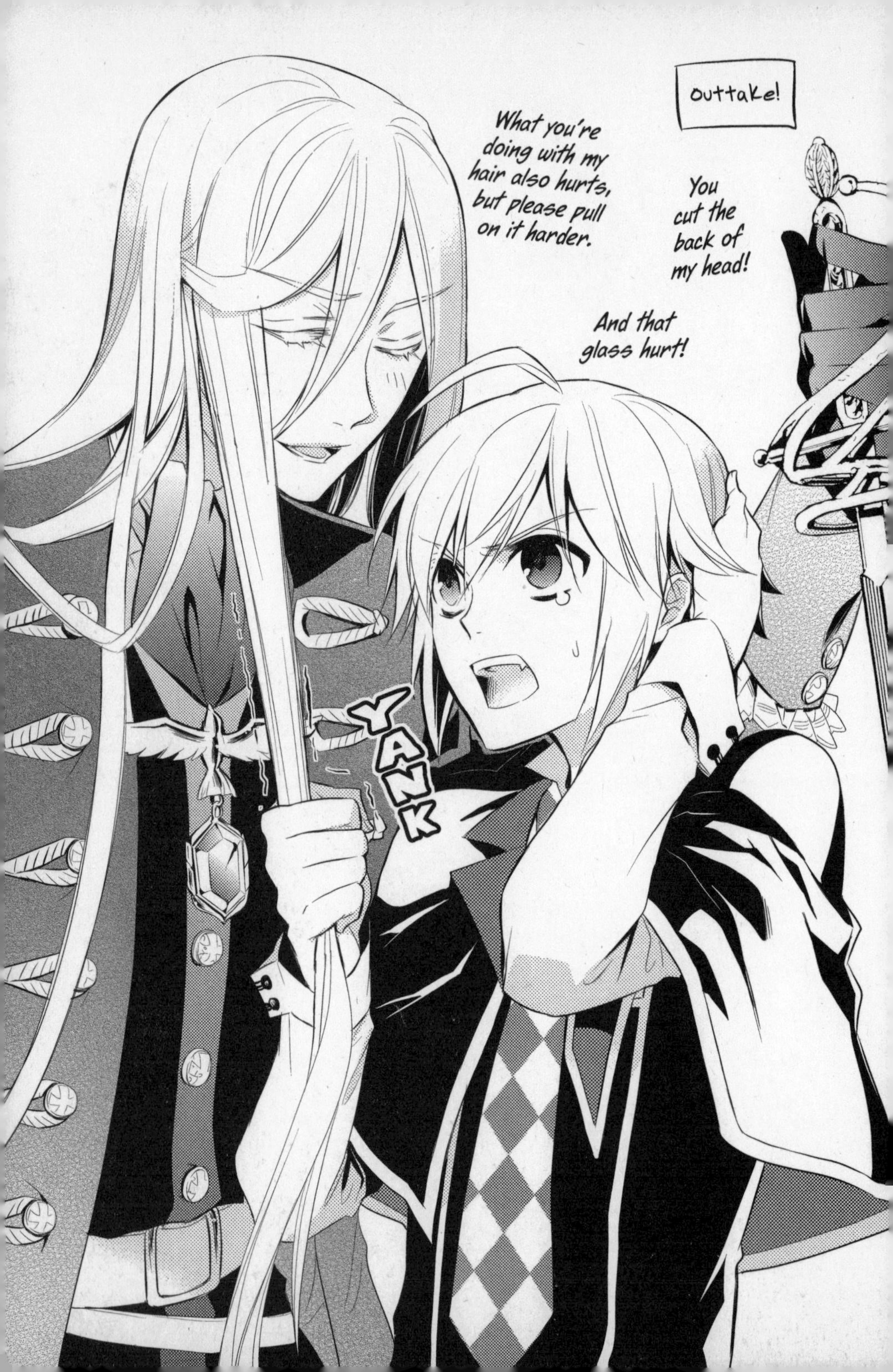
Outtake!
You cut the back of my head!
And that glass hurt!
What you're doing with my hair also hurts, but please pull on it harder.
YANK

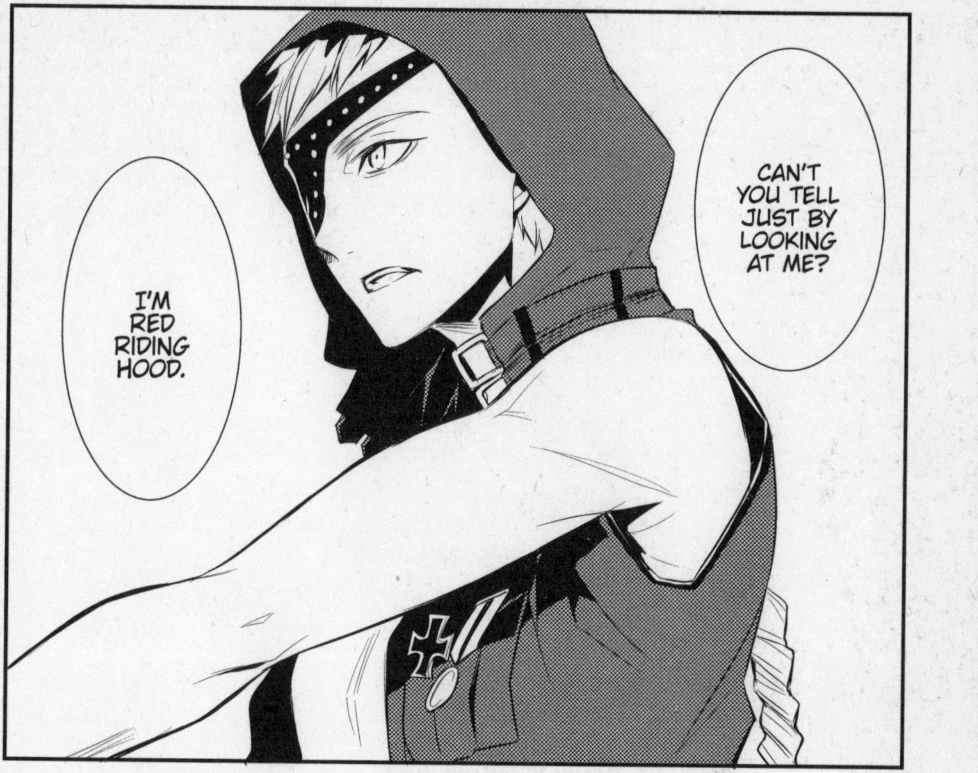
CAN'T YOU TELL JUST BY LOOKING AT ME?
I'M RED RIDING HOOD.

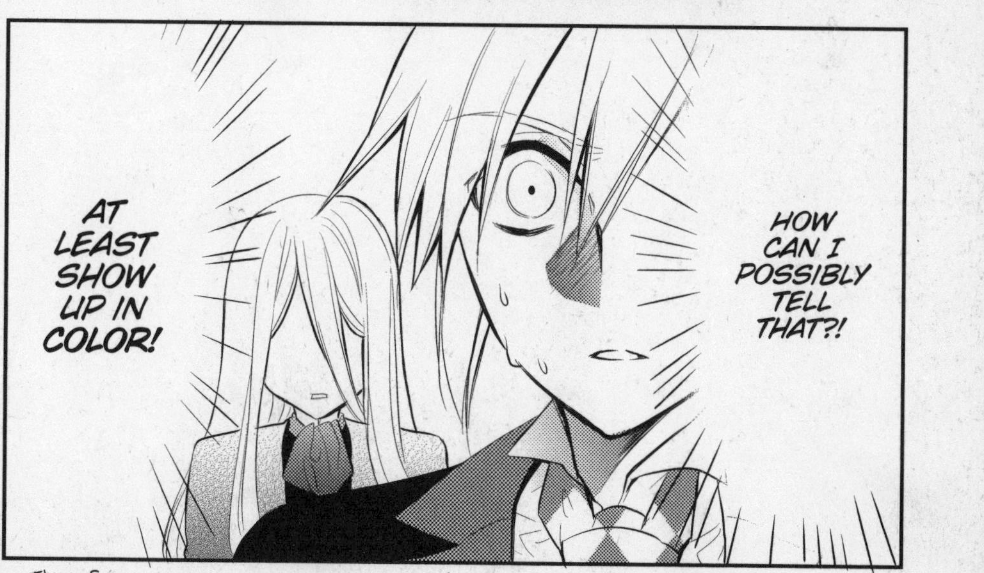
HOW CAN I POSSIBLY TELL THAT?!
AT LEAST SHOW UP IN COLOR!

This is funny.

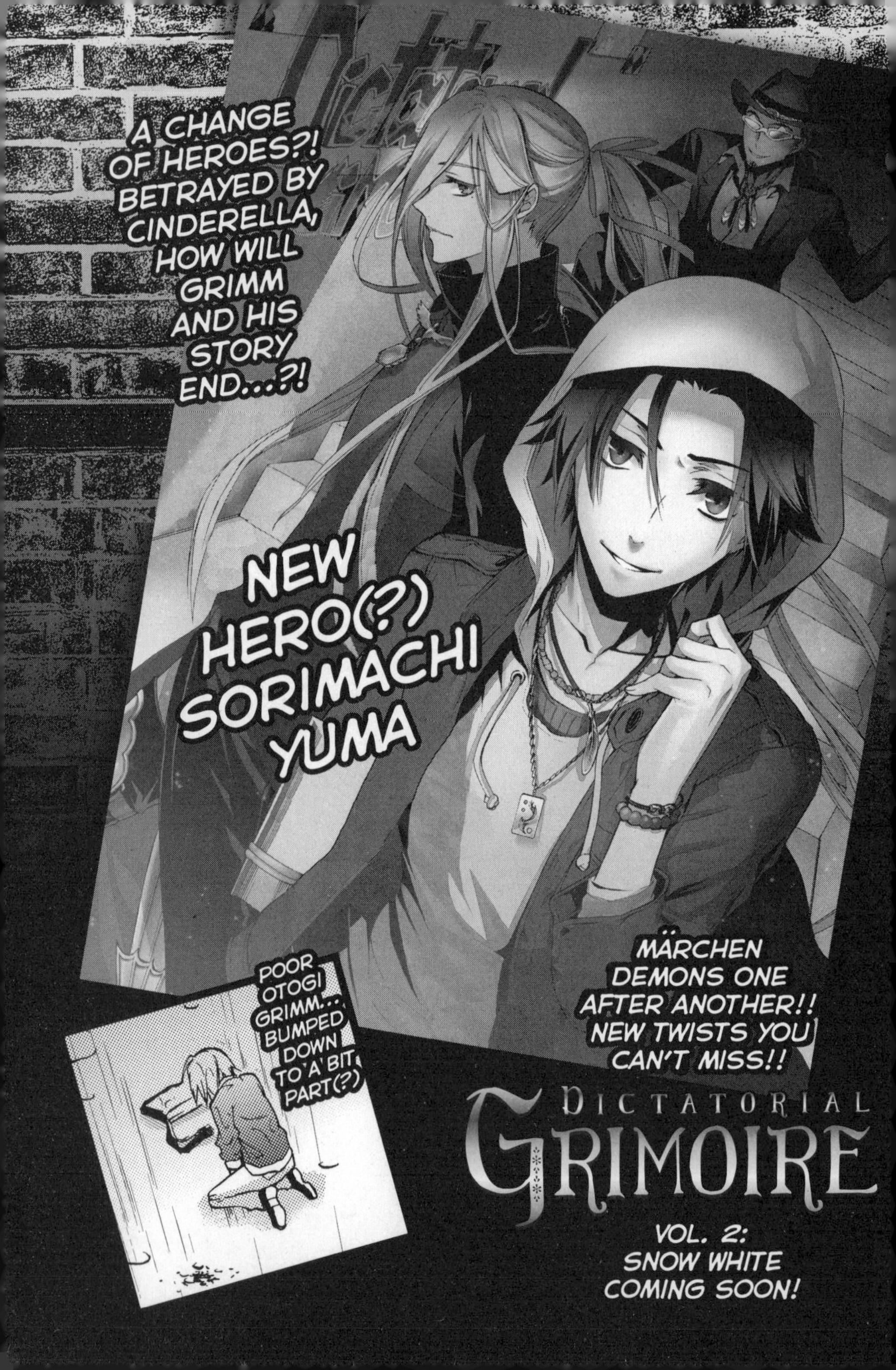
A CHANGE OF HEROES?! BETRAYED BY CINDERELLA, HOW WILL GRIMM AND HIS STORY END...?!
NEW HERO(?) SORIMACHI YUMA
POOR OTOGI GRIMM... BUMPED DOWN TO A BIT PART(?)
MÄRCHEN DEMONS ONE AFTER ANOTHER!! NEW TWISTS YOU CAN'T MISS!!
DICTATORIAL GRIMOIRE
VOL. 2: SNOW WHITE COMING SOON!

独裁グリムワール
Dictatorial Grimoire

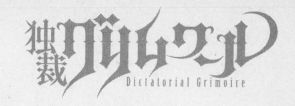

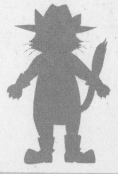

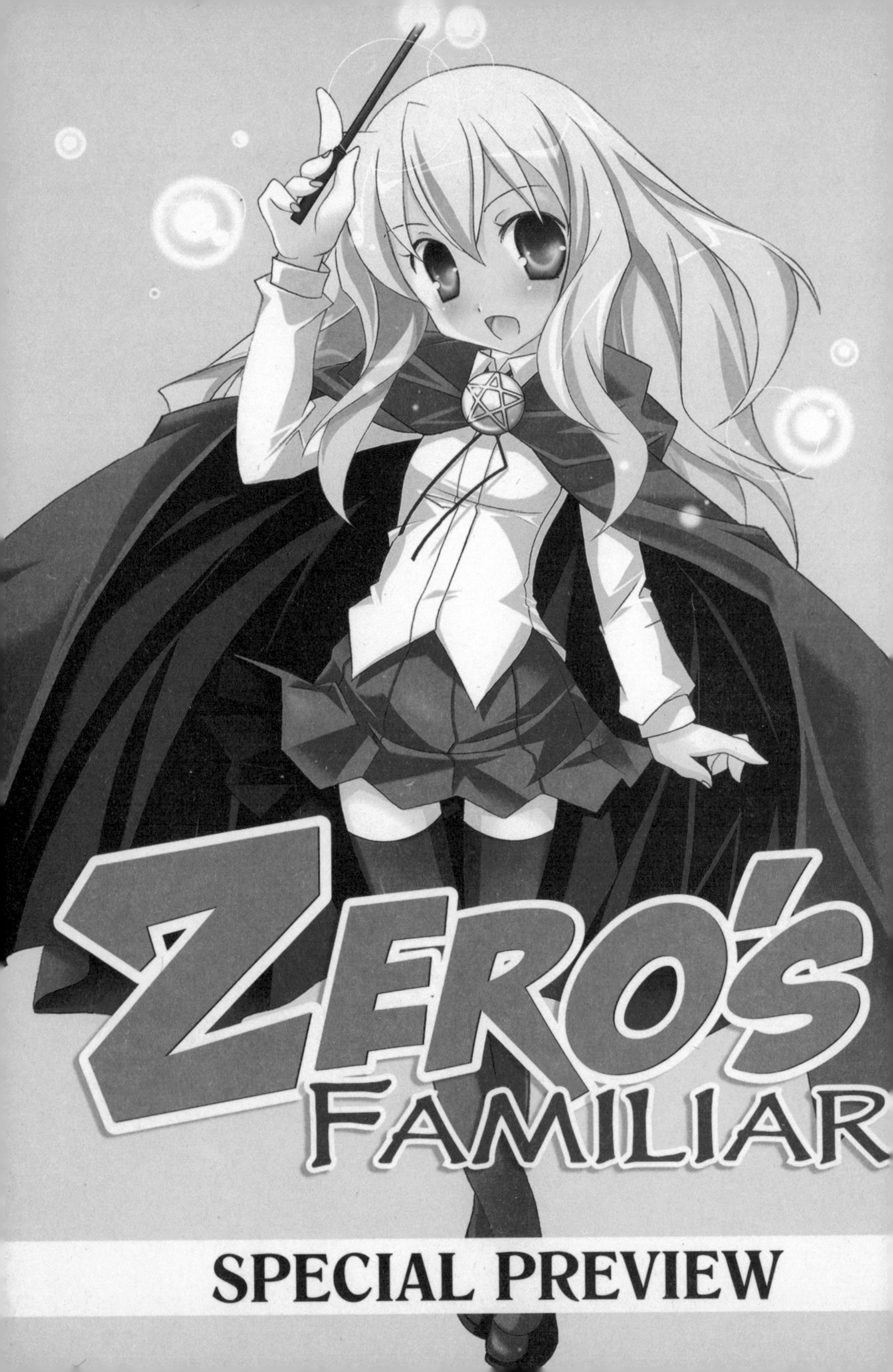
ZERO'S
FAMILIAR
SPECIAL PREVIEW

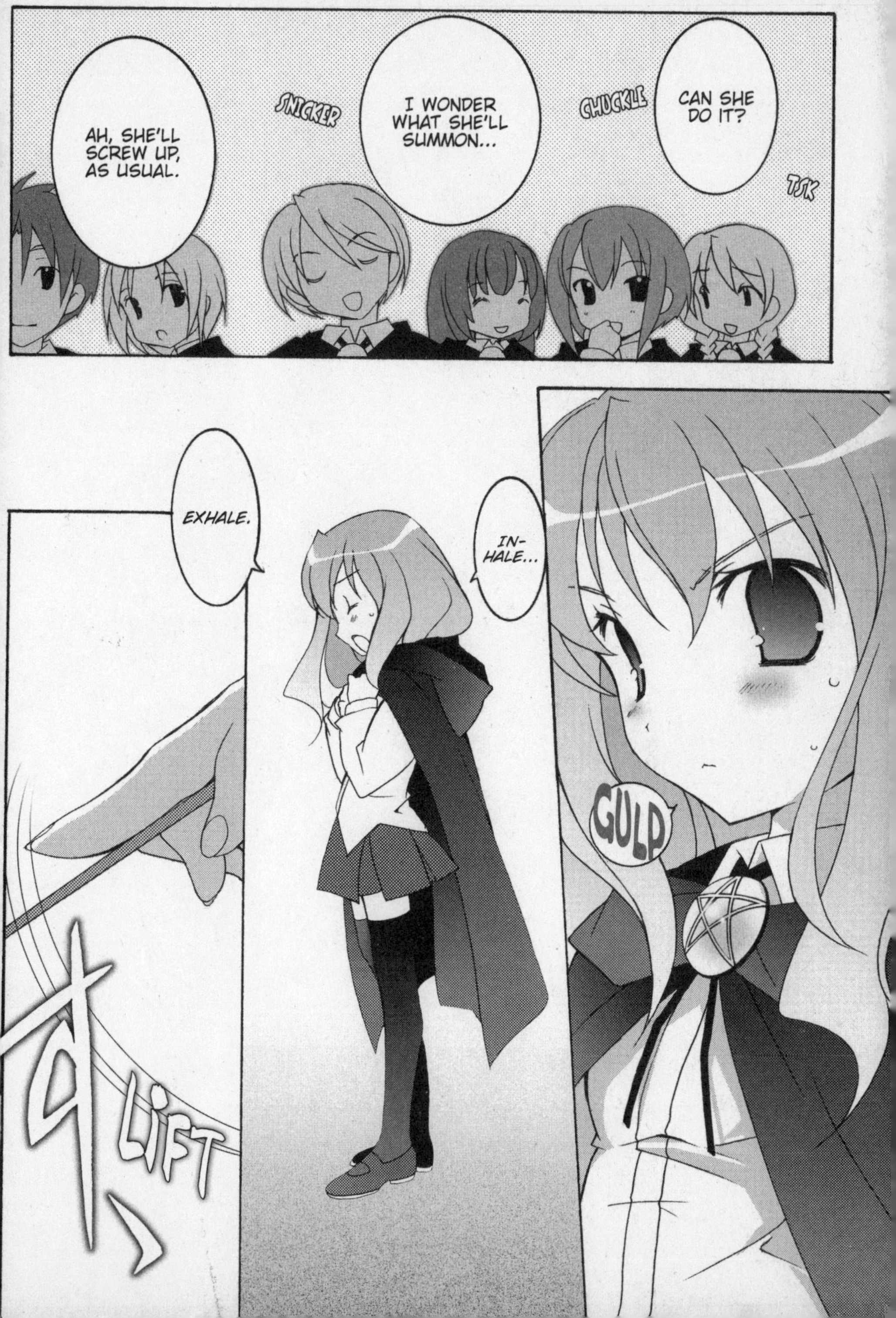
CAN SHE DO IT?
TSK
CHUCKLE
I WONDER WHAT SHE'LL SUMMON...
SNICKER
AH, SHE'LL SCREW UP, AS USUAL.
GULP
IN-HALE...
EXHALE.
LIFT

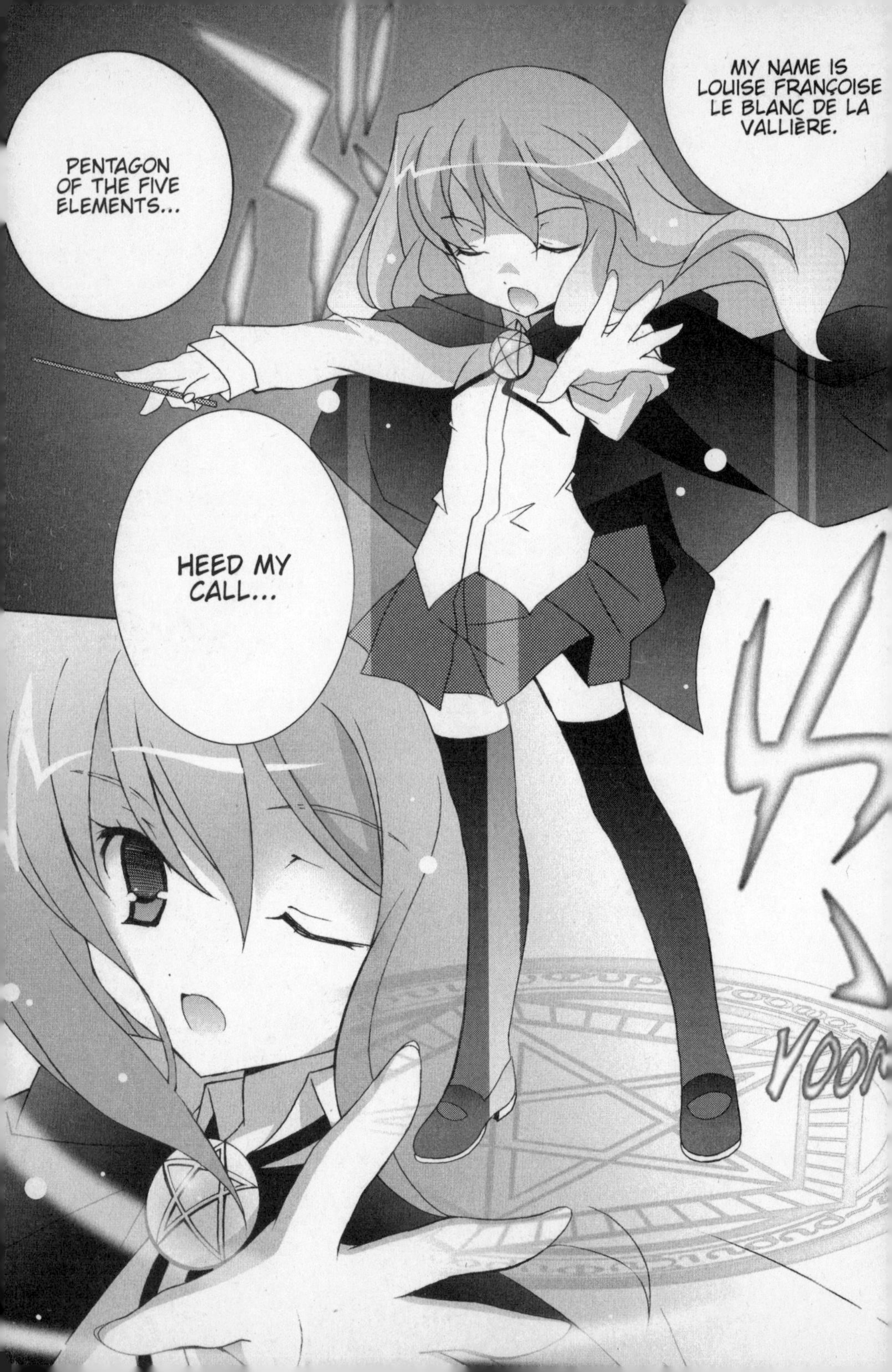
MY NAME IS LOUISE FRANÇOISE LE BLANC DE LA VALLIÈRE.
PENTAGON OF THE FIVE ELEMENTS...
HEED MY CALL...
VOOM

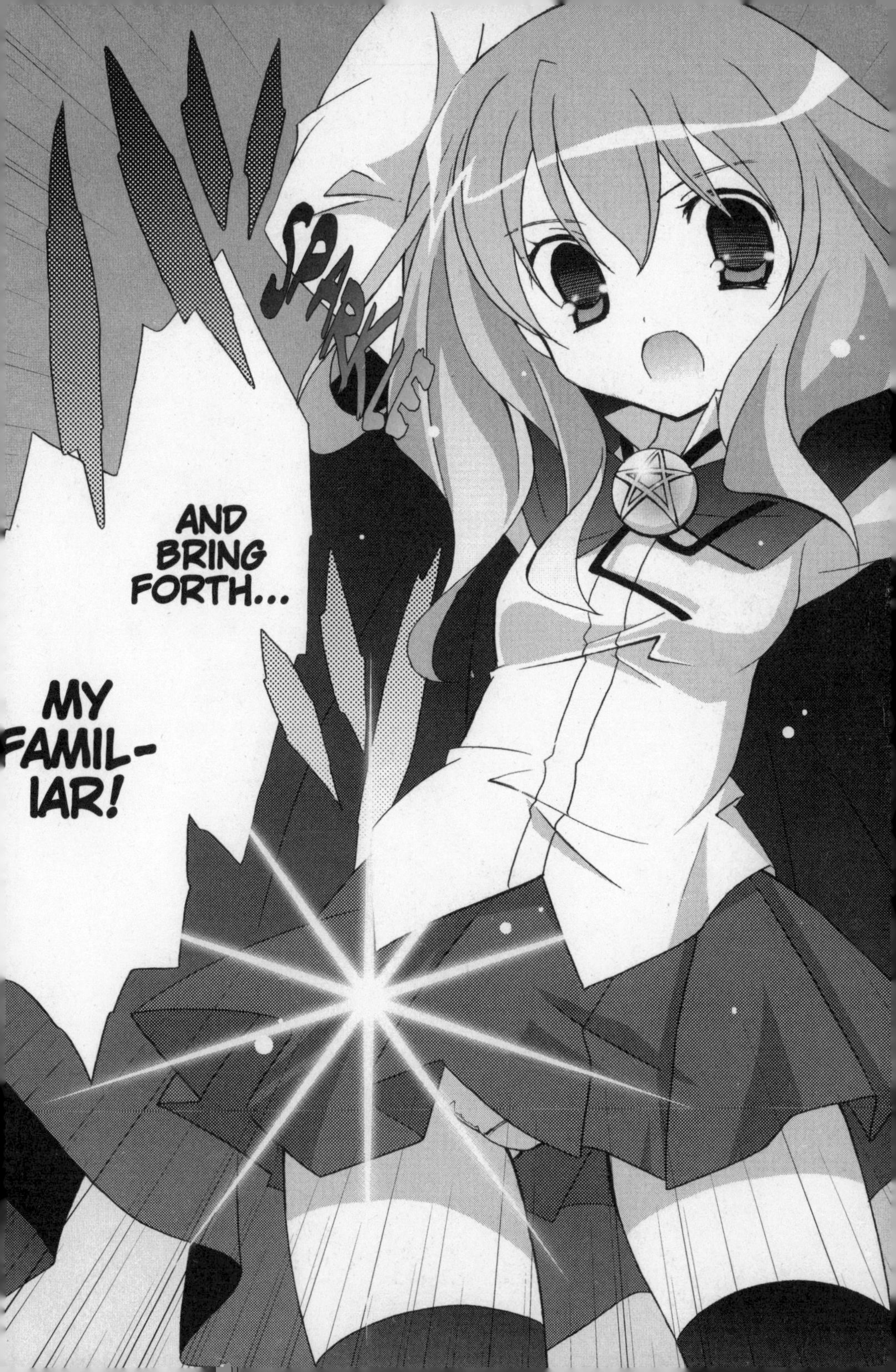
SPARKLE
AND BRING FORTH...
MY FAMIL-IAR!

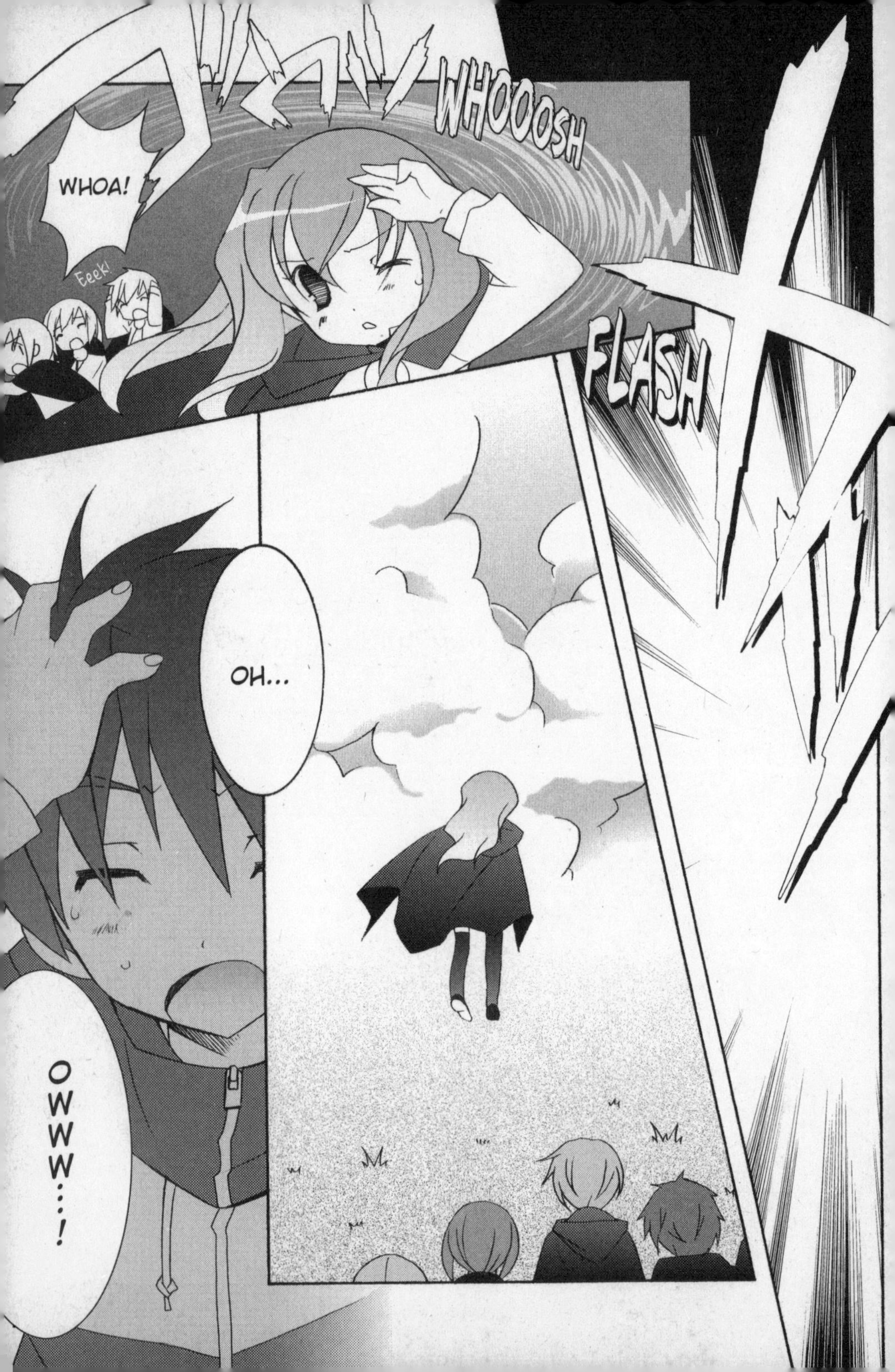
FLASH
WHOOOSH
WHOA!
Eeek!
OH...
OWWW...!

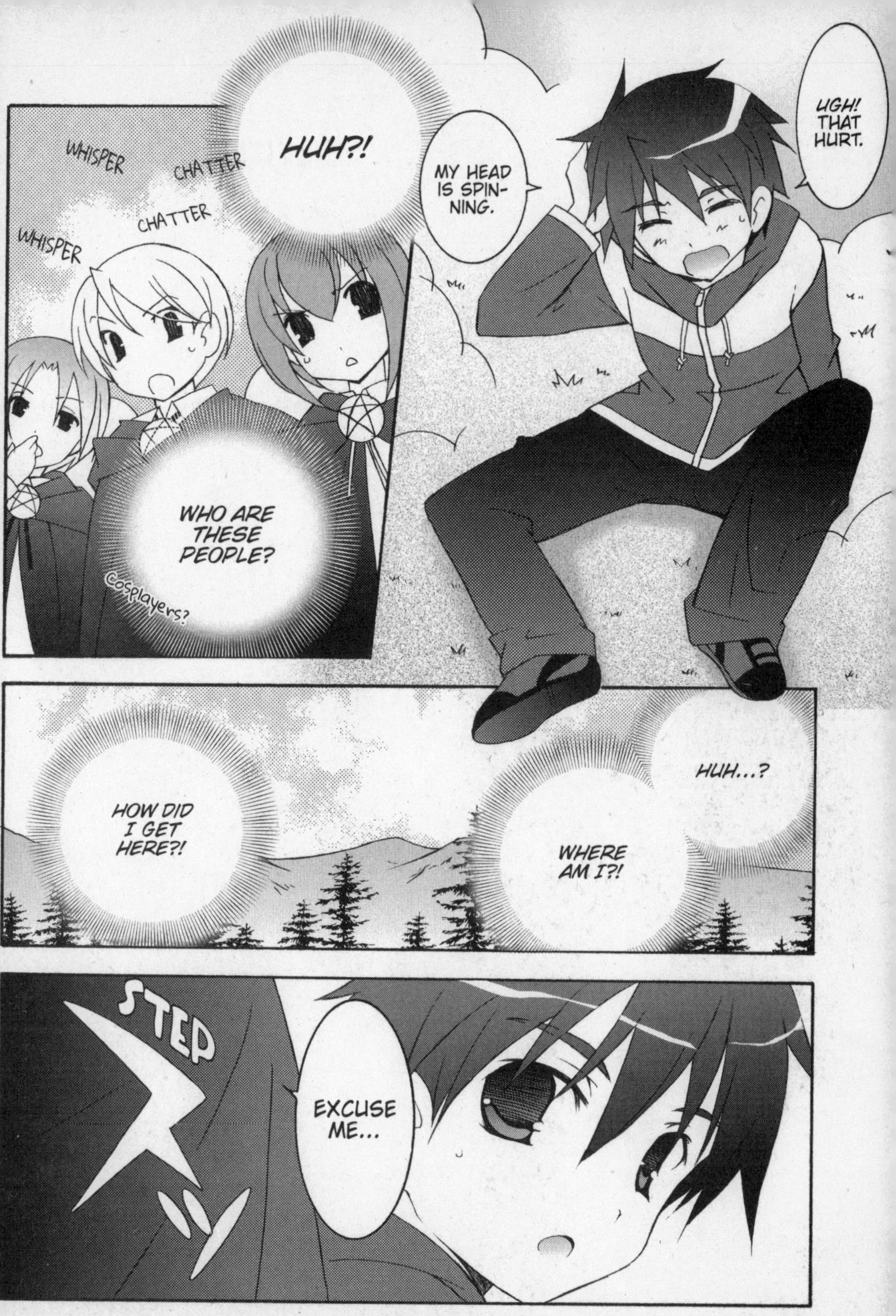
UGH! THAT HURT.
MY HEAD IS SPIN-NING.
HUH?!
WHISPER
CHATTER
CHATTER
WHISPER
WHO ARE THESE PEOPLE?
Cosplayers?
HUH...?
WHERE AM I?!
HOW DID I GET HERE?!
STEP
EXCUSE ME...

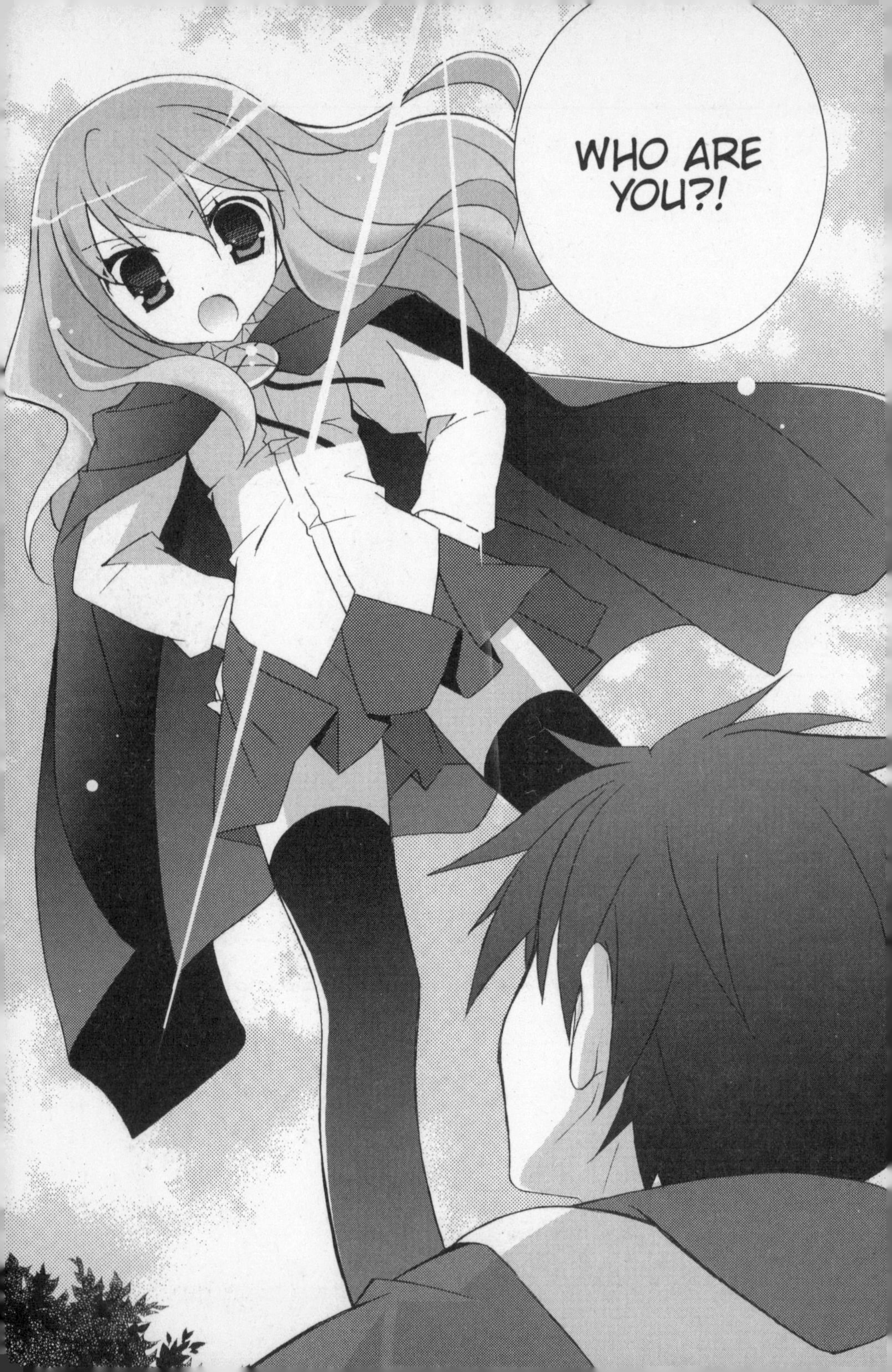
WHO ARE YOU?!

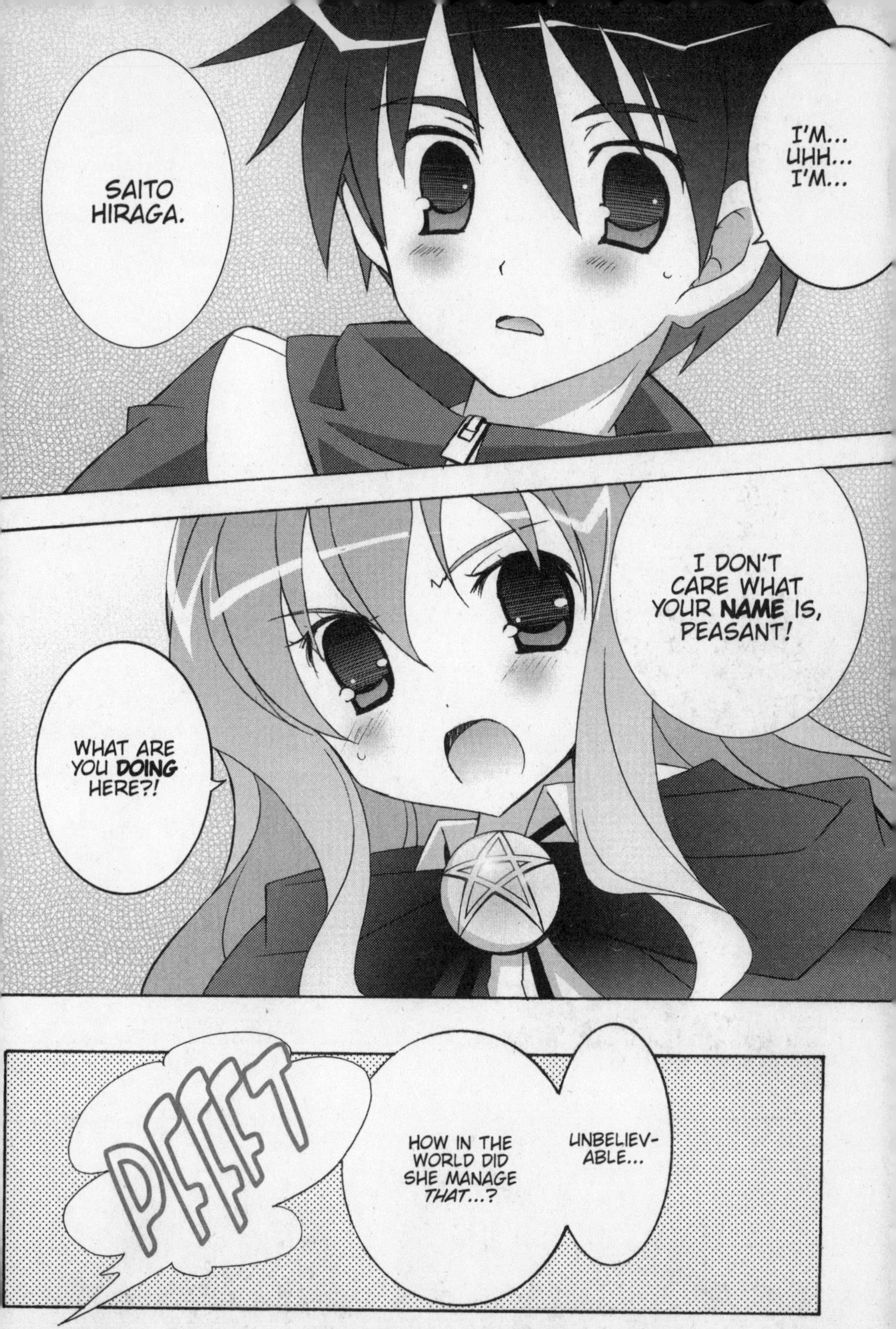
I'M... UHH... I'M...
SAITO HIRAGA.
I DON'T CARE WHAT YOUR **NAME** IS, PEASANT!
WHAT ARE YOU **DOING** HERE?!
UNBELIEV-ABLE...
HOW IN THE WORLD DID SHE MANAGE *THAT*...?
PFFFT